T0312180

Managing
Environmental Data

Managing Environmental Data

Principles, Techniques, and Best Practices

Gerald A. Burnette

CRC Press
Taylor & Francis Group
Boca Raton London New York

CRC Press is an imprint of the
Taylor & Francis Group, an **informa** business

Cover photo courtesy of Richard Tippit.

First edition published 2022
by CRC Press
6000 Broken Sound Parkway NW, Suite 300, Boca Raton, FL 33487-2742

and by CRC Press
2 Park Square, Milton Park, Abingdon, Oxon OX14 4RN

© 2022 Gerald A. Burnette

CRC Press is an imprint of Taylor & Francis Group, LLC

Library of Congress Cataloging-in-Publication Data
Names: Burnette, Gerald A., author.
Title: Managing environmental data : principles, techniques,
and best practices / Gerald A. Burnette.
Description: First edition. | Boca Raton, FL : CRC Press, 2022. |
Series: Principles, techniques, and best practices, 2381-2613 | Includes index.
Identifiers: LCCN 2021024858 (print) | LCCN 2021024859 (ebook) |
ISBN 9780367654405 (hardback) | ISBN 9780367675929 (paperback) |
ISBN 9781003131953 (ebook)
Subjects: LCSH: Environmental sciences–Data processing. | Environmental
management–Data processing. | Environmental protection–Data processing.
Classification: LCC GE45.D37 B87 2022 (print) |
LCC GE45.D37 (ebook) | DDC 363.70285/57–dc23
LC record available at https://lccn.loc.gov/2021024858
LC ebook record available at https://lccn.loc.gov/2021024859

ISBN: 978-0-367-65440-5 (hbk)
ISBN: 978-0-367-67592-9 (pbk)
ISBN: 978-1-003-13195-3 (ebk)

DOI: 10.1201/9781003131953

Typeset in Times
by Newgen Publishing UK

Access the Support Material: www.routledge.com/9780367654405

To my beautiful wife Kimberly Spargo, the true writer of our family. I could not have written this without your guidance, patience, and encouragement.

Contents

PART 2   Environmental Data Management Realities

Acknowledgments

I would like to thank the US Army Corps of Engineers for multiple contributions that made this book possible. First, the database and user interface development I have done over the course of my career as a contractor to the Corps was instrumental in acquiring the knowledge I attempt to convey in this work. Second, I would like to explicitly thank the Corps for granting me permission to relate the events described in Part 2. And finally, I would like to explicitly express my gratitude to the three individuals who provided the most input and guidance for the work presented in Part 2: Bob Sneed, Mark Campbell, and Richard Tippit.

Cover photo courtesy of Richard Tippit.

About the Author

Gerald Burnette is a Senior Project Manager with Civil and Environmental Consultants, Inc. He earned a Bachelor of Arts in Mathematics (with a minor in Physics) from Maryville College in 1983. He has over 35 years experience in developing analytical and management applications related to land, ecosystem, and natural resources issues. He specializes in developing complex database management systems, including desktop and web interfaces. In addition to performing these services for numerous private clients, he has a long history of working for numerous state, local, and federal government clients. Notable examples include the US Army Corps of Engineers, the US Department of Energy, and NASA.

1 About This Book

1.1 THE PURPOSE AND OBJECTIVES OF THIS BOOK

Scientific investigations are driven by data. If you accept this as a valid premise, then one unavoidable conclusion is that improving the quality of data is a desirable aspect of good science. Given this, it should be the objective of all organizations involved in scientific investigation to do the best job possible for ensuring data quality. One of the largest contributing factors to data quality is effective data management. Toward that end, the primary purpose of this book is to educate the readers about the concepts, principles, and best practices for managing environmental data. There are three goals that further refine this purpose:

- defining the concept of data management;
- identifying general data management techniques and exploring how they may be best applied to environmental data; and
- illustrating environmental data management principles using real-world examples.

The purpose is supported by a series of objectives. The objectives are implicit in the titles and content of the chapters in Part 1. If all objectives are achieved, by the end of Part 1, the reader will:

- be able to identify effective methods for managing data;
- have a working knowledge of relational database management systems;
- understand the options available for establishing an effective environmental data management system;
- be able to design a database that addresses the needs of their organization; and
- have sufficient information to manage the creation of a custom user interface.

1.2 STRUCTURE OF THE BOOK

This book consists of three parts. The introductory material establishes the common vocabulary used throughout the remainder of the book. This is a critical foundation for the discussion. Once the preliminary basis is established, the presentation of

DOI: 10.1201/9781003131953-1

detailed information can proceed. Part 1 describes the entire process of creating a proper data management system under ideal conditions. Part 1 can be considered the formal education portion of the book. Part 2 then presents examples of the application of the principles and practices of Part 1. Part 2 thus serves two purposes. First, it demonstrates proper application of concepts and practices discussed in Part 1. Second, it describes what happens when the best practices of Part 1 conflict with requirements imposed by the real world.

1.3   WHO SHOULD READ THIS BOOK

The target audience of this book encompasses several groups. These include:

- students enrolled in courses related to Environmental Studies who recognize the need for knowledge concerning management of large data sets;
- environmental professionals who are already involved in collecting and managing data but are searching for ways to improve their techniques;
- computer scientists who may be called upon to assist environmental professionals with data management; and
- anyone with an interest in a more thorough understanding of the process of environmental data management.

This list does not necessarily identify every category of readers who could benefit from the book, but it identifies the major ones. The first group is academically focused and should consider the content much like any other text book. The second group will be looking for practical applications that can help solve situations they are already facing. Members of the third group likely already know much of the database-related information contained in the book. For them, the advantage to be gained is insight into the nuances of applying their knowledge for environmental endeavors. The last group defies clearer delineation. Each group may be curious as to the chapters most pertinent to their goals. Our recommendations are as follows:

- For the first group, Chapters 2, 3, 4, and 6 are essential. Chapters 5, 7, and 8 may be instructive depending on interests or inclinations.
- For the second group, Chapters 2 through 6 plus the first part of Chapter 8 are the most important (with special emphasis on Chapter 5). Chapter 7 and the remainder of Chapter 8 will be helpful depending on the choice made based on information presented in Chapter 5.
- For the third group, Chapters 6 through 8 identify how important elements of database management are best implemented for environmental activities.
- For the last group, all of Chapters 2 through 8 should be interesting and informative.

Everyone should read Part 2 if for no other reason than to understand that you can never anticipate everything up front.

1.4 WHAT THIS BOOK IS NOT

We've identified what this book is (or at least what it's intended to be), but it's just as critical to understand what this book is not. It is not a step-by-step guide for creating a specific data management system for a particular environmental study. The information contained herein should convince you that every environmental data system's objectives are sufficiently unique that such a guide could only be written after the fact – and would be only moderately useful for future efforts. This book is also not intended to be a definitive primer on structured query language (SQL). There are many fine books and other resources that cover this topic in detail. This book is not a technical treatise on or a comprehensive exploration of database theory. We leave such weighty subjects to our colleagues who are academically more advanced than we.

2 Data Management Concepts

2.1 WHAT DOES IT MEAN TO "MANAGE DATA?"

As scientists, we are accustomed to a certain level of consistency when we approach an unfamiliar subject. We start with the definitions of basic terms and proceed to exploration of the theoretical framework that supports the subject. As an example, consider how you might start learning about migration of contaminants in groundwater. The first steps are acquiring an understanding of concepts such as hydraulic conductivity, soil porosity, and the vadose zone. These are rigorously defined terms and everyone agrees on a common definition. You can choose any resource and be reasonably sure that the definition and explanation of each term will be consistent. From this starting point you move on to the mathematical bases for analysis (Darcy's law, etc.). Now you have the foundation on which you can start to construct your particular interest or investigation.

Is this framework applicable to data management? That is, can we start by finding a common, consistent definition of "data management?" Perhaps. As an interesting exercise, try searching the web for one. I just now tried it – I entered "definition of data management" (as a phrase) into Google and the summary reported more than 7.2 million pages! If you explore a few of these pages, you'll discover a wide variety of "definitions" of the term. Fortunately, you'll also discover that a great number of the differences are simply contextual and that a common terminology emerges. Here are the first sentences from a few of the pages my search returned:

From an Oracle Corporation page: "Data management is the practice of collecting, keeping, and using data securely, efficiently, and cost-effectively."[1]

From a TechTarget page: "Data management is the process of ingesting, storing, organizing and maintaining the data created and collected by an organization."[2]

From a SAS Institute page: "Data management is the practice of managing data as a valuable resource to unlock its potential for an organization."[3]

---

[1] Oracle Corporation. 2020. What is Data Management? www.oracle.com/database/what-is-data-management/.

[2] TechTarget. 2020. What is data management and why is it important? https://searchdata management.techtarget.com/definition/data-management.

[3] SAS Institute. 2020. Data management: What it is and why it matters. www.sas.com/en_us/insights/data-management/data-management.html.

DOI: 10.1201/9781003131953-2

Note the self-reference in that last one. This tautology pops up a lot, as in this definition from the Wikipedia page for data management: "Data Management comprises all disciplines related to managing data as a valuable resource."[4] At this point we can argue that attempting to apply the scientific method and develop an underlying theory of data management is an exercise in futility. I propose the reason for this is that organizing and storing data is such a basic part of the human experience that it defies deconstruction. This is what we do as humans – we gather information (data) through our interactions with the world, then store and organize it (manage it) in our internal database (our brain). The concept is so fundamental that it doesn't require a definition.

Is "Data" a singular or plural noun? Throughout most of my career I've been a stickler about insisting that data is a plural noun. The word is Latin and is the plural form of datum. End of story. But language is an ever-evolving entity, and we learn to adapt. The large dictionary on my shelf is "Webster's New Universal Unabridged Dictionary" from 1983, and it states that data is a plural noun. But it also notes that it is "construed as singular." (Oddly, the paperback dictionary on my shelf includes neither "data" nor "datum.") The AP Stylebook (1984) lists it as plural, but also includes it in a list of "collection nouns" that can represent a group of like items treated as a unit, in which case it is singular. The way I use the term is similar to that described in the AP interpretation, but not an exact match. I've come to use data as a plural noun when referring to specific examples – as in "The data for the Smith project have been reviewed" – and as a singular noun when invoking a more generic meaning – as in "Data is the life's blood of most scientific endeavors." Even within this framework, however, I'm not always consistent. Don't hold that against me. Also, don't make fun of the dates of my reference books.

There are some common threads, however, that help illustrate why there is so much literature about managing data. Two of the citations above explicitly list data as a "valuable resource." That phrase speaks volumes about the importance of proper data management: data is the life's blood of most (some might say all) scientific endeavors. We spend a lot of time, effort, and capital collecting data; therefore, it is vitally important that we take all precautions necessary to manage it properly.

The point of this exercise is to establish that "data management" is an incredibly broad subject with an almost unlimited number of nuances and variations to be explored. We don't necessarily need an exact definition of the term because it is intuitive enough that we can just accept an understood definition. Even if we abandon attempts to rigorously define the term, there is value to be gained by examining the characteristics of the process of data management. In particular, we want to identify the criteria by which we will judge the effectiveness of a particular data management approach. Fortunately, the similarities in the definitions provide sufficient commonality to do this.

---

[4] Wikipedia. August 2020. Data management. https://en.wikipedia.org/wiki/Data_management.

For simplicity, let us begin by stating that a data management system has two primary characteristics: data storage and data retrieval. We will stipulate it is acceptable to describe any system that meets these two objectives as a data management system. These two characteristic descriptors are also themselves such basic terms that we will accept them as having their commonly interpreted meanings. We can then proceed to the following description of a data management system:

> Any process that allows us to store data and retrieve it at a later time can be considered a data management system.

Note that we're not calling this a definition but rather a description. The description allows us to evaluate whether a given scenario can be called a data management system, but does not rule out using other criteria if the need arises. We recognize that being able to call something a data management system without a formal definition might be an uneasy compromise for us scientists, but it's a compromise we are willing to make.

As an exercise, try to think of a system that meets only one of the two characteristics – either storage or retrieval – but does not meet the other. It's not easy. I suppose you could argue that making observations of the physical world is, in some sense, retrieving data that was not previously stored. That argument relies on a strict interpretation of the word "data" that leads directly down the proverbial rabbit hole. In that case, are we retrieving data, or are we creating data? If we're retrieving it, then the counterargument would be that the data were actually stored in whatever physical condition or object we observed. As another exercise, we can describe an incredibly silly situation in which we gather data, put it into a container, and launch the container into space on a trajectory that takes it forever away from Earth. These data can never be retrieved. Or perhaps not. Who is to say that many years in the future, man might explore so far beyond Earth that this artifact is found and opened – thus retrieving the data. So even this far-fetched scenario potentially meets our description of a data management system.

What if we put the data in an electronic file and encrypt it using a complex key generated by a computer and the key is not recorded anywhere. Would these data be forever unretrievable? Would we therefore not consider this a data management system at all? Advances in number theory and cryptanalysis suggest that no such encryption is unbreakable forever, so the data could someday be retrieved and therefore this would qualify as a data management system. What about our measures to evaluate the system (see below)? It certainly fails the data accessibility assessment. It also likely fails the data integrity measure because until we are able to retrieve it, we have no way of knowing if it was retained in its original form (would we consider this Schrödinger's data?). Hopefully you get the point: if we have data, we have a data management system essentially by default.

Being able to acknowledge something as a data management system is in itself insufficient for discussing principles and best practices. The more interesting investigation lies in the determination of whether a particular data management system meets our needs – we need to evaluate the effectiveness of a particular data management system. We need some measures. Fortunately, at the most basic level, we don't require very many. For our purposes, two will be enough: data integrity and data accessibility.

Data *integrity* refers to the ability of the system to retain information in its accepted form while providing all other services required of the data management system.

Data *accessibility* measures the level of difficulty required to interact with specific data from the system under normal conditions.

"Accepted" is an important word in the data integrity definition. We might consider using "original" instead, but that implies a lack of change in the data. We know that data can change over time, so intuitively we know that it may not remain in its original form. The data can change because it is accessible and therefore subject to correction and modification. This observation illustrates an important point: the characteristics and measures are not concepts to be treated individually but instead have multiple levels of interdependence. Choices we make regarding storing data affect both the other characteristic and both measures. The processes we implement for accessing the data must protect the integrity of the data. The interactions between these concepts make them virtually inseparable. Consider another simple situation. Let's say our data management approach is to save the paper copies of the laboratory results reports in a filing cabinet in the basement. We can retrieve the data but in this case data retrieval is not very efficient because of the physical inconvenience. We would deem the data accessibility measure as not particularly good. Furthermore, the pages may age and become unreadable over time, which renders the data integrity questionable. (Also, there is a rather suspect looking water pipe directly above the filing cabinet …) We must accept the characteristics and the measures as a single package.

Further consideration of the data accessibility measure quickly leads us to another important aspect of a data management system: organization. The critical phrase in our definition of data accessibility is "level of difficulty." Disorganized data – data without some logical method that guides how it is arranged – is accessible, but target data may only be retrieved by searching through all the data. We can therefore add a corollary to our data accessibility measure.

Data accessibility is dramatically improved by the imposition of a method of organizing the data.

There are many ways of organizing data, and once again it is something we humans tend to do intuitively. As we continue our exploration of data management approaches, we will quickly observe that the most efficient systems offer multiple ways of organizing data. (This paragraph is the text equivalent of a movie teaser. Stay tuned.)

In the next chapter we will examine different potential ways in which we might manage data. For each approach, we'll use the characteristics to decide if we're willing to call the approach a data management system. (Based on the discussion so far, it's not hard to anticipate that they will all pass this first test.) We'll then use the measures to assess how effective each approach will be.

2.2   OTHER FUNCTIONS OF A DATA MANAGEMENT SYSTEM

So far we've focused on the most basic concepts associated with managing data, but there are other significant tasks we will want a data management system to be capable of completing. Common examples are analyzing data, generating reports, and sharing data with other data management systems. These capabilities are desirable but they should not be considered inherent characteristics of the data management system because all of them can be performed outside the data management system itself. If you can retrieve data effectively, you can generally accomplish these goals. Still, including some additional functionality in the data management system leads to more efficient workflows.

The distinction between analysis and reporting is somewhat amorphous. Reporting typically refers to presenting the data in a predetermined format, but a great many reports perform data analysis as part of the report. Many systems for managing environmental data include the capacity to create a report that identifies values that exceed regulatory limits. In order to make that determination, the system must perform the rudimentary analysis of comparing the values to the limits. More complex reports usually require more complex analyses. Conversely, displaying the results of any analysis requires generating a report by definition. This conflation is why few commercial data management solutions offer "analysis" as part of their interface but almost all will include an option for reports.

The most basic level of reporting is essential to every data management system. Without any ability to present data in a manner that makes it capable of being manipulated or interpreted outside the system, we isolate the data and therefore render it less useful. Without this functionality, all required analysis and reporting capabilities would have to be part of the data management system itself. This is a burden that is almost insurmountable. Think of all the different types of analyses you perform on your data; now consider what it would take to make all those analyses part of the data management system.

Other than this most basic report, additional analysis and reporting options become a matter of choice based on the requirements of your specific endeavor. These choices require balancing competing objectives: the ability to expedite a repeated process versus adding complexity to the data model. In Chapter 6 we will more closely examine the implications of deciding which options are required.

Sharing data with other data management systems can be another important capability. (Note that we specify the target as another data management system. Sharing data with an analysis system is accomplished as described above.) Environmental data are inherently part of science, and the spirit of science is infused with the sharing of information. There are a great many systems managed by governments and other agencies that warehouse environmental data. Each system's ability to accept data from external sources is defined and guided by the developers and managers of the individual system, so your ability to send data to a given system may require that your system be capable of producing specific formats and metadata. This also means that you should be cognizant of these targets as you evaluate potential data management solutions to ensure that external system requirements are adequately addressed.

2.3   IS MANAGING ENVIRONMENTAL DATA DIFFERENT FROM MANAGING OTHER TYPES OF DATA?

A natural question to ask at this point is whether managing environmental data is different from managing other types of data. More to the point: is there guidance that can be gleaned from this book that can't be obtained from other, more generic treatises on data management?

At the most basic level, the answer is "no" – the practice of managing environmental data is not significantly different from managing any other type of data. The basic concepts and principles of effective data management are, at the root level, the same regardless of the specifics of the data being managed. On a more practical level, however, managing environmental data is different because managing every category of data is different. The variations are due to differing characteristics of the data being managed. On the surface, these variations would seem to be trivial. If you're managing financial transactions, you need to record the amount; and if you're managing soil properties, you need to record the pH. Big deal … you have a different column header. As you contemplate the data needs more completely, though, you quickly realize that the metadata requirements are different, and the relationships between data elements are different, and the data confidence levels are different, and so on. (Also, the examples in this book focus on environmental data. The familiarity of that paradigm eliminates the distraction of having to consider the meaning of the data in addition to absorbing the information about how it's being managed.)

This introduces the incredibly important concept of data modeling. Data modeling is the practice of identifying the data elements and relationships required to accomplish your goals. Proper data modeling requires that you first understand your business model. Here "business model" refers not to financial considerations but rather to the mechanics of the processes you follow to perform your business. What characteristics do you record about the sites where you collect samples? What type of preservatives do you use for samples associated with specific categories of chemical analyses? Which test methods are appropriate for which parameters? (To be clear, there can be some carryover from the financial aspects of your operation, but these tend to be at a relatively obvious level. For instance, your data are likely project-specific, and there could be some connections between project, client, and data quality objectives.) Essentially, you want to break down every aspect of your business model to a level sufficient for identifying data requirements. After that, you create a data model that mimics the data elements of the business model. The data model involves identifying the data elements, the descriptors that further characterize the data elements (the metadata), the relationships between data elements, how the data elements will be organized, and other considerations (e.g., which characteristics will be important for grouping data elements during retrieval). We'll discuss data modeling in more detail in later sections, but the main point here – and the point that will be emphasized over and over in this book until it's either ingrained in your thought process or you're sick of hearing it – is that you absolutely must create a data model before you can start effectively managing data.

As you move back up the conceptual ladder, you realize that data modeling is critical to every data management practice. So once again, we're back to a level at which managing environmental data is no different from managing any other type of data.

This brings us to our first best practice.

> **Best Practice #1   Always Create a Data Model Before You Start Attempting to Manage the Data.**
>
> Ideally you should create the data model before collecting any data, but this may not always be practical due to previous activities or the existence of legacy data. The data model is an incredibly valuable tool for identifying all the data elements and metadata you need to accomplish data objectives. The data model must be based on the business model.

2.4   DATA MANAGEMENT PLANNING

Before we dive more deeply into the main course, we should address one other topic that is germane to every data management project: the data management plan. (I can hear the audible groan from those of you who have been in this business awhile, but bear with me.) While not actually a part of the data management system *per se*, it is an important aspect of using the data management system and a significant component of every project for which environmental data are collected. A data management plan is absolutely critical to any project involving a large volume of data, but a plan can be very beneficial even for small projects.

Therein lies the key to getting over your distaste for data management planning: the scale of the plan should match the scale of the overall project. The level of detail required in the plan is dependent on both the volume and complexity of the data to be collected. These factors are independent but cumulative. Both are scalable. If your project involves a relatively small volume of complex data, it suggests the need for a moderately robust plan. A project that generates a large volume of relatively simple data results in the same recommendation. Only a small volume of simple data can be addressed with a simple plan. Data volume is simple to assess, even if the judgment of what constitutes a lot of data is relative. Data complexity is more subjective. This is where a complete data model evaluation becomes important. With some practice, you should become more adept in determining data complexity.

It is also possible to create a generic data management plan under certain circumstances. If your business includes performing the same type of activity repeatedly and those activities involve a consistent volume and type of data – for instance, removing underground storage tanks – then you can create a generic data management plan for all those projects. If you do this, though, you must review the data management plan for every project before applying it.

The basic information contained in the data management plan is generally consistent regardless of the overall size of the project and document. Note, however, that very large projects (from a data perspective) may need to repeat some of the elements with different details. This can be the case when different aspects of the project vary with respect to the topic being addressed. An example would be a project with differing data quality objectives for different phases or locations. Significant components of the data management plan are presented below.

Data Model: This portion of the plan presents the data model that will be used for managing the data. The entire data model should be described in a single section in order to summarize the relationships between each of the data elements. If aspects of the data model apply only to certain categories of data, this can be addressed in more detail in the affected section(s) of the plan. It's still important to present the entire data model in one place for easier reference. It's also acceptable to have a separate data model document that is either incorporated or referenced in the data management plan if appropriate. Acceptable situations would include those cited above in which projects are of similar nature and scope.

Data Standards: This is often called the Data Quality Objectives. This segment identifies the level of quality the data must achieve in order to meet project goals. These can be expressed in a variety of terms. Examples include specifying the limit on the number of statistical outliers and identifying data quality flags reported by the laboratory that disqualify the data from use. For projects that involve multiple categories of data, the standards can be different for each category.

Roles and Responsibilities: This portion describes each category of activity associated with collection and management of data (roles) and identifies individuals who will be assigned to each as well as the procedures associated with the activities (responsibilities). The level of detail regarding roles can be as generic or specific as required. For instance, the plan for a small project might identify a single role of data manager whose responsibilities include all the activities involving electronic data, whereas the plan for a large project might identify separate roles for data entry/import, analysis, and reporting. A significant role that should always be included is that of Quality Assurance (QA) review of data. Responsibilities of this role typically include both review of data received from laboratories (to ensure, for instance, that all requested analyses were performed according to the project plan) and review of data after entry into the data management system (to verify that no errors occurred during data loading). Obviously the QA review role should never be assigned to anyone with other responsibilities associated with the data being reviewed. Responsibilities assigned to roles that involve collecting field data should include a comprehensive list of the parameters to be measured in the field and the methods used to observe them. Responsibilities assigned to roles that involve collecting samples that are analyzed elsewhere should include sample collection procedures, instructions on sending or delivering the samples to the lab(s), and chain of custody form guidance. Individuals associated with each role may be identified either by name (as is common with smaller organizations) or by job title or description (as is common with larger organizations). A combination of these is also acceptable.

Data Platform: This piece of the plan identifies the specific software that will be used to manage the data (if any ... but who doesn't use something for this these days?). Multiple platforms may be specified for different categories of data if desired, but this should be avoided if possible.

Data Procedures: This part of the plan identifies specific procedures associated with the data management platform that will be used for each step in capturing, analyzing, and reporting the data. If the platform is a comprehensive data management tool designed or adapted for the specific category of data being managed, it can be sufficient to simply cite the activity in the software that accomplishes the task (example: "Laboratory results will be loaded using the standard data import tool provided by the software."). If the platform is more generic – a spreadsheet program, for instance – more detail is required in order to ensure consistency and accuracy of data acquisition.

User Interface(s): The data management plan should also address how users with different roles and responsibilities will interact with the data. You don't have to get into a lot of detail in the data management plan, but you should identify any and all user interfaces that will be used. If any users require customized applications for data access, briefly describe their origins and capabilities. If custom user interface tools will be developed, the specifics of each will be detailed in their respective project plans.

Finally, don't think the plan has to provide the answer to every conceivable situation that might arise in the project. The data management plan should be a living document that is adapted as necessary as new challenges and requirements are encountered during the course of the project. The "final" data management plan is seldom realized until the project is completed.

> **Best Practice #2   Every Project That Involves the Collection and/or Analysis of Data Should Have a Data Management Plan.**
>
> The data management plan does not have to be a tome – it should be of a size and scope that fits with the overall project. The size of the data management plan coincides with both the volume and complexity of the data being managed.

Part 1

**Environmental Data
Management Principles**

3 Techniques for Data Management and Their Effectiveness

3.1 THE FRAMEWORK FOR THIS CHAPTER

Congratulations on your new job! You were hired a month ago by We Sample Stuff, Inc. (WSS) as a field technician. Now you've been assigned the additional role of data manager. The company has a small volume of data from its short history as a sampling contractor, and those data need immediate attention. The existing data are not very diverse because all sampling to this point has been for wells. Still, the company has plans to expand into many other types of environmental sampling. Your broader assignment therefore is to create the procedures and mechanisms for managing many varieties of analytical data as the company grows. We Sample Stuff has only been in business a short time, so there is no formal legacy data management approach – you can design the system from the ground up. Your primary objective is to figure out the best and most efficient system for managing the analytical data.

Being a smart person, you've already analyzed the business model in preparation for crafting an appropriate data model. It's not necessary to present that entire analysis in detail here, but we will note some important considerations that will affect how you proceed. These are summarized in the following:

- Each sampling activity is associated with a specific project for a specific client. The company's accounting system tracks client information, contract details, and generates a list of projects. The data management system will need the list of project numbers and names but otherwise will operate independently of the accounting system.
- Each sampling location is associated with a site. When writing reports, project managers have varying requirements for grouping sampling events – individually, combined by site, and combined for the entire project.
- The locations sampled by WSS so far are all wells, but they have different purposes. Some are drinking water wells, some are used as industrial process water sources, and some are water quality monitoring wells. WSS has additional capabilities and plans to sample other types of wells in the future. The company also plans to collect samples from other types of sources.
- For every sample, the date and time at which the sample was collected are noted on a field data sheet. Each sample is also assigned an identifier.

DOI: 10.1201/9781003131953-4

- When performing sampling, the standard operating procedure is to record a number of physical conditions at the site at the time the sample is collected. Examples include water temperature, well depth to water, and water pH. These are entered manually on a field data sheet.
- The list of parameters for which analysis is performed varies with the purpose of the well. Analysis of wells with the same purpose may require analysis for different parameters based on client or project requirements.
- WSS has existing contracts with two different analytical laboratories. These labs have the same capabilities and similar performance ratings. They charge nearly the same for corresponding analyses. The lab to which any given batch of samples is sent is therefore decided by each project manager based on factors related to how quickly results are needed and the current workload level at each lab. WSS also frequently evaluates other laboratories as potential partners, so more labs may be used in the future.
- WSS has standard operating procedures (SOPs) that describe the actions required for collecting, preparing, and handling samples. Each SOP is specific to the type of equipment used to collect the sample. Another SOP describes the procedure for shipping samples to a laboratory. Clients are provided copies of these SOPs, and contracts state that WSS will reference the specific SOPs followed for each sampling event when reporting analysis results.
- WSS has a Quality Assurance (QA) officer whose responsibilities include validating all field and laboratory results.
- Depending on the project, some sampling events include the collection of Quality Control (QC) samples. WSS offers a limited number of QC sample types: duplicate samples (collecting multiple samples from the same source), split samples (dividing a sample into multiple containers to be analyzed independently), blanks (reagent grade water), and spiked samples (reagent grade water spiked with a known quantity of a specific substance). The objective of collecting duplicate samples is to assess the performance of field personnel by helping determine if the samples are collected and processed correctly. Split samples, spiked samples, and blanks provide a basis on which to evaluate the lab's handling and analysis of the samples. WSS retains information about the relationships between QC samples and regular samples. This information is used for generating an analytical data QC report. Laboratories should have no way of recognizing that a sample is a QC sample.

This may seem like a trivial list because it contains elements of just about every sampling program ever. It is worth reviewing, however, because it illustrates the level of detail required when translating the business model into a data model. This level of granularity is necessary in order to ensure complete identification of all the required data elements.

We can now use this enumeration of important business model characteristics as a checklist for evaluating various approaches to managing the data.

3.2   THE FILING CABINET SYSTEM

Before you accepted the role as data manager, WSS managed their analytical data by maintaining paper copies of all documents and storing them in filing cabinets. The "data model" for this system therefore is defined entirely by the types of documents that are retained and how they are organized in the file drawers. Currently all paperwork for a given project is stored together in the same drawer. Different types of documents are stored in different folders and the list of folders for each project is standardized. The folders for each project include contract documents, sampling and analysis plans, all field data sheets, all chain of custody forms, all laboratory analysis reports, and others. Given this scenario, we now ask the following question: can a paper-only model be an effective data management strategy? To answer this question we start by performing an evaluation to determine if this system successfully captures the business model. First, let's see how well the documents themselves capture the characteristics of the business model. This can help determine both the sufficiency and efficiency of the system.[1]

- Field activity associated with a specific project – The field data sheets and chains of custody are in the file drawer for the project, so this is acceptable.
- Sampling location associated with a site – The contract documents identify the site; so since the contract document, the field data sheets, and the chains of custody are all in the same file drawer, this would seem sufficient to define that appropriate association for the sampling activities. However, some clients have multiple sites; therefore, a potential problem exists if a given project involves more than one site. We need to make sure that there is some way to identify which locations are part of each site. The best solution occurs when the field data sheets and/or chain of custody forms have spaces to indicate the site – these documents can then be used when the project manager starts compiling results. If neither of these forms indicates the site, this information could also be in the sampling and analysis plan. This enables the project manager to connect sampling events with sites, but now it requires information from another source.
- Sampling location type – The same discussion for sites applies to sampling location types. The field data might have a way to indicate the type of well. The chain of custody form is less likely to include this information but it could. Lacking either of these options, we're back to requiring project managers to consult the sampling and analysis plan, so once again we are using data from different folders.
- Date, time, and a unique sample identifier (ID) are recorded for each sample – These items are likely on both the field data sheet and the chain of custody,

---

[1] The analysis presented here is relatively robust in that it addresses most aspects of the collection and management of environmental data at WSS. While the particulars cited are specific to the filing cabinet system, the overall structure and objectives of the analysis are generic and should be used to evaluate any potential data management system. The level of detail in this example is intended to illustrate an example of a thorough approach. Analysis of subsequent potential data management systems may omit some of these elements. This does not mean they were not considered, only that commentary on them was deemed unnecessary.

so technically this requirement is met as long as the lab includes the sample ID in the results report (this is almost always the case). One potential issue is the uniqueness of the sample ID. Ideally we want each sample collected for a given project to be unique within the project and not just within the location or site. There are a number of ways to ensure this, with varying degrees of difficulty for implementation. One obvious solution is to generate a list of unique IDs and then mark them off as they are used. In most cases this is done in the office before deploying to the field by pre-entering sample IDs on the field data sheets and chains of custody. The problem with this approach is that it doesn't allow for any deviation from the sampling plan. This essentially eliminates any freedom the field team might have to decide additional samples should be gathered based on anything that occurs in the field. A better approach is to generate the sample ID using some combination of the site, location, date, and time at which the sample was collected. This can be done at any time, allowing for deviations from the plan.

- Recording of physical conditions on the field data sheet – Acceptable. The field data sheet is a paper form that is stored in the appropriate folder.
- Different analyses for different location types or projects – This situation has a high potential for error unless there are variations of the field data sheet and chain of custody form for each specific configuration. Such an arrangement is unlikely, so this is an unacceptable implementation.
- Use of multiple laboratories – This is not inherently a difficult aspect of the system. Even if the labs produce dramatically different analytical reports, the data elements reported should be remarkably consistent. Acceptable.
- SOPs for collecting, preparing, and handling samples – In order to meet this requirement, the field data sheet(s) and/or the chain(s) of custody must have spaces to document these activities. It could be acceptable to simply have a check box on one of these forms to denote that the methods identified in the sampling and analysis plan were followed, but once again this puts additional burden on whoever is compiling data for the report by forcing them to consult another folder.
- Quality Assurance validation – Some method must exist for documenting QA reviews. It could be as simple as a signature line on the field data sheet and a stamp with a signature line that is applied to the lab results reports. In that case the QA documentation becomes part of each form. Alternatively there could be a QA review sheet, in which case the documentation is separate. These documents might be stored in the same folders with the field data and lab results reports, or they might be in a different folder specifically for QA reviews. By now you should be able to recognize that the latter arrangement is noteworthy because it requires information from yet another folder when evaluating the data.
- Collection and analysis of QC samples – The same chain of custody forms are used for both regular and QC samples, and the uniqueness of each sample ID suffices to meet this requirement.
- Relationships between QC samples and regular samples – The acceptability of this practice is entirely dependent on the method of identifying QC samples. The

method must be managed entirely within the company to assure that labs don't have the ability to recognize QC samples. This means, for instance, that the chain of custody form can't have any marker that designates QC samples. How then do we manage this information? One possibility would be to provide space on the field data sheet to record the identifying information for all samples (both regular and QC) collected at the location in sufficient detail to define any association between the two categories (e.g., the regular sample for which each QC duplicate sample is a duplicate). An alternative would be a supplemental form that records this same data. This option, however, has the now-expected effect of introducing another data source. Another alternative might be to standardize some aspect of the sample metadata in a way that can be easily decoded. For instance, the sample collection SOP might specify rounding the time of all regular samples to the nearest 5 minutes and then assigning time offsets to designate specific types of QC samples (e.g., QC split samples have the same date as their regular companions but the time is increased by 1 minute ... duplicate sample times are increased by 2 minutes, etc.). The caveat to this approach is that your regular sample times need to be sufficiently spaced to accommodate all possible QC samples in between.

A key point that emerges from this evaluation of the filing cabinet system is that simply capturing all the data elements is often insufficient to enable robust data management. The relationships between various elements define connections that are required in order to place data in the correct context. How the data are organized – in this simple case it means how the various paper documents are stored – becomes a critical factor. This will be true in the more robust cases as well.

As with our discussion of the business model, this exercise is just as trivial as the system itself. Once again, though, the point of the exercise is to illustrate the analysis that goes into the mapping of business rules to data elements and relationships. Our examination of this paper-only system has shown that it meets our characteristics sufficiently to be called a data management system, but it struggles with some aspects of data retrieval. We'll end this exercise by providing (admittedly subjective) grades for our two main evaluation criteria. The results are shown in Table 3.1. We conclude with the determination that this system is not acceptable.

3.3   MANAGEMENT OF ELECTRONIC COPIES OF THE DATA

If we had limited our requirements to simply reading the data, our paper management system would have achieved better grades. Such a limitation, however, is wildly unrealistic. The two most common uses for environmental data are analysis and reporting. It's rare to collect data and not be required to generate some form of summary report, so including data extraction and compilation is a reasonable requirement to impose. This is also our primary motivation for choosing data accessibility as one of our measures of the effectiveness of a data management system. Data accessibility is critical to all applications and uses of data – we need the ability to easily retrieve and organize the data in order to meet the most basic goals of just about any project. We easily identified two major inherent problems with the paper-only system when it comes to accessing the data: finding the data and transcribing the data. Consider in more detail the steps

TABLE 3.1
Grading the Paper-Only System

Metric	Grade	Notes
Data Integrity	D	The data are stored and maintained in their original form, so there is no realistic scenario we can expect under normal conditions that provide potential for affecting data integrity. Any subsequent use of the data for analysis or reporting requires manual transcription – a process that has high potential for error – which poses a significant threat to data integrity in that context.
Data Accessibility	F	Accessing the data for any purpose requires the physical action of interacting with the paper copies. Compiling the data for analysis or reporting requires both physical action and transcription.

required to accomplish the task of summarizing the results of a sampling event involving three locations under the paper-only system. First, we must retrieve the field data sheets and lab analysis reports for all the samples for the three locations. Next, we need to create a table grid into which the data will be transcribed. We might choose a layout in which the rows correspond to samples and the columns correspond to parameters, but the exact layout is not important to this discussion. Finally, we examine each field data sheet and lab analysis report and for each parameter we transcribe the value on the source document to the appropriate cell in the report grid.

Okay, that's not a terribly onerous list of tasks, but the process does get very tedious if you have results for several hundred parameters. Given the inefficiencies of the process, there are questions we should ask and checks we should perform to ensure a complete and true compilation:

- Did I make any errors while manually transcribing the data?
- Am I sure I captured all the parameters and results from all the forms and lab results reports?
- How do I know the lab performed analysis for all the requested parameters in every case?

The answers to these questions require more hours of review and comparison, and the last question likely entails examining more paper document sources (the sampling and analysis plan and the chain of custody forms, for instance). Our conclusion is that the paper-only system requires significant investments of time and effort to accomplish even the most basic analysis or report. Now let us consider whether there is a minor change we can make to the system that reduces this effort. What if, instead of relying on paper copies of all the documents, we use electronic versions instead? Does this address the data access problem with the previous solution?

Under this new approach our wooden or metal file cabinets are replaced by one or more storage solutions on our network, the drawers and folders in the cabinets are replaced by directories and subdirectories on the network, and the paper files are now electronic. Otherwise this new system is identical to the previous one, so we need not bother with the analysis of its capacity to store the appropriate data. The outcome would be no different. Instead we examine the effects on the data retrieval and accessibility aspects by repeating the report generation exercise.

The overall report generation process is not significantly altered (this is basically true regardless of the system we use ... generating this report requires the same steps in all cases). The only real difference is that instead of manually entering the results into the report grid, we can now copy and paste data from the source to the destination.[2] That will save some time, but is it a significant savings? Probably not. What about the Quality Assurance (QA) review described by the above questions? Does this system improve that process? Yes, but again, not substantially. Copying and pasting is typically more reliable than manual re-entry of data, but is not guaranteed to be error-free. (The most likely error using copy and paste in this scenario is that the data ends up in the wrong cell of the report grid.) Furthermore, the new approach does nothing to address the question of data completeness.

You could argue that, since the electronic files can be searched in order to identify parameters and analysis request details, the time required to compile the data will be reduced by a large margin. Note, however, that a reliable text search requires a consistency of data that is not assured under either of the systems described thus far. Consistency is particularly important when considering parameter names. Many organic compounds are known by multiple names, so different labs may report the same parameter using different nomenclature. Identifying constituents using a coded identifier such as those assigned by the Chemical Abstract Service (CAS numbers) helps, but some parameters you collect may not have commonly used identifiers. Physical observations often fall into this category; there are, for instance, no CAS numbers for Secchi depth and water temperature. The lack of standard identifiers in these situations places additional burdens on the use of text searches when identifying data. Another issue with searching electronic files is that many search utilities

---

[2] Actually, our ability to copy and paste text and/or to search for text is dependent on the format of the electronic versions of the documents. If we have source documents in a native electronic format (e.g., the documents were produced using word processing, spreadsheet, or other software) then we can copy and paste provided we ourselves have software capable of opening the source documents. Many electronic deliverables, though, are provided in a static version. The most common software for this is Adobe's™ Portable Document Format (PDF). The rationale for delivering products in these formats is twofold. First, you typically don't need any specific software to view the files (assuming the format is sufficiently common that it is widely supported by computer operating systems). Second, and perhaps more important, the files are configured to prevent alteration after delivery. These static file formats come in two variations: generated and scanned. Generated versions are produced by using a printer driver that creates the desired format. For instance, most versions of Microsoft Windows® come with printer drivers for producing PDFs. Generated files are of high quality and in most cases text within these documents can be selected and copied. Scanned files are created by scanning a paper version of a document and are therefore just images. You will likely be unable to copy text from a scanned document and paste it into another application in any meaningful way. If the scanned image is of sufficient quality, you can attempt to convert the image to text using optical character recognition (OCR), but that process is notoriously prone to error and requires significant review before use. Scanned documents also cannot generally be searched.

are limited to a single directory and its subdirectories. There are text search programs that allow you to specify multiple disparate directories, but these may be third-party programs with additional licensing fees. Without one of these specialized programs, you may not be able to search for data to be included in a particular report without first copying all the files to a single location prior to the search. Any time savings realized by the actual search may be negated by the required preparatory steps.

Just as the organization of the paper files in the filing cabinets affected data retrieval, how you organize the electronic copies within your storage device will affect the level of effort required to create a particular report. As an example, let's say you've standardized your file structure according to the following plan. You have a main directory called "Projects." Immediately below the Projects directory are directories for each specific project. Each project directory has a consistent set of subdirectories – for contract documents, sampling plans, field logs, chain of custody forms, analytical results, and reports. Under this arrangement, searching for data for a single project is easy because all the data are under the appropriate project directory. What happens when you get a second project for the same site? You could store the data for this project in the same directories previously used, but then you end up with two projects in the same directory. You will likely have to either change the directory name to include the multiple project references (an undesired inconsistency) or rely on remembering that the original project directory name includes multiple projects. Also, a search of the directory for data for one project would retrieve data for both projects. What if we modify the directory structure so that we have a Sites directory at the top level and then repeat the Projects structure as necessary under each site? That works until we have a single client with multiple sites who wants a consolidated report of all their data. No problem … we make our top level Clients and then subjugate the Sites directory structure under that. Now we're ready for anything, until someone asks us to generate a report of all the data we have for a particular state.

The regression continues: no matter how we choose to organize the data in this system, there may always be data needs that challenge our ability to retrieve the required data in an efficient manner. Our conclusion is that managing the data simply by capturing and using electronic versions of files does not offer significant improvement over the paper-only approach. There are some minor advantages, but these are not noteworthy. Grades for this approach are shown in Table 3.2.

3.4   USING SPREADSHEETS

It was tempting at the end of the last section to define another best practice ("don't rely on the intact source documents as the basis for managing data"), but that seems a bit pointless because it would restate the obvious: the source documents are macro-level entities that are not easily parsed in a manner that would be effective for accomplishing the objectives of a data management system. In reality, no one would suggest actually using either of the approaches we've examined thus far as real-world solutions. The point of these exercises has been to better understand the level of discrimination required to enable the desired functionality – to realize that our data consist of individual pieces of information instead of documents, reports, and other aggregations. Effectively managing our data requires decomposing and

TABLE 3.2
Grading the System That Uses Electronic Copies of the Data

Metric	Grade	Notes
Data Integrity	C	As before, the data are maintained in their original form. Assuming proper backup procedures, there is once again little threat to data integrity. We've eliminated the need for manual transcription when compiling data, but as noted, there are still challenges. No significant improvement here.
Data Accessibility	D-	All we've really accomplished with this change is that we no longer have to visit the file room.

discretizing the individual elements so that each is isolated and accessible. With that lesson in mind, let us now turn to an approach that is often applied to actual data: the use of spreadsheets.

Spreadsheet software is readily available, spreadsheets are easily constructed, and the spreadsheet paradigm offers rudimentary analysis tools. All these traits are contained within a framework that (with some patience and experience) is easily understood. On the surface, storing our data in spreadsheets would appear to accomplish the primary objective of isolating individual pieces of information, making data identification and analysis easier. For these reasons, spreadsheets have become ubiquitous data analysis tools. We therefore logically ask the next-level question: can we use spreadsheets as the basis for the overall data management system? Implementing this approach typically starts simply by requesting that your labs provide their reports in spreadsheet format. At the most basic level this does provide access to the sampling results at the discrete data element level: each cell in the spreadsheet contains an entry that is isolated, distinguishable, and easily extracted, copied, or otherwise manipulated. Upon closer inspection, however, you should realize that this approach is not significantly different from our previous idea of managing more static electronic copies of the lab reports. We still have all the same issues regarding file organization and accessing data from multiple sources. Also, any observations recorded during field data collection will not be present using this approach unless we enter them into their own spreadsheet(s). What we actually want to consider, then, is a system that consolidates the data (at some level) into one place – perhaps a single spreadsheet for all our data. Let's return to our We Sample Stuff example in an attempt to construct such a spreadsheet with sufficient efficacy for environmental data.

We'll start with an exercise that involves compiling data for several samples collected at a single location. As our test case, we choose an industrial process site with several monitoring wells. We begin by consolidating the data for a single well (designated as MW-1). At this location, samples are collected every other month at three fixed depths (1, 5, and 10 m). At each depth, physical observations of pH and Total Hardness are recorded and a grab sample is collected. Grab samples are sent to a laboratory where they are analyzed for arsenic, barium, cadmium, and chromium. Results are requested for both dissolved and total fractions for each parameter. After

	A	B	C	D	E	F	G	H	I	J
1		pH	Total Hardness	Dissolved Arsenic	Total Arsenic	Dissolved Barium	Total Barium	Dissolved Cadmium	Total Cadmium	Dissolved Chromium	Total Cl
2	Sample ID		mg/L	mg/L	mg/L	mg/L	mg/L	mg/L	mg/L	mg/L	mg/L
3	8710-387	7.6	85	0.001	0.001	0.001	0.001	0.0002	0.0002		0.0002
4	8710-388	7.8	86.7	0.0011	0.0012	0.0222	0.0246	0.0002	0.0002		0.0011
5	8710-389	7.8	91.2			0.0225	0.0248	0.0002	0.0002		0.0012
6	2366-011	7.6	55.8	0.0012	0.0013	0.0186	0.0205	0.0002	0.0002		0.0002
7	2366-012	7.9	62.3	0.0015	0.0015	0.02	0.0211	0.0002	0.0002		0.0002
8	2366-015	7.8	60.6	0.0012	0.0016	0.025	0.0218	0.0002	0.0002		0.0002
9	0107-255	7.5	55.3	0.0014	0.0016	0.018	0.0238	0.0002	0.0002		0.0002
10	0107-256	7.6	70.8	0.0014	0.0014	0.0187	0.0249	0.0002	0.0002		0.0002
11	0107-257	7.7	77.7	0.0014	0.0015	0.0206	0.0255	0.0002	0.0002		0.0002

FIGURE 3.1   A spreadsheet for recording results for sampling events.

receipt of the analytical results, a summary of the field and laboratory results is created for each sample. These reports are our primary resource for compiling the data into a single repository. How might we construct a spreadsheet for managing these data?

Figure 3.1 illustrates a possible approach. To facilitate the most efficient capture of the data in the summary reports, the structure of the spreadsheet mimics the layout of those reports. Each row represents a specific sample. The sample ID is located in column A. Columns starting at B contain the results for the sample (not all results are shown in the figure). Does this spreadsheet effectively manage the data for well MW-1? Here are some observations, comments, and additional queries to help evaluate that question.

- The sample ID by itself is insufficient to provide temporal context for the results – we don't know when each sample was collected. This makes it impossible to know if the samples are shown in ascending order, descending order, or, in fact, any order. The sample ID is also inadequate for complete spatial context. We know that samples are collected at multiple depths each time the well is visited, but this format also doesn't include any indication of the depth for each row. The additional information should be indicated on the chain of custody form, but this format requires us to consult another document in order to obtain the needed metadata.
- There are no arsenic values in row 5. Why not?
- There are many repeated values. This is especially true of the cadmium readings. Are the values for cadmium truly that consistent?

How can we improve this spreadsheet to address the shortcomings and additional concerns identified by these comments and questions? The obvious solution to the first issue is to add more columns that identify sampling particulars – date and depth. The answers to the questions we posed can be obtained by an examination of other documents for the project. Let's assume that a closer examination of the chains of custody has determined that no analysis was performed for arsenic for sample ID 8710-389 because the field crew failed to check the box to request it. Now that we know this, a simple solution is to indicate no analysis was performed by entering NA in the appropriate cells. What we are essentially doing with this procedural change is specifying that no result cell can be blank … we're making this a required entry.

Examination of a different set of documents – the laboratory analysis reports – provides the answer to the question about all the 0.0002 values for cadmium and chromium. It

	Sample ID	Date	Depth (m)	pH	Total Hardness mg/L	Dissolved Arsenic mg/L	Total Arsenic mg/L	Dissolved Barium mg/L	Total Barium mg/L	Dissolved Cadmium mg/L	Total Cadmium mg/L	Dissolved Chromium mg/L	Total Ch mg/L
3	8710-387	9/12/2013	1	7.6	85	<0.001	<0.001	0.001	0.001	<0.0002	<0.0002	<0.0002	<0.0002
4	8710-388	9/12/2013	5	7.8	86.7	0.0011	0.0012	0.0222	0.0246	<0.0002	<0.0002	0.0011	
5	8710-389	9/12/2013	10	7.8	91.2	NA	NA	0.0225	0.0248	<0.0002	<0.0002	0.0012	
6	2366-011	7/10/2013	1	7.6	55.8	0.0012	0.0013	0.0186	0.0205	<0.0002	<0.0002	0.0002	
7	2366-012	7/10/2013	5	7.9	62.3	0.0015	0.0015	0.02	0.0211	<0.0002	<0.0002	<0.0002	<0.0002
8	2366-015	7/10/2013	10	7.8	60.6	0.0012	0.0016	0.025	0.0218	<0.0002	<0.0002	<0.0002	<0.0002
9	0107-255	5/11/2013	1	7.5	55.3	0.0014	0.0016	0.018	0.0238	<0.0002	<0.0002	<0.0002	
10	0107-256	5/11/2013	5	7.6	70.8	0.0014	0.0014	0.0187	0.0249	<0.0002	<0.0002	0.0002	
11	0107-257	5/11/2013	10	7.7	77.7	0.0014	0.0015	0.0206	0.0255	<0.0002	<0.0002	0.0002	

FIGURE 3.2   The spreadsheet has been improved by adding more sample descriptors and indicators to show when data are missing.

turns out that the method detection limit for these tests is 0.2 µg/L and the lab records the detection limit as the result when the analysis returns less than that value. This is denoted by a value qualifier (U) in the lab report, so we need to somehow indicate this situation in the spreadsheet. One way to accomplish this is to insert the less than symbol before all the values for which the "below detection limit" qualifier is noted. We also discover that this is the case for some of the arsenic values as well, so by questioning the implications of the suspiciously consistent numbers, we have improved our data quality with this review. The data now appear as shown in Figure 3.2.

In addition to improving the data quality, the changes we've made give us additional analytical capabilities as well. Adding the date column allows us to sort the data in the spreadsheet temporally, which gives us the option of creating a time series graph showing how values for a given parameter change at MW-1 over time. Including a column for sample depth allows us to distinguish the results vertically, which properly segregates the data for our time series analysis appropriately.

At this point, our spreadsheet approach to data management appears to be an effective way to manage simple data. Environmental data, however, are rarely simple. Let's see what happens when we begin adding the next batch of results for MW-1. Immediately we encounter another challenge: we discover that there are results for two different samples for MW-1 on the same day and for the same depth. There are at least two distinct possibilities that explain this situation. The first is that one of the samples could be a QC sample – a duplicate. If so, we need a strategy for managing QC data. We could add another column to the spreadsheet that denotes the QC sample type, thus consolidating all the regular and QC data for the well into a single spreadsheet. Another option would be to add another spreadsheet to the MW-1 workbook file. This allows us to store both the regular and QC data for the well in the same file while simplifying the process of distinguishing between the two. There is much to consider about how to handle the QC data, and we'll return to that issue later. In this specific case, though, the second explanation turns out to be the correct one: the second sample is not a QC sample, but rather an additional sample that was collected because the field team was concerned about potential contamination of the first sample. The difference here is subtle but important. Proper QC analysis takes careful planning and preparation. Specific types and numbers of QC samples are identified prior to the start of field activities based on anticipated conditions or project objectives and are documented in the sampling and analysis plan. The purpose of the second sample in this case is not to support QC assessment, but rather to ensure an accurate analysis of the routinely collected specimen. For this reason, it should not be logged as a QC sample – it is just another regular sample. The only distinction between the first and second of these samples is the time at which it was collected, so we can accommodate this situation by adding a sample collection time to our spreadsheet.

We need all the details for all our data (including results previously recorded in the spreadsheet), so the addition of the sample collection time requires researching the previously entered samples to obtain that information. While examining the source files, we discover another important category of metadata that needs our attention. It's one we should have realized in our last revision when we addressed the values less than the test method detection limit: there are other value qualifiers in the lab results reports as well. Value qualifiers are critical to effective analysis because they note conditions observed in the lab that can significantly affect the interpretation of results. Some qualifiers may be so important as to invalidate any results that were obtained. An example would be a qualifier that identifies results for which the sample hold time was exceeded. The importance of these value qualifiers suggests that they should be included in our management of the data. To accommodate this need, we must add another column for each parameter in which any qualifiers are recorded. To save space, we will enter only the codes in the qualifier columns and include an explanation key at the bottom of the spreadsheet (or perhaps on another tab). Our MW-1 spreadsheet now appears as shown in Figure 3.3.

The more we explore additional lab reports in preparation for including more data in our spreadsheet, the more new details we discover that are significant and need to be captured. The client collected samples prior to contracting with WSS, and they have supplied us with lab reports for those samples. Those old lab reports contain details that carry important implications regarding the data. Key new features are summarized in the following:

- The analyses were conducted by a different lab, so we'll need to record which lab performed each analysis.
- The previous lab reported results in µg/L rather than mg/L. We'll either have to carefully convert these values before loading them into our spreadsheet, or we'll need to specify units for each observation.

	A	B	C	D	E	F	G	H	I	J	K	L	M	N	O	P	Q
1						pH	Total Hardness	Dissolved Arsenic	Qualifiers	Total Arsenic	Qualifiers	Dissolved Barium	Qualifiers	Total Barium	Qualifiers	Dissolved Cadmium	Qualifiers	Total Cadi
2	Sample ID	Date	Time	Depth (m)			mg/L	mg/L		mg/L		mg/L		mg/L		mg/L		mg/L
3	0107-255	5/11/2013	9:17	1	7.5		55.3	0.0014		0.0016		0.018		0.0288		<0.0002	U	<0.0002
4	0107-256	5/11/2013	9:24	5	7.6		70.8	0.0014		0.0014		0.0187		0.0249		<0.0002	U	<0.0002
5	0107-257	5/11/2013	9:33	10	7.7		77.7	0.0014		0.0015 G		0.0206		0.0255 G		<0.0002	U	<0.0002
6	2366-011	7/10/2013	10:08	1	7.6		35.8	0.0012		0.0013		0.0186		0.0205		<0.0002	U	<0.0002
7	2366-012	7/10/2013	10:14	5	7.9		62.3	0.0015		0.0015		0.02		0.0211		<0.0002	U	<0.0002
8	2366-015	7/10/2013	10:22	10	7.8		60.6	0.0012		0.0016		0.025		0.0218		<0.0002	U	<0.0002
9	8710-387	9/12/2013	8:44	1	7.6		85	<0.001	U	<0.001	U	0.001		0.001		<0.0002	U	<0.0002
10	8710-388	9/12/2013	8:49	5	7.8		86.7	0.0011		0.0012		0.0222		0.0246		<0.0002	U	<0.0002
11	8710-389	9/12/2013	8:54	10	7.8		91.2 NA			NA		0.0225		0.0248		<0.0002	U	<0.0002
12	6404-120	11/8/2013	9:52	1	7.2		74.5	<0.001	UA	<0.001	UA	0.08 A		0.1 A		<0.0002	U	<0.0002
13	6404-121	11/8/2013	9:55	1	7.2		74.5	<0.001	U	<0.001	U	0.001		0.001		<0.0002	U	<0.0002
14	6404-122	11/8/2013	10:04	5	7.4		71.2	0.0012		0.0014		0.0228		0.0248		<0.0002	U	<0.0002
15	6404-123	11/8/2013	10:11	10	7.4		71	0.0015		0.0018		0.023		0.0254		<0.0002	U	<0.0002
16																		
17	Qualifier Key:																	
18	A	Lab duplicate not acceptable.																
19	G	Lab performance check not acceptable.																
20	U	Undetected or below MDL																
21																		

FIGURE 3.3 More details about the sampling events have been added, as well as columns to indicate value qualifiers.

- Some samples were diluted before analysis. This is often done in the lab in order to reduce the concentration of the target constituent to a range compatible with the analysis equipment, or in some cases to eliminate interference from other constituents. Regardless of the reason, it's important to know if the sample was diluted.

- A significant gap exists between when some samples were collected and the date when analysis was performed (as noted in the lab reports). We're not sure whether these delays exceed the hold time for some of the analyses, so we'll need to capture the analysis date and evaluate this situation ourselves.

- Some reports include results for the same parameter and fraction using different test methods. The different methods have different detection limits. In some cases, we find detectable results (i.e., values above the detection limit) for the same parameter and fraction for which the values are different. This is useful information, so we need to record the test method for each result as well.

What we learn from this examination is that there are more metadata elements we need to document in order to assure a complete and accurate record of all the lab results. Our previous approach of adding new columns for each parameter to capture each additional metadata element quickly becomes unmanageable. A new format is necessary. The new format is shown in Figure 3.4. We could describe the previous versions as sample-centric because each row contained information for one sample. This format is result-centric in that each row contains information regarding the analysis results for a single parameter from a given sample.

	A	B	C	D	E	F	G	H	I	J	K	L
1	Sample ID	Date	Time	Depth (m)	Parameter	Lab	Test Method	Result	Units	Qualifiers	Dilution Factor	Analysis Date
2	0107-255	5/11/2013	9:17	1	pH			7.5				
3	0107-255	5/11/2013	9:17	1	Total Hardness			55.3	mg/L			
4	0107-255	5/11/2013	9:17	1	Dissolved Arsenic	Analysis Lab, Inc.	ASTM D2972-08	0.0014	mg/L		1	5/14/2013
5	0107-255	5/11/2013	9:17	1	Total Arsenic	Analysis Lab, Inc.	ASTM D2972-08	0.0016	mg/L		1	5/14/2013
6	0107-255	5/11/2013	9:17	1	Dissolved Barium	Analysis Lab, Inc.	ASTM D4382-18	0.018	mg/L		1	5/14/2013
7	0107-255	5/11/2013	9:17	1	Total Barium	Analysis Lab, Inc.	ASTM D4382-18	0.0238	mg/L		1	5/14/2013
8	0107-255	5/11/2013	9:17	1	Dissolved Cadmium	Analysis Lab, Inc.	ASTM D3557-02	<0.0002	mg/L	U	1	5/14/2013
9	0107-255	5/11/2013	9:17	1	Total Cadmium	Analysis Lab, Inc.	ASTM D3557-02	<0.0002	mg/L	U	1	5/14/2013
10	0107-255	5/11/2013	9:17	1	Dissolved Chromium	Analysis Lab, Inc.	ASTM D1687-17	<0.0002	mg/L	U	1	5/14/2013
11	0107-255	5/11/2013	9:17	1	Total Chromium	Analysis Lab, Inc.	ASTM D1687-17	0.001	mg/L		1	5/14/2013
12	0107-256	5/11/2013	9:24	5	pH			7.6				
13	0107-256	5/11/2013	9:24	5	Total Hardness			70.8	mg/L			
14	0107-256	5/11/2013	9:24	5	Dissolved Arsenic	Analysis Lab, Inc.	ASTM D2972-08	0.0014	mg/L		1	5/14/2013
15	0107-256	5/11/2013	9:24	5	Total Arsenic	Analysis Lab, Inc.	ASTM D2972-08	0.0014	mg/L		1	5/14/2013
16	0107-256	5/11/2013	9:24	5	Dissolved Barium	Analysis Lab, Inc.	ASTM D4382-18	0.0187	mg/L		1	5/14/2013
17	0107-256	5/11/2013	9:24	5	Total Barium	Analysis Lab, Inc.	ASTM D4382-18	0.0249	mg/L		1	5/14/2013
18	0107-256	5/11/2013	9:24	5	Dissolved Cadmium	Analysis Lab, Inc.	ASTM D3557-02	<0.0002	mg/L	U	1	5/14/2013
19	0107-256	5/11/2013	9:24	5	Total Cadmium	Analysis Lab, Inc.	ASTM D3557-02	<0.0002	mg/L	U	1	5/14/2013
20	0107-256	5/11/2013	9:24	5	Dissolved Chromium	Analysis Lab, Inc.	ASTM D1687-17	0.0002	mg/L	U	1	5/14/2013
21	0107-256	5/11/2013	9:24	5	Total Chromium	Analysis Lab, Inc.	ASTM D1687-17	0.001	mg/L		1	5/14/2013
22	0107-257	5/11/2013	9:33	5	pH			7.7				
23	0107-257	5/11/2013	9:33	5	Total Hardness			77.7	mg/L			
24	0107-257	5/11/2013	9:33	5	Dissolved Arsenic	Analysis Lab, Inc.	ASTM D2972-08	0.0014	mg/L		1	5/14/2013
25	0107-257	5/11/2013	9:33	5	Total Arsenic	Analysis Lab, Inc.	ASTM D2972-08	0.0015	mg/L	G	1	5/14/2013
26	0107-257	5/11/2013	9:33	5	Dissolved Barium	Analysis Lab, Inc.	ASTM D4382-18	0.0206	mg/L		1	5/14/2013
27	0107-257	5/11/2013	9:33	5	Total Barium	Analysis Lab, Inc.	ASTM D4382-18	0.0255	mg/L	G	1	5/14/2013
28	0107-257	5/11/2013	9:33	5	Dissolved Cadmium	Analysis Lab, Inc.	ASTM D3557-02	<0.0002	mg/L	U	1	5/14/2013
29	0107-257	5/11/2013	9:33	5	Total Cadmium	Analysis Lab, Inc.	ASTM D3557-02	<0.0002	mg/L	U	1	5/14/2013
30	0107-257	5/11/2013	9:33	5	Dissolved Chromium	Analysis Lab, Inc.	ASTM D1687-17	0.0002	mg/L	U	1	5/14/2013
31	0107-257	5/11/2013	9:33	5	Total Chromium	Analysis Lab, Inc.	ASTM D1687-17	0.0002	mg/L		1	5/14/2013

Results | Samples | Qualifiers | ⊕

FIGURE 3.4 The format of the spreadsheet has been modified in order to capture more details about sampling events and results.

This iteration of our spreadsheet is a distinct improvement, but there are still some inefficiencies and concerns with it. First, note that we must repeat the sample details on every row that contains results for the sample. We could reduce the number of repeated columns by creating a separate spreadsheet for sample details (this is depicted by the spreadsheet tabs at the bottom of Figure 3.4). In fact, this probably becomes a requirement when we note that there are more metadata elements that describe the sample than we have included thus far (e.g., the collection method), and complete documentation of the samples is essential. We would then decide which of the sample descriptors are important enough to include in the results spreadsheet. Not surprisingly, the distinguishing elements depicted in Figure 3.4 are necessary because they make it easier to filter the results spreadsheet contents without having to switch back and forth between tabs.

A second potential problem with this spreadsheet is that because pH and Total Hardness are measured in the field, we don't have an entry for these results in either the lab or test method columns. The lack of these entries could be interpreted ambiguously by others who might have reason to use the data: was this information not documented, or were the details just not inserted into the spreadsheet for some reason? We can clarify this by entering a notation in the lab column that clearly indicates these observations were made in the field ("Field Data" seems a likely choice). We could also use the "Field Data" designation for the test method column, but instead we should take this opportunity to improve our data quality by specifying the actual method used to perform the analysis in the field.

Pondering the test method situation for field observations leads to the recognition of an important limitation that suggests a potential problem with the whole spreadsheet data management paradigm: how to effectively ensure that required entries are recorded. Earlier we mentioned that the lab reports for some of our samples include results for the same parameter and fraction using different test methods. From this we conclude that an entry should be required in the test method column for each result. Implementing this requirement, though, can become difficult and depends largely on your choice of spreadsheet software. Some spreadsheet programs may not have the ability to require entries at all. Others offer this capability but may implement it through the use of formulas or macros. If a formula is possible, you will likely have to copy it to every cell in the column. In the case of using a macro, you might only be able to evaluate it when the user takes an additional action such as saving the spreadsheet. In either case, requiring entries in particular columns can be difficult.

A third concern with our spreadsheet is in data consistency and validation. Funneling data into a spreadsheet is done typically either through manual data entry or copy/paste activities. The human element in both these endeavors offers great potential for mistakes, many of which can be difficult to identify even during careful review. Consider, for instance, the contents of the test method column in Figure 3.4. The method specified for arsenic in each case is ASTM D2972-08. During manual data entry, it would be very easy for someone to transpose digits and enter ASTM D2792-08 instead. Now ponder the effect this has on the ability to search or filter data. If you want to find all the results that were obtained using test method ASTM D2972-08, you would miss any that were incorrectly entered. The situation is even more extreme regarding parameter names, especially inorganic compounds. Inorganic compounds are often identified by complex names that include numbers and symbols. Different labs may report these complex names differently, making consistent data entry difficult. One difference that occurs frequently is that some labs will report constituents with numeric components with the name first while others will report them with the numbers first (e.g., tetrachlorobenzene-1,2,4,5 vs. 1,2,4,5-tetrachlorobenzene). [As an aside, we know that some of these differences are likely due to limitations in the lab's data management system. Their system may limit the number of characters available for parameter names, resulting in abbreviated nomenclature. For example, there are situations where one lab reports a constituent by its formal name – 1,2,3,4,6,7,8-heptachlorodibenzofuran – and another reports it as 1234678-heptachlorodibenzofuran.] Some constituents are also legitimately identified with different names – 2-butanone is also known as methyl ethyl ketone, and furthermore is frequently abbreviated simply as MEK. It might require a chemical engineer with a compulsion for detail to ensure consistency in the spreadsheet.

A fourth issue lies in our specific implementation. Because our current approach evolved from previous efforts, we've retained potentially troublesome entries in the parameters column. In the first spreadsheet they were column headers that mimicked what existed in the reports we used for our source material. We made the mistake of keeping them in their original form as our format changed over time. The issue here is that we've actually combined two descriptors – parameter and fraction – into a single entry. This poses a challenge when we want to retrieve all values for a constituent regardless of fraction.

It is possible to construct a spreadsheet system in such a way that some of these problems are minimized. For instance, you could program the spreadsheet so that the contents of a particular cell are chosen from a list rather than entered manually. The code for your programmed spreadsheet might discretely identify the possible valid values, or it might also populate the list from a range of cells contained somewhere else in the spreadsheet. This second option adds complexity to the original spreadsheet design but reduces maintenance activities that would otherwise be required when, say, a previously undocumented test method needs to be recorded. When you undertake this approach, you are basically turning the spreadsheet file into a custom application. Dropdown lists of valid values are common in custom applications, and users are familiar with how they work. Lists, though, can become difficult to navigate (and therefore not user-friendly) when they contain a large number of entries. This is especially the case when the entries may be very similar (e.g., 1,3-dichloropropane and 1,3-dichloropropene). As an added concern, these and other customized functions will result in a highly modified spreadsheet system with many programmed elements. A major problem with this scenario is that the spreadsheet does not operate independently of the spreadsheet software – it's just a file that requires the software in order to work. This puts you in a position of being dependent on the software vendor to continue to support all the functions and programming you've so carefully crafted into your solution. Even a minor change to how a particular function works can wreak havoc with your custom code.

Despite all the problems, we conclude that, with some tweaks, the structure depicted in Figure 3.4 can be effective for managing relatively small amounts of

Sample Loc	Sample ID	Date	Time	Depth (m)	Parameter	Fraction	Lab	Test Method	Result	Units	Qualifiers	Dilution Factor	Analysis Date
MW-1	0107-255	5/11/2013	9:17	1	pH	NA	Field Observation	multiparameter probe	7.5	None			5/11/2013
MW-1	0107-255	5/11/2013	9:17	1	Total Hardness	NA	Field Observation	SM2340B	55.3	mg/L			5/11/2013
MW-1	0107-255	5/11/2013	9:17	1	Arsenic	Dissolved	Analysis Lab, Inc.	ASTM D2972-08	0.0014	mg/L		1	5/14/2013
MW-1	0107-255	5/11/2013	9:17	1	Arsenic	Total	Analysis Lab, Inc.	ASTM D2972-08	0.0016	mg/L		1	5/14/2013
MW-1	0107-255	5/11/2013	9:17	1	Barium	Dissolved	Analysis Lab, Inc.	ASTM D4382-18	0.018	mg/L		1	5/14/2013
MW-1	0107-255	5/11/2013	9:17	1	Barium	Total	Analysis Lab, Inc.	ASTM D4382-18	0.0238	mg/L		1	5/14/2013
MW-1	0107-255	5/11/2013	9:17	1	Cadmium	Dissolved	Analysis Lab, Inc.	ASTM D3557-02	<0.0002	mg/L	U	1	5/14/2013
MW-1	0107-255	5/11/2013	9:17	1	Cadmium	Total	Analysis Lab, Inc.	ASTM D3557-02	<0.0002	mg/L	U	1	5/14/2013
MW-1	0107-255	5/11/2013	9:17	1	Chromium	Dissolved	Analysis Lab, Inc.	ASTM D1687-17	<0.0002	mg/L	U	1	5/14/2013
MW-1	0107-255	5/11/2013	9:17	1	Chromium	Total	Analysis Lab, Inc.	ASTM D1687-17	0.001	mg/L		1	5/14/2013
Pond1	P1D-20130516	5/16/2013	14:15	0.3	Water Temperature	NA	Field Observation	multiparameter probe	13	deg C			5/16/2013
Pond1	P1D-20130516	5/16/2013	14:15	0.3	Dissolved Oxygen	NA	Field Observation	multiparameter probe	9.8	mg/L			5/16/2013
Pond1	P1D-20130516	5/16/2013	14:18	3	Water Temperature	NA	Field Observation	multiparameter probe	13.1	deg C			5/16/2013
Pond1	P1D-20130516	5/16/2013	14:18	3	Dissolved Oxygen	NA	Field Observation	multiparameter probe	9.6	mg/L			5/16/2013
Pond1	P1D-20130516	5/16/2013	14:22	6	Water Temperature	NA	Field Observation	multiparameter probe	13.1	deg C			5/16/2013
Pond1	P1D-20130516	5/16/2013	14:22	6	Dissolved Oxygen	NA	Field Observation	multiparameter probe	9.6	mg/L			5/16/2013
Pond1	P1D-20130516	5/16/2013	14:28	10	Water Temperature	NA	Field Observation	multiparameter probe	13.1	deg C			5/16/2013
Pond1	P1D-20130516	5/16/2013	14:28	10	Dissolved Oxygen	NA	Field Observation	multiparameter probe	9.6	mg/L			5/16/2013
Pond1	P1D-20130614	6/14/2013	10:00	0.3	Water Temperature	NA	Field Observation	multiparameter probe	14.6	deg C			6/14/2013
Pond1	P1D-20130614	6/14/2013	10:00	0.3	Dissolved Oxygen	NA	Field Observation	multiparameter probe	9.6	mg/L			6/14/2013
Pond1	P1D-20130614	6/14/2013	10:03	3	Water Temperature	NA	Field Observation	multiparameter probe	14.6	deg C			6/14/2013
Pond1	P1D-20130614	6/14/2013	10:03	3	Dissolved Oxygen	NA	Field Observation	multiparameter probe	9.3	mg/L			6/14/2013
Pond1	P1D-20130614	6/14/2013	10:06	6	Water Temperature	NA	Field Observation	multiparameter probe	14	deg C			6/14/2013
Pond1	P1D-20130614	6/14/2013	10:06	6	Dissolved Oxygen	NA	Field Observation	multiparameter probe	9.4	mg/L			6/14/2013
Pond1	P1D-20130614	6/14/2013	10:09	10	Water Temperature	NA	Field Observation	multiparameter probe	13.8	deg C			6/14/2013
Pond1	P1D-20130614	6/14/2013	10:09	10	Dissolved Oxygen	NA	Field Observation	multiparameter probe	9.4	mg/L			6/14/2013

Tabs: **Results** | Samples | Locations | Qualifiers

FIGURE 3.5 The spreadsheet approach has reached its maximum potential with this iteration.

simple analytical data. What happens when the scope of our data expands? To this point we've only considered the situation in which our spreadsheet houses data for one location. We've previously stated that our best solution will be a single repository for all our data, so let us now consider whether this approach can be effective as an overall strategy for managing all our sampling results. We will repeat the same escalation of levels we performed in Section 3.3 and see how each added level affects our file.

We start by giving the spreadsheet the ability to manage all data for a site. This change requires adding a column to the samples spreadsheet that identifies the specific sampling location at which each sample was collected within the site. If we want to reduce the need for cross-referencing between multiple spreadsheet tabs when analyzing data, we will also want to add this column to the results spreadsheet as well. Because the file now contains data for multiple locations at the site, we should also add another new spreadsheet tab for location details. Suggested columns in this new spreadsheet would include the location ID, the location type (monitoring well, drinking water well, reservoir, etc.), coordinates of the location,[3] and the state, province, or other geopolitical entity in which the location exists. Additional columns would be useful for different location types. For instance, for monitoring wells, it is often desirable to know the elevation of the top of the well casing. Many users also find a general purpose description of the location helpful. Figure 3.5 shows the resulting configuration. Note the new tab for the location information. Rows 2 through 11 on the Results tab contain the same first sample as our previous versions. Rows starting at 12 show a new location of a type we have not yet discussed. This

---

[3] There are multiple options for specifying coordinates, and the specific columns required can vary among them. Simple latitude and longitude values could be entered in only two columns if decimal degrees are used, or they might require six columns if each is specified in degrees, minutes, and seconds. For maximum efficiency when plotting locations in a Geographic Information System, a datum reference is also required. Universal Transverse Mercator (UTM) coordinates require specifying a Northing, an Easting, and a Zone. In the United States, state plane coordinate systems vary.

location is a pond that is sampled each month at depths of 0.3 (near surface), 3, 6, and 10 m for water temperature and dissolved oxygen. In this iteration, we've also separated the parameter name and fraction. Otherwise there is not much difference in this version.

The next three levels of our discussion at the end of Section 3.3 involved incorporating first the project for which a particular sample was collected, then the site at which the project occurred, and finally the client who controls the site for which the project was performed. As you would anticipate, we can roll that information into our master spreadsheet by adding columns for these elements to our results worksheet and additional tabs for new worksheets that contain more details about each project, site, and client. With these additions we find ourselves in possession of a system that manages all our environmental data in one container but still may impose a high cost in terms of the effort required to retrieve a particular subset of the data. The major concerns we identified earlier are now more prevalent and contribute significantly to the unwieldy nature of the overall file. Furthermore, two of these issues are diametrically opposed so that any attempt to address one contributes more problems to the other. Those two issues are data simplicity and data identification. To maximize the efficiency of our system, each worksheet tab should completely describe each member of the class the tab is managing. That is, all details about our sampling locations should be on the Locations tab, all details about the samples themselves should be on the Samples tab, all details about projects should be on the Projects tab, and so forth. However, important relationships exist between the tabs; for instance, each location is associated with a site and each result is associated with a sample. We must have some mechanism for identifying these relationships. Once again in our crusade for efficiency, we would prefer to have a single element for each row on each tab that serves as a primary identifier that can then be referenced on related tabs. The use of a unique alphanumeric identifier as the primary distinctive entry for each sample is an example. Efficiency demands, then, that we use only this sample identifier in the Results spreadsheet to specify the sample with which each individual result is associated. That puts us back in the same situation with which we started this section and reintroduces the problem of being able to easily determine important details required to place results in context. We find ourselves having to compromise between efficiency of data storage (reduction in the repetition of data) and efficiency of data identification (presenting the data in a proper context). Every new report or analysis requires manipulation of the data to achieve the proper balance between these two competing interests.[4]

---

[4] There is one final argument against using a spreadsheet system for our analytical data, and it's something I find incredibly annoying: spreadsheets have a nasty habit of trying too hard to interpret the meaning of what you enter. One situation in which this becomes particularly troublesome occurs when you make an entry that can be interpreted as a date. The spreadsheet may display the data in the cell exactly as you entered it, but internally it still considers it a date. Any external program that attempts to read the data will receive a return value formatted as a date, which may cause unexpected problems. For example, the CAS number for methylene chloride is 75-09-2. Enter that in a spreadsheet cell (just as text), and the entry may be stored internally as a value that indicates September 2, 2075 (or perhaps February 9, 2075 depending on your system's default settings). There are ways to force the spreadsheet program to interpret the entry simply as text, but you must be cognizant of them and take extra actions to make that happen. Very annoying.

TABLE 3.3
Grading the Spreadsheet-Based System

Metric	Grade	Notes
Data Integrity	B-	This grade is conditional based on how much effort we've put into standardization and customization and reflects the best possible outcome. The grade gets progressively worse as these levels decrease.
Data Accessibility	C+	Decomposing the source documents into discrete elements and storing each in a unique container (cell) is a big improvement over the paper system. The level of effort required to manipulate the layout in order to construct a specific data set brings the overall grade down.

What we need is a system that allows us to focus on data efficiency but provides inherent capabilities for assembling the data in different ways as needed. Our grades for the spreadsheet system are presented in Table 3.3.

We conclude this section with another best practice.

Best Practice #3

A spreadsheet can be an effective tool for managing environmental data but should only be used when both the volume and complexity of data are limited. If either of these conditions is not applicable, attempting to use a spreadsheet-based system for analysis will require significant manipulation of data. More manipulation introduces more opportunities for error.

3.5   DATABASE MANAGEMENT SYSTEMS

At the conclusion of the previous section we determined that the best solution for managing our environmental data was a system that stores the data in a very efficient manner but still allows the data to be easily organized in different ways to meet specific analysis and reporting needs. Fortunately, there is just such a framework that is widely available. To no one's surprise, that approach is the use of a database management system. If you've studied particular subjects in higher level mathematics, you have likely realized by now that many of the various concepts we've identified thus far can be mapped to mathematical principles, especially in the fields of set theory and relational algebra. Because database management systems are practical applications of these theoretical realms, it makes sense that they offer the best solution for applied management of environmental data.

In Chapter 4 we will dig more deeply into how database systems work and get a better understanding of how to model environmental data; however, before we get there it may be helpful to explore database management systems in general. First, it's worth noting that there are different implementations of the underlying mathematics that result in different classes of database management systems. The different names of these classes of systems are based on the model used to implement the underlying math.

Two organizations are generally credited with the research and development that produced the first implementations – IBM Corporation and the Conference on Data Systems Languages (CODASYL). (It is noteworthy that the members of these two groups are not disjoint sets.) IBM manufactured computers and CODASYL was a consortium of government and industry professionals organized to establish standards for data systems and analysis. (Perhaps the highest profile outcome of the overall group was creation of the business-oriented programming language COBOL.)

The Hierarchical Model was developed by IBM in the 1960s and is acknowledged as being the first database framework. It is based on the familiar concept of a tree diagram. A tree diagram consists of a set of nodes that are linked by established relationships. Each tree has a single unique starting point called the root node. All remaining nodes exist at some level below the root node, but isolating any node and its children effectively produces a new tree. A key feature of the tree is that the collection of children of a given node is a disjoint set; that is, no node within the tree can be a member of the set of children of multiple parents. The Hierarchical Model specifically implements what is known as an ordered tree, meaning that the relative order of the connections between the various node levels is important (an organization chart is an example of an ordered tree). The nodes of the tree in the Hierarchical Model represent record types. The links between nodes represent one-to-many relationships. Data management implementations using the Hierarchical Model are still quite popular, but are typically created from native source code (as opposed to based on a third-party framework) and used in individual applications to address a specific need. The registry in Microsoft Windows® is an example of a Hierarchical Model data structure, and the registry editor is an example of a hierarchical application. It's difficult to find a database management system based on the Hierarchical Model that is designed to allow users to create their own databases.

A subgroup of CODASYL known as the Database Task Group refined the Hierarchical Model when exploring methods for accessing data. The first standard they issued (1971) defined the Network Model. The Network Model specifies two categories of data constructs: records and sets. The record structure represents an entity with a common set of characteristics. The database can have multiple collections of different record data types, but each record within a given collection carries the same set of characteristics. The set defines a directional relationship between two record types: the owner and the member. All relationships are understood to be one-to-many, meaning a given owner can have multiple members. An instance of a set type is defined as one owner record and any number of its related members. The most significant advancement offered by the Network Model is that it allows a given record to be a member of multiple sets, provided the sets are unique instances within a given set type. An illustration of these concepts is apparent if we apply the Network Model to the basic environmental data we've described thus far. Samples and results would be instances of records. An obvious set would be one that specifies the relationship between samples and results. We might call this set "sampling events." The sampling events set would define the sample as the owner and the result as the member. The definition of the sampling events set would specify that each sample owns multiple results, and each result is associated with one and only one sample. Modern database management systems based on the Network Model still exist but are most commonly found in embedded systems at this time.

Accessing specific data in either the Network or Hierarchical Model is accomplished by traversing the connections between various types of data elements (records or nodes, respectively). For this reason, these models are collectively called Navigational Models. When querying a Navigational Model data structure, the objective is to instruct the system how to navigate to the desired record. The primary drawback of the Navigational Models is that each desired data retrieval format must be identified at design time; creating a view of the data that was not planned in advance is difficult if not impossible. For systems that process a large number of standard procedures, though, they can be remarkably fast. For this reason they are still common in certain business sectors, such as banking and financial markets.

Most examples of general-purpose database management systems – software frameworks that allow you to create your own application-specific data model – use the Relational Model. The legendary British computer scientist Edgar F. Codd is largely credited with creating the Relational Model in 1969. In this model, all data are represented simply by relations. Relations are defined as associations between entities, which Codd called "tuples," but we more commonly refer to as records. The most basic relation defines the set of records of the same type. Other relations define how these basic relations connect to each other. A significant difference between the Navigational Models and the Relational Model is that when querying an instance of the Relational Model, you specify only what data you want. The underlying data management system uses the relations to determine how to find the data.

There are several advantages offered by the Relational Model, but the primary one – the one that makes commercial relational database management software possible – is flexibility. The traditional Navigational Models are notoriously hard to modify after data have been entered, whereas changes to a Relational Model can often be made without affecting existing data. The Relational Model also enables simple methods for enforcing data consistency between entities; this may not even be possible with the Navigational Models. This flexibility, however, is important in identifying the most significant drawback to the Relational Model, which is overall performance. Navigational Model databases are typically capable of completing actions faster than Relational Model databases. However, as previously noted, these systems may be incapable of data retrievals that were not anticipated at design time. We can safely say that this level of certainty is almost impossible when dealing with environmental data; therefore, the Relational Model is an appropriate choice.

Deployment of a relational database may require installation and understanding of multiple pieces of software that operate at different levels. There is no standard definition of the term "middleware," but a common interpretation is that middleware is any software that communicates between the operating system and software applications. Under this definition, the database engine – the heart of any database management system – can be considered middleware. You won't typically be required to understand how the database engine works, but you may be required to configure and adjust it. Rather than interacting directly with the database engine, a software application will be the primary means through which you and other users will access the database. Your ability to manipulate the data in the database is therefore directly controlled by the functionality provided by the user interface. This means that in some cases, operations that are possible within the database engine may not be possible due to limitations of the user interface. We will discuss user interface functionality in more detail in Chapter 4.

Before we leave the discussion of general database variations, it is worth mentioning a movement in recent years toward novel implementations of the models. Many of these are hybridized approaches that were created in response to the increasingly distributed nature of storing large data sets (e.g., data warehousing and cloud-based storage). The Relational Model has not found widespread implementation in distributed environments due to inefficiencies introduced by data segmentation. A class of database management systems collectively referred to as "NoSQL"[5] databases has evolved primarily from the Navigational Models because these models are inherently more conducive to distribution of data. The ability to distribute data is not without its own difficulties, however. The biggest flaw in these implementations is identified by what's known as the consistency, availability, and partition tolerance (CAP) theorem. The CAP theorem was proposed by Eric Brewer (professor emeritus at the University of California at Berkeley), which states that any distributed system that offers sufficient redundancy to support partition tolerance (the P in CAP) cannot simultaneously guarantee both data consistency (C) and data availability (A). As a result, many NoSQL systems emphasize data availability while sacrificing immediate data consistency. Consistency is achieved by progressively updating data across the database incrementally. This occurs over very small periods of time, mitigating the potential effects of data anomalies.

NoSQL databases are often categorized by the type of element on which they are based. Examples include the following:

- key-value – in which records essentially consist of tables of values, each of which is identified by a unique key;
- wide column – a variation on a two-dimensional key-value structure in which the format of columns can vary between rows in a table;

---

[5] The term "NoSQL" is a generic moniker that is generally accepted to mean "non-SQL." SQL refers to the Structured Query Language that is a central feature of the relational model. SQL is the language used by most relational database management systems for interacting with the underlying database management system. SQL sometimes elicits negative reactions due to its potential for extremely complex statements – a by-product of the combination of its power and simplicity. It seems odd that these systems have come to be known as NoSQL since it is possible to interact with a relational database without the use of SQL. "NoRelation" would have been a better name. Ironically, some of the NoSQL database systems have introduced very SQL-like query languages. This is why we consider them to be hybrids. We'll discuss SQL in more detail in Chapter 4.

- graph – in which data elements and relationships are modeled on concepts from mathematical graph theory (nodes and edges); and
- document – another variation on key-value in which tables are replaced by documents, allowing for less structural rigor.

Emerging database approaches may ultimately provide platforms and environments that make them viable alternatives to more mainstream implementations. However, when we limit our considerations to the needs of a typical environmental data management system, the primary motivation behind the NoSQL paradigm becomes insignificant: the volume of data managed by most environmental applications is not sufficiently substantial enough to introduce the need for "big data" infrastructure. To be sure, there are environmental applications that meet this criterion. The United States Environmental Protection Agency (EPA) has multiple systems whose objectives are to warehouse all data collected in the United States related to a particular environmental realm (e.g., water quality data). To accommodate such voluminous data, EPA has created a network of servers and databases called the Exchange Network. The Exchange Network is structured in such a way that it allows virtually any organization that collects environmental data to incorporate their data into the appropriate Exchange within the Network. Because the variety of sources from which these data originate is so diverse, EPA uses a method for data submittals based on the document variation of NoSQL data management. Uploaded documents are posted using an eXtensible Markup Language (XML) format that conforms to the underlying data model. (It is important to note that this applies only to the data submission process. The repositories in which data are ultimately stored are independent of this process and may adhere to different data management techniques.) This volume of data is rare, though, in the practice of front line environmental management. Rather than a data warehouse, the volume of data managed by most organizations is sufficiently limited that a more traditional approach is sufficient. For this reason – and the fact that the technology is readily available and widely supported – we will limit our discussion for the remainder of the book to relational databases.

For the previous example approaches we proposed for managing the WSS data, we conducted an evaluation of their effectiveness using the metrics identified in Chapter 2. We will defer that analysis for the relational database choice until Chapter 8. This may seem unfair, but there are valid reasons for the deferral. First, there are many more variations possible in the design of a database than in any of the other options we have discussed. (You could argue that this also applies to the spreadsheet system, but we believe the deficiencies we identified in that discussion will pertain to any spreadsheet variation you may concoct.) Also, while it is certainly possible to create a poorly designed database that fails just as badly as anything we've analyzed so far, we strive to develop good solutions, so we will discount this possibility. We want to evaluate a solution that at least satisfies the basic requirements of our data model, so we need to better define the proposed database before we can analyze it. Second, we still have a lot to learn about how relational databases work. Both proper creation of the database solution and effective evaluation of the metrics require an understanding of the intricacies of the proposed system. While virtually everyone is familiar with the other methods we've described, we shouldn't presume that familiarity with database principles and practices is as widespread. The purpose of Chapters 4 through 7 will be to provide the knowledge and understanding required to create an effective database. In Chapter 8 we will explore an example similar to the solutions presented earlier in this Chapter. We therefore choose to delay the evaluation until then.

3.6 ADDITIONAL CONSIDERATIONS

While a relational database system is the best choice for managing environmental data when the volume and/or complexity of data exceed the simplest case, databases do not offer a panacea. There are additional considerations that should be taken into account before making a final decision on the method you will use. First, be aware that many people – many very smart people – find databases conceptually challenging. The reason for this is not clear. One possibility is the multidimensional nature of a relational database. Most of the software we use on a daily basis presents information in formats that are easily related to our familiar three-dimensional world. Word processing documents correlate nicely with books, journals, and other printed matter. Graphics programs produce results similar to photographs, charts, and other artwork (potentially, given recent developments, even in three dimensions … but no more). Spreadsheets correspond to the ledger sheets after which spreadsheet software was modeled. Relational databases, on the other hand, connect bits of information from multiple tables into n-dimensional data objects. (Don't confuse the presentation of data contained in a database with the conceptual basis. The presentation takes place on a screen or page, which must therefore ultimately be reduced to two dimensions. The relational model, on the other hand, offers connections beyond the third dimension.) Your job as database architect and administrator, therefore, is to serve as the distiller who translates the multidimensional connections into more relatable forms. You apply your insight and experience to provide others with information critical to applying their insight and experience. The point is that you should not expect everyone to be adept in or comfortable with the distribution of data within the data model. This places more burden on the capabilities of the user interface – the lens through which most users will view the data.

Reliance on the interface raises another issue that often occurs when developing a relational database management system: the tendency to overbuild. It's easy to get caught up in the creation and development of a system and fall into the trap of adding too much contingency to the design. Combating this enticement goes back yet again to an effective analysis of the business model and subsequent translation to the data model. That effort in turn requires a thorough understanding of the various uses of the data. A typical environmental data management system will have data consumers both within and outside your organization. Evaluate the specific needs of each category of data user carefully. It may be helpful to consider the frequency and applicability of each function in order to determine the required breadth of the interface. Ask yourself these questions about each analysis and report you consider when designing the interface:

- How often is this process used?
- To how many projects does it apply?

- Are there other software tools that can adequately perform this function?
- If so, how easy is it to make the data available to the other tool(s) in the required format?
- How difficult is it to create this capability within the interface?

The last question requires especially careful consideration because it has the potential to significantly affect the database design as well as the interface. If a particular analysis demands altered interpretations to data elements that are otherwise unchanged in form throughout the remainder of the system, additional fields or tables may be required to accomplish the metamorphoses. Such additions can burden the system and may have the potential to corrupt other data if improperly used.

Another potential issue depends on which specific relational database software you use. That issue is the level of effort required to manage the underlying database platform. The range of capabilities varies within relational database management systems, but generally speaking, the more capabilities a system possesses, the more complex it is to manage. Simpler platforms require very little effort to administer and in fact don't provide many opportunities for fine-tuning. More complex platforms introduce significantly more capabilities but also require more attention. To illustrate the differences, compare two products sold by Microsoft: Access and SQL Server. Access offers very few options after the database is created: you can limit access to the data by password protecting it, and there is a short list of built-in utilities that perform functions such as compaction and repair or analysis of performance. SQL Server, on the other hand, offers numerous management interfaces and utility programs and a large universe of configuration and tuning options. If your business utilizes a large platform with many functions and options, you may find the need to hire a full-time system administrator dedicated just to the database platform.

Not all the additional considerations have a negative effect. In particular, relational databases quite often facilitate connections between your data and Geographic Information Systems (GIS). GIS software can be an extremely powerful tool for understanding the connection between data and, in fact, GIS is likely the best possible approach for placing environmental data in a spatial context. All modern GIS software has the capacity to link to a variety of relational database management systems. These connections are configurable and often provide querying capabilities within the GIS that create additional options for spatial analysis. Housing your data in a system that is compatible with your GIS software will save a lot of time that would otherwise be required for data extraction and reformatting.

Another factor that is also important in some cases is a requirement to provide your data to other systems. Either your organization or the clients for which you collect data may be contractually or legally obligated to provide data you collect to other parties. These arrangements may be project-specific or more broadly defined. A common example of such a requirement in the United States is found in many projects funded by the Environmental Protection Agency (EPA). When EPA provides financial resources to support a project that involves collecting environmental data, that funding often includes an obligation to make the data available to the general public. Facilitating this requirement is one of the reasons EPA developed the Exchange Network mentioned earlier. Other examples in the United States include large database systems managed by the Department of Defense that serve as repositories for environmental data collected at various military installations. In many of these situations, a relational database serves the data storage needs of these repositories. In all cases, submission of data to these systems requires assembling data into specific formats. Experience shows that these exports are easier to complete if your data already reside in a database.

3.7 SUMMARY

In this chapter we have explored several ways in which we might choose to manage environmental data. The first examples were unrealistic and would never be attempted in a real-world situation, but they were nonetheless useful as exercises to get us thinking critically about how we access and use data. For each system, we applied the metrics discussed in Chapter 2 to evaluate the effectiveness of the method. We determined that it is possible to use a spreadsheet-based approach, but if the data are voluminous or complex, we discovered that this method lacks critical features that ensure data integrity and help prevent errors. We determined that a database is a better choice for most endeavors, that relational database management systems are the most commonly available, and that relational databases are therefore the best choice of platform for managing environmental data.

Using a relational database to manage your data may be intimidating because the technology is less familiar to you than other options. However, the advantages offered by a relational database produce a convincing argument. Adopting a relational database approach will ultimately prove to be the best choice.

> **Best Practice #4**   For most situations, the best choice for managing environmental data is a relational database.

At this point, a decision guide to help you determine the best approach on which to base your own environmental data management system would be helpful. Unfortunately, the breadth of endeavors that involve environmental data makes creating a single comprehensive decision tree impossible. As an alternative, this book will offer a few decision guides that are focused on specific topics. The first one is presented below.

At this point you understand that deciding to use a relational database is almost never the wrong approach, and later we'll explore how to determine variations within that context. For now, though, you may be dealing with data that could potentially be effectively managed with a simpler program. For that situation, we offer Table 3.4 – an attempt to answer the question "can I manage my data with a spreadsheet?"[6]

---

[6] You may have been expecting a traditional flow chart and frankly that's what we originally had in mind. Some of the evaluations and questions that guide this decision, however, may not be appropriate to answer with a simple "yes" or "no." We opted for a tabular presentation instead.

TABLE 3.4
Can I Effectively Manage My Data with a Spreadsheet?

Question	If the answer is "yes," then	If the answer is "no," then	Comments
Do I have a lot of data?	Probably not	Maybe	"A lot" is a subjective call. Consider this comparison. Suppose you wrote each individual result for every sample you collect on a single sheet of standard paper. If this collection of pages would not fit in one drawer of a typical filing cabinet, you have "a lot" of data.
Do I have a large number of different data classes?	Not recommended	Maybe	"Classes" in this context refers to conceptual objects that have the same set of characteristics (e.g., samples, results, labs, etc.). Ten is a sufficiently large number of classes to justify a "yes" answer.
Are there complex relationships in my data?	No	Maybe	Draw a diagram that contains one box for each data class. Now draw lines between the boxes that denote a relationship between the classes. If more than one box connects to multiple other boxes, your answer is "yes." Analysis requirements can also have a significant effect on this answer.
Is there a lot of variety in some of my data elements?	Probably not	Maybe	Less diverse data improves your chances of being able to control input. Only consider the spreadsheet option if all your data elements lack diversity.

If you are able to answer all these questions in the negative, then there is a good chance that a spreadsheet will suffice.

4 Relational Database Management System Basics

4.1 COMPONENTS OF A RELATIONAL DATABASE MANAGEMENT SOLUTION

Thus far we have determined that our best method for managing environmental data requires the use of a relational database management system (DBMS). To prepare for implementation of this recommendation, we need a more thorough understanding of the components of such a solution, the function and capabilities of each piece, and how the various parts interact.

4.1.1 THE DATABASE MANAGEMENT SOFTWARE

We start at the lowest level with the DBMS itself. The DBMS is the software that performs all the basic interactions between the actual database and the higher level components such as the operating system and the database user interface (the actual database – the container for your specific data – is a separate item … see Section 4.1.2). The DBMS consists of background programs and processes contained in function libraries and other bits of code that are not directly accessible by users. So, for instance, when a user enters a command in some higher level software to perform an action such as updating the value in a record, that command gets passed to the DBMS. Code within the DBMS interprets the command and performs the action. This situation is actually no different from how most other software works. To better understand this process, consider what happens when the user of a spreadsheet program enters a formula to add together the contents of a series of cells. The spreadsheet program parses the entry and takes appropriate action by applying its interpretation of the user's instructions. The actions available to the spreadsheet program – like those available to the DBMS – are contained in multiple function libraries and other support files. If the user chooses to sum the cells using simple arithmetic operations (A1 + A2 + A3 … etc.), the specific process invoked by the spreadsheet software may be different than if the user invokes one of the software's internal functions (a typical syntax might be SUM(A1:A5). In that respect, the spreadsheet software performs similar actions as the DBMS.

DOI: 10.1201/9781003131953-5

There are limits to the amount of control you have over the DBMS beyond the initial selection of software. The limits vary with the sophistication and complexity of the DBMS, but ultimately the various settings within your control are typically adjustments that mostly affect the performance of the DBMS rather than having more significant effects. For this reason, it is less critical that you have a detailed understanding of the intricacies of how the DBMS accomplishes its tasks. A more productive use of your time is spending it gaining knowledge about the functions of the DBMS from a higher level.

That said, selecting an appropriate DBMS as the basis for your system is still very important. This is due to variations and limitations that exist between commonly available systems. At the end of Chapter 5 we will present a decision guide that may help with this determination, but in the meantime we need more knowledge in order to better understand these differences. At this point it is worth introducing a few of the most widely available DBMS software packages. There are dozens of relational database systems currently available. Rather than attempting to catalog and describe them all, we will confine our attention to a small number of the most commonly used varieties (an admittedly subjective measure). We will provide a brief introductory description here and continue to focus on these packages as we discuss more details of relational database capabilities in the remainder of this chapter. The intention of our list is not to suggest that these platforms are superior to alternatives. Rather, we focus on these particular DBMSs primarily due to their popularity.

It is important to note that the examples presented will be confined to those relational DBMS platforms that can be implemented on personal computers or local servers. The principles and general functionality of relational databases discussed in this chapter apply to relational DBMS systems on any computer. However, there are two reasons limit our scope for this discussion. First, if you are reading this book, the expectation is that you are doing so in order to learn about this technology. Most people learn better in environments over which they have more control. The personal computer platform offers this level of control better than any other option. You may want to experiment with ideas found in this book, and the easiest way to do so is to use a DBMS on your personal computer or local network. Second, the majority of environmental data are initially managed on these platforms. There are certainly organizations that are responsible for large data warehouses full of environmental results that are housed on mainframe systems. The groups that use environmental data most intimately, however, are those groups with direct responsibility for primary data collection and analysis. These organizations are more likely to utilize a DBMS of this type than one of the mainframe-based systems. The advent of cloud storage may alter the physical location of the database but has less effect on the platform. With that discussion as background, here is our chosen list.

4.1.1.1 Oracle (Oracle Corporation)

Oracle is perhaps the most widely used relational DBMS in the world today. It was first created in the late 1970s and has grown steadily in usage ever since. You can install and run the Oracle database system on a moderately powerful personal computer, but it is often deployed on a network server. Oracle runs on many server platforms and many operating systems. Of the example DBMSs discussed in this book, Oracle tends to be the most expensive option.

4.1.1.2   SQL Server (Microsoft Corporation)

As Microsoft focused on the growing server market in the late 1990s, it introduced SQL Server to address its customers' need for a more integrated DBMS. Like Oracle, it can also be deployed on a single personal computer or a network server. Unlike Oracle, SQL Server is only available (at the time of this writing) for the Windows Server platforms and some varieties of Unix.

4.1.1.3   Jet (Microsoft Corporation)

You may not recognize the Jet name as a DBMS platform, but you are likely to recognize the most prominent application that uses it: Microsoft Access™. Included with many versions of Microsoft Office™, Access is the relational database product through which a large number of users get their first exposure to database management. The Jet database engine has been distributed as a core component for all versions of Microsoft Windows since 3.1. Since Jet is considered a part of the Windows operating system, applications can be developed and distributed without requiring installation of the Access software. (JET is an acronym for "Joint Engine Technology" and was developed with the objective of providing a common database back end for both consumer-level database products such as Access and development platforms such as Microsoft Visual Basic.)

4.1.1.4   MySQL (Open Source)

MySQL was originally developed in the mid-1990s as an open source alternative to proprietary systems for which licensing fees are required. MySQL runs on a wide variety of operating systems for both personal computers and servers. In addition to its use for developing local applications, it has gained widespread popularity as a DBMS for developing web-based applications.

4.1.1.5   PostgreSQL (Open Source)

PostgreSQL (commonly referred to as "Postgres") is another open source DBMS. Its origins seem to pre-date those of MySQL, although its use appears to have accelerated at about the same time.

4.1.1.6   Conclusion

While there are some differences in implementation of the query language and some variations in overall capabilities between these DBMS platforms, your specific choice is likely to be driven by factors not directly related to these disparities. What are the factors, then, that guide your decision when selecting a DBMS? Details about these decisions will be explored in Chapter 5.

4.1.2 THE DATABASE

It is vitally important to distinguish between the DBMS and the database itself. As previously discussed, the DBMS provides the framework and conditions that control your interaction with the database. The database is the structure that contains your specific data. If, for instance, you use Microsoft SQL Server for your DBMS, then your installation of SQL Server is unlikely to be dramatically different from that of someone else who uses SQL Server. Your actual database, though, is almost guaranteed to be remarkably different from theirs.

The definition of what constitutes a database varies across different platforms. Although true in some cases, it is best to avoid conflating the database with a specific physical file. Most commonly, a database conceptually encompasses all the objects and data created to manage an identifiable set of related information. Some DBMSs utilize discrete files for each distinct database, while others incorporate all the data they manage in a single physical file. This file may contain multiple, disconnected data frameworks. For clarity, we would call these disconnected frameworks separate databases. (Some DBMSs use different terminology, calling the various data frameworks "instances," with the term "database" then referring to the physical file. We will avoid the use of the term "instance" and will instead use the term "database" to refer to a collection of related information.)

The facets of implementing a database system that are most affected by your understanding of the distinction between DBMS and database are configuration planning and management. The storage and system requirements for different DBMSs vary, even when identical data models are created. Additionally, some database platforms are transparent regarding the name and location of the database, while others are more obscure. This can effect plans you make for system backups. These variations in system complexity may also affect your ability to create targeted backups of your data beyond routine, scheduled events.

Finally, while not the concern it once was, knowledge of the storage efficiency and capacity within the database can still be a factor that affects your data model. The importance of an effective data model has been emphasized throughout this discussion – and will continue to be in remaining discussions – but you may find yourself facing important decisions regarding specific aspects of implementation. You may discover situations in which multiple equally viable options exist for how to address a particular data model requirement in your database. In some DBMSs, the database size is limited or performance is affected as the database gets larger. In such cases, the best choice may be influenced by effects on the database itself.

4.1.3 THE USER INTERFACE

The level at which most users will experience the data is the user interface – the programs through which you and others interact with the database. Use of the plural ("programs") is appropriate here because the use of multiple user interface tools is common. Your role as a designer and administrator will almost certainly require you to interact with the database on a more detailed level than most users. You never want to isolate yourself from the same tools as those used by the regular user community, however, so your specific work will likely require the use of multiple interfaces. At minimum, initial design steps will require you to work with programs that are part of the DBMS itself. Depending on the level of experience possessed by your user community, you may not want general users to have access to these programs. An interface program with more limited capabilities is generally advisable.

The required capabilities and functions of the primary user interface – the one used for data entry, analysis, and reporting – are determined both by the variety and experience level of the users. If you will be the only person interacting with the data, it may be acceptable to essentially have no user interface beyond the tools provided by the DBMS. A well-designed database can be managed effectively through direct queries, but this approach requires a thorough understanding of the data model (a quality that you, as the database architect, possess). More commonly, however, an alternative is desirable that does not rely on knowledge of either the data model or the query syntax supported by the DBMS. In most instances, the primary functional requirements of this alternative interface will be data entry and editing. An interface that handles only these functions might be acceptable, for example, if a limited number of coworkers will be responsible for entering data while you maintain responsibility for all other functions such as data analysis and reporting. If you have a wider variety of users with different roles, you may need a more complex interface or (optionally) multiple interface programs. This would be appropriate if, for instance, you have one group of users who enter and/or edit data, another group that performs QC review of the data, yet another set of users who extract and analyze the data, and a final group responsible for generating reports (or any combination of these responsibilities).

Before you start designing and developing your solution, these decisions should already have been addressed in the data management plan and other documents. "Other documents" might include the system design document, which is part of the project plan created for any software development required for the system. Also note that decisions related to the user interface may be moot if you choose a complete existing environmental data management system. In Chapter 5 we will debate the advantages and disadvantages of using an existing software system or creating your own. For now, there are many more details to learn about the various elements of a relational database.

4.2   ELEMENTS OF A RELATIONAL DATABASE SYSTEM

Section 4.1 identified the pieces that constitute the conceptual framework for the system. We now turn our attention to a more detailed investigation of the elements common to all (or at least most) relational database implementations.

4.2.1   STRUCTURED QUERY LANGUAGE (SQL)

Every software platform has a language that enables communication between users and the software. For instance, with spreadsheet software this language consists of the functions and macro statements that can be used to perform calculations or other manipulations. Different spreadsheet software packages are likely to have different function syntax and macro statements. The vast majority of relational DBMSs, on the other hand, use a common syntax: Structured Query Language (SQL ... often pronounced like the word "sequel"). Be aware that there are subtle variations in SQL among different DBMSs, and some systems have implementations that are either more or less robust and capable when compared to others.[1] The basics of SQL, though, are relatively well defined and consistent. This is primarily due to both its flexibility and origins, which date back to the earliest developed relational database systems.

Presenting a comprehensive reference on SQL is beyond the scope of this volume. There are countless books and websites that offer explorations and instructions to address that need. The fact that there are entire compendia devoted to specific implementations of SQL is sufficient reason to avoid a complete attempt in this space. That said, some basic SQL syntax examples will be provided in this chapter. The primary purpose of including these statements is to familiarize you with general SQL syntax and statement structure. A complete understanding of these statements requires knowledge of the database objects being referenced, so examples will be deferred until after discussion of the objects themselves. Additionally, be aware that the online resources that support this book contain detailed examples that perform specific functions related to more definitive needs.

For our purposes, we will assert that common implementations of SQL offer two main categories of statements: those that constitute the Data Definition Language (DDL) and those that constitute the Data Manipulation Language (DML). DDL statements create and modify database objects – elements we will present in the remainder of this chapter. DML statements operate on those objects by performing actions such as adding or updating records, or retrieving records that match specific criteria. You will need to know both categories, although you will typically use the DML statements much more often than the DDL statements. You may use the DDL statements frequently during initial database creation, but once your database structure is completed, they will not be required as frequently. This might be a good circumstance, though, since execution of some DDL statements requires careful planning to avoid unintended consequences on existing data.

Note that many DBMSs include tools that offer graphical or other methods for creating database objects as an alternative to use of DDL. You might infer from this that intricate knowledge of the DDL statements is not needed. From our perspective, more knowledge is always better. Furthermore, the power of the DDL commands requires that they be used with caution. At the very least, you should be aware that DBMS tools for creating and modifying database objects work by soliciting your input and then generating the appropriate DDL commands to accomplish the task at hand. Your level of trust that the action performed by the tool is exactly the action you desired correlates with your level of confidence in the source of the tool. This level of confidence is enhanced if you understand DDL processes as a separate approach. *Caveat emptor.*

---

[1] The American National Standards Institute (ANSI) adopted a standard for SQL in 1986, and the International Organization for Standardization (ISO) adopted a standard in 1987.

Before presenting examples of DDL and DML statements in later sections, we should note that there are SQL commands that perform other categories of activities as well. The most commonly used of these are usually classified as Data Control Language (DCL) statements. DCL statements accomplish things like creating user accounts and establishing privileges. These actions tend to be much more DBMS-specific, and so the DCL statements tend to be less standardized. In Sections 4.2.2 and 4.2.3 we'll discuss users and roles. As you investigate these concepts, keep in mind that these objects are created and manipulated by DCL statements. Some reference materials may also identify another class of statements called Data Query Language (DQL). Since querying can be considered a form of data manipulation, we choose to think of DQL statements as a subset of DML statements.

One more item is worth mentioning before we proceed. The SQL standard specifies that each SQL statement must end with a semicolon, but some implementations forgo this requirement. We will include it in our examples since requiring the semicolon is more standard.

4.2.2 USERS

On a macro level, "users" refers to individuals with accounts that give them access to the database. In a more technical sense, the term "users" refers to the accounts themselves. The user concept is relatively consistent across most database platforms, but the implementation of user objects varies greatly. Creation of user objects is done through DCL statements. As mentioned above, DCL statements can have significantly different syntax from one DBMS to another. As a result, the exact statement required to create a user in your database will depend entirely on your platform. In most cases, the statement that creates the user object also creates the password for the account.

Creation of users poses an interesting conundrum. Like all other database objects, user accounts must be created by a user (with appropriate privileges … see Section 4.2.3), but who creates the first user? The answer is that the first user is always generated during the creation of the database. This typically happens during the installation of the DBMS. The first user is known as the system administrator. The system administrator then creates all the other user accounts.

The nomenclature employed to identify users is a local management issue, so it's up to the system administrator to determine. For many organizations, users are identified by part or all of the name of the person who owns the user account. For instance, Raul Ortega might have a user account identified by "rortega" or some other configuration. While simple to understand and easy to manage, such practices can lead to security concerns, particularly for users with high level privileges. Consider using more cryptic identifiers when possible.

It's worth noting that some platforms include another entity that can be easily confused with the user entity. The name by which these entities are identified may vary, so we will illustrate this concept using an example from one specific DBMS. SQL Server has an entity called a login. A login is similar to a user in that it involves an object name and some method of authentication. Logins and users can both be created and managed using the same primary interface (typically SQL

Server Management Studio). The difference is that the login object provides access to the server (the instance of SQL Server), whereas the user object provides access to a specific database. SQL Server allows you to allocate capabilities (privileges) to both entity types, although the available capabilities vary between the two. SQL Server provides a mechanism for linking instances of the two entities so that a user object is tied to a login object. The important concept here is that accessing a particular database on a given instance of SQL Server requires the use of both a login object and a user object. Making the situation even more complicated, Microsoft allows different configurations so that logins can be verified either using Windows authentication (managed by the server) or SQL Server authentication (managed within the DBMS).

Essentially, the login object is a system-level security feature and the user object is a database-level security feature. Not all database platforms address system-level security, but both levels still exist nonetheless: in order to access a database, you must be able to connect to the computer on which the database resides as well as to the specific database itself. Those DBMS packages that do not offer system-level security features rely on network functions to provide this capability.

In this book, the term "user" always implies the database-specific entity.

4.2.3   ROLES AND PRIVILEGES

Roles are standard designations of the capabilities that may be granted to users. The individual capabilities themselves are called privileges. Separating these two concepts can be challenging at first because they are often managed by the same DDL statements. Different platforms may use different terminologies for the same roles and privileges, and sometimes there may be subtle differences between privileges on different DBMSs that have the same name. Table 4.1 describes some of the most common privileges found in most DBMSs.

The names shown in Table 4.1 are typical, but may vary within specific DBMSs. Some platforms also include modifiers that either enhance or limit a particular privilege. Many platforms also have additional privileges beyond the basic ones listed here.

TABLE 4.1
Typical DBMS Privileges

Privilege Name	Users with this privilege are able to ...
CREATE	create new instances of the object specified (e.g., "CREATE TABLE...")
ALTER	modify the structure of the object specified (e.g., "ALTER TABLE...")
DROP	delete instances of the object specified (e.g., "DROP INDEX...")
INSERT	insert rows into tables
DELETE	delete rows from tables
UPDATE	modify the contents of columns in tables
SELECT	retrieve data from tables.

In every relational DBMS, the user who creates an object is considered the owner of that object. The owner has full privilege on any object they create, regardless of any privilege settings associated with their account. Privileges are best thought of as capabilities granted to other users by the owner of the object. Of course, this means that if a particular user does not have CREATE privileges in the database, they usually may not grant other users any privileges since they have no way of creating new objects. In practice, all the objects in many databases are created by the system administrator. This is especially true of databases created to manage data at a local level – environmental data, for instance.

Privileges may be granted to users on an individual basis, but there are shortcuts that allow users to be granted multiple privileges without requiring enumeration. Roles are essentially predefined sets of privileges, so granting a user a specific role gives them permission to perform the actions available to each associated privilege. Most DBMSs include default roles that are appropriate for different types of typical users. For instance, the system administrator referred to in Section 4.2.2 is a role that is predefined on most platforms. Most DBMSs also provide a mechanism for creating new roles. As an example, consider the case where you need to grant certain users the ability to insert new data and retrieve any data, but not to delete or update any existing data. You might create a role called "NEWDATA" that grants SELECT and INSERT privileges only.

Management of users, roles, and privileges is a significant part of system administration and requires careful planning and execution.

4.2.4 SCHEMA

Different sources define the word "schema" differently. Some sources describe it as applying to the database ("The schema is the logical description of the entire database."[2]), while others describe it as having a more limited scope ("A schema is simply a collection of database objects that are owned by a particular user."[3]) These differences may seem important due to the potentially significant ranges of applicability, but ultimately the underlying concept of schema is consistent. Regardless of the level at which the idea is applied, the constitution of the schema is the same: the schema consists of all the tables, constraints, views, and other objects – as well as the data contained in the objects capable of housing data – associated with the item at the level at which the term is applied. Given this duality, we might more properly require a modifier in order to differentiate between the cases: the database schema and the user schema.

In practical terms, however, this difference is not significant in the context of most environmental databases. In the majority of environmental data management applications, the system administrator or system architect creates all the tables, constraints, and other elements that constitute the database schema. Individual users are granted access to perform actions at various appropriate levels but are often not allowed to create new objects with the system. We will therefore refer to the schema as applying to the entire database.

---

[2] An Introduction to Database Systems, Bipin C. Desai, West Publishing Company, 1990, p. 403.
[3] CodeNotes for Oracle 9i, Gregory Brill, ed., Random House Trade Paperbacks, 2002, p. 30.

4.2.5 COLUMNS

Columns are the fundamental storage locations for specific pieces of information. Every column has a name and a data type. Some columns have additional restrictions (constraints) that limit what can be entered (see Section 4.2.8 for more information about constraints). The user who defines the column establishes all the characteristics of the column, including any constraints. Columns are often called "fields" and we will use the terms interchangeably. Columns are defined during the creation of a table (see Section 4.2.6) and only exist within that context – that is to say, there is no such thing as a column not contained in a table.

As hinted above, there are only two items required when defining a column – name and data type. All other characteristics of the column are optional and have default settings. Columns may typically have any name desired, but be cognizant of the fact that some DBMSs may limit the length of column names. The effects of typographic case can vary between DBMSs as well. In some instances these variations affect functionality. To illustrate this point, consider examples from Oracle and SQL Server. When defining a column in an Oracle table, if the name is enclosed in quotes, the name is stored in the database using the exact typography as entered (e.g., entering "First_Name" – including the quotes – records the column identifier as First_Name). If the name is not enclosed in quotes when defined, the name is stored in upper case (e.g., entering First_Name – no quotes – records the column identifier as FIRST_NAME). When column names are cited in the SELECT portion of a query statement, column names stored in all upper case may be referenced using any case if the name is not enclosed in quotes. (This is true regardless of whether the name was originally entered without quotes or was entered with quotes but still in all upper case, by the way.) If the column reference in the SELECT clause is enclosed in quotes, the name must match exactly to the name recorded in the database. Furthermore, when referenced in the WHERE clause of a query, field names must exactly match the recorded name (and cannot be enclosed in quotes). SQL Server, on the other hand, stores the column names exactly as entered during creation regardless of the presence of quotes. Thus, entering "First_Name" and First_Name result in creation of the same column identifier, whereas entering First_Name and first_name result in creation of different column identifiers. Column names cited in either SELECT or WHERE clauses are not case-sensitive, meaning you can use any mix of typographic cases with or without quotes. Other DBMSs vary on this subject as well, so knowing the typographic rules for your particular software platform is important.

> **Best Practice #5** When creating tables, avoid defining column names using mixed upper and lower case letters, and do not enclose column names in quotes. For best results, use a consistent pattern in all your SQL statements – either enter everything in upper case or lower case at all times. This approach defers identifier capitalization to the DBMS and will reduce the likelihood of bad references later.

TABLE 4.2
Numeric Data Types Commonly Available in Relational Database Systems

Type	Notes
Integer	Integers are usually defined as 4 bytes, providing an available range of -2,147,483,648 to 2,147,483,647.
Small Integer	These are integers stored in 2 bytes, giving a range of -32,768 to 32,767.
Large Integer	These are 8-byte integers (-9223372036854775808 to 9223372036854775807).
Decimal	An exact number; expressed as Decimal(p,s) where s is the scale (total number of digits) and p is the precision (number of decimal places).
Number	An exact number; expressed as Number(p,s) where s is the scale (total number of digits) and p is the precision (number of decimal places).[a]
Float	An approximation of a decimal number; expressed as Float(n) where n is the number of decimal places; these are approximations because they are stored as binary representations using the number of bytes required to attain precision n; the maximum precision varies by platform.
Real	Also an approximation, but the precision is defined by the DBMS (by fixing the number of bytes used) rather than the user.
Double Precision	Same as Real except that it uses a greater number of bytes.

[a] The differences between DECIMAL and NUMERIC are subtle and are defined by an American National Standards Institute (ANSI) Standard. According to the Standard, NUMERIC specifies both the precision and scale, whereas DECIMAL specifies the exact scale but identifies only the minimum precision – the actual precision may be greater than what is entered. For this reason, on some platforms there is no difference between DECIMAL and NUMERIC.

As you might expect, when compared to names, you have fewer choices when deciding on a data type for each column. Options are limited to the list of data types supported by the DBMS. While there are data types common to all DBMSs, most platforms also offer unique or extended data types. We will discuss these as appropriate, but we will focus on the data types common to all platforms.

We can start by noting that most common data types can be classified into one of the two categories: text or numbers. These carry the connotations that you would expect – numeric types are intended to contain numeric values and text types are intended to contain words or symbols.[4] There are, however, multiple variations within each category. Your choice of the specific numeric or text data type requires further knowledge. Consider the numeric data types first. The numeric data types available most frequently in relational DBMSs are presented in Table 4.2.

The names for each of these data types may vary between DBMS platforms, but every DBMS we've encountered supports all these types. A commonly used

---

[4] There is some possible cross-over between the categories. You can, for instance, store a number in a text-based field. There are legitimate reasons for doing this, and the process is simple and obvious. You can also store textual data as numbers – ultimately this is what binary storage does at the most basic level anyway – but you must be much more clever and obtuse about it.

name for the small integer type, for instance, is SMALLINT, but Oracle uses the name SHORTINTEGER for this data type. In addition to these standard ones, many platforms have more types that are slight variations on the common ones. For example, MySQL has TINYINT (1 byte) and MEDIUMINT (3 bytes) data types in addition to its standard INTEGER, SMALLINT, and BIGINT types. SQL Server also has a TINYINT type, but no MEDIUMINT. Another common practice is to support decimal approximations with only fixed precision capabilities (essentially offering Real but not Float). In these cases, you may see data types defined as Single and Double which typically denote 8 bytes and 16 bytes respectively.

A complete understanding of the numeric data types offered by your platform of choice is essential, but in some cases the names by which data types are defined may not be easily identified with the terms noted above. This is particularly true in situations where table creation is done using some form of graphical user interface instead of direct DDL commands. Microsoft Access is a good example of such an interface (recall that Access is an application that interacts with the Jet database engine). When designing a table in Access using the Table Design option, you make a selection from a column labeled "Data Type." You then must further define the actual data type (the specific type of numeric field) by selecting from another list. Choices in that list that correspond to the items we've discussed so far are Single, Double, Integer, Long Integer, and Decimal.

As with numeric data types, there exists a common set of text data types and names used in most DBMSs. These are summarized in Table 4.3.

There are fewer basic options for text as compared to numbers, but in practice many DBMSs offer multiple variations on this short list. The fixed length character field is often defined by the CHAR keyword, with the fixed length being specified in ensuing parentheses [e.g., CHAR(2)]. The variable size character field is often called VARCHAR, again with the maximum allowable size identified in parentheses [e.g., VARCHAR(100)]. There are notable differences between Character and Variable Character fields. The obvious difference lies in how they are stored in the database. A CHAR(25) field that is not null will always occupy 25 bytes in the database regardless of the actual data length. Alternatively, a VARCHAR(25) field that is not null will occupy a number of bytes that is close to the actual length of the data (it will typically be the length of the data plus one or two additional bytes for delineators). VARCHAR fields thus offer a more compact storage option than CHAR fields. Another difference

---

TABLE 4.3
Text Data Types Commonly Available in Relational Database Systems

Type	Notes
Character	A character string stored in a fixed length field; fixed length specified at table design time.
Variable Character	A character string stored in a field whose length varies with content length; the maximum allowable length is specified at table design time
Large Character Objects	Character fields that can store large blocks of text.

occurs when data are retrieved from the table. CHAR fields will always return the exact number of characters specified in the field size. If the field contains fewer actual characters, empty characters (spaces) will be added to attain the required length. This can be particularly important when comparing retrieved data. As an example, consider the use of Chemical Abstract Service (CAS) numbers for parameter identification. CAS numbers can contain up to 10 digits in 3 sections separated by dashes for a maximum total of 13 characters, so let's say you define the CAS number field as CHAR(13). Now suppose you are searching for results for benzyl chloride. Its CAS number is 100-44-7, so you may be inclined to include a predicate in your search condition that states

```
CAS_NUM='100-44-7'
```

(assuming the field name is CAS_NUM). Unfortunately, this will not match any records because when comparing table values to your search condition, the lengths of the two strings will be different.[5] In order to match the desired records, you must enter

```
CAS_NUM='100-44-7     '
```

which contains five spaces after the last digit so that the strings are the same length. This is terribly annoying and easy to forget.

Why use CHAR fields at all then? The arguments for their use are somewhat limited but nonetheless valid. One practical use occurs in situations where the contents of the field will always be the same length. This is often the case in some reference or lookup tables (lookup tables are defined in Section 4.2.6). If the length of the value used to reference a record in a lookup table does not vary, the use of a CHAR column is logical because it provides the most compact possible storage of the data. Consider an example that is very common in environmental data management systems designed for use in the United States: a lookup table of states. Every state in the United States has a standard postal abbreviation that is always two characters. The use of a CHAR(2) column for the state abbreviation is therefore appropriate.

We noted earlier that some platforms offer slight variations to these standard text field data types. In some cases these variations are designed to accommodate international applications and are related to the character set used to store the text. By default, every system will interpret data stored in a fixed or variable length text field according to the standard character set defined in the DBMS. Default standard character sets are specified within the DBMS but may be altered by configuration changes. The default standard character set can vary between platforms. For global applications, the use of Unicode characters is desirable, so some platforms offer explicit support for Unicode characters by identifying distinct text data types. Oracle, for instance, offers

---

[5] This is true assuming you construct the query without resorting to the use of functions to manipulate columns. We will demonstrate some of the more common SQL query syntax in Section 4.2.6, so we're jumping ahead a bit. But the assumption in this case is that your query is similar to

```
SELECT * FROM RESULTS WHERE CAS_NUM='100-44-7'
```

where RESULTS is the table from which the data are to be retrieved. We don't mean to imply that it is impossible to find results for this parameter if the CAS_NUM field is of type CHAR.

NCHAR and NVARCHAR data types for Unicode text. The behavior of NCHAR and NVARCHAR columns are identical to the behavior of CHAR and VARCHAR columns, respectively. The only differences are interpretation of the field contents and (potentially) different storage requirements (the number of bytes). SQL Server offers NCHAR and NTEXT, which are the Unicode-capable equivalents to their standard fixed and variable size character data types. DBMS platforms that do not provide Unicode support through explicit data typing may offer add-ins or libraries that enable this functionality. If your database is required to accommodate Unicode characters, refer to the documentation provided with the software.

The last type of character data noted above is for large volumes of text. There is considerable variation in the naming convention and capabilities related to handling of these fields within different platforms. Generally speaking, the purpose of a field of this type is to capture a large block of text. Some platforms include multiple large text options for different purposes. Oracle, for instance, includes a CLOB data type that can store multiple terabytes of data (and the expected NCLOB variation as well), but also offers a data type called LONG with more limited capacity (gigabytes instead of terabytes). In addition to the size limits, Oracle appears to handle these data types differently within the database, as evidenced by the documentation for the LONG data type which suggests using it in cases where data may need to be shared with other systems. A major drawback to large text fields is that, in addition to storage capacity, they often have additional limitations regarding usage. For instance, most systems do not allow you to use a large text field as part of the retrieval order, and you may not be able to search these fields directly.

You will probably have limited need for any of these large text data types in an environmental data management system. The most probable use will be to capture comments provided during field observations or laboratory analyses. Even in those situations, it may be more appropriate – and offer better options for data search and retrieval – to use a variable character field with sufficient capacity for accommodating expected text lengths.

If you determine that your system needs to store complete versions of certain documents – for instance, images of lab reports – you may consider another data type supported by many platforms: binary large objects, often called BLOBs. As the name implies, fields of these types store binary data of any type. These may be images such as JPEGs or bitmaps, or they may be binary versions of documents created by other software. Even if your database platform supports BLOBs, however, they should be used sparingly if at all. BLOBs can quickly fill space better used for more discrete data. Furthermore, some implementations of support for BLOBs are inefficient or awkward. A better approach might be to store binary data in their original forms just as ordinary files within the file system and use a text field to store the path and name of the file within the database. Many user interfaces can be made to interpret contents of a text field as a file location and name, allowing retrieval and display of the source file without resorting to BLOB data types. Note that this may require the use of additional software for displaying the files, but this is true even when the files are incorporated as BLOBS as well.

Beyond the common data type for numeric and text data, every relational DBMS supports one other important data type: date/time fields. Date/time fields are used for storing exactly what you would expect – dates and/or times. The basic date/time data type stores both date and time, although most systems allow you to omit one or the other in a given record (i.e., you can enter just the date portion or just the time portion).[6] There are also other variations of date/time data types supported by some platforms. For instance, Oracle offers only one option for date/time fields (identified by the DATE data type), but SQL Server offers three different date/time data types – with differing possible ranges and levels of time accuracy – as well as distinct separate date-only and time-only data types, plus a special date/time that automatically applies time zone settings.

Before concluding this section, we need to introduce another concept that is important to any discussion of data types – the idea of a null value. Unless otherwise declared (see Section 4.2.6), the default value of every field in the database is NULL. NULL means that the column has no value. If you've ever written a program in any computer language, this idea may require some adjustments to your thinking. When you declare a variable in most programming languages, the language assigns an initial value based on the variable type. This is often 0 for numbers and an empty string (which is different than NULL) for text. Databases behave differently, however. While options exist to explicitly specify an initial value, the act of simply assigning a data type to a column has no effect in this regard. In the absence of the identification of a default value, the addition of a new record to a table creates a new instance of the column but the column's value is essentially empty – NULL. Null values are so pervasive and important that all relational databases have procedures and commands related to identifying them. Examples of these will appear in the next few sections.

As a final note for this section, we should mention that many DBMSs also offer other data types that are not considered standard. Some of these will actually be variations on the standard data types but targeted for specific purposes. As such, they may support special formatting or handling within the DBMS. One of the most common such type you may encounter – especially if you use some form of graphical user interface for creating tables instead of relying on DDL commands – is for values that are either true or false. These may be identified as yes/no, true/false, or Boolean data types. The reason you will see this most often in an interactive interface for defining tables is that surprisingly few platforms actually support a Boolean type directly. Because the DBMS interacts with the operating system using the same methods as other programs, the smallest available storage unit is typically 1 byte. Since the DBMS likely has other single-byte options (e.g., CHAR(1) or TINYINT), it is more efficient for the platform to manage Boolean values using these other options rather than explicitly supporting another distinct data type. So even if your interface

---

[6] If you've ever experimented with date/time entries in a spreadsheet program, you probably know that spreadsheet programs typically store date/times internally as floating point numbers where the date is the integer part (representing the number of days since some arbitrary start date encoded in the software) and the time indicates the percentage of the 24-hour day that has passed (e.g., 0.25 = 6:00 AM). In a spreadsheet, you can enter a decimal number in a cell formatted to display date/time and the number will be converted and displayed appropriately. While the internal workings of some DBMSs may use this same approach, generally speaking, this type of behavior is not permitted when entering database records. You will have to enter a valid date and a valid time in a recognizable format in order to insert data.

TABLE 4.4
Atypical Data Types

Platform	Data Type	Notes
Oracle	XMLType	Oracle provides functions for extracting and manipulating XML data; XMLType is not recognized within DDL but can be used in DML statements.
SQL Server	Money	As you would expect, this data type is used for monetary values; a wide variety of different monetary units are supported.
MySQL	ENUM	An enumeration of possible values – a list.
PostgreSQL	Point	The (x,y) coordinates of a point on a plane; other geometric data types are also supported.
Access	Calculated	A value calculated from the values in other fields.

allows you to specify a Boolean data type, it may actually be implemented in another way. If your platform does include an explicit Boolean data type, use of it may be an acceptable choice when appropriate. It may be more practical in some cases, however, to simply use a small character or number data type instead. We generally recommend avoiding the use of Boolean and other odd types and instead suggest using only the more standard ones. Table 4.4 lists some other interesting data types found in some popular systems. (Some types shown are available in more than one of the referenced systems.)

If you're already familiar with databases, you may have noticed that we did not mention automatically incrementing fields in any of the above discussion despite the fact that many systems support them. The omission is intentional. These data types have different names in different DBMSs: AutoNumber in Access, UniqueIdentifier in SQL Server, Serial in PostgreSQL, etc. (Oracle does not explicitly have an auto-matically incremented data type. Instead, Oracle supports a separate database entity called a SEQUENCE. You get the next item from a SEQUENCE by accessing a pseudo-table called DUAL, but the values are stored in fields of other data types. It's not as complicated as it sounds.) Fields assigned to one of these data types are most often used to generate unique, sequential ID numbers for new records. Because the behavior of automatically incremented fields can be dramatically different between DBMSs, we don't recommend using them. A better approach is to create a stored pro-cedure to retrieve the ID of the last record and manipulate it as needed.

Best Practice #6   When designing your database, strive to use only common and basic data types that are supported by the majority of database platforms. It is often necessary for data models to expand over time to include new cat-egories of data not originally planned. As needs get more expansive, you may encounter limitations in your original platform that limit the ability to grow the database. You should therefore consider the possibility that you may have to migrate your data to another DBMS in the future. Use of uncommon or platform-specific data types can introduce significant complications to the process of data migration.

4.2.6 Tables

At the most basic level, tables are collections of columns. While columns represent the most fundamental data elements in a relational database, tables are more important conceptually. This is mostly true because the table is the starting point for all data manipulations – columns do not exist as stand-alone entities and SQL does not offer any way to access a column without referencing a table. In the Relational Data Model, the formal name for a table is simply "Relation" which points out the obvious clarification that tables are actually collections of related columns. We'll discuss the finer points of efficient table structure in Section 4.3, but for now it will suffice to accept the intuitive notion that a given table represents something that has characteristics, and those characteristics are found in the table's columns. As an example, consider a well. There are a number of characteristics we might use to describe the well: depth, diameter, type of casing, ground elevation, intended use, etc. If we need to document the attributes of a group of wells in our database, it makes sense to create a WELLS table that contains columns for those attributes we wish to document. The table should contain columns for all the characteristics we deem sufficiently significant, even if there are wells to which some of these characteristics do not apply. Referring back to our example in Chapter 2 in which we attempted to manage data using spreadsheets, the final iteration of that exercise contained multiple worksheets within the same spreadsheet file. Each of those worksheets contained columns for entering information needed to describe the item represented by the worksheet. The individual worksheets are essentially our tables in that example.

In a more practical sense, a table is a collection of both columns and rows. The columns identify the attributes and the rows are individual instances of the item the table describes. When we refer to a table, we are referring both to its construction (the columns) and its data (the rows). The only real limitation placed on tables in the Relational Model is that duplicate rows – rows in which values of all columns are the same as corresponding columns in another row – are not allowed.

Once you grasp the concept of a table, there is not much else to discuss. Instead, let us explore the process of creating and modifying tables, inserting records, and retrieving data. As noted earlier in this book, a comprehensive SQL primer is not included here. While no attempt is made to cover all possible SQL syntax variations associated with creating and working with tables, there are two desirable goals that may be accomplished with these examples. First, the examples demonstrate how the different column data types are created and used. Second, the examples provide a sense of the structure of the most basic SQL commands.

As a first example, consider a table for storing information about samples that are collected. We will assume that the data model has already been constructed. Table 4.5

TABLE 4.5
An Example of Data Elements for a Sampling Events Table

Element	Notes
Location	The location at which the sample was collected.
Sample ID	A unique identifier for this sample; used to associate the sample with other tables (e.g., Results).
Trip ID	Identifies the sampling trip during which the sample was collected.
Sample Date	The date and time at which the sample was collected.
Sample Depth	The depth from which the sample was taken.
Collection Procedure	A reference to a Standard Operating Procedure regarding sample collection.
Equipment	The type or specific piece of equipment used to collect the sample.
Source	The source of the sample (e.g., well, open water, industrial plant discharge, etc.).
Medium	The sample medium (surface water, groundwater, soil, sediment, etc.).
COC Number	The identifying number on the chain of custody form (COC) on which the sample is recorded.

lists the data elements we have identified associated with sampling events. The table is not intended to be comprehensive, but should give you some ideas about the types of information that could apply to a sample.

Note that many of the data elements refer to items that may themselves have important descriptors. Likely candidates are the location, trip, and collection procedure elements. This suggests that we will also need to create additional tables whose columns describe the characteristics of each item. For instance, we will need a table for sampling locations that identifies things like location type, coordinates, geopolitical containers, etc. The locations table will itself have a unique identifier for each record, which we will use in the samples table in much the same way that our unique sample ID will be used in the results table. We will discuss how these connections are established in Section 4.2.8, but for the moment we should mention another class of data elements often found in discrete tables.

The elements of interest are those for which a limited number of possible choices can be made but for which there are not a significant number of additional descriptors. Your first instinct might be to think such elements do not warrant a separate table. Let's use the sample medium as our example. There are only a few distinct media for the samples we will collect, so we could just make the medium a text field in our samples table and be done. Let's say we follow that approach. Furthermore, in the user interface, let's assume we allow users to enter the text directly. This will introduce the possibility of data inconsistency that may make proper interpretation difficult. For example, someone who does not fully appreciate the specificity we desire might simply enter "water" as the medium. While this is a valid identification of the medium, we prefer a more qualified descriptor such as "surface water" or "groundwater." We can overcome this hurdle relatively easily by changing the behavior of the interface so that we offer users a dropdown list of options rather than a simple text box. This addresses the immediate problem but poses another challenge regarding data maintenance. Suppose we wish to specifically distinguish water from a runoff collection system as a unique medium, so we add "storm water" as an option in our dropdown list. After several months of use, we have hundreds of records in which the medium is listed as "storm water," at which time we realize that the preferred designation is "stormwater." To correct this situation, we must find and edit all the affected entries. To avoid such a scenario, we can instead begin by creating a separate table for our medium names that includes a coded identifier associated with each record. We can then use this coded identifier as the medium entry in the samples table. Changing "storm water" to "stormwater" now requires editing just one record in the media table. Note that this also has the additional benefit of allowing us to use the records in the media table as the source for our user interface dropdown list, thus eliminating the need to tweak the interface when a new medium is added. Tables used in this manner – that is, tables used to control the entries that can be accepted in columns of other tables – are sometimes called lookup tables or reference tables. We'll discuss more about the role of lookup tables in Section 4.3.

We're now ready to use SQL DDL statements to create our samples table. The general format of the statement to create a table is as follows:

```
CREATE TABLE tname (cname_1 ctype_1, cname_2 ctype_2, ...);
```

where tname is the name of the table, $cname_n$ is the name of column n, and $ctype_n$ is any valid data type. Let's decide on some column names for our data elements and sort out what type is required for each. The results are shown in Table 4.6.

Interestingly, the only field that will contain a text entry is the chain of custody form number. The reason is because these forms are sometimes obtained as standard printed forms that may contain both numeric and alphabetic characters, so we need some flexibility here. The frequent use of identifying numbers suggests that we intend to create related tables for locations, trips, collection procedures, equipment, sample sources, and media. Also note the choices we've made for integer sizes for those columns that will involve related tables. The sizes are reflective of the anticipated

TABLE 4.6
Possible Definitions of Data Elements for a Sampling Events Table

Element	Column Name	Data Type
Location	LOC_ID	Integer
Sample ID	SAMPLE_ID	Integer
Trip ID	TRIP_ID	Integer
Sample Date	SAMP_DATE	Date/Time
Sample Depth	SAMP_DEPTH	Decimal(4,1) or Float
Collection Procedure	COLLECT_MTHD	Small Integer
Equipment	EQUIP_D	Small Integer
Source	SOURCE_ID	Small Integer
Medium	MEDIUM_ID	Small Integer
COC Number	COC_NUM	Variable Character (15)

number of items in each table. We don't expect the number of collection procedures, equipment types, sources, or media to be greater than 32,767, so small integers are appropriate for those columns. (If our DBMS supports TINYINTs, those could actually be better choices in some of these instances.) It is conceivable that over time we may have more than 32,767 locations, sampling trips, and samples, so we need the larger regular integer data type for these.

We're now ready to translate the contents of Table 4.6 into an SQL DDL statement that will create the samples table:

```
CREATE TABLE SAMPLES
     (LOC_ID INT,
     SAMPLE_ID INT,
     TRIP_ID INT,
     SAMP_DATE DATETIME,
     SAMP_DEPTH DECIMAL(4,1),
     COLLECT_MTHD SMALLINT,
     EQUIP_ID SMALLINT,
     SOURCE_ID SMALLINT,
     MEDIUM_ID SMALLINT,
     COC_NUM VARCHAR(15));
```

(In all these examples, the exact syntax may vary slightly between platforms. This is especially true for the data type names. Note also that in this case we have separated the list of columns so that each one is on a separate line. This is not required but makes reading and understanding the statement easier. Most implementations of SQL will allow you to enter statements in this form. Once a keyword such as "CREATE" is recognized, the interpreter will consider everything you type as part of the statement up to the semicolon at the end.)

This statement is all that is required to create the basic structure of the samples table, but there is more we can include to improve on this definition. We'll revisit this statement in Section 4.2.8 when we introduce how to define relationships between tables, but there is one simple yet important revision we can make right now. Recall in Chapter 3 our discussion of the need to require entries in certain columns. All we require is a few simple modifications to our DDL statement to identify the columns for which we want to require an entry. We do this by adding the modifier "NOT NULL" after the data type. As an example, let's assume that the required columns will be the location, the sample ID, and the sample date. Our DDL statement then becomes:

```
CREATE TABLE SAMPLES
     (LOC_ID INT NOT NULL,
     SAMPLE_ID INT NOT NULL,
     TRIP_ID INT,
     SAMP_DATE DATETIME NOT NULL,
     SAMP_DEPTH DECIMAL(4,1),
     COLLECT_MTHD SMALLINT,
     EQUIP_ID SMALLINT,
```

```
SOURCE_ID SMALLINT,
MEDIUM_ID SMALLINT,
COC_NUM VARCHAR(15));
```

When considering which columns to define as NOT NULL, be aware of the difference between a NULL value and an empty string in a text column. As hinted earlier in this chapter, databases treat these entries differently. A column specified as NOT NULL can still contain an empty string as a value. You won't be able to tell the difference when viewing the data, but the fact that the DBMS treats NULLs and empty strings differently can affect data retrieval operations.[7]

Another column characteristic that can be specified is less common but still potentially very helpful: specification of a default value. This is accomplished by including the keyword DEFAULT and then the default value in the text that defines the column. As an example, let's say we sometimes collect special samples that we don't wish to associate with a sampling trip. According to the definition above, we allow NULL values for the trip ID, but suppose we prefer to designate samples not associated with a trip as having a trip ID of 0. Then the line that defines the trip ID field in the samples table becomes:

```
TRIP_ID INT DEFAULT 0,
```

You won't always get the definition of the table perfect on the first try. You might determine at some time in the future that you need to modify the table definition. If the changes are significant and you have not yet inserted any data into the table, the simplest approach is simply to delete the table and start over. The simple DDL statement for this is as follows:

```
DROP TABLE tname;
```

where tname is the name of the table to be deleted. If you have already inserted data, or if the changes are relatively minor, it may be more efficient to modify the existing table definition. The general format of the DDL statement for changing an existing table varies slightly depending on whether you are adding a column, changing something about a column, or removing a column. To retain consistency with the other general form templates in this section, we will present each separately instead of attempting to show all variations in a single template. The general syntax for adding a column to a table is:

```
ALTER TABLE tname ADD cname₁ ctype₁, cname₂ ctype₂, ...;
```

where tname is the name of the table to modify, $cname_n$ is the name of new column n, and $ctype_n$ is a valid data type. You can add a single column or as many columns as needed for the new table definition.

The general syntax for modifying a column in a table is:

```
ALTER TABLE tname ALTER COLUMN cname newctype;
```

---

[7] We're jumping ahead a bit to Section 4.2.8, but one way to prevent empty strings in a column is to define a CHECK constraint that compares the column contents with an empty string. An example would be: CONSTRAINT kname CHECK $cname_x <> ``$.

where tname is the name of the table to be altered, cname is the name of the column being altered, and newctype is a valid data type to which the column will be changed. In some SQL implementations, MODIFY COLUMN is used instead of ALTER COLUMN. Note that you can only change the data *type* using this statement – not the column name. If you need to change a column name, you'll have to add the column with the new name and then delete the original version. Changing the data type may affect the contents of any existing records, depending on the type and magnitude of the change. Generally, staying within the same data type category but increasing the size of a column has no effect on existing data. This is the case if, for instance, you change a column from an integer to a long integer or from variable text of length x to variable text of length x+c. If you retain the same category but reduce the size, text data are typically truncated at the new length. Applying the same type of change to numeric columns may produce unexpected results. Note that most DBMSs will not allow you to modify multiple columns with a single ALTER TABLE command. Some platforms, though, may include non-standard alternatives that are capable of this. MySQL, for instance, supports a variation in which CHANGE replaces ALTER COLUMN in the ALTER TABLE statement; the CHANGE variation has the ability to modify multiple columns with a single statement.

As is the case with deleting an entire table, the syntax for deleting a column from a table is once again simple:

```
ALTER TABLE tname DROP COLUMN cname₁, cname₂,…;
```

where tname is the name of the table and $cname_n$ is the name of a column to be removed. In some implementations, you can omit the word COLUMN in this statement.

> **Best Practice #7**　When creating your data model, use appropriate column data types for the categories of data in your business model, but try to avoid the use of data types that are not widely supported on multiple platforms. It is not uncommon to encounter issues after deployment that result in a change to a different platform. Use of unusual data types can make migration of data from one DBMS to another significantly more difficult.

That will suffice for the time being. Let's now turn our attention to the DML statement for inserting data. The general form is:

```
INSERT INTO tname (cname₁, cname₂, …) VALUES
(cvalue₁, cvalue₂, …);
```

where tname is the table into which data will be inserted, $cname_n$ is the name of a column in the table, and $cvalue_n$ is a value of the type that corresponds to the data type of column n. As you would expect, there must be the same number of columns and values in each parenthetical list, and the values are inserted into the columns assuming the same order applies to both lists.

Constructing an example that inserts values for all columns in our samples table, we get:

TABLE 4.7
Contents of the Record Inserted into the Samples Table

Column	Value	Notes
LOC_ID	27	There will be a record in the table that stores location information with a unique identifier of 27; that record provides the details for the location referenced here.
SAMPLE_ID	9082	This ID is the unique identifier for this particular sample. It may be generated by the user interface or in some other manner.
TRIP_ID	325	There will be a record in the table that stores sampling trip information with a unique identifier of 325; that record provides the details for the trip referenced here.
SAMP_DATE	June 25, 2019 at 9:47 AM	(See the discussion in the first full paragraph following this table.)
SAMP_DEPTH	12.5	Note that no units are indicated. This implies that we are making an assumption that all our depths are recorded in predetermined standard units. If this is not the case, then our table definition is insufficient and should be modified to explicitly indicate depth units.
COLLECT_MTHD	4	There will be a record in the table that stores collection method information with a unique identifier of 4; that record identifies the specific collection procedure referenced here.
EQUIP_ID	NULL	By setting the value to NULL, we are basically indicating that the specific type or piece of equipment bears no significance regarding this sample.
SOURCE_ID	2	There will be a record in the table that lists our valid sources with a unique identifier of 2; that record provides the name of the source referenced here.
MEDIUM_ID	2	There will be a record in the table that lists our valid media choices with a unique identifier of 2; that record provides the name of the medium referenced here.
COC_NUM	19-017765	This corresponds to the sequence number printed on the chain of custody form.

```
INSERT INTO SAMPLES (LOC_ID, SAMPLE_ID, TRIP_ID,
SAMP_DATE, SAMP_DEPTH, COLLECT_MTHD, EQUIP_ID,
SOURCE_ID, MEDIUM_ID, COC_NUM) VALUES (27, 9082,
325, '2019-06-25 09:47:00 AM', 12.5, 4, NULL, 2, 2,
'19-017765');
```

Breaking down each entry, we note the contents of the new sample record in Table 4.7.

Most of these entries are relatively obvious and you could probably have correctly guessed how to create the insert statement for them using just the template description. The field that requires the most discussion is the sample date field, and this is because every platform seems to offer multiple different ways of specifying dates in an insert statement. The use of literal strings for specifying dates in an insert statement is supported in almost all DBMSs, but delimiters and standard order of date components can vary. The syntax used in our example should work for SQL Server, MySQL, and PostgreSQL. The syntax for Access is similar, except that the date value must be delimited using the pound sign character rather than quotes (#2019-06-25 09:47:00#). As originally installed,[8] Oracle's syntax assumes a different construct for the components – two digits for the day, a three-character abbreviation for the month, and then four digits for the year ('25-JUN-2019') – that appears to work when you specify a date only (no time component). The reason we say "appears to work" is because Oracle explicitly discourages the use of literals when entering dates. Instead, they recommend the use of the TO_DATE function. This function allows you to specify the date and time in any format you choose, but requires that you also specify a format string that tells Oracle what each component represents. An example would be (omitting the other fields):

```
INSERT INTO SAMPLES (…SAMP_DATE…) VALUES (…TO_
DATE('06/25/2019 09:47', 'mm/dd/yyyy hh24:mi')…);
```

Note that the components of the format string must follow standard nomenclature as described in the Oracle documentation. Many other platforms also support variations on this approach, providing functions in their SQL implementations for converting strings to dates. These functions offer flexibility in the exact format of the date/time string so long as you use a valid format string to describe the entry. Some platforms support multiple variations; consult the documentation for your specific DBMS for details.

Our example INSERT statement listed the columns in the order in which they were specified during table creation and the values for each column in that same order. This is not necessary: the columns and values can be specified in any order provided that the order is the same within each clause. It's also not necessary to cite every column in the table in every insert. You can omit columns and values if there is a default value (see Section 4.2.8) or if the column can be NULL. For instance:

```
INSERT INTO SAMPLES (LOC_ID, SAMPLE_ID, SAMP_DATE)
VALUES (27, 9082, '2019-06-25 09:47:00 AM');
```

would be acceptable given the most recent table definition we've discussed.

One more variation is noteworthy. If you specify values for all the columns, most platforms will allow you to omit the clause that explicitly specifies the columns. Such a statement skips directly to the parenthesis-enclosed list of values. This only works if you specify values for all columns, regardless of default values or nullability. We will not offer an example of this because this practice is generally frowned upon by database administrators (DBAs) and developers. It is considered bad form, but more importantly it has the potential to produce unintentional and/or bad data. As an example, consider a simple table for storing equipment identifiers. As originally

---

[8] Oracle, like many of the other platforms, offers configuration settings that can modify the default behaviors.

created, the table had three columns: an equipment ID (small integer), an applicability description (variable text), and a serial number (variable text). Later, the DBA determines that the applicability is not needed but the original source from which it was acquired would be helpful. The DBA drops the applicability column and appends the new vendor column. The columns are now (in order): equipment ID (small integer), serial number (variable text), and vendor (variable text). If you've been inserting records into this table and have grown accustomed to not specifying the columns explicitly, you might issue a statement that is acceptable and will succeed, but now inserts incorrect data. If you had listed the columns, the statement would have produced an error, thus avoiding insertion of the invalid data.

Another common requirement is that of updating an existing record. The general SQL syntax for an UPDATE statement is:

```
UPDATE tname SET cname₁ = cvalue₁, cname₂ = cvalue₂, …
WHERE conditionals;
```

where tname is the name of the table to be updated, $cname_n$ is the name of a column, and $cvalue_n$ is the new value for column n. Note that this syntax is somewhat different from the INSERT syntax. The INSERT statement lists the columns as a discrete set and the values as a separate discrete set. The UPDATE statement pairs them for each desired column to be updated. This obviously has the desired effect of allowing specification of only the column(s) being changed. Here is an example using our sampling events table:

```
UPDATE SAMPLES SET EQUIP_ID=6 WHERE SAMPLE_ID=9082;
```

This example will update the record for sample number 9082 to indicate the identifier of the equipment used (6) when we first saved the sample record.

The UPDATE example also introduces an extremely important concept not present in our previous examples: the WHERE clause. The WHERE clause defines the set of records that will be affected by the statement. The WHERE clause is used in other SQL statements as well (see below). The text following the WHERE keyword constitutes the conditional portion of the WHERE clause, and consists of one or more specifications of column names and desired values. In the simplest case, a single identification of one column and a target value is used. This does not necessarily mean that only a single record will be affected. Rather, all records for which the condition is true will be affected. That may be one record or many. It is more common to find WHERE clauses that specify multiple conditions that may be required to designate the affected records. In cases where multiple conditions are needed, the standard Boolean operators (AND, OR, and NOT) are used and groupings within the logic are done using normal parentheses. As an illustration, let's say we have a lookup table of test methods (it has two fields: MTHD_CODE short integer and MTHD_NAME variable text) and we've added a bunch of methods by examining analysis reports from various labs. We discover later that we inadvertently added the same method with three different name variations (the records are as follows, where the first item of each pair is the method code and the second item is the method name: 6 SM4500HB, 27 SM4500, 51 SM4500H). All versions have already been referenced in records in the results table, but we determine that only the first one (code=6) should be retained.

We need to update all results records that cite the erroneous test methods so that they now indicate the correct one. We issue this statement:

```
UPDATE RESULTS SET TEST_MTHD=6 WHERE (TEST_MTHD=27
OR TEST_MTHD-51);
```

Statements that can include a WHERE clause are valid without one. Note, however, that omitting the WHERE clause causes the statement to be applied to all records in the table. Thus,

```
UPDATE RESULTS SET TEST_MTHOD=6;
```

would update *every* result record to indicate the same test method.[9]

WHERE clauses involving numeric or date comparisons can utilize any of the mathematical operators you would expect: equality (=), inequality (< >), greater than (>), and less than (<). WHERE clauses involving text comparisons can determine if the strings are the same by using the equal sign (=) or different by specifying greater than and less than consecutively (< >) in every DBMS. Most platforms also support the use of greater than and less than operators individually when comparing strings. These conditions are determined based on the internal order in which the DBMS interprets individual characters (called the collating order). This means that, for instance, 'A'<'B' would likely return TRUE but 'A'>'C' would return FALSE.

Most platforms also provide functions that can manipulate values within the WHERE clause (as well as in some other places). The names and syntax for these functions may vary, so as usual, consult your system's documentation for details. One text comparison function that is universally supported is sufficiently important to discuss here – the LIKE function. The LIKE function allows you to compare text strings using wild card characters that serve as substitutes for one or more characters. All implementations of the LIKE function offer two wild cards: one that represents a single character and one that represents a group of characters. The specific wild card characters can vary. Oracle, SQL Server, MySQL, and PostgreSQL use the underscore (_) to represent a single character and the percent sign (%) to represent multiple characters. Access uses the underscore for a single character but uses the asterisk (*) for multiple characters. Here is an example of a WHERE clause that would match all chains of custody that start with 91-HN:

```
...WHERE COC_NUM LIKE '91-HN%';
```

Note that some platforms offer additional variations on LIKE. For instance, in PostgreSQL, the ILIKE function will disregard cases when comparing strings.

Another frequently used function found in WHERE clauses is IN. The IN clause is followed by a list of values enclosed in parentheses and separated by commas. Here is an example of a WHERE clause that might be used, for instance, to retrieve data about sampling locations in North and South Carolina:

```
...WHERE STATE IN ('NC','SC');
```

---

[9] Here is an interesting anomaly that applies only to Microsoft Access: the UPDATE statement in Access SQL does not support a WHERE clause. If you specify one, the query will be rejected as invalid. Thus, in Access, you can only issue an UPDATE statement that will update all records. Very odd.

(assuming the locations table has a field that identifies the state and that the state abbreviations are the standard postal service ones). Note that the specific format of the list of values depends on the data type of the field being matched – values must be enclosed in quotes to match character-based fields, but not in quotes to match numeric fields. The IN clause becomes even more powerful when you don't explicitly populate the list of target values but instead generate the list using a subquery. The subquery is a standard SQL SELECT statement that retrieves data (almost always from a single column) in another table. To expand our example above, suppose we have another table called REGIONS that defines groups of states. The following WHERE clause might be included in a query that returns data about states in region #4:

```
...WHERE STATE IN (SELECT STATE_ID FROM REGIONS WHERE
REGION_NUM=4);
```

We now (finally) turn our attention to the most commonly used SQL statement: the SELECT statement, which is used to retrieve data. The general syntax is

```
SELECT cname₁, cname₂, ... FROM tname WHERE
conditionals;
```

where tname is the name of the table from which data will be retrieved, $cname_n$ is the name of a column in the table, and the conditionals identify the specific records to be retrieved. An example is as follows:

```
SELECT LOC_ID, SAMPLE_ID, COC_NUMBER FROM SAMPLES
WHERE SAMPLE_ID<100;
```

You don't necessarily have to include the column identified in the WHERE clause in the list of returned columns. Also, if you want to retrieve all the columns in the table, you can use the asterisk as a wild card:

```
SELECT * FROM SAMPLES WHERE SAMPLE_ID<100;
```

This will display the columns left to right in the order in which they occur in the table definition. If you want all the columns but in a different order, you'll have to list them explicitly. Without further modification, the rows will be returned in the order in which they are stored in the database.[10] This is rarely the desired order. Fortunately, there is an ORDER BY clause that lets you determine the ordering of the rows:

```
SELECT * FROM SAMPLES WHERE LOC_ID=22 ORDER BY SAMP_
DATE;
```

You can list multiple columns in the ORDER BY clause. As you would expect, each additional column simply adds a sort order for the records with the same values in preceding columns. By default, an ORDER BY clause returns the rows in ascending order. You can modify this by adding the keyword "DESC" after the column names (... ORDER BY SAMP_DATE DESC;). You can also explicitly use ASC for ascending.

---

[10] Many people assume this will always be the order in which they were inserted, but this is an erroneous assumption. The DBMS may manipulate the file in which the database is stored, resulting in a physical rearrangement of data within the actual disk file.

SELECT statements can also include SQL aggregate functions that treat groups of records as one unit. The most commonly used aggregate function is probably COUNT, which (not surprisingly) counts the number of records that match the condition. COUNT requires an argument that identifies a single column [e.g., COUNT(LOC_ ID)], but you can substitute the asterisk to count all affected records [COUNT(*)]. This example counts all the samples for a given trip:

```
SELECT COUNT(*) FROM SAMPLES WHERE TRIP_ID=7;
```

Barring other factors, SELECT queries that include aggregate functions return a single value (e.g., the example above might return the number 4). It's often helpful to limit an aggregate function to unique values in the data being evaluated. The DISTINCT modifier addresses this need. This query:

```
SELECT COUNT(DISTINCT TRIP_ID) FROM SAMPLES WHERE
LOC_ID=5;
```

will return the number of trips during which the location whose identifying number is 5 was visited.[11]

Before we conclude our general discussion of the SELECT statement, there is one more tip worth passing along. It is especially important when dealing with environmental data for reasons that will soon become apparent. You have likely noticed that in all our examples that include strings of characters, we delineated each string using the single quote character. The use of single quote characters to identify strings is an SQL standard. (Some platforms may also support the use of double-quotes, but you should avoid them if possible.) When managing environmental data, you will often need to refer to strings that themselves include single quotes. This is particularly true for many chemical names (e.g., p,p' DDT). Special care must be taken when referencing strings that contain the quote character in a SELECT statement (or any other SQL statement for that matter). Consider the case in which you want to find all parameters whose names begin with "1,1'-Sulf." Your first inclination might be to use this syntax:

```
SELECT * FROM PARAMETERS WHERE PARAM_NAME LIKE
'1,1'-Sulf%';
```

This statement will produce an error because the command interpreter will consider the single quote following the second digit 1 as the end of the string. It will subsequently try to interpret "-Sulf%" as part of a command, which will fail. Fortunately, there is an easy solution to this issue. Any time you need to include a single quote character in a string, simply repeat it within the string. The command interpreter will interpret two consecutive single quotes as one single quote that is part of the string. This is the correct interpretation and will therefore result in an appropriate action. Thus, the correct syntax for the situation described above is:

---

[11] Here is one more deficiency in the Access implementation of SQL: it does not support COUNT (DISTINCT).

```
SELECT * FROM PARAMETERS WHERE PARAM_NAME LIKE
'1,1''-Sulf%';
```

(Note that what follows the second digit 1 is two consecutive entries of the single quote character and not a double quote character.)

The SELECT statement has many more capabilities for organizing and manipulating the returned data. We've barely scratched the surface of its functionality. As your experience and comfort with SQL grow, you will have many opportunities to explore these uses.

So far we've learned how to add records, update records, and retrieve records. The other significant operation involves deleting records. The general DELETE query syntax is

```
DELETE FROM tname WHERE conditions;
```

where tname is the name of the table from which records will be deleted and the WHERE clause identifies the specific records to be removed. You should be sufficiently knowledgeable at this point to construct your own examples of a DELETE statement.

4.2.7 INDEXES

Indexes[12] are entities that define a logical order of the records in a table based on the values in one or more columns. The order of retrieval for records in a particular query is determined using an ORDER BY clause, so you might wonder why you would bother creating an index that specifies a particular order. The answer is performance: if the list of columns in an ORDER BY clause matches those in an index (in both number and sequence), then the query will return the data much more quickly. For this reason, a single table can have as many indexes as you like. Be cognizant, however, that creating an abundance of indexes both increases the storage requirements of the database and has the potential to increase the response time for data inserts, updates, and deletions. The rule of thumb is that you should consider creating indexes on fields or combinations of fields that are used often in the WHERE clause of SQL commands you expect to issue on the database. In these cases, the index will have the desired effect of expediting retrieval of the data. As noted above, though, an index that uses a combination of fields will only be used if all fields cited in the index are present in the WHERE clause.

The general syntax for creating an index is

```
CREATE INDEX iname ON tname (cname₁, cname₂,...);
```

where iname is the name of the index, tname is the name of the table, and $cname_n$ is the name of a column in the table. Indexes that reference a single column perform best, indexes that use a combination of columns from the same category (e.g., all

---

[12] Similar to the question regarding proper use of "data" in Chapter 2, "Indices" should be the proper plural of "Index." But I've given up on this fight.

variable text fields) generally perform acceptably, and indexes that include columns of different data types perform worst.[13]

Using the general syntax above to create an index permits situations in which multiple identical entries of the combination of data in the columns referenced in the index exist. For example, let's say our table for analytical results includes columns for sampling location, the lab that performed the analysis, and the test method used – all as numeric fields that link to lookup tables. Then creating an index using this statement:

```
CREATE INDEX IDX_RESULTS ON RESULTS (LOCATION, LAB,
TEST_METHOD);
```

creates an index that allows multiple records that have identical location, lab, and test method. There are times when this is undesirable because you wish to ensure that each record contains a distinct combination of the columns. To accomplish this goal, insert the UNIQUE key word in the CREATE INDEX statement:

```
CREATE UNIQUE INDEX iname ON tname (cname₁,
cname₂, ...);
```

Unique indexes create additional constraints on the records in the affected table by prohibiting insertion of data that would result in duplication in the index expression. Similarly, attempting to create a unique index on a table with existing data that conflicts with the index expression will result in an error. Unique indexes are sometimes created automatically by other SQL statements. For example, specifying the primary key (see Section 4.2.8) for a table always creates a unique index on the key field(s).

There is no ANSI SQL standard for an ALTER INDEX statement, but some DBMSs do offer one. The options in these cases are most often related to aspects other than the construction of the index. Typical operations offered by these statements are renaming or rebuilding of the index.

4.2.8 Constraints

Constraints are defined as database objects or characteristics that limit the ability to add or change records in undesirable ways. What makes these actions undesirable is that they negatively affect data integrity. Constraints therefore offer a significant method for increasing the quality of your data.

There are two basic categories of constraints: data integrity rules and data relationships. Data integrity rules come in two varieties. The first variety specifies that entries in a given column or combination of columns must be unique. This is accomplished by creating a unique index on the table using the column specified as requiring unique values. In this case, you don't create the unique index explicitly.

---

[13] You can use available functions to modify the type of a column in the index and thus produce an index that uses the same data types throughout when otherwise the types would be different. In order to utilize the index, however, you must also manipulate the corresponding columns in the query statement so that the type of each element in the query matches the altered type in the index.

Instead, the DBMS interprets the instructions you provide that specify the uniqueness requirement and creates the index on its own. Note that you may be able to specify a uniqueness constraint on a column that is nullable, but on most platforms this means you will only be allowed one record in which that column is NULL.

Constraints can be created at the same time the table is created by including a CONSTRAINT identifier in the list of objects that constitute the table.[14] The general format for creating a table with a uniqueness constraint in most SQL implementations is

```
CREATE TABLE tname (cname₁ ctype₁, cname₂ ctype₂, ...,
CONSTRAINT kname UNIQUE (cnameₓ, cname_y, ...));
```

where tname is the name of the table being created, $cname_n$ is the name for column n, and $ctype_n$ is the type for column n. The elements of the additional CONSTRAINT clause are: kname, which is the name given to the constraint being created; the keyword UNIQUE; and the list of fields ($cname_x$, etc.) that together define the combination that is required to be distinct. Just as with columns, you can add multiple constraints when you create the table. It may also be possible to mix constraint definitions in among the column definitions, and even reference a column in a constraint that has not yet been defined at that point in the DDL statement. This produces awkward syntax that can be confusing and is highly discouraged.

You can also add a uniqueness constraint to an existing table using the previously discussed ALTER TABLE statement:

```
ALTER TABLE tname ADD CONSTRAINT kname UNIQUE
(cnameₓ, cname_y, ...);
```

where tname is the name of the table being altered, kname is the name of the constraint, and the list of fields ($cname_x$, etc.) is the list of fields that, combined, must be unique. As with creating a unique index, you may not create a uniqueness constraint on an existing table if records within the table contain data that would violate the condition. Note that ANSI SQL does not support modifying an existing constraint, just like it does not support altering an index. You can, however, drop a constraint and then redefine it. For completeness, the syntax for dropping a constraint is

```
ALTER TABLE tname DROP CONSTRAINT kname;
```

where tname is the name of the table and kname is the name of the constraint. For an explicit example, we revisit our previous CREATE TABLE statement, this time with the additional specification of a uniqueness constraint:

```
CREATE TABLE SAMPLES
    (
    LOC_ID INT NOT NULL,
    SAMPLE_ID INT NOT NULL,
    TRIP_ID INT,
```

---

[14] In our previous examples, we only identified the columns that make up the table being created. This is our first encounter with other objects that can be part of a table definition. This should encourage you to explore the SQL implementation for your specific platform to discover what other types of objects may also be included.

```
SAMP_DATE DATETIME NOT NULL,
SAMP_DEPTH DECIMAL(4,1),
COLLECT_MTHD SMALLINT,
EQUIP_ID SMALLINT,
SOURCE_ID SMALLINT,
MEDIUM_ID SMALLINT,
COC_NUM VARCHAR(15),
CONSTRAINT LOCDATE UNIQUE
        (LOC_ID,
        SAMP_DATE)
);
```

This constraint specifies that the combination of location ID and sample date/time must be unique. Imposing this limitation helps avoid a situation that could occur if we inadvertently attempt to enter the same sample twice. When discussing indexes, we noted that indexes that combine columns of different data types can slow overall database performance. This suggests that our constraint in this case is ill-advised since it creates just such an index. In this specific case, however, we judge the creation of this constraint to be sufficiently beneficial that we can ignore the performance penalty.

The second variety of data integrity constraint is the CHECK constraint. A CHECK constraint acts as a validation check, only allowing column values that satisfy the condition identified in the CHECK clause. The general syntax of a CHECK constraint is similar to that of a UNIQUE constraint:

```
CONSTRAINT kname CHECK (kcondition)
```

where kcondition defines a Boolean expression that must be true in order to accept the data.[15] (We've omitted the semicolon here to emphasize that this is not a complete SQL statement.) The condition specification can take multiple forms but generally follows typical rules for identifying columns and applying standard logical and mathematical operations. This capability provides a simple method for establishing controls such as limiting a numeric entry to a range of values. A simple and obvious example would be a constraint that ensures the trip identifier entry is a positive number less than 1000:

```
CONSTRAINT CHK_TRIP CHECK (TRIP_ID > 0 AND TRIP_
ID<1000)
```

---

[15] Of the DBMS platforms we've been discussing in this book, MySQL and PostgreSQL also offer additional options for creating constraints. In both cases, constraints can be created by including constraint keywords in the column definition. For instance, requiring a unique value for a single column can be accomplished by specifying the UNIQUE keyword when creating the column (e.g., LAB_NAME VARCHAR(25) NOT NULL UNIQUE). Both platforms also allow the use of a variation in which you list the constraints separately from the column names but omit the CONSTRAINT keyword and any explicit name for the constraint – just use the required keyword and the parenthetical list of columns or the condition when defining a constraint. Both, however, also support the ANSI standard syntax. We encourage use of the standard format at all times.

CHECK conditions may compare or otherwise reference multiple columns, as in this one that requires the lab analysis date to be after the date on which the lab received the sample:

```
CONSTRAINT CHK_DATES CHECK (ANALYSIS_DATE > RECD_
DATE)
```

CHECK conditions can also accept any functions and operators supported in DML statements. This allows you to use, for instance, the LIKE clause discussed above. Another common use of a CHECK clause that leverages the use of other supported DML functions limits entries to a specified list of values, as in this case that restricts the medium code to odd-valued single-digit integers:

```
CONSTRAINT CHK_MEDIUM CHECK (MEDIUM_ID IN (1, 3,
5, 7, 9))
```

The next obvious leap would be to use a subquery to populate the list of valid values in the CHECK constraint by returning values from a lookup table. Unfortunately, this is not permitted. We are therefore faced with two options (foreign key – see below – and CHECK constraint) that may serve the same function. How, then, do you decide which method to use? This may be determined by personal preference, but some factors can sway the decision one way or the other:

- If the list of valid choices is limited in number and will remain static throughout the life of the database, a CHECK constraint may be the most efficient and compact enforcement method.
- If the list of valid choices has the potential to change frequently, a lookup table will reduce administrative task load since a CHECK constraint would have to be recreated with each addition to the valid values list.

It is also important to note that NULL values for columns referenced in the CHECK condition may cause unexpected results. This is because NULL is considered an indeterminate condition with regard to the standard true/false Boolean dichotomy. How a particular platform reacts to a NULL is buried deeply within the platform's internal logic – does the condition pass only if true, or does the condition fail only if false? (You can perform some experiments to determine which is the case in your DBMS if you are sufficiently curious.) Depending on the platform's internal logic, then, a NULL value may result in the check condition being ignored.

Most platforms will allow you to temporarily disable CHECK constraints. One situation in which this is desirable occurs when loading data in bulk from another resource. This happens frequently when there is a need to include data from an obsolete system that did not abide by the same data integrity rules as those of the current database. You may determine that the ability to include these data is more important than enforcing the rules that are applied to new data. Disabling the constraint will allow loading of the legacy data successfully. Remember to reinstate the constraint before returning to normal operations.

We now turn our attention to the other category of constraints: data relationships. Data relationship constraints define how different tables relate to each other. It is this concept that lies at the very heart of the relational database model. As with data integrity constraints, there are two types of relationship constraints: primary keys and foreign keys.

A primary key is a column or combination of columns in a table that create a distinct identifier for each row of the table. It is thus very similar to a uniqueness constraint and many people conflate the two, especially when first learning about relational databases. While there are definite similarities, there are also significant differences. Like uniqueness constraints, primary keys are managed through the automatic creation of a unique index (often cited as the "primary index"). One significant difference between a primary key and any other uniqueness constraint is that NULL values are not allowed in any of the columns that constitute the primary key. Also, each table can have as many uniqueness constraints as necessary but only one primary key. A more important difference is that the primary key is used as a reference in other tables to identify a specific record in the table for which the primary key is defined.

A foreign key is a column or combination of columns in a table which links records in that table to records in another table. This relationship is established when a foreign key value exactly matches the primary key in the other table. The table containing the primary key is referred to as the parent table, and the table containing the foreign key is called the child table. Essentially, the link establishes that the data in a specific record in the parent table contains additional information about the corresponding record in the child table.

An illustration may help clarify these definitions. Consider the samples table we described in Section 4.2.6. The objective of the samples table is to describe each sampling event as completely as possible. A robust description of a sampling event would include extensive information about the location at which the sample was collected, including such details as coordinates. Because we expect to collect multiple samples at each location, listing the coordinates of the location in every sample record would result in redundant data. We therefore create a parent table for the locations that contains a unique location ID as its primary key. The child table (samples) then includes a column for the location ID that specifies the column as a foreign key into the locations table.

We will revisit this example shortly with specific DDL statements for creating the two tables. Before we get there, however, we need to present the general form of the statements. We'll first examine the creation of a primary key. There are two variations that produce the desired outcome. For single column primary keys, ANSI SQL allows you to simply include the keywords PRIMARY KEY in the column definition, as in this snippet:

```
cname ctype NOT NULL PRIMARY KEY
```

where cname is the name of the primary key column and ctype is its data type. Some platforms will allow you to omit the NOT NULL portion of this definition, but will still create the column as non-nullable since primary keys may not be null. Other platforms may report this attempt as an error. If your primary key is a composite of multiple columns, you define it the same way you define other constraints – by listing it explicitly in the list that includes column definitions and other constraints:

```
CONSTRAINT kname PRIMARY KEY (cname_x, cname_y, ...)
```

where kname is the name of the constraint and the cname entries are the names of the composite primary key fields. The same general scenario applies to defining foreign keys; that is, you may define single-column foreign keys within the same snippet that defines the column, and you may define any foreign key by explicitly listing it in a CONSTRAINT clause. The only significant difference between defining primary and foreign keys is that foreign keys require a REFERENCES keyword and the identification of the parent table. Thus, the first variation for creating a foreign key is:

```
cnamec ctypec FOREIGN KEY REFERENCES ptable(cnamep)
```

where cnamec and ctypec are the name and type of the foreign key field in the child table, ptable is the name of the parent table, and cnamep is the primary key column in the parent. The second variant is:

```
CONSTRAINT kname FOREIGN KEY (cnamec₁, cnamec₂, …)
REFERENCES ptable(cnamep₁, cnamep₂, …)
```

where kname is the name of the foreign key constraint, $cnamec_n$ is the name of a column in the child table, $ctype_c$ is the data type of the column in the child table, ptable is the name of the parent table, and $cnamep_n$ is the name of a component of the primary key in the parent table. When generating a composite foreign key, the constituent columns must be listed in the same order as that used when defining the corresponding primary key. It is considered good form to define the same names for the corresponding columns in each table, but this is not a requirement. As with unique indexes and uniqueness constraints, you may create a composite key with columns of different data types, but some loss of performance may result. Data types for corresponding components of a composite key must be identical in both the primary and foreign keys. As with most other elements of a table, you can add keys after the table is defined and you can delete existing keys. Both activities utilize the ALTER TABLE command. We leave it as an exercise for you to discover the exact syntax.

We can now return to our test case for specific examples of the syntax. Since we have not yet previously created the locations table, we will create the primary key at the same time we create the table.

```
CREATE TABLE LOCATIONS
    (
    LOC_ID INT NOT NULL PRIMARY KEY,
    LOC_NAME VARCHAR(15) NOT NULL,
    LAT_DD FLOAT(24) NOT NULL,
    LONG_DD FLOAT(24) NOT NULL,
    LL_DATUM VARCHAR(10) NOT NULL
    );
```

(An actual locations table would have more columns than this, but we omit them here for simplicity.) The LOC_ID field is specified as our primary key. The name is the more common identifier of the location (e.g., MW-1). The latitude and longitude fields are intended to specify values in decimal degrees. When specifying latitude and longitude coordinates, the reference datum used is essential, so we include that as well. Since we have already created our samples table, we will create the foreign key using an ALTER TABLE statement.

```
ALTER TABLE SAMPLES ADD CONSTRAINT FK_LOC FOREIGN
KEY (LOC_ID) REFERENCES LOCATIONS (LOC_ID);
```

Note that the order of these actions is important: you cannot create a foreign key that references a primary key that does not yet exist. (Actually, this may be possible on some platforms as long as the column or combination of columns in the parent table is specified as unique. It is, however, considered bad form.)

> **Best Practice #8**   When creating multiple tables that contain columns that refer to the same conceptual item, use the same column name in all tables. This will help you avoid confusion when defining relationships between the tables.

The true advantage of establishing foreign key relationships is that these constraints can prevent data integrity problems that arise when data in a parent table are modified or deleted. In our example that links the locations and the samples, for instance, if the identifier (Loc_ID) for a location is changed, the foreign key relationship should update the location ID field in any samples associated with that location. Similarly, if a location is deleted, the relationship constraint should delete all samples collected at that location. This behavior may not always be the best outcome in all cases, however. Most platforms offer options to specify how updates or deletions are propagated to child tables. It is also permissible to specify different options for update and deletion actions. For DBMSs that adhere to the ANSI standard, the available options for how to address changes in parent data are to cascade the operation (e.g., delete child records when the parent is deleted), to set the foreign key column in the child to NULL, to set the foreign key column in the child to some default value, or to take no action. The cascade option is most frequently the default, but in order to avoid unexpected behaviors, it's always best to explicitly identify the desired outcome. Our ALTER TABLE statement above, then, would be more complete in this form (exact syntax may vary by platform):

```
ALTER TABLE SAMPLES ADD CONSTRAINT FK_LOC FOREIGN
KEY (LOC_ID) REFERENCES LOCATIONS (LOC_ID) ON DELETE
CASCADE ON UPDATE CASCADE;
```

Be cognizant that the specifications regarding how to treat delete and update actions are only specified in the definition of the child table, and that they refer to delete and update actions performed on the parent.

As you define more relationships between various tables, these relationship constraints can produce great efficiencies in data maintenance operations. For example, in addition to the relationship defined above for locations and samples, every conceivable environmental data management system should also have a relationship that defines the samples table as the parent and a results table as the child. Thus, deleting a location record would delete all associated records in the samples

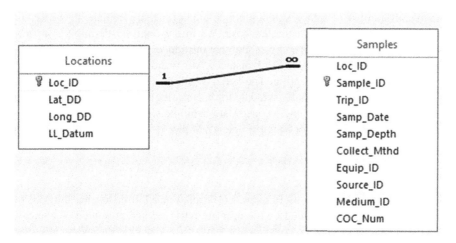

FIGURE 4.1   A small portion of a typical entity relationship diagram.

table, which would in turn delete all records in the results table for the samples that are deleted.

Keeping track of all these relationships can be cumbersome. Fortunately, most platforms offer a visual depiction of them. A graphical representation of the relationships is called an Entity Relationship Diagram (ERD). An ERD for our simple locations/samples example is shown in Figure 4.1.

A typical ERD will list all the columns in each table, with lines connecting the columns that constitute the foreign key relationships. The key symbol beside a column indicates that the column is part of the primary key for that table. The line in the figure correctly denotes that the LOC_ID column in both tables is used for the relationship. The digit 1 on the end of the line connected to the locations table indicates that the locations table is the parent. The end of the connecting line at the samples table is anchored at the LOC_ID column, indicating that this is the foreign key column. The infinity symbol at the samples end of the line indicates that this relationship is a one-to-many relationship, which means that a single record in the locations table may have as many associated records in the samples table as needed. While this is the most common type of relationship, another type is sometimes desirable in environmental data management systems: the one-to-one relationship. In this type of relationship, each parent record can have only one record in the child table. This may seem counterintuitive – if there can be only one record in the child, why not simply include the columns in the child table in the parent? For justification, consider this scenario. Suppose there are both common and distinct characteristics between different categories of samples we collect. For instance, let's say we collect samples for evaluating bacteriological toxins in water (e.g., *Escherichia coli*). The metadata requirements for our bacteriological samples are the same for other types of samples, but there are additional pieces of information that need to be recorded because of their potential to affect the results (e.g., if waterfowl or other wildlife are present). Because the volume of bacteriological samples is small compared to the overall number of samples, including columns for these influencing factors for all samples wastes space in the database. We might consider defining a separate table just for bacteriological samples, but that introduces the complication of having to search multiple tables when, for instance, we want a summary of all samples collected at a particular location. The better solution, then, is to create a separate table that houses the additional metadata for bacteriological samples. For data integrity considerations, then, a one-to-one relationship between the main samples table and the supplemental one for bacteriological samples is appropriate.

4.2.9 QUERIES

Queries represent the most useful aspect of a relational DBMS in that they are the means by which data specified by the user are retrieved and presented. Technically they probably should not be considered a part of the database proper because they do not persist – queries are defined, executed, and then discarded. They are better considered simply as an aspect of SQL. They are so important, however, that we feel obligated to discuss them in their own section.

We introduced the basic syntax of a query and presented simple examples in Section 4.2.6. Our examples in that section were simple because they retrieved data from only one table at a time. Such simple queries are rarely informative in the real world. The details we learned in Section 4.2.8 explain why this is so: data in a single table are often represented by coded values that point to other tables. In order to make the data understandable by a human reader, information from multiple tables must often be amalgamated. Fortunately, this is relatively easy using additional capabilities of the basic SELECT statement syntax we learned previously.

Displaying data from multiple tables in a single SELECT statement is accomplished using a JOIN clause. There are various types of joins, but the one used most often while managing environmental data is the INNER JOIN; therefore, we will confine most of our attention to this variation here. At the end of this section, we will briefly discuss other types of joins.

The simplest syntax of a SELECT statement with an INNER JOIN clause is:

```
SELECT cname_1, cname_2,... FROM tnamec INNER JOIN tnamep
ON tnamep.cnamep = tnamec.cnamef;
```

where tnamep is the name of the parent table, tnamec is the name of the related child table, cnamep is the name of the primary key column in the parent, cnamef is the name of the foreign key column in the child, and $cname_n$ is a column name in either table. This gets easier to understand by examining a specific example, so let us return to the samples table we described earlier. There are several columns in that table which should be designated as foreign keys into parents other than the locations table. We can create one of them (collection methods) with this statement:

```
CREATE TABLE COLLECTID
    (
    COLLECT_MTHD SMALLINT NOT NULL PRIMARY KEY,
    COLLECT_NAME VARCHAR(20) NOT NULL
    );
```

To establish the proper relationship, we define the column in the samples table that acts as a foreign key:

```
ALTER TABLE SAMPLES ADD CONSTRAINT FK_COLLMETH FOREIGN
KEY (COLLECT_MTHD) REFERENCES COLLECTID (COLLECT_
METHOD) ON DELETE SET NULL ON UPDATE CASCADE;
```

Note the variation here regarding what happens when we alter records in the parent. As before, we choose the option to apply the same changes to child records when a related parent record is updated (ON UPDATE CASCADE). However, in this case, we choose not to delete the child record (the sample) if we delete a related collection method record. We learn from this that some relationships are more important than others – we don't want a sample to reference a location that does not exist, so it makes sense to cascade delete in that relationship. But we deem it acceptable to have a sample for which no collection method is specified, so in this relationship, we set the collection method to NULL if the parent record is deleted (ON DELETE SET NULL).

Let's assume that the following data have been added to the collection methods table:

COLLECT_MTHD	COLLECT_NAME
1	Multi-parameter sampler
2	Kemmerer bottle
3	Nansen bottle

Let us now attempt to identify the method used for sampling events at a specific location (LOC_ID=12). We can retrieve these data from just the samples table:

```
SELECT LOC_ID, SAMP_DATE, SAMP_DEPTH, COLLECT_MTHD
FROM SAMPLES WHERE LOC_ID=12;
```

We get the results, but they look something like this:

```
LOC_ID    SAMP_DATE       SAMP_DEPTH        COLLECT_MTHD
12        12-JUN-2019     1.0               3
12        12-JUN-2019     5.0               3
12        12-JUN-2019     10.0              1
```

This query produces all the data we requested, but without further information, we don't really know what methods were used. Including a JOIN in the query returns the data in a more understandable format:

```
SELECT LOC_ID, SAMP_DATE, SAMP_DEPTH, COLLECT_NAME
FROM SAMPLES INNER JOIN COLLECTID ON COLLECTID.
COLLECT_MTHD=SAMPLES.COLLECT_MTHD WHERE LOC_ID=12;
```

```
LOC_ID    SAMP_DATE       SAMP_DEPTH      COLLECT_NAME
12        12-JUN-2019     1.0             Nansen bottle
12        12-JUN-2019     5.0             Nansen bottle
12        12-JUN-2019     10.0            Multi-parameter
                                          sampler
```

This is more informative, but still a bit obtuse because the location is identified only by its internal number. We can get a better overall report of these data if we also display the actual location name instead of the ID, which also affords us the opportunity to demonstrate the use of multiple joins within the same query.

```
SELECT LOC_NAME, SAMP_DATE, SAMP_DEPTH, COLLECT_
NAME FROM SAMPLES INNER JOIN COLLECTID ON COLLECTID.
COLLECT_MTHD=SAMPLES.COLLECT_MTHD INNER JOIN
LOCATIONS ON LOCATIONS.LOC_ID=SAMPLES.LOC_ID WHERE
LOC_ID=12;
```

Assuming location ID 12 is named "Carter Spring," we get the following results:

```
LOC_NAME          SAMP_DATE      SAMP_DEPTH  COLLECT_NAME
Carter Spring     12-JUN-2019    1.0         Nansen bottle
Carter Spring     12-JUN-2019    5.0         Nansen bottle
Carter Spring     12-JUN-2019    10.0        Multi-parameter
                                             sampler
```

While there is no limit imposed by SQL on the number of JOINs contained in a single query, every platform places a limit on the total number of characters it will accept in a statement. If you are approaching that boundary, though, your query is likely to be so complex that it cannot be debugged in the all too probable case that it contains one or more errors. Also, while the SQL standard does not require the use of parentheses when using multiple JOINs, some platforms may require them. The SQL interpreter for Microsoft Access is one such example.

Another thing you may notice in the examples above is that in each case, the actual key columns of the joined tables are not specified in the list of returned fields – we do not display the collection method ID in either query, and the second one does not display the location ID. As with all other SELECT queries, the list of columns returned is independent of other clauses in the statement. It may be desirable to include key columns, however, but including them requires additional clarification if the columns have the same name in both the parent and child tables. This is accomplished by specifying both the table and the column name, separated by a period. This identifies the specific column to be reported in the same way that the specific columns that define the join conditions are designated. Thus, to include the location ID in our query, we issue this statement:

```
SELECT LOCATIONS.LOC_ID, LOC_NAME, SAMP_DATE,
SAMP_DEPTH, COLLECT_NAME FROM SAMPLES INNER JOIN
COLLECTID ON COLLECTID.COLLECT_MTHD=SAMPLES.
COLLECT_MTHD INNER JOIN LOCATIONS ON LOCATIONS.LOC_
ID=SAMPLES.LOC_ID WHERE SAMPLES. LOC_ID=12;
```

The query returns these results:

```
LOC_ID    LOC_NAME          SAMP_DATE      SAMP_DEPTH  COLLECT_
                                                       NAME
12        Carter Spring     12-JUN-2019    1.0         Nansen
                                                       bottle
```

```
12          Carter Spring   12-JUN-2019   5.0       Nansen
                                                     bottle
12          Carter Spring   12-JUN-2019   10.0      Multi-
                                                     parameter
                                                     sampler
```

Note that we could just as easily have specified the LOC_ID field from the SAMPLES table. Since the values are the same, the choice of table has no effect on the returned data. Since the column name is ambiguous, though, we must explicitly select one or the other.

The other type of join available in standard SQL is called an outer join. There are three different variations of outer joins, and each requires a slightly different syntax in the query statement. An inner join only returns records matching the specified join condition(s) – no records will be displayed for which the join condition(s) cannot be met – but an outer join will return all records in one or both tables being joined (depending on the type of outer join). The three outer join variations are:

- the left outer join, which returns all records in the table referenced on left side of the equal sign in the join condition;
- the right outer join, which returns all records in the table referenced on the right side of the equal sign in the join condition; and
- the full outer join, which returns all records in both tables.

The SQL standard syntax for the three outer join types are LEFT JOIN, RIGHT JOIN, and FULL JOIN, respectively. To illustrate the results of an outer join, consider this variation on our original inner join example:

```
SELECT LOC_ID, SAMP_DATE, SAMP_DEPTH, COLLECT_
NAME FROM SAMPLES LEFT JOIN COLLECTID ON COLLECTID.
COLLECT_MTHD=SAMPLES.COLLECT_MTHD WHERE LOC_ID=12;
```

The original version (using the inner join) only returned rows that included a collection method ID that could be matched to a parent record in the collection methods reference table. In particular, that original version would not return any rows in which the collection method is NULL. The outer join version will return all samples for location ID #12, regardless of the value in the collection method column. If the collection method in the samples table is present and can be matched to a record in the collection methods table, the appropriate name will be displayed. If no match is found, the query will return NULL for the collection method name.

```
LOC_ID        SAMP_DATE       SAMP_DEPTH       COLLECT_NAME
12            12-JUN-2019     1.0              Nansen bottle
12            12-JUN-2019     2.5              NULL
12            12-JUN-2019     5.0              Nansen bottle
12            12-JUN-2019     10.0             Multi-
                                              parameter
                                              sampler
12            14-AUG-2019     3.0              NULL
```

The obvious situation in which an outer join is appropriate occurs when the objective is to list all the records in one of the joined tables, regardless of whether it contains a valid reference to a parent record. In this example, the outer join ensures that all samples from location #12 are reported. A more subtle use of an outer join offers an opportunity for checking data status. If we include both the collection method ID and the collection method name in our query:

```
SELECT LOC_ID, SAMP_DATE, SAMP_DEPTH, SAMPLES.
COLLECT_METHD, COLLECT_NAME FROM SAMPLES LEFT JOIN
COLLECTID ON COLLECTID.COLLECT_MTHD=SAMPLES.COLLECT_
MTHD WHERE LOC_ID=12;
```

the data that gets returned can identify any samples that reference invalid collection methods (invalid because the codes are not present in the collection methods parent table):

LOC_ID	SAMP_DATE	SAMP_DEPTH	COLLECT_MTHD	COLLECT_NAME
12	12-JUN-2019	1.0	3	Nansen bottle
12	12-JUN-2019	2.5	18	NULL
12	12-JUN-2019	5.0	3	Nansen bottle
12	12-JUN-2019	10.0	1	Multi-parameter sampler
12	14-AUG-2019	3.0	14	NULL

Reviewing the results, we note that two collection method IDs (18 and 14) are recorded in the samples table but are not found in the collection methods parent table. This can be a useful exercise when the need arises for modifying the data model after data are already present.

4.2.10 VIEWS

At the beginning of the last section we stated that queries cannot be saved as objects in the database. After learning more about the complexities of queries, you may be confounded by this. Imagine carefully crafting a query with many joins and other intricacies and honing it until it returns exactly the data you need in exactly the desired format ... and then realizing you need to issue this query repeatedly. Your first inclination would likely be to save the text of the query in a text file so that you could retrieve it for subsequent use. That's a valid approach, but fortunately there is a better option. It's one that calls our previous statement about queries into question. While technically true, our statement about queries not being saved is a little bit misleading because of something that can be saved in the database – views.

Views are essentially pseudo-tables constructed by issuing a query. Thus, in the example we just mentioned regarding that incredibly complex query you crafted, if you create a view using the same query syntax, the definition of the view essentially saves that query for later use at any time.

The syntax for creating a view is

```
CREATE VIEW vname AS sql statement;
```

where vname is the name of the view and sql statement is the standard SQL SELECT statement (in its entirety) that is used to retrieve the desired data.

One of the most significant features of views is that you can issue other queries to retrieve specific data from them. Suppose we have created a view called SAMP_RESULTS that retrieves all data for all records in the results table, with numerous joins that translate various coded fields in the results table to their meanings obtained from parent lookup tables. We could then issue the following query statement to retrieve all the results for the year 2019, presented in a completely translated, readable manner:

```
SELECT * FROM SAMP_RESULTS WHERE SAMPLE_ID IN
(SELECT SAMPLE_ID FROM SAMPLES WHERE YEAR(SAMP_
DATE)='2019');
```

(This assumes that our DBMS supports a YEAR function that returns a string that identifies the year in a specific date.)

By now you should be able to anticipate the syntax for deleting a view, which is:

```
DROP VIEW vname;
```

where vname is the name of the view to be deleted. To alter an existing view, there is a variation on the CREATE VIEW statement that lets you replace the query statement used to generate the view:

```
CREATE OR REPLACE VIEW vname AS sql statement;
```

4.2.11   STORED PROCEDURES AND TRIGGERS

The last major component we will discuss that is part of most DBMS platforms consists of sets of statements and commands that perform desired functions. There are two variations available in most systems: stored procedures and triggers. Stored procedures are snippets of code that are contained within the database that can be invoked at any time to perform the actions defined in the code. The code that constitutes the stored procedure consists of standard SQL statements and other commands supported by the specific platform. Some platforms support multiple languages for the non-SQL statements used to construct the procedure, while others offer only a single language option.

The code that constitutes the stored procedure is saved in the database as an object. There is an ANSI standard SQL syntax for creating a stored procedure object. It begins (as you might guess) with CREATE PROCEDURE and includes other keywords. Most platforms support this approach, although there are significant variations in the expected structure of the CREATE PROCEDURE statement. There are also variations in how you save the procedure. The SQL standard is to issue the single command "GO;" at the end of the process. Many platforms deviate from this standard, instead defining explicit keywords that denote the end of the procedure. DBMS packages also differ in how procedures are invoked. The two most common invocation commands are EXEC and CALL. The documentation for your specific DBMS will include instructions that guide you through the process (and hopefully provide examples).

Creating a stored procedure by defining it within the platform's text-based interface is fraught with peril however – the procedure will be created using the statements you enter with exactly the same syntax you type. Even the simplest procedure is likely to require multiple commands and statements, and if you mistype any of them while creating the procedure, the procedure will be doomed to fail. For that reason, many platforms include more robust components for creating procedures within their management framework. These components behave like mini-software development packages. They include a code window that allows you to interactively edit the entire procedure definition before committing it to the database.

Regardless of all these nuances, stored procedures can include very important tools for common data maintenance activities. You can pass parameters to stored procedures – for instance, table column values – and you can have stored procedures report the results of their calculations as return values. Stored procedures can be referenced (called) from external programs, allowing them to be included in more complex data operations associated with a user interface. As an example, let's say that state regulations require you to document and report all releases of rhodamine, and that you have a piece of equipment used in dye tracing that emits a fixed amount of rhodamine on a regular basis. You could incorporate a table in your database schema that records details of usage of rhodamine and create a stored procedure that inserts a record into this table automatically. This procedure could be called from your data entry interface each time you indicate the equipment was used. The user interface could pass the date and duration of the test to the procedure, and the procedure could then calculate and save a record containing the appropriate data. The ultimate outcome is that all uses of rhodamine associated with dye tracing would be available to report without additional data entry.

A trigger is very similar in that it consists of a set of coded instructions that get executed when the trigger is invoked. One major difference is that a stored procedure can be called at any time but a trigger only fires in response to a specific database action. Another significant difference is that a stored procedure can be more interactive in that it can accept input and provide return values, whereas a trigger has neither capability. Triggers are used primarily to perform actions on other tables that are associated with the action that sets off the trigger (an example might be inserting a record into a table that logs activity in the table with which the trigger is associated). The SQL standard statement for creating a trigger is (not surprisingly) CREATE TRIGGER. Triggers are always associated with a specific table and can be configured to execute when either an insert, update, or delete event occurs. You can also specify whether the trigger fires before or after the triggering event. Because of their context, there is no additional requirement for modifying any settings or definitions in the table with which the trigger is associated. Like stored procedures, the specifics of the process of creating a trigger can vary sufficiently between different platforms to justify omitting a more complete exploration in this space. Consult the documentation for your specific platform for details and syntax.

4.2.12 FORMS

Many people consider forms to be an integral part of their DBMS. While this is true from an overall perspective, forms are not technically part of the DBMS. They are often a critical part of the total data management solution, but few DBMS platforms actually include the capabilities for creating and managing forms.[16] To be clear, some DBMS vendors have companion products for creating forms, and these products are tightly integrated with their respective platform software. For instance, Oracle Corporation offers a package called Oracle Forms. These forms packages may be one component in a complete user interface, and in some cases may be sufficient alone to meet the user interface needs of a particular application. Forms creation software may be tied to a specific database platform, or may be flexible enough to connect to multiple platforms. Licensing of forms software may require either one-time or annual fees.

4.3   OTHER RELATIONAL DATABASE CONCEPTS

In this section we discuss other concepts that are important to grasp when acquiring complete knowledge of DBMSs.

4.3.1   DATA NORMALIZATION

In the preceding chapters, we've discussed numerous times the importance of creating a proper data model before you begin defining the tables and relationships in your database. We've covered the essential steps, but there is one final topic that should be addressed to ensure the most complete understanding of the data modeling process: data normalization. Of all the topics presented in this book, data normalization is probably the one with the most widely analyzed theoretical basis. There are many textbooks written on the subject. The traditional presentation of the subject is steeped in terminology and nomenclature associated with theoretical mathematics. We encourage you to explore such resources if your interest is sufficient, but here we will attempt to summarize the information in a way that is more focused on the practical implications.

The purpose of data normalization is to reduce the possibility of data errors as data are inserted, modified, and deleted in the various tables of the database. Normalization is a tiered activity – there are different levels of normalization, each of which builds on the previous levels. The successive levels are referred to as "forms," producing descriptions such as "first normal form," "second normal form," and so forth. The

---

[16] The most obvious exception to this is Microsoft Access. Access includes Visual Basic for Applications (VBA) which allows users to create forms that are retained as part of the individual database.

first three normal forms were defined by Edgar F. Codd in his original treatise on the Relational Model. Let's start at the beginning: first normal form.

A database is in first normal form if the following conditions are met:

1. All information is contained in tables.
2. Each record in each table has a unique identifier (primary key).
3. Each column contains an atomic element.
4. There are no repeating groups.

Some terms in this definition have already been discussed extensively, but others may require clarification here. First, what is an "atomic element?" An atomic element is a single basic piece of data – one that cannot be decomposed any further into individual items. Furthermore, every entry in the column is an item from the same category of data. This last qualification means that first normal form prohibits the use of generic columns into which any entry may be inserted. You can't, for example, create a table for test methods with a column called ATTRIBUTE_1 and have some records in which the value identifies a method identifier and other records in which the value identifies the method source.

It may be helpful in understanding what constitutes an atomic element by considering counterexamples. Consider a table for storing information about laboratories. Suppose the table contains a field called ADDRESS. Possible records in this table are presented in Table 4.8 (not all fields likely found in a table for labs are shown).

The LAB_ADDRESS column in this table violates the atomic element definition because the entries can be decomposed into more basic elements – street address, city, state, and zip code.

The second new term in the definition of first normal form is "repeating groups." A repeating group is a group of columns that contain entries from the same domain (i.e., entries that represent different instances of the same piece of information). An example of a repeating group can be obtained by considering a table of parameters

TABLE 4.8
Representative Records in a Table for Laboratories

LAB_ID	LAB_NAME	LAB_ADDRESS
1	Continental Services	101 N. Buckman St., Columbus, OH 43035
2	Technical Analytics	1553 Tucson Blvd., Phoenix, AZ 85005
3	Simpson Associates	2205 Del Rey Road, Knoxville, TN 37920

TABLE 4.9
Partial Listing of Columns and Data in a Table for Parameters and Appropriate Test Methods

PARAM_ID	PARAM_NAME	TEST_MTHD_1	TEST_MTHD_2
205	Mercury	EPA 245.1	ASTM D3223-17
800	Magnesium	EPA 608.3	ASTM D5790-18
17	pH	EPA 150.1	SM 4500-H+B

TABLE 4.10
Table for Laboratories in First Normal Form

LAB_ID	LAB_NAME	LAB_STREET	LAB_CITY	LAB_STATE	LAB_ZIP
1	Continental Services	101 N. Buckman St.	Columbus	OH	43035
2	Technical Analytics	1553 Tucson Blvd.	Phoenix	AZ	85005
3	Simpson Associates	2205 Del Rey Road	Knoxville	TN	37920

and the test method(s) appropriate for each. Table 4.9 contains a (partial) potential structure and some possible records.

The rationale behind the construction of this table is clear: to identify multiple valid test methods for a given parameter. The most obvious problem with the construction of this table is equally clear: there is no way to record more than two valid test methods for a given parameter. You might consider adding a TEST_MTHD_3 column but that only exacerbates the problem and quickly leads to a repetitive nightmare of column additions. From this example it should be obvious why this situation violates the first normal form.

First normal form is easily achievable as you design the data model if you simply keep the definition in mind. Let's see what needs to be done to bring the two example tables into first normal form. The solution to the laboratories table issue is obvious. All that is required is to break the address field into its constituent parts. Table 4.10 shows the results using the same records as those in Table 4.8.

The parameters table issue requires a bit more effort. Resolution comes with the realization that the original table definition is essentially trying to serve two purposes. The primary goal of the parameters table is the identification of parameter names and characteristics. While identifying applicable test methods for a given parameter is important, this is not quite a characteristic of the parameter. Instead, it is an identification of how a parameter relates to another class of data – test methods. Normalization of this relationship is achieved by creating a separate table of test methods and then

TABLE 4.11
Three Tables Are Required for Relating Parameters and Appropriate Test Methods

Parameters Table

PARAM_ID	PARAM_NAME
205	Mercury
800	Magnesium
17	pH

Test Methods Table

TEST_MTHD_ID	TEST_MTHD_NAME
6	ASTM D3223-17
14	EPA 245.1
11	EPA 608.3
94	ASTM D5790-18
54	EPA 150.1
37	SM 4500-H+B

Parameter Test Methods Table

PARAM_ID	TEST_MTHD_ID
205	6
205	14
800	11
800	94
17	54
17	37

creating a table that signifies each proper pairing of records from the two primary tables, as shown in Table 4.11.

You should not be surprised that we created a unique numeric identifier for each test method. Note also that the table which relates the parameters and test methods is an extreme example of a table that would require the use of multiple joins in order to translate the coded values to their human-readable meanings. Nonetheless, these relationships are now first normal.[17]

---

[17] Hopefully by now you're thinking far enough ahead to recognize a more efficient way to describe the relationship between parameters and test methods. Many test methods are applicable to a wide range of specific parameters because they apply to a class of parameters (e.g., volatile organic compounds). As described, this structure produces many references to the same method in the parameters/tests methods relational table we have created. We can therefore increase the efficiency of the data model by defining classes of parameters (another parent lookup table), assigning each parameter to a class, and then listing the parameter class for which each test method is appropriate. We end up with the same number of tables as before, but fewer total records.

We're now ready for the next normalization level.

A database is in second normal form when the following conditions are met:

1. The table is in first normal form.
2. All non-key columns for a given row are dependent on the entire primary key.

Once again we encounter a new term, but its meaning is obvious: a non-key column is any column that is not part of the table's primary key. In other words, the second requirement means that no non-key column can be dependent on only part of the primary key. More insight into the implications of second normal form can be obtained by considering some trivial cases in which the second normal form is guaranteed. First, consider the situation where the primary key of a table consists of a single column. In that case, the attributes (columns) for every record in the table represent specific characteristics of the element identified by the record (assuming the table is in first normal form). The second trivial situation occurs when there are no non-key columns. At first blush you might think this is a truly trivial case – how useful is a table that doesn't contain any information other than the primary key? – but such tables occur frequently. In fact, we've already encountered one in Table 4.11. The table that relates the parameters and test methods can have only one possible primary key, which is the combination of the only two fields present.

As before, let's consider a nontrivial table that is not second normal form. Suppose we create a table for sampling information that includes the following columns (all are required entries):

- SAMPLE_ID (unique number assigned to each sample);
- LOCATION_ID (unique ID for each location; primary key in the LOCATIONS table);
- SAMPLE_DT (date and time when the sample was collected);
- SAMLE_DEPTH (depth at which the sample was collected); and
- SAMPLE_TZ (time zone designation to clarify the interpretation of the sample time).

Before we sort out why this table is not in second normal form, we need to briefly return to our discussion of primary keys. The obvious primary key choice in the above list is the SAMPLE_ID column since it is by itself a unique identifier of the specific sampling event. It is not the only candidate for a primary key, however. We cannot physically collect multiple samples at the same location, date/time, and depth, so the combination of LOCATION_ID + SAMPLE_DT + SAMPLE_DEPTH represents a potential valid composite primary key. When there are multiple options for the primary key for a table, they are each referred to as candidate keys until one is chosen. What's interesting in the table described here is that the SAMPLE_ID is (probably) generated by the system when the sample is recorded in the table. Unlike the composite candidate key, it does not have any physical meaning. There are certainly some advantages of using the single SAMPLE_ID column as the primary key,[18] and by definition the presence of a single column primary key means the table is in second normal form. But is it really? If we choose the composite candidate as the primary key, then we note that the SAMPLE_TZ column is dependent only on one part of the primary key (since the time zone is an attribute of the sampling location). In that case, the table does not fit the definition of second-order normal because it violates item #2.

The solution in this case is simple: all that is required is adding the time zone indicator to the LOCATIONS table and removing it from the SAMPLES table.

The next level of normalization is third normal. Unfortunately, in order to describe third normal form we must introduce some additional terminology from the theoretical realm of relational theory. Since we're on the subject, we'll also revisit some terms we've already learned but have not formally defined.

A superkey is any set of attributes that can be used to uniquely identify a row.

Obviously, the set of all columns is a superkey. In most cases, other superkeys exist that do not include all columns.

A candidate key is a superkey with the additional qualification that no component of the candidate key can be removed without eliminating the ability of the key to uniquely identify records.

Columns that can be removed from a superkey without affecting the ability to identify uniqueness of records are said to be redundant; therefore, the restriction that disallows redundant columns in candidate keys is referred to as nonredundancy. Every candidate key is a superkey, but not every superkey is a candidate key.

Attribute A is said to be functionally dependent on attribute B if, for any valid value of A, the value of B determines A.

---

[18] In particular, we'll need to include the primary key from the SAMPLES table in the RESULTS table (which contains analytical results for the sample). If the SAMPLES table has a composite key, each constituent of that key must be present in the RESULTS table. Using the simpler key reduces the number of columns required in the RESULTS table.

Functional dependence is typically denoted either using the familiar mathematical nomenclature A=f(B) or as B → A. The latitude of a sampling location is functionally dependent on the location ID since the location ID determines which location is being described. Functional dependence is important in identifying all types of keys, so the left side of the definition can actually be a set of attributes (e.g., BC → A means that A is functionally dependent on attributes B and C). If the left side includes multiple attributes, it is often designated by X to indicate a set of attributes. We can use the familiar mathematical designations of variables as independent and dependent to describe both sides of a functional dependence: if B → A, then we can call B the independent attribute(s) and A the dependent attribute. In relational algebra, it is acceptable to include the dependent attribute in the set of independent attributes (e.g., AB → A), but such dependencies are designated as trivial.

We're now ready to define the third normal form.

A database is in third normal form if the following conditions are met:

1. It is in second normal form.
2. For all nontrivial functional dependencies X → A, either
   • the set of attributes in X is a superkey, or
   • A is a member of a candidate key.

Loosely translated, this definition states that every non-key column in each table is either part of a candidate key or is functionally dependent on a superkey. (Another common translation is that each attribute is "a function of the key, the whole key, and nothing but the key."[19]) Essentially, the third normal form is violated when a non-key field is a fact about (is functionally dependent on) another non-key field.

Continuing with our previous pattern, let us discuss an example that is not in third normal form. Consider the table we introduced earlier in which we record details about our sampling equipment. When we last mentioned this table, it had only three columns (equipment ID, serial number, and vendor). Suppose we decided it would be helpful (for whatever reason) to also note the vendor's website in this table. That modification would mean the equipment table would no longer be in third normal form because the vendor's website is an attribute of the vendor and not the specific piece of equipment. The obvious way to correct this would be to create a separate table for vendor information.

We've now discussed Codd's original set of normalization levels. There are other, more sophisticated normalization levels. Like the first three, each of these assumes the previous levels are enforced and then identifies more restrictions. These more advanced normalization forms tend to address specific conditions that may lead to data update anomalies, but with each succeeding level, the likelihood that you will

---

[19] This quote is found in many references and is generally attributed to William Kent in "A Simple Guide to Five Normal Forms in Relational Database Theory." In references that are more whimsical in nature, it is also followed by "so help you, Codd."

encounter the targeted anomalies becomes less likely within a system for managing environmental data. Explore them at your leisure if you are interested, but don't focus on them unless and until you discover mistakes in your data that cannot be attributed to other sources.

> **Best Practice #9**   When creating your data model, strive to achieve third normal form. Remember, though, that normal forms are guidelines and not hard and fast rules. There may be legitimate reasons for violating a normal form. If your business model requires deviation from normality, don't hesitate to accommodate it.

We'll end this section with a list of guidelines that you should follow when designing your data model. The items in the list essentially summarize the conditions required to meet the third normal form, but we thought it might be helpful to present them all in one place. Situations may require flexibility, so don't worry if you can't adhere to all the guidelines. Following as many as possible will help you normalize your database to a reasonable and appropriate level. Keep these guidelines in mind during the initial stages of your data design.

- Each column in each table should contain only atomic values.
- Identify repeating data groups and create separate tables to contain them.
- Every record in each table should have a unique identifier (primary key).
- Connect related tables through the use of primary keys and foreign keys.
- Each distinct category of data should reside in its own table. (In other words, all the data in a given table should be directly related to the primary key.)
- Each non-key column should identify an attribute of the entire primary key. Non-key columns that relate to only part of the key should be removed.

4.3.2   DATA VALIDATION

Data validation is an essential feature of any DBMS. In broad terms, validation means guaranteeing that entries in any given column satisfy the data requirements of that column. Valid data may be limited to a specific set of entries, a range of numeric values, or other restrictions. Multiple techniques may be employed to validate data. Most data validation restrictions can be implemented using techniques we described earlier (e.g., foreign keys, constraints, stored procedures, etc.). However, it may not always be possible to completely define all the requirements associated with a column using just the tools available in the database itself. We previously discussed why dispersing data into different tables places emphasis on the need for a user interface. We now observe that the user interface can offer another advantage beyond simply presenting the data in a more understandable manner – it can also implement data validation procedures that are too complex to capture in other ways. This can, in fact, be a significant tool when moving data from one DBMS to another. Due to variations in how different platforms implement the same relational concept, migrating to a new platform may not always result in complete adherence to the data model if all validation is handled within the database. Modifying the user interface to reference a different platform, however, may be as simple as redefining the data source. Don't fall into the trap of thinking you have to perform all validation within the database.

4.3.3 Transactions

We mention transactions only for purposes of completeness. Some relational platforms support transactions, but others do not. The transaction model is a method of delaying data actions until a defined set of conditions is met. A transaction consists of multiple SQL statements that are treated as a single unit. Transactions are used when a change to data in one table affects data in one or more other tables. Even then, they are most applicable to systems that must support a large number of users or processes simultaneously. In those cases, data modifications to all affected tables must be committed at the same time in order to preserve a persistent state to the relationships between the various tables. The transaction therefore serves as a sort of queue that pauses execution of the individual statements until all have been processed. At that point, the transaction can either be committed or abandoned (often referred to as rolled back).

SQL implementations that support transactions may have a statement that identifies the beginning of the transaction.[20] All subsequent statements are considered part of the transaction. The transaction ends when a statement is entered to either commit or roll back the changes.

Transactions are important in many systems, but their utility in managing environmental data is limited.

---

[20] In some cases, transactions are always implied. When accessing an Oracle database using the SQL*Plus command window, for instance, all statements issued during a given session are part of a transaction. You can commit at any time, and that action initiates a new transaction. Pending transactions are committed automatically when you exit SQL*Plus normally or rolled back if your connection terminates irregularly. On the other hand, SQL Server considers all T-SQL statements entered without the explicit declaration of a transaction to be independent and auto-commits them as each one is entered.

5 Buy, Borrow, or Build

A Decision Guide for Choosing between an Existing Solution and Creating Something New

5.1 OPTIONS FOR A COMPREHENSIVE DATA MANAGEMENT PROGRAM

Previous chapters have discussed the general principles of proper data management, identified some loosely organized systems that may be sufficient in limited situations, determined that a relational database is the best option for environmental data, and introduced the basics of how a relational database system works. Armed with this knowledge, we are now ready for the first major decision related to establishing a system particular to our needs: identifying the specific system components. There are multiple aspects of this decision, and they intersect and overlap in numerous ways. Three of the most critical elements are:

- which DBMS should be used for the database;
- which methods are appropriate for user interactions with the data; and
- how and by whom will the user interface be created and/or maintained?

The general knowledge and detailed information about specific database platforms presented in Chapter 4 should be sufficient to provide a starting point for assessing the first issue. Proper application of the principles and methods presented thus far creates a suitable foundation on which to build the solution regardless of the specific platform. This foundation (the database) by itself, however, is not a complete solution. The most well-designed database in the world is of little value unless an effective means exists for enabling interactions between users and data. A good user interface is essential for any system. (This is a true statement even if you are the only user. Knowing how data gets segregated into individual tables, you should now recognize that a meaningful presentation of information requires retrieving data from multiple tables. Do you want to deal with all the table relationships every time you enter results for a sampling event?) The last two items in the list above relate to the user interface and are therefore just as important as the first.

The second item in the above list may need a little clarification. We use the term "methods" here to denote the variety of environments in which users expect to interact with the database. These environments include typical office settings as well as

DOI: 10.1201/9781003131953-6

potentially multiple scenarios in the field. Understanding the requirements associated with each environment and scenario helps identify the technology, equipment, and infrastructure needed to address each variation. Common choices (at least at the time of this writing) include standard personal computers and laptops, hardened laptops, tablet devices, and cell phones. The capabilities of these devices vary, as do the methods available on each that address the capture and transfer of data. The user interface or interfaces – you may need more than one – should accommodate as many user scenario variations as possible.

Clearly, then, the capabilities of the interface(s) are just as critical as the database back end. The effectiveness of the user interface is another responsibility of the system designer/developer/manager. For some environmental professionals who find themselves in the role of data manager, this realization might be considered a step too far. It may be reasonable to expect you to learn about, construct, and manage the data repository, but do you have to become a software developer as well? Thankfully, the answer is "no." Within the environmental data world, there are many technical resources available that can assist the process of creating a complete data management approach. These resources come in a variety of formats. When the various options are considered, we can identify three distinct pathways to arrive at a comprehensive solution:

- purchase a commercial, off-the-shelf (COTS) software package;
- acquire and adapt a system from an organization that performs similar activities; or
- create a new database schema and/or user interface(s).

Exploring these approaches sheds light on our observation regarding the overlap and interaction between the original list of aspects.

5.2   USING COMMERCIAL SOFTWARE

There are many commercial software packages that claim to provide management, analysis, and reporting of environmental data. Because "environmental data" can be interpreted differently under varying circumstances, these claims should mostly be considered legitimate. However, this means that identifying a particular COTS package that meets your specific needs requires extreme diligence. This includes careful comparison of your particular requirements with the actual capabilities of each package, as well as discovery of any limitations that exist. Undertaking this evaluation can be difficult and requires judicious selection of your sources of information. It's reasonable to start with the website for a particular product, but remember that the goal of these web sites is to sell the product. These sites tend to display screen shots and bullet lists identifying a plethora of capabilities, some of which may stretch the limits of truthfulness. Furthermore, important specific details related to product functionality and technology are often missing. A particular product may, for instance, require the use of specific DBMS, but this fact may not be present in the information shown on the site. You are thus not likely to get as thorough an understanding of a commercial product as needed from the website alone.

In many cases, you may be able to use the software for a trial period before paying for it. Exercise caution and plan carefully when accepting this offer. Make sure to allocate sufficient time to perform a comprehensive comparison of the product to your organization's needs and practices. Prepare a set of test data that includes a representative cross-section of all the types of data your organization collects. Testing should include assessing the ease with which data in your specific formats can be incorporated into the software. If you have standard formats for inclusion of analytical data in your reports, determine how much (if any) additional manipulation is required to wrangle the output of the software into the needed arrangement. If you export data to other systems, those targets may require data to be submitted in a specific format; check to see if the software can export the required files without further modification. If you evaluate multiple COTS options, use the same test data in all cases in order to avoid biased conclusions.

Ultimately, your best source of information about a package is likely to be other users. Check with other organizations whose missions and practices are similar to yours in order to determine who may now be using (or have used in the past) any software you are evaluating. Conferences, symposia, and other professional meetings provide excellent opportunities for this type of discussion. If you are interested in a particular COTS and can't find users within your community of practice, scan the support forum(s) for information and post questions that identify the types of data you manage.[1] Establish conversations with respondents whose data are similar.

Cost can be a major factor when considering a COTS solution. In the past, software was primarily sold as a product for which you paid a fixed price for licensed use of a specific version. While some vendors required licensing fees each year (and included updates to the latest versions in the price), the predominant approach was that vendors would supply users with a licensed copy of the software on some tangible media (e.g., CD or DVD). There were often explicit limits on your use of the media (e.g., you would likely have to purchase separate licenses for each computer on which the software was installed), but basically you had use of that version as long as you wanted. The advantage to this model (for users) was that if the current version of the product met your needs, there was less motivation to pay for updates. Recent years have seen a rise in the popularity of the "software as a service" model under which the software is centrally hosted and provided to the user on demand. This model shifts control of usage entirely to the provider and (usually) requires license renewal on a regular basis. Thus, you must now include the cost of the software as part of your budget every year.

In addition to this change, be aware that some vendors divide the capabilities of the software into different modules and require licensing of the modules separately. For instance, there are environmental data management COTS packages that don't include data validation capabilities in the basic product or that require extra components in order to import data and thus avoid requiring manual data entry. In

---

[1] If they exist. If no such forum exists, it's probably a bad sign. If a company is selling a product and does not provide a community discussion forum, they may not be able to provide adequate support in the likely event you need it.

these cases, the modules are often interdependent in such a way that you may be required to license modules you rarely use in order to acquire capabilities that are essential. And of course, the more modules you have to license, the more you will pay each year.

Another practice of which you should be aware is that some vendors go to great lengths to hide the database schema. This means, for instance, that you may not be able open the database directly using the underlying DBMS in order to understand the data model. You will likely also be unable to find a comprehensive data dictionary. The rationale used to justify this position is that the vendor invested their own time and money in creating the schema, so they consider it as intellectual property worth protecting. This position, however, sets up two potentially very large impediments for end users. First, this means your only method of interacting with the data is through the interface(s) provided by the developer. You have no easy way of verifying that the data are being stored as you intended. More troubling, this approach may significantly limit your ability to create your own methods of analysis and reporting. Addition of new capabilities will likely require acquiring the services of the original developer – a service for which they may charge a high price. Second – and even more troubling – a closed data model has a better chance of locking you into a particular system for longer than desired. If you grow dissatisfied with the product, your ability to migrate your existing data to a new system is highly dependent on your knowledge of how the data are stored in the current database. Imagine using a system for a few years and loading thousands of locations, samples, and results records. If you can't migrate those data to another database, your only choices are to either continue with the current system or re-enter the data from scratch. Neither choice is satisfactory.

Another recent trend within many COTS data management packages is the storage of data on the cloud. There may be numerous arguments that support cloud storage in general, but with regard to managing environmental data specifically, these are the most cogent:

- access to the live data from anywhere using multiple device types;
- automated backup of data; and
- reduction in support requirements for the DBMS.

Of these, only the first offers a compelling rationale for using cloud-based storage. Even that reason is tempered, however, with the realization that field data collection has a high potential for occurring in locations where access is limited or nonexistent due to the unavailability of mechanisms for connectivity. Cellular coverage – the most obvious and cheapest method for connecting to the Internet from remote locations – is not present everywhere (despite the claims of all the major telecom vendors). Even if all areas in which you sample have available cellular networks, the networks may be different for each.

A better solution is to create your data collection procedures such that they do not require direct access to the live database at all times. This can be accomplished in a variety of ways, ranging from the use of technology-free approaches (e.g., paper forms) to identifying and incorporating required lookup data during pre-deployment staging of data collection devices. Consider that the most significant factor in the cost of field data collection is typically manpower and deployment. Strive to make field data collection as quick and simple as possible, but not at the increased risk of data loss or inability to acquire a signal.

Another potential argument against cloud-based solutions is the loss of control of the data. When you store your data externally, you are relying on multiple parties (at minimum, the network provider and the cloud vendor) over which you have little or no control. Your data safety net depends on their abilities to provide security and access. The quality and reliability of these services is growing, but you should maintain a healthy skepticism about their claims. In short, there is no one perfect solution for everyone. Choosing between a locally managed data repository and an off-site scenario largely depends on your comfort level with the technology required for each option.

[As an aside, the obvious question you might now be asking is "if I'm just going to use a commercial software package, why did I bother learning all that stuff in Chapter 4?" While the potential exists that you may be able to find a package that meets all your needs and you will never have to step outside the capabilities created by the system vendor, that likelihood is relatively small. A more likely scenario is that even if you identify and adopt a system from a commercial source, there will be specific requirements that you must meet that are not available within the original framework. Knowledge and understanding of how the database works will allow you to seize the initiative in such cases and enable you to be more self-reliant.]

5.3 ADAPTING AN EXISTING SOLUTION

The first alternative to licensing a COTS software package is the adaptation of an existing system from a source other than a traditional software vendor. Sources for candidate systems include government agencies, professional associations, and other organizations that collect and manage data that is similar to yours.

Various government agencies involved with monitoring environmental conditions are likely to have the same requirements, adhere to the same practices, and follow the same procedures as the private sector. Their data needs are therefore the same. When faced with collecting, managing, and analyzing environmental data, they follow the same paths presented here in order to identify an acceptable and appropriate solution. In some cases, they determine that the use of COTS software is appropriate. When a COTS solution is not chosen, they often opt to develop a custom system. Depending on the importance of the objective and the scope of the data, their systems may be quite comprehensive.

An advantage that many government organizations have over the private sector is that they are often integral participants in establishing the policies driving environmental analysis and thus have the ability to focus data analysis in the most important areas. They may sometimes also have a significantly larger budget that can be dedicated to development. It's common for government entities to define system requirements and then contract the actual development to the private sector while providing oversight to ensure systems meet performance and analysis goals. (This is especially true in the United States at the federal government level.)

The big advantage when considering systems developed by government agencies is that, since they are typically developed using public funds, they are often considered public domain. Thus, licensing fees and other costs are often not applicable.[2] In some cases, the source code for the software may also be available. This offers the best opportunity for adapting the existing system if it meets most but not all your specific requirements. The biggest drawback of using software developed by a government agency is that technical support (and even detailed information) may be severely limited or even non-existent. To be clear, some government data management projects are broad in scope and intended for wide applicability. These systems may have dedicated support staff whose responsibilities include providing guidance and technical information to users. Even in the best cases, however, the level of support may not be as comprehensive as what you may expect from a commercial software vendor.

A second potential source for non-COTS software is professional organizations associated a given activity or data category. There are many such organizations at numerous levels of concentration: local, regional, national, and international. At the regional level, an example might be an affiliation of municipal water treatment plant operators within a given geographic area. The purpose of the association is to share information, technologies, and best practices related to treating drinking water. Because they also have regulatory monitoring and reporting requirements, the association may sponsor development of a custom application for managing certain types of water quality data. There are numerous organizations at the other levels with similar foci and reach. Examples in the United States include the American Water Resources Association, the Air and Waste Management Association, the National Municipal Stormwater Alliance, and the American Society of Civil Engineers to name just a few. International examples include the Society of Environmental Toxicology and Chemistry and the North American Lake Management Society.

Organizations such as these often participate in grants with colleges and universities to develop applications. In many cases, source code for these packages may be available at no charge. As with software from government agencies, software sponsored by professional organizations may tend to be very targeted and its applicability may not be sufficiently broad to meet all your needs. It may, however, offer a good starting point for further development.

The best way to acquire information about solutions developed by professional organizations is to participate in their meetings and conferences. Many of their symposia will include sessions on tools for managing and analyzing the types of data with which they deal. Better still are the opportunities these meetings offer for directly interacting with other scientists involved in similar endeavors. There is no substitute for one-on-one discussions with your colleagues.

---

[2] Note, however, that there may be fees associated with licensing the DBMS on which a solution is constructed.

5.4 BUILDING A CUSTOM APPLICATION

If none of the other options adequately addresses your needs – or if you're just feeling adventurous – your other option is to create an entirely new system. While this option might seem intimidating, it does provide one significant advantage not available with the other choices: total control over every aspect of the database design and the user interface(s). It will be well within your means to craft the resulting application in such a way that it looks and behaves exactly as you determine. We'll examine this option in more detail in Chapters 6 and 7, and in Chapter 8 we'll apply what we learn to an example. For now we'll limit our discussion to the overall approach required to create a new system. Our discussion here will treat the entire solution – both the database and the user interface(s) – as a single topic.

We've emphasized the importance of system planning throughout this book, so it should come as no surprise when we state once again that the single most important thing you can do to ensure an acceptable solution is to analyze your business model and then craft the data model in such a way that it encapsulates the business model. Formalize your analysis of the business model by capturing everything in a single and complete document. Describe details of every type of sample you collect and every type of analysis you either perform within your organization or request from others. Include examples of electronic data sources in the documentation. Identify the capabilities of all equipment you use (or plan to use) for collecting field observations and samples. If you have standard operating procedures for collecting samples, describe them. If you don't have existing procedures, create them. If you have an in-house laboratory that performs some or all of your analyses, describe their requirements for handling and receiving samples as well as the nomenclature they use for identifying parameters. Do the same for any labs with which you contract analyses. If you subcontract any data collection efforts, describe the requirements each subcontractor must meet in order to perform quality work. Include samples of any standard reports you are required to generate as well as the format(s) in which you summarize data for clients. Identify any external systems to which you submit data, either under obligation or voluntarily. Document the requirements for submitting data to each.

After completing the analysis of the business model, tailor your expectations regarding automation. It may not be worthwhile to expect the solution to automate every analysis and report. There may be sufficient similarities between some required outputs that a single format can satisfy multiple objectives if you're willing to do a little post-processing. Identify the time requirements to manipulate a given output to serve a different purpose and estimate how often this situation occurs. Compare that level of effort to what is required to include each variation as a separate option. Generating graphical analyses typically requires more effort than generating tabular or statistical analyses. Don't hesitate to include this capability in your solution if necessary, but consider using third-party tools if possible. Creation of Geographic Information Systems (GIS) data should be relatively easy when managing your data with a database. Focus only on the data requirements for GIS rather than trying to incorporate this capability within the system.

It is impossible to overstress the importance of accurate and efficient data capture. Forms for manually entering data should address all data elements related to their objective without resorting to secondary pages or subforms if possible. Prompts should be clear and unambiguous. If your organization has a history of collecting data using paper forms, the transition to electronic data collection will be less disruptive if the digital versions of the forms appear as similar as possible to the familiar hard copy ones. Some creativity may be required if there are variations in the data requirements for forms with the same general purpose. There are multiple distinct solutions to this situation. A single form that always includes all possible entries is typically a source of confusion and should be avoided. A single form whose appearance changes according to the specifics of a particular situation can be more effective. If the data variations are substantial, it may be more efficient to create entirely unique forms. As an example, documentation of sampling events is significantly different for surface water samples collected in a reservoir and groundwater samples collected from a monitoring well. The requirements for each of these scenarios in your business model will determine which option is best.

Developing an entirely new product involves creating software that will present forms for user input, properly collect the data, and perform retrieval and analysis functions – in other words, software that will serve as the user interface. You must be prepared to commit adequate resources in order to complete this goal. Furthermore, if you are unfamiliar with the process of software development, understand that coding is only the first of two significant aspects of the undertaking. The other aspect is testing. Software testing can demand a large investment in time and effort, especially if conducted under any of the various formal protocols. However, since the community of users for your environmental data solution is likely to be more limited, you don't have to go overboard with testing. At minimum you should confirm accurate and complete interaction between the interface and the database. Also, you should strive to provide your users with an interface as free from bugs as possible. Software that frequently crashes or introduces unnecessary difficulties in operations will often be rejected as unacceptable. Finally, note that the testing requirements apply if you adapt an existing product as well – any modifications you make to the previous version of the software should be tested as rigorously as any completely new endeavor.

5.5   ADVANTAGES AND DISADVANTAGES OF EACH OPTION

Deciding between these three approaches can be difficult. In this section we present the advantages and disadvantages of each option.

Use of Commercial Software
  Advantages

- This option presents the fastest possible route to deployment. Note that it may still not necessarily be a very short route.
- This is also typically the cheapest option, although the monetary advantages may decrease the longer you use the system.

- Costs for implementation of a COTS solution are typically easier to identify. When evaluating costs, don't forget to include any training that may be required for proper usage.
- Use of the existing data model provided by the software vendor eliminates the need for developing a new database.
- There is usually no requirement for developing a new user interface when using a commercial application.
- Resolution of any bugs or product shortcomings is the responsibility of the vendor.

Disadvantages

- Because the data model is already defined, there is the potential temptation to skip the business model analysis step. You should avoid this temptation. A complete understanding of your business model is still required in order to assess the ability of the software's data model to adhere to your practices.
- Use of a COTS package usually requires the use of specific database platform. This cost element may or may not be included in the price of the software.
- A more careful evaluation of capabilities of the system is required before selecting a product. You may also have to perform this rigorous assessment multiple times.
- Options for customization of the system may be limited or non-existent.
- If any modifications are desired, the cost for developing them is typically higher. The original vendor may be your only source for these changes. Even if other options exist, the programming language on which the system is based or the data model details may discourage third parties from considering modifications.
- Deployment of a solution developed by an outside entity may require changes to established procedures for data collection and/or analysis within your organization.
- The vendor may be unable to provide support that is adequate in expertise or detail, or may limit the time of day during which support is available. Vendors may also charge a premium for different levels of support.
- The ongoing costs for licensing can be significant over time.
- There may be possible issues with data migration if the product is determined to be insufficient to meet your needs.

Adapting an Existing Product
Advantages

- This is likely the second fastest route to deployment.
- Because you are adapting an existing system, you don't have to design the entire data model from scratch.
- Significant portions of the user interface(s) will already be developed and (presumably) debugged.
- Depending on the original source and popularity of the system being modified, access to other users for community support may be more prevalent.

Disadvantages

- Even though you are not starting from scratch, this option still requires a complete analysis of your business model (did you think we would say otherwise?).
- A thorough understanding of the data model and capabilities of the product being adapted is also essential. (So now you have two data models to analyze.)
- Care must be taken to ensure that data types and procedures in the existing data model are compatible with your practices. If possible, discuss your needs and practices with multiple other users of the software. Try to identify any differences between their procedures and yours; check to see if appropriate deviations are already coded in the system.
- If some business rules are implemented through stored procedures in the database, you will need sufficient knowledge of or support for the underlying language in order to evaluate them.
- This option may still limit your choice of DBMS.
- Availability of technical information about the product is likely to be more limited than for a commercial application.
- There may also be little to no technical support available. This emphasizes the importance of the size and breadth of the user community for the product.
- In order to identify the changes that will be required, side-by-side comparisons of all aspects of your practices and those included in the existing system should be documented.
- The actual modifications to the system may require acquiring expertise in the language in which the interface is written. If you have in-house expertise in the language, those resources may still not be adequately familiar with databases or with the nuances of data you collect.

Creating a New Product
Advantages

- The choice of database platform is not limited by outside influences.
- You get to design the database from scratch.
- You can define the entire form and functionality of the user interface(s).
- You have the ability to determine the appropriate language of the interface(s). This may allow you to use existing developer resources (if available).
- You can adapt the software to existing procedures and practices rather than forcing users to adapt to the software.
- Costs related to development, deployment, and ongoing usage are within your control.
- If your needs or practices change in the future, you have assurance that the system can be modified accordingly.
- There are no ongoing licensing or maintenance fees for the software.

Disadvantages

- This may be the most costly option, both in terms of time and money.
- You have to design the database from scratch.
- There may still be licensing costs for use of the DBMS.
- Unless you are an expert in all types of data your organization collects, manages, and analyzes, design of the data model and software will require input from others. (This can actually be a good situation, provided you limit the number of people involved.)
- Creation of the complete solution requires an understanding of the management of software development projects. This may be beyond your skill set or comfort level.

5.6   GUIDANCE: DECIDING ON THE BEST OPTION

We conclude this chapter with some assistance to help you determine your best option regarding how to choose a path. When providing guidance such as this, a common practice is to present a decision tree that functions similarly to a flow chart. The decision tree usually offers a series of questions with limited potential responses that define pathways to an ultimate answer. Unfortunately in this case, the questions to be asked are not easily answered with a short list of responses. Many of them are subjective, further clouding the picture. In the end, the complexities of attempting a flow chart approach produce a tangled mess of interconnections and far too many indeterminate conditions. As an alternative, we offer a series of questions with commentary on how to use your answers as guidance. These questions are not comprehensive; consider them as seeds from which your own questions will grow.

"Does my organization have unique requirements regarding data management?"

Everyone likes to think their organization fills a unique role in the world of environmental practice. Some do, but most don't. More to the point, even those that provide specialty services as their main business generally support their activities using data that mostly fits well into traditional environmental data practices. (We're referring here to the *data model* – locations, samples, and results – rather than the specifics of parameter choices, unusual collection methods, or advanced analysis techniques.) For this reason we would argue that the answer to this question for most organizations is "no."

If you answer this question negatively, then the question does not offer any special insight or guidance – all the options are still open to you. If the answer is "yes," however, the chances that a commercial product will satisfy all your requirements decrease significantly. COTS packages are by nature designed to address the most common needs. If you truly have a special situation, then a commercial solution may not be a good fit. It may still be possible to gain some benefit from a commercial package however. This may be the case if – in addition to your specialty – your business model also includes elements more commonly found in traditional environmental practices, or if your specialty can be addressed through post-processing of more routine activities. At best, though, you will likely need a higher level of customization than most users. So if your answer to this question is "yes," then either modifying an existing (noncommercial) package or developing an entirely new system is probably a better choice.

"What services does my organization offer that are not generally available from other organizations?"

This question is similar to the previous one, but the focus here is a little different. The data your organization collects may be essentially the same as most other environmental practitioners, but may include unusual metadata requirements. Perhaps you collect data under specific conditions that introduce the need for adherence to special procedures and/or documentation of conditions. Maybe you've created a new collection method that requires extensive and frequent calibration. For whatever reason, if you can identify significant factors that are atypical, the discussion of the previous question applies in this case as well: the likelihood of finding a predefined solution decreases.

"What are other organizations similar to mine using?"

We've touched on this earlier in this chapter, but it bears repeating. If you don't know what other organizations with a similar focus are using, find out. Talk to colleagues and competitors. Go to conferences and professional meetings. Do your research. Don't stop at simply finding out what others use: ask them detailed questions about what they like and what they don't like about their choice. Keep in mind that use by other organizations does not necessarily imply that a particular product is best for you. Find out why others chose a particular solution. Other organizations are likely to use different evaluation criteria than you, so their decision may not be entirely compatible with your goals. Ask questions about how they settled on the solution they deployed. Ask if they tried other options first. Ask if they performed an analysis as extensive as the one you are conducting. If so, are they willing to share their results? If you get significant positive feedback from another organization whose requirements and business model are sufficiently similar to yours, the probability that the same solution will work for you increases.

"What is my budget?"

Money plays a role in the decision process, so you should conduct at least a rudimentary cost–benefit analysis. In this case, determinations of benefits should be based only on comparisons with other options under consideration. Consider applying scale factors to both the costs and benefits in order to avoid premature elimination of a high-cost option that might otherwise offer superior technical capabilities. Base your comparisons on a reasonable time frame. Costs tend to be incurred more heavily during earlier time periods (but don't forget about ongoing support and maintenance costs), whereas benefits tend to increase over time. Create a common basis for comparison of costs and benefits. This can involve placing a monetary value on efficiencies associated with products, or it can utilize translating both factors to a normalized scale. Above all, try to be as objective as possible when rating the alternatives. While deploying a COTS product will frequently be the cheapest option, it may not be the best choice.

"What capabilities for software development do we have in-house or available through contracting?"

This question can significantly affect your choice, especially when seriously considering either adapting an existing system or creating something new. Note, however, that the answer to this question involves much more than simply discovering if your organization employs or otherwise has access to individuals who routinely develop software. If the answer is "no," then you should probably focus your attention on commercially available options. If the answer is "yes," however, it does not necessarily automatically level the playing field. Find out more about the knowledge and experience of these human resources. Talk to other departments in the organization to get feedback on any development performed in support of their activities. A great many very talented software developers don't routinely write code that interacts with a database. Your environmental data management system will be database-based, so you must gain confidence that the resources at your disposal have sufficient experience to meet that challenge. If you've already definitively selected a database platform, their experience should be specific to the chosen DMBS. On the other hand, if significant expertise using a particular platform exists within your organization, you might alter your evaluation criteria of DBMS software based on that knowledge. General programming capabilities and database knowledge are extremely important, but don't discount the significance of an understanding of the science associated with your endeavors. Engaging developers who also have experience or training in more traditional scientific fields will greatly decrease the amount of time you will spend explaining procedures, and will greatly increase your confidence that the end product is sound. Determine other commitments and responsibilities of the individual(s) who will be developing your system. Understand who sets software development staff priorities and agree to your system's place in that hierarchy. Discuss software development philosophy with potential members of the coding team, especially as related to input from the user community. Avoid coders who prefer to isolate themselves from the end users.

All these issues must be addressed if the developers are in-house, but they become even more significant if development is assigned to another organization. Additional concerns also arise in this scenario because your ability to control events is one more step removed. If possible, focus on contractors with which your organization already has a relationship. Be extremely cautious about assigning development to an outside entity with which you have little or no experience. In all cases, obtain references from other clients of the contractor – preferably for software with somewhat similar requirements to yours.

NOT Best Practice #1

If you were hoping for a best practice for the end of this chapter, you're going to be disappointed. The focus of this chapter is on the decision regarding whether it's best to deploy a commercial software solution, adapt an existing database and interface package, or create an entirely new program from scratch. That is a decision that is based entirely on the specific situation that exists in your organization and is therefore always a one-off. What's best and appropriate for my organization may not be best or appropriate for your organization. Determining the best course of action requires thorough consideration of your situation. There simply is no one best solution.

6 Designing and Building a Database

6.1 PRELIMINARY STEPS

The first requirement for creating an efficient and effective database is a thorough analysis of your business model. (If this comes as a surprise, you have not read any of the other chapters … we've mentioned this in almost every one of them.) Thus far we have described this endeavor only in general terms. Since the focus of this chapter is implementation, we should now provide a bit more detail. It's important to note, however, that business model analysis is not an exact process due to the many variations in business practices. Also, because business models vary so much, a detailed exploration of the process is beyond the scope of this book. The guidelines identified below are therefore purposely somewhat vague.

Begin the process by recognizing that the analysis will be limited to only those aspects of your business practices that are related to analytical data – elements such as the standard terms of your invoicing system or other monetary facets can be ignored. You should, however, include all aspects that affect your analytical data even peripherally. As an example, if you associate analytical data with specific projects (as most organizations do), then some aspects of your project management paradigm should be incorporated into the analysis.

For an overwhelming majority of environmentally oriented organizations, a common set of concepts related to analytical data lies at the heart of their business model. These concepts define a standard basic hierarchy of data organization:

- sampling events occur at sampling locations;
- a single location may have multiple associated sampling events; and
- each sampling event is likely to have results for multiple parameters.

A good place to start analyzing your business model is therefore with this essential framework. From there, elaborate on variations within each of these primary categories. Do your organization's sampling activities involve multiple different classes of locations? If so, are the sampling protocols and procedures different for each? Perhaps sampling locations can be categorized into types with similar requirements. Are there different classifications of samples for which the results are reported for different sets of parameters (e.g., chemical vs. biological vs. radiological)? A good

DOI: 10.1201/9781003131953-7

technique for answering these questions is to start with one instance of an item (e.g., a single sampling location) and identify all the activities that are performed there. Carefully consider each activity, documenting how other actions and items become involved. Now repeat the exercise for a different variation of the same starting item. At each step, ask yourself what differences in approach must be accommodated in order to capture all the variations. Repeat until you're comfortable that you've accounted for all variations. Now go back and see if there are logical groupings that point out the need for different data elements.

As you document the characteristics of these essential activities, additional connections to other business practices will emerge. Do you use multiple labs for sample analysis? How do you track which samples are sent to which lab? What review procedures are involved in assessing the quality of the analytical results? Do you have one or more standard report formats?

Continue to follow these paths of connected business elements until each reaches a point at which there are no more items to describe. At that point you will have a document that represents a complete model of your business practices as they relate to your environmental data collection, management, and analysis. If you're like most people, the information you have entered will be almost in stream of consciousness form. As a final step, review the document and organize it in such a way that there are distinguishable sections that focus on identifiable segments of your operations. Deciding which descriptions apply to which segments won't be easy because of the connections between entities – this is, after all, the motivation for using a database for managing the data – but do your best.

6.2 DESIGNING THE DATA MODEL

With the business model completed, you're now ready to translate what you've documented into a data model. The process here is comparable to the one you just completed with the business model, except that it should be easier because you can leverage the information obtained in the business model exercise. Also, instead of narrative, the objective of this step is identification of the tables that will make up the data model. The end result will therefore be more akin to a list. As before, start with the standard concepts: locations, samples, and results. Pick a name for each table that will manage a separate element. Next, for each table, document the characteristics needed to completely describe the element from a data perspective. Some descriptors are so inherent to the element that you may not have documented them in the business model analysis – the test method, parameter, value, and units for the results, for instance. Other descriptors that may be more specific to your particular organization will be apparent from the business model analysis. The descriptors are the metadata for each entity within an element class and will be captured by columns in their respective tables. Define names for each column. (A common practice is to use plural names for tables and singular names for columns. This provides an intuitive level of distinction to the referenced items: tables are collections of multiple instances of the pertinent object – rows – and each column entry contains a single instance of that descriptor for a particular row.)

At this point, it's not necessary to specify details of the data types for the columns; in fact, it may be undesirable. You may be inclined toward assigning a particular category of data type to a given column (e.g., column X should be a text entry). This is acceptable, but don't be surprised if you later decide on a different category. Even if the category remains the same, it's best to avoid further refinement of column specifications until after sufficient examples of column data are examined and relationships between tables are identified.

After you've completed the initial structure of the three base tables, examine the columns created for them and consider if some should be tied to valid value lists. Depending on the number and fluidity of the candidate values, it may be appropriate to define lookup tables for managing them. Create tables for any characteristics that you determine are best managed this way, and define appropriate columns in each. Later you will create relationships between these lookup tables and the tables they support, so consider using coded indicators for the records in the lookup tables. In accordance with Best Practice #8 (Chapter 4), use the same names for the columns in both tables. Table 6.1 lists some columns commonly found in implementations of the three basic tables that are frequently associated with valid value lists. The examples are not intended to be comprehensive. Rather, they are offered as suggestions that may help you evaluate your specific table definitions.

At this point you have described the three basic tables that are typically included in any environmental data management system, and you have described tables that support lookup values in some of their columns. Now review your business model analysis and identify other categories of data elements related to the tables already created. It's possible that you may need to define lookup tables related to tables that are themselves lookup tables in addition to the main tables.

Continue checking your business model for references to additional elements not yet incorporated. Repeat the same process for these as described above for the basic elements. You may encounter some situations where a single lookup table (parent) supports multiple data tables (children). For instance, a table of state names and

TABLE 6.1

Common Columns in the Three Basic Tables That Are Likely Candidates for Valid Value Lists

Table	Possible columns for which valid value lists may be appropriate
Locations	Location type
	State
	Hydrologic unit
	Coordinate datum reference
Samples	Medium
	Sample Type
Results	Lab
	Parameter
	Parameter fraction
	Test method
	Units

abbreviations could be used for both sampling locations and labs. Repeat this process until you have accounted for all the entities referenced in your business model. The list of tables and columns in the data model is now completed.

The next step is to define the relationships between tables. If we had already created the tables in the database, we might consider using the database interface component for creating entity relationship diagrams (ERDs), provided that there is one (see Appendix A for examples of ERDs). However, we're still in planning mode, so we've not actually created any entities in the database, and that option is not available. We can, however, perform the same process off-line using either a graphics package or even just pencil and paper. Start by drawing a box for each table and list the columns for each within the box. Now would be a good time to define the primary key for each table. Mark elements of the primary key in some manner (maybe put an asterisk beside them). Now draw connecting lines between each related table. If possible, have the endpoints of each line connect to the box at a point beside the name of a column that is included in the definition of the relationship. Designate the parent in each relationship by putting the digit 1 above the connecting line at the end next to that box. If the relationship is one-to-one, also put a 1 at the other box as well. If the relationship is one-to-many, use a different symbol at the other end (common choices are either the letter M or the infinity symbol [∞]). Finally, below the connecting line at each end, jot down the names of all the columns that are required to define the relationship. The information you've recorded in this exercise will be essential later when you define the actual relationship in the database.

Now you're ready to assign the data types and sizes to the fields. There are two primary considerations for the choice of each column's data type and size. First, for non-coded columns (i.e., columns that contain explanations of coded values ... columns such as parameter name or value qualifier meaning), gather as many examples as possible of the data that needs to be captured. Use the characteristics of the examples to select a data type and size. If the examples are all numbers – and you are confident that the values will always be numbers – use of a numeric data type is appropriate. If you anticipate that a column may at times need to store text (even if it normally is a number), then a character data type is required. Other characteristics of your best choice are likely to emerge as well. For numbers, if the values are always integers, use an integer sized to accommodate the highest anticipated value. If the values are not integers, scale the column to accommodate storage for both the value range and the appropriate number of decimal places. For character-based columns, try to anticipate the longest text entity that may be required by examining examples. The objective is to make text columns as large as needed but no larger. Going overboard on text column sizes wastes database resources.

For coded fields, you typically have more leeway regarding both data type and size. This is because the coded values are (in most cases) referenced only within the database. A code you use to designate a particular parameter, for instance, has meaning within every table that includes a parameter identifier but has no meaning outside the bounds of your database.[1] How you use this freedom often comes down to personal preference. Numeric codes are simple to implement using integers that

---

[1] While generally true, this situation is not cast in stone. If you exchange data with other data management systems, having common identifiers for corresponding data elements can offer significant advantages during data exchanges.

get incremented with each new record. (While there is nothing that prohibits the use of non-integer numeric fields as coded values, you should avoid them because of the possibility of inexact matches due to round-off error.) The size requirement of a coded integer column can be determined by estimating the maximum number of records in the table. For instance, you may consider it unlikely that you will use more than 255 different laboratories for analysis, so perhaps a TINYINT is an appropriate choice for the numeric code assigned to each lab.[2]

An integer may not always be the best option for a coded field. Sometimes there is a choice that affords an opportunity to create additional meaning to the code. A classic example is test methods. Test methods are documented by various scientific and professional organizations, and every group of test methods uses some sort of abbreviation as a designator. For instance, the American Public Health Association (APHA) – in combination with other organizations – publishes an often-referenced work called "Standard Methods for the Examination of Water and Wastewater," commonly referred to as "Standard Methods." Methods are grouped into parts (e.g., part 3000 is metals) and each method in the part is described in a section that is assigned a number within the category's range. Further method refinements are identified by subsections designated by letters. Test method references cited from this source are often abbreviated using the letters SM (for Standard Methods) followed by the complete section and subsection identifiers. Thus, method SM 3500-Ba-B refers to identification of barium using the atomic absorption spectrometric method. This designation conveys multiple levels of meaning, so it is a good candidate for use as a coded field.

The most critical factor for assigning types and sizes to coded columns is that these columns are typically used for defining relationships between tables. You must ensure that the column type and size is the same in all tables for which these columns will be used for relationships.

6.3 OTHER DATA CONSIDERATIONS

At this point you've created the most critical part of your data model – the part that manages the environmental data properly. However, there are other aspects of the data model to consider that may affect the database design.

The first of these aspects is identifying who will use the system – more specifically, how will you manage who has access to the data and what will you allow them to do? The range of answers to this question is wide, but the implications of your answer can have a dramatic effect on additional design concerns within the database.

The simplest scenario is the one in which you are the only person who interacts with the database in any way. In the environmental field, this is not an unreasonable scenario: there are many examples of smaller organizations in which one person holds all the responsibility for the database. This one person loads all the data, generates all the reports, and executes all the queries required for data retrievals to support other

---

[2] It is only appropriate if you are comfortable with using non-standard SQL data types. Don't forget that not all database platforms support the TINYINT data type. If you think you might someday need to move your data to another platform, you may have to deal with data-type conversion issues.

analyses. In that situation, there is no need to define any additional roles or users. In every DBMS considered in this book, the person who creates the database is by default the database owner and therefore has full privileges on all database objects.

Although this scenario is reasonable, it's not the most common. More often, the person who creates the database must accommodate other users who require access to the data. In these instances, the database administrator should create roles and users to address the specific needs of the organization. The options for how best to do this are not always obvious and are affected by more than just a simple enumeration of who needs what type of access to which data. Other factors include the inter-related considerations of how the database will be deployed, what type(s) of interface(s) will be created, and even which DBMS platform is used.

A very traditional paradigm involves creating roles that identify commonly implemented database access categories: a read-only role that can retrieve data but cannot enter new data or edit existing records, a read-write-insert role that can retrieve data as well as insert new records or edit existing data, and so forth. If the database stores data that are administered or analyzed in such a way that there are significantly different schemas for different data, it may be judicious to create roles that also limit the specific tables that can be accessed. In this paradigm, the roles are then assigned to user accounts as appropriate. This creates a clearly delineated set of capabilities for any given user account. This approach is supported by the capabilities of most of the relational database platforms identified in this book. (The exception is Microsoft Access, which dropped all functionality related to roles and users beginning with Access 2007).[3] This approach is most appropriate when the number of users is relatively small and static. If all users are sufficiently proficient with database technology, it can even be implemented in those rare situations where no customized user interface is deemed necessary.

If the user community is large or tends to change frequently, the method above for managing user accounts becomes unwieldy due to the time required to manage accounts. In this situation, an alternative is to define a set of fixed database user accounts and add tables to the database that support a reduced set of the functions traditionally implemented through database user objects. The existence of a wider range of user experiences in this case almost certainly requires the creation of a user interface. This approach therefore offers the opportunity to manage user accounts through a custom interface, eliminating the need to constantly manipulate accounts using raw database tools. It also affords the opportunity to increase the metadata associated with users as necessary (e.g., adding a telephone number or e-mail address) and shifts the responsibility of maintaining the additional metadata to the users themselves. Under this scenario, more complex roles can also be created that provide more nuance to the associated capabilities (e.g., defining privileges on the basis of record contents rather than just a table basis). Implementation of these custom roles requires either the use of stored procedures in the database or coding within the user interface, but the advantages can be significant. If you choose to implement this approach, the specific

---

[3] https://support.microsoft.com/en-us/office/what-happened-to-user-level-security-69b362cd-503f-4e8a-a735-fb923ffb9fa3.

tables and columns you will need to add to the database schema are determined through careful consideration of the control and access mechanisms desired.

Other factors that should be considered affect decisions made in Section 6.2 regarding data types and sizes. If there are external systems with which you want or need to exchange data, a careful examination of the data models for those systems should be performed in order to ensure compatibility of data exchanges. Results of these analyses may lead to expansion of column sizes or the creation of additional columns for characteristics required by the target systems. It may also be worthwhile to examine other systems with which there is no need to exchange data, but that offer procedures or code examples that are useful. The familiar phrase about not reinventing the wheel is applicable here. Examining these resources provides an opportunity to validate your own schema or gain insight into viewing data elements in a different way.

6.4   CREATING THE DATABASE

At last, you're finally ready to create the database. If you have not yet done so, you must now choose a platform. Several factors can affect your selection. If your complete volume of data is expected to be somewhat small, it probably doesn't make sense to invest in a DBMS such as SQL Server or Oracle due to the comparatively high licensing cost. On the other hand, if your organization already licenses one of these products, they have great capabilities and are therefore excellent choices. If you have past experience with a particular product, your comfort level alone could be the deciding factor. Another consideration is the level of support that may be required from your information technology (IT) department. It is virtually inevitable that you will at some point encounter a problem that necessitates their involvement. Seek input from them as part of the decision process.

Before you can dive in and create your database schema, the DBMS software must be installed. Depending on the chosen platform, the DBMS may need to be installed on a server. This may require permission and/or assistance from the IT department. Some organizations even place restrictions on individual users' ability to install software on their assigned computers, which means involving the IT department in those installations as well. If someone else installs the software, you should be present and take notes on what transpires. In most cases, the system administrator account and password are established during installation. You may need that information in order to proceed. Once the DBMS is installed and working, you are finally ready to create your database schema.

On most platforms, there are at least two distinct variations available for creating your schema – either through entry of standard SQL commands or use of an interface tool. Which do you choose? That's a personal choice that depends on your comfort level with command line processes and graphical user interfaces. There is a bit of a learning curve either way, especially if we assume your experience level with the database design process is relatively low. There will be ample resources at your disposal for learning either method. The optimal approach – from an educational perspective – might be to use both methods at times.

The procedure for creating the database in some ways mimics what we discussed when creating the data model. Start by creating the tables. Use the information you recorded during the data model exercise as a guide. It's a good idea to specify the primary key for each table during the initial creation, but it may be best to delay the creation of foreign key relationships until all the tables have been generated. That's a statement of opinion, but it's justifiable. The creation of any relatively complex database schema takes some time. Even with the careful preparation you've done, it can be easy to assign different types or sizes to related columns in different tables. If this happens, attempting to define relationships at the same time that you create the tables can become a frustrating endeavor. Completing the table definitions accomplishes a recognizable milestone and generates a boost of self-confidence. Deferring creation of the table relationships to a second activity may require you to make minor adjustments to some column definitions, but this is easier to address on a case-by-case basis.

As you create the relationships between the tables, you may encounter situations that require alternative methods for integrity enforcement – approaches that are not available within the standard relational framework. Here is an example: laboratories frequently assign value qualifiers to parameter results. These qualifiers provide important metadata about the result. Typical qualifiers indicate things like "equipment failed validation check," "analyte detected in associated blank," "holding time exceeded," and so on. Any given result may have zero to multiple value qualifiers. How do you handle the necessity of capturing multiple qualifiers? One option would be to include multiple qualifier columns in the table that contains the results (e.g., val_qual_1, val_qual_2, etc.), but this violates the first normal form ban on repeating groups (see Section 4.3.1). To reach third normal form for the schema, the solution is to create a separate table for the value qualifiers that are recorded for each result, but this introduces another set of complications. In order to relate the qualifiers to their associated results, the qualifiers table must include all the columns that constitute the primary key in the results table. If your primary key for the results table is a single column – say, a long integer that is generated automatically for each record inserted – that's not a big deal. A valid case can be made, though, that a simple numeric value is not a suitable primary key for the results table. The goal is to ensure no duplicate records, which will almost certainly require the creation of a unique index on whatever combination of columns is determined to define a unique result. If this combination is used to define a unique index, shouldn't it be the primary key? If such an index exists but is not the primary key, then the schema is not in third normal form. A commonly used alternative in situations like this is to create a single column capable of capturing multiple entries (in this case, a single column in the results table that stores all the associated value qualifiers for the result).[4] This can be done in two ways. First, all the

---

[4] You could argue that this violates the definition of first normal form since such a column would not contain an atomic element, and you would have a valid point. However, if we consider the column entry to contain the set of value qualifiers that apply to the result, we can sleep better ... until we recognize that we're distorting some of the principles of set theory on which the relational model is based. If you haven't already, you can hopefully now realize why we stated in Chapter 2 that data management is not a hard science.

value qualifiers can have single-character primary keys. The value qualifiers column in the results table would then be a character type field (probably VARCHAR) sized to accommodate the maximum number of qualifiers we want to allow for any given result. Each individual character in the value qualifiers column of the results table is then considered an identifier of a single qualifier descriptor. Alternatively, the value qualifiers records can have variable length primary keys. The value qualifier column in the results table in this case again contains multiple qualifier codes, but since the codes themselves may be of different lengths, they must be delineated. The size of the value qualifier column in the results table is then determined by the size of the primary key in the value qualifiers table times the maximum number of qualifiers allowed, plus the maximum number of qualifiers minus 1 (to account for the separator … which is presumably a single character). Optimally, the value qualifier primary key should be small (maybe two characters) in order to limit the size requirement of the column in the results table. Either approach makes it impossible to define traditional relationship constraints between the two tables. Such constraints are still desirable, but they must be defined using either stored procedures in the database or code in the user interface.

The discussion about deferring establishment of table relationships until after creation of all the tables – as well as the illustration of relationships that cannot be defined through traditional means – leads to a very important conclusion: you will likely have to modify your database several times as you progress through development. Collection, management, and analysis of environmental data constitute a complex undertaking with many nuances. It would be unreasonable to believe that creation of the perfect system is possible on the first effort. Recognize and understand that change is good because it reflects either an evolution of your understanding of the processes you are modeling or a change in the scope of your database. Both of these signify an increase in the value of the system.

At the same time, realize that some changes – especially those implemented after a significant amount of data has been collected – will require a great deal of work. Minor changes such as altering the size of a character field can typically be executed without substantial effort. Other changes such as modifying a column's data type can require a more intensive endeavor. Keep the potential evolution of your system in mind as you define the schema and create the user interface(s).

6.5   LOADING DATA

The final step in preparing the database portion of your system for deployment is loading data. There are two categories of data that can be loaded into the raw database. The first category of data is the data that populates the lookup tables; you must insert these records into the database before anything else. The reason should be obvious: if table A contains a foreign key into table B, you can't insert a record into table A that references the lookup value record in table B until the record in Table B exists. For example, let's say your sampling locations table is called LOCATIONS. LOCATIONS includes a required column that identifies the state in which it is found, and this column is a foreign key into a table called STATES. Before you can insert a location record for a sample point in a given state, the state must be identified in the STATES table.

Because lookup tables can themselves require values from other lookup tables, the starting point for loading lookup data is to identify tables that contain reference data at only the lowest level. These will be tables that have primary keys but no foreign keys. A good practice is to make a list of all the tables in the schema and all the foreign keys of each. Begin by loading data into those tables for which no foreign keys are identified. As you enter data into each of these tables, remove the references to them as foreign keys in the remainder of the list. Repeat this process as necessary until there are no more foreign keys listed in the reference data tables.

The specific processes available to you for inserting data will be entirely dependent on the capabilities of the DBMS. Every system will allow you to insert data through the use of SQL commands, so this is always an option. (If a table contains only a few records, it's a good idea to use this option. This will increase your familiarity and experience with SQL commands.) Some platforms offer tools for loading data from spreadsheets or other electronic files. If you have data for a given table in an acceptable format, these tools can save time and boredom by avoiding the need to repeatedly type SQL insert statements. Most tools of this nature follow a predictable pattern of steps you will be required to follow (order of some steps may vary):

- Select the table into which data will be imported.
- Select the file that contains the data to be imported. The tool will parse the file in an attempt to create identifiers for the columns. In most cases, the tool will consider entries in the first row of the file to be headers and use those as identifiers.
- Identify how you want to map the columns in the import file to the columns of the database table.
- Execute the import.

If all goes well, the data will be loaded successfully. Errors may halt the operation. Typical errors include text entries that are too long for the assigned column, or the inability to coerce the import data into the expected format (e.g., attempts to store character data in numeric columns, or date entries in unrecognizable formats). Well-designed tools will reject the entire import operation if any errors occur, resulting in none of the import records being saved. Some tools may retain any records that do not contain errors. Sometimes data may be reported as successfully imported, but unanticipated manipulations and interpretations render the data unusable as intended. Review the results of each import operation carefully to verify correct loading.

In addition to preparing your database for deployment, loading reference data is a good way to verify your data model. Failed attempts to insert data often lead to the discovery of errors in the definitions of relationship constraints. Missing constraints will be harder to detect at this stage, but not impossible.

The second category of data that may be desirable to load is data from past work. These would be the product of previously completed activities and would involve (at minimum) sampling locations, sampling events, and results. In general, the same process should be followed as for reference data. Assuming you included all tables in the schema when producing the list of relationships as recommended above, that document contains the information you need to successfully load these data as well. Follow the same procedures and advice as for the reference data.

If you also deem it necessary to create at least one user interface that includes an option for importing data into one or more of the higher level tables (locations, samples, and results), it can be a good idea to withhold some of your past data from loading at this point. As the interface progresses, you will need test data to evaluate how well the interface performs its data capture functions. Data with which you are already familiar can be particularly useful for this purpose.

In Chapter 8 we will create an example database that illustrates the concepts and processes described in this chapter.

6.6 DATABASE CREATION SUMMARY

In stark contrast to Chapter 5, this chapter is essentially one long best practice. We therefore conclude with a summary of the key points related to creating the database. Consider this a sort of checklist for the process.

Best Practice #10   Database Creation Procedures

- Analyze the business model that drives your data. You can't create an effective database unless you understand the processes involved in collecting, managing, and using the data.
- Be expansive in your consideration of what aspects of the business model require attention in the data model. It's better to pursue a path that proves fruitless than to miss something because you didn't think it was important to the data.
- Structure the data model to follow the business model. The data model must adhere to business model in order to avoid loss (through failure to capture) of important details.
- The data model should adequately support all project operations and decisions that are affected by the analytical data.
- Consider any special requirements for final reporting needs. Also consider any special analyses that are performed to help meet project goals. Decide which of these needs are performed often enough to warrant inclusion in the schema and which are better addressed through either a user interface or an external process.
- Select a DBMS platform that is capable of meeting your requirements. Consider using the preferred platform of your organization if there is one.
- Don't attempt to create the database without first generating a plan that defines tables, columns, and relationships.
- To identify the required tables, start at the heart of the system (locations, samples, and results) and work your way out.
- When assigning column data types and sizes, examine as many examples as necessary to ensure that all variations are addressed.

- Strive to be consistent in naming corresponding columns in related tables. The data types and sizes must be the same in order to establish referential integrity constraints, but the names do not. Using consistent names will reduce the opportunity for confusion.
- Enforcement of complex relationships may not be possible using standard relational techniques. Define stored procedures or include code in the user interface(s) to overcome these limitations.
- Load as much data into supporting tables as possible before releasing the database for use. Supporting tables are those that identify valid values for columns in higher order tables (e.g., test methods). Use past data to generate the initial list of records for these tables.
- Be prepared to modify your schema both during development and after deployment.

7 Creating the User Interface(s)

7.1 THE PURPOSE OF THE USER INTERFACE

Creating the database is a significant milestone but likely does not signify completion of the system. As discussed in Chapters 4 and 6, a normalized database can present comprehension challenges to even very astute individuals due to the deconstruction of familiar conceptual elements into interconnected pieces. For this reason, we must now consider what steps should be taken to enable users to interact with the data effectively.

One option would be to require anyone who accesses the database to learn the intricacies of database technology – plus the details of the specific schema – for themselves. This suggestion is just as ridiculous as requiring someone to learn Newtonian physics and mechanical engineering before being allowed to drive an automobile. Furthermore, implementing this approach means the only tools available to users for data interaction are those provided by the DBMS itself. Very few of these tools are intended or designed for this audience.

A more appropriate option, then, is to create a custom application that performs common activities by soliciting input from users and performing actions in a controlled, pre-planned manner. This is the purpose of the user interface: to provide users with the ability to enter, edit, delete, and retrieve data (as appropriate for their role) without requiring them to become database experts.

Actually, we should place one additional qualifier in the statement that describes the purpose of the user interface: it should not only enable the entry, editing, deletion, and retrieval of data, but should do so in an efficient manner. Efficiency in the context of a user interface relies heavily on effective communication with users. As the system architect, consider the user interface as your avatar in a conversation with the user in which the discussion is about how to perform various data activities. By now you should have more technical knowledge about how databases work than most of your users (and you will most certainly have more understanding of your specific schema). Given this, a potential trap into which many developers fall is that they create programs that make too many assumptions about how well the user understands the data structure and how it is affected by the process being performed. The interface should explain each situation well enough to convey the required

DOI: 10.1201/9781003131953-8

knowledge without becoming condescending. Because of their technical orientation, many developers struggle with this approach. There is a very good book by Mike Gunderloy (*Developer to Designer: GUI Design for the Busy Developer*) that offers great insight into effectively communicating with users. See Appendix C for details about this book and consider reading it.

7.2   IDENTIFYING USER INTERFACE REQUIREMENTS

The first step in creating an appropriate user interface is determining user requirements. That process actually begins by answering a very basic question: who will use the database? It is possible that the answer will be "only me." If that's your situation, then the interface can be effective with far fewer functions. You'll probably still want to create forms and processes for managing data in high level logical groupings – for instance, a form that displays all results for a sampling event with all coded values translated into their more understandable meanings – but you can consider omitting forms and processes for some or all of the lower level tables. These tables may be accessed less frequently even in the most active situations, and if you are the only database user it will probably be just as convenient and efficient to simply interact with these tables directly in the database.

Although possible, this situation is relatively rare; therefore, for the remainder of this section we will assume that your database must be accessible by others also. Even if you will be the only user, framing the remaining discussion in the context of a single user can still reveal important considerations.

An appropriate point at which to start the process of identifying user interface requirements is to return to the business model analysis performed when creating the database. That document will already contain information regarding all the activities captured in the data model, so now you simply need to re-examine those activities from a slightly different perspective. This time, instead of focusing on the data requirements, focus on how each activity presents itself in the physical world. For sample collection activities, this means considering the actions performed in the field. For analytical lab data, the real-world presence is typically represented by files provided by the lab. For analysis and reporting activities, examine the formats into which data are assembled. As you evaluate each of these areas, consider the interactions between users and data. Solicit input from people who actually perform the work. If there are standard forms involved in an activity, you should have collected them while completing the business model analysis; revisit those forms to learn how users are accustomed to viewing or recording data.

In previous chapters, we've often referred to "users" within the context of the database user object. When considering user interface options, we must switch to the broader definition of users as the individuals who interact with the data. In this context, "user" has some similarities with the database object in that a user needs to access particular data and functions in the database. Now, however, instead of organizing users in relation to database roles, we need to organize them from a functional business standpoint. Thus, instead of role-based terms such as "read/write," our categories are described by terms such as "field crew." Also, database roles are defined using a limited set of database functions which means there are a limited range of possible combinations. Functional business roles are far less constrained. A good approach for grouping users, then, is to define classes based on activities.

After identifying the appropriate classes of users, the next step is to identify the specific data elements that are associated with the activities of each. The type of data access required for each data element can also be stipulated at this point. The data access decisions are not always straightforward and may require some unexpected levels of consideration. Don't automatically conclude that a particular category of activity requires full control over a data element simply because the element is an important part of the activity. As an example, consider the medium for each sample. Many different activities will require documentation of the sample medium, but it is probably not wise to allow users to enter new media at will. Furthermore, failing to constrain user entries may have strong negative effects on the quality of the data. This observation suggests a situation that requires constant assessment as you plan the interface. There are two competing interests within any program that manages data: data access and data integrity. Users typically need the ability to enter data, and the interface should strive to provide them with sufficient latitude to address any situation they may encounter. In order to do this, the interface needs to be very flexible – it should be capable of accepting whatever data is entered. However, as we've discussed multiple times in this book, the strength of the relational model is derived from the connections between different data elements. These relationships cannot exist without some degree of restraint regarding allowable entries.

The conundrum is presented graphically in Figure 7.1. The two arrows represent data quality and data flexibility. Quality is determined by the ability of the system to enforce referential integrity and reduce data errors. Flexibility is a characteristic of the system that describes its ability to accept data in a variety of forms and formats. The vertical bar represents the overall capabilities of the user interface with regard to users' ability to enter, edit, and delete data. The bar behaves like a slider control – you can shift it in either direction to select a position within the range of each attribute, but it remains vertical at all times. Thus, increasing the flexibility of the system gives

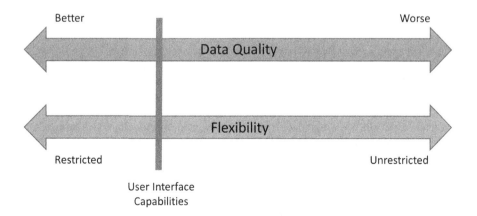

FIGURE 7.1   The user interface must strike a balance between data quality and flexibility.

users greater freedom to manipulate data but it comes at the expense of potentially affecting data quality. Improving the data quality requires reducing the flexibility by restricting access or user options. The outer ends of the diagram represent two opposite but equally unappealing extremes. You can allow users maximum flexibility by eliminating restrictions on data entry and not applying validation rules, but this will quickly render your data useless due to lack of relational integrity. On the other end of the spectrum, you can ensure maximum data quality by not allowing anyone access, but this eliminates users' ability to perform their jobs. When designing your user interface, you must identify your comfort level with regard to these competing interests and set the bar in the appropriate area.

After defining classes of users, identifying the data needs of each, and resolving the data integrity/data access conundrum, the final step in completing the requirements analysis is a consideration of the operating environment for each class. By this we mean: in what environment and under what conditions will each class of users interact with the data? The answers to this question will help decide the platform on which the user interface will be constructed. There are a limited number of options, but they can have a profound effect on the utility of the interface. You may, in fact, determine at this point that different interfaces are required for different classes of users. For example, if you focus the interface on users performing data extraction and analysis in an office setting while working from personal computers issued by your organization, it makes sense to create the interface with tools designed to interact with whatever computer operating system your organization utilizes (e.g., Windows, Unix, etc.). Consider, though, what happens if one of these users attempts to execute the user interface from a remote location where a different operating system is used (for instance, what if they need to work from home using their personal computer?). Also, chances are that personnel who collect data in the field will find this solution unacceptable even if it's possible due to the physical demands of lugging a laptop around. They are likely to find an interface that runs on a lightweight tablet computer or smart phone more amenable. Since the purpose of the interface is to allow users to effectively interact with the database, it must be conducive to implementation within their typical work environment. This may often require multiple interface variations that connect to the same database.

7.3   INTERFACE DEVELOPMENT TOOLS

After the requirements are defined, the next consideration is a determination of the tool(s) that will be used to construct the interface(s). The tools available for building a user interface can be broadly categorized into three classes: tools that are part of the database platform, third-party tools that are designed specifically for creating database interfaces, and generic programming tools.

7.3.1   INTEGRATED TOOLS

Development tools in this class are provided by the same organization that creates the database platform. In some cases these tools may truly be an integrated part of the database platform; in other cases they may be add-ons that must be acquired separately but are tightly integrated with other database system tools from the same vendor. This class probably has the fewest members of the three and is generally limited to commercially developed platforms. (An interface development tool for an open-source DBMS is by definition a third-party tool.)

The classic example of a DBMS that includes tools for developing an interface is Microsoft Access. As we learned in Chapter 4, describing Access as a database platform is a bit of a misnomer – Access is instead an application that interacts with the Microsoft Jet database engine. However, Access is so ubiquitous that attempting to distinguish between Jet and Access is virtually impossible. Most users simply consider Access to be the platform. We will bow to that perception and treat Access as a DBMS. All versions of Access released since 1995 have included some form of robust programming language capable of creating a complete user interface. Beginning with Access 95 and up to the point of this writing that language was/is Visual Basic for Applications (VBA), but that may be subject to change in the future. Access is also unusual among DBMSs in that it isolates each schema into a separate file and makes that fact obvious to the developer (by forcing the developer to specify a file name). Thus, every Access database has the ability to contain objects created by VBA that can together constitute a user interface for the tabular data contained in the file. Within Access you can open a VBA window that allows you to build interface components. The primary interface component is a form, and forms typically have controls that are linked to columns in tables. The forms and controls can include code snippets that perform data validation, formatting, and other functions (this serves as the Access equivalent of stored procedures). Forms can be programmed to invoke other forms, so building a complete user interface is possible using nothing more than Access itself. Note, though, that the interface is embedded within the file so it cannot be used to interact with another Access database even if the structures are identical. Transferring the interface from one Access database to another is possible but requires much copying and pasting. An alternative (if you need another copy of the same database that will be used for different data) is to simply copy the entire Access database file and then remove data as appropriate, but again this requires a lot of selecting and deleting. Finally, a cautionary tale is in order if you choose to create a user interface within Access: while the database is managed by Jet, VBA is a component of the Access product. If you update Access to a newer version, changes in VBA may make it impossible to modify the existing interface. In some cases, the existing interface may also be rendered unusable.[1]

A less extreme example of an integrated interface development tool can be found with Oracle. Oracle has for many years offered various software packages that must be acquired separately but that are designed to interact with an Oracle database. These

---

[1] This has happened to me. More than once I've been asked to modify the interface for an Access database that I did not create. In all cases the interface was created with VBA, incorporated into the database, and had stopped working after the client had moved to a newer version of Access. The problem was typically either that (A) a function was no longer supported, or (B) one of the controls on a form had been replaced with a newer version in VBA, the new control had different properties and events, and it was not backward compatible.

are similar in form and capabilities to the third-party tools described below, except that they are created by the same company that creates the database software. This can mean that any changes to the database software may be supported more quickly in these tools than in third-party variations.

7.3.2 THIRD-PARTY OPTIONS

The largest number of user interface creation options are found in the category of third-party frameworks. These are application development packages created by vendors other than the organization that created the DBMS that are designed to facilitate the creation of forms and other user interface components. Many such packages will be database-specific. This can be an issue if you later decide to change DBMS platforms because it could render your interface inoperable. That said, some of these packages offer versions whose only difference is in the database to which they are designed to connect. If you choose one of the tools with multiple database versions, the chances that your existing interface development will be lost is greatly decreased.

There are two variants within this class. The first variant creates an interface that utilizes proprietary components to connect users and data. Creating an interface using one of these tools typically involves generating forms and reports using a graphical layout tool and then specifying table and column information that identifies the data associated with individual elements of the form or report. There will also usually be an option for writing additional code in some sort of programming language to expand the inherent capabilities of the controls. Distribution of the resulting interface often requires distribution of additional modules or other program components provided as part of the development framework. Be aware that some of these packages may require paying a licensing fee for each installed instance of any interface you develop using the package. Determining the true cost of using such a system therefore requires careful analysis of the number of users you need to support because every copy of the interface you install must be licensed. If the cost per seat is low and/or the number of users is small, it may still be cost-effective. However, in these cases you will want to monitor installations carefully in order to avoid unnecessary expenses. Another potential drawback exists if the framework's extensibility relies on the use of a proprietary macro language. This can lead to future difficulties related to support or additional development. If you create the interface yourself using one of these packages, you may have to relearn the system when changes are needed. Finding someone else who knows the system can also be difficult, depending on the longevity and popularity of the tool.

The other variant in this class may work similarly during the design and programming phase, but create an interim product that is based on a standard programming language. Depending on the language, the interim product is either then compiled to produce an executable program or consists of a language designed to interact with a commonly supported interpreted environment (e.g., HTML). (Software packages like this were originally called "program generators.") In either case, the interim product is the most valuable asset generated by the system. Because it is in a non-proprietary language, opportunities to expand or enhance the code are more attainable. Packages that fit this description are therefore often used to create "first generation" interfaces that are then appended with additional functions not already available within the development framework.

7.3.3 Traditional Programming Languages

The final class involves the use of traditional programming languages and development tools to create the interface. This option can require more effort but provides the ultimate level of control – you have total control over the appearance and functionality of the interface. (There are, however, limits to this control. For instance, you are confined by the capabilities of the operating system on which the interface will be deployed – Windows, Unix, Android, etc.) You have numerous options for the choice of language as well. The only requirement is that the language and development framework include low-level components designed to connect to whichever database engine you have chosen. Most modern languages have such components for all the most popular DBMSs. This flexibility gives you an opportunity to leverage programming capabilities that are already available in your organization – other software developers or even yourself.

Creating an interface from scratch this way might seem intimidating, but it's not significantly different from creating any other program. The only real difference is that you need a thorough understanding of database principles, the specific schema to which the interface will connect, and the object models of the components and controls that connect to the data. If you choose to develop the interface yourself, you understand the database principles because you've read this book, and you understand the schema because you created it. The object models of the data connection components may be new to you, but there is a tremendous amount of information available on the Internet for all of them. You can also find innumerable examples of how to do just about anything you can imagine with the data connection components.[2] If you opt to have someone else create the interface, choose your resources wisely. For best results, find someone who has used the selected language to create database applications in the past – preferably ones that connect to your DBMS of choice. They will have the requisite knowledge about database principles and the database connection components; all you have to do is bring them up to speed on your schema.

In addition to maximizing your ability to control the product, there can be other significant advantages of this option. First, should the need arise to change database platforms, such transitions may have less effect on the user interface code base than you think. That seems counterintuitive since the most essential elements of the user interface are the data connection components. Experience demonstrates, however, that while the components themselves are platform-specific (in most cases),

---

[2] One problem may be filtering out information about prior versions. The Internet is filled with pages that describe – in great detail and with ample code examples – how to accomplish something using a particular component. But when you try applying the technique, it doesn't work because the example was created with version 2.0 and you're using version 5.1. Sadly, the lack of version identification is very common in many technical web resources. Paying close attention to the dates of web pages helps.

the events, properties, and methods are not so different. Many, in fact, use the same names for the most often used methods. Given this situation, a change to a different platform can often be accomplished with some minor adjustments to the code. The modifications will be unnoticeable from the users' perspective. Second, this approach offers the opportunity to isolate the interface from the database. Ideally you want the relationship and data integrity constraints to exist in the database as much as possible. If the schema defines all data integrity rules, you can modify either the database or the interface without concerns over affecting the other item. This applies not only to changes you might make, but also to version changes to the database. For instance, updating from Version 10 to Version 11 of your DBMS platform can be done with the reasonable expectation that your interface will not be affected. Third, the use of a standard programming language to create an interface that is a completely separate entity increases the sustainability of the system. Finding computer programming resources for future maintenance and modifications is much simpler if the interface is coded in a well-known language.[3] For all the reasons discussed in this section, development of a user interface using a standard programming language is often the best choice.

Evolution of Database Interface Development

As an aside, I will offer a personal opinion and a bit of a history lesson. It should come as no surprise that I am a proponent of the approach described above – separating the database and the interface and using a standard programming language for development of the interface. The advantages listed in the last paragraph have been identified through long years of experience. I will admit, however, that adhering to that paradigm has gotten more difficult over the years, and the reason is that the way we work with computers has changed significantly. Believe it or not, at one time most interactions between humans and computers were done with text only – you typed some text and the computer responded with text. In that scenario, a database interface was very procedural: the user would select an option from a single menu (by typing a letter or number), which would lead to either another menu of choices, a display of data retrieved from the database, or a data input form. If it was a form, you filled out the first field, then the second field, and so on. Programming an interface like that was as simple as the interface itself because there was no way for users to perform actions out of order. That all changed with the advent of the graphical user interface (GUI). In a GUI, users expect the freedom to click around on the screen and potentially enter information in the order they

---

[3] It's not always easy to predict whether a given language will survive the test of time. Not that long ago, everyone was coding in Pascal. There doesn't seem to be a glut of programs being developed in Pascal anymore. A few years ago, ColdFusion (developed by Macromedia, which was purchased in 2005 by Adobe) gained tremendous popularity for developing web-based database interfaces. It's still around, but appears to be losing steam. (That's a shame because it's actually an excellent platform for that purpose. The ColdFusion Macro Language (CFML) is very similar to HTML in structure but was obviously created with databases in mind. That made it very easy and fast to learn.)

prefer. This can present challenges if you make traditional assumptions about the presence of data in specific fields. Furthermore, GUIs are event-driven, which requires coding responses to a wide variety of actions that may occur. It's more complicated, but the richness of the user experience makes it completely worthwhile.

7.4 USER INTERFACE FUNCTIONS

So far you've identified the user community for your database, determined the types of activities required of your interface(s), and selected the approach you will use for creating the interface(s). Now it's time to sort out the functions that will be included. We will classify functionality into six basic categories for the purposes of this discussion. This assortment may not include every possible function in every case, but it will cover all the common needs and perhaps provide ideas for addressing anything you require that is not covered.

7.4.1 USER ACCESS AND PRIVILEGES

In Chapters 4 and 6 we explored different approaches to the process of managing user accounts. Presumably by now you will have already decided the specifics of which method to use and incorporated the appropriate mechanisms into your database. In this section we examine implementations in the user interface for handling the mechanics of enabling access to the database and assigning privileges. Fortunately, even though some of the details vary, the basic methods are not significantly different regardless of which approach you use for managing user accounts.

First and foremost, the entry point for every user interface should be a login form. If you manage specific user accounts in the database, the format and behavior of the login form is the same regardless of whether your user management model is based on database user objects (see Chapter 4) or a table of users (see Chapter 6). The form must accept entries of both the user's name and their password. It is considered good form to echo the input of the user name to the screen, but to avoid doing so for the password. It is customary (and perhaps preferable) to use a marker character instead of the actual password character entries – the asterisk is the most common choice – but it is also acceptable to leave the password box completely blank as the user types. The login form code verifies that the user name is recognized and that the password matches the information in the database. If the login information is deemed invalid, the login form should remain open. If the login information is valid, the user's privileges are retrieved from the appropriate source and applied to the current session.

An alternative to this traditional approach is acceptable in some cases, particularly when the number of users remains small and there are a limited number of privilege classes. That alternative involves defining privileges based solely on the entered password. In this scenario, no individual user accounts exist – there are no database user objects and no table of registered users. Instead, a table in the database associates a password with each privilege class. That is, there is a password that grants full access, a password that grants read-only access, and so on as needed. In this scenario, the login screen presents only an option for entering a password. If the password matches any of the privilege class records, that access level applies to the current user's session. If the password does not match any privilege class record, the login screen remains open. In another variation of this approach, the privilege class definitions include only privileges beyond read-only. If the password entry on the login form does not match any existing privilege class record, the user is logged in with read-only privileges.

7.4.2 ENTERING, UPDATING, AND DELETING DATA

The next essential category of functionality that must be included in some form for every effective user interface is that of basic entry, editing, and deleting of data. Note that this does not necessarily mean that you must provide all these functions for every table in the schema. If the interface is for a database that you manage, it may be overkill to create forms for managing data in every table. If you are developing a user interface for someone else, though, it is considered poor form if there are data that cannot be managed through the interface.

In general, you must at least include forms that manage data at the highest level, and those forms should present data in ways that are familiar or intuitive. As discussed many times in this book, most environmental schemas include the classic monitoring pyramid consisting of locations, samples, and results. When we say "the highest level" and "in an intuitive way," then, we mean that you should include, for instance, a form that shows all metadata for all the results of a sampling event in one place. Forms that include a grid are best for this purpose. Needless to say, these forms should translate coded values into their meanings ... show the parameter name instead of the parameter ID, for example.

The need for forms for data at lower levels is determined by the functional requirements as determined by the process in Section 7.2. It may be unwise to allow users to enter new sample source definitions, for instance, because there may be business rules concerning defining sample sources that must be taken into account. If so, this is a function best reserved for a system administrator rather than a read-write user. On the other end of the spectrum, it is probably desirable to allow users to enter and edit information about parameters. Consider how frustrated a user will become if, while entering results for a sample, they encounter a parameter that is not yet in the database and must halt their data entry activity until someone with higher privileges creates the required parameter record.

It's considered best practice to allow entry, update, and deletion of data on the same form in most cases. Users will find it annoying if you require them to change forms when performing each of these activities. Note also that forms for data entry, editing, and deletion require error handlers in order to avoid problems when an attempted action violates a database integrity rule. If these errors are not trapped, the interface may stop executing. This is a very frustrating experience for users.

Another common problem occurs frequently when programmers with limited experience create a user interface for a database: creating multiple forms that have very similar appearance. This issue tends to arise most frequently for lower level tables. The forms that interact with lookup tables are frequently the ones with the least diverse options, so often the only differences are text prompts and labels. It's an easy trap into which many developers fall. The inherent problem is that an interface with many forms that appear very similar can be disorienting. It can be difficult to pick up subtle visual cues that signify the specific data currently being managed. Avoid this situation by striving to make every form visually distinct.

7.4.3 IMPORTING AND EXPORTING DATA

Most interfaces for environmental databases will require the ability to import data from one or more sources. Manual data entry in volumes typically encountered in environmental endeavors is not practical as a sole option. When addressing import needs, consider not only the different categories of data that may be imported but also variations that exist within each category. Most environmental data management systems must be capable of importing electronic data deliverables (EDDs) because laboratories frequently provide results using these files. If your organization has sufficient clout to define a specific EDD format and can require that each lab with which you work provide EDDs in your format, the process of importing results is simplified. In that case, you can create a single form and expect successful processing of all incoming data. If your organization is not able to enforce a single EDD format, however, you may need a way to deal with a variety of data layouts. The traditional way to handle this is to create forms for each format. This can grow into a maintenance nightmare because labs may change their EDD format without warning. A popular alternative is to create a single form that is adaptable. This can be accomplished by allowing users to define mappings of incoming data columns to their corresponding table columns in the database. In this way a single form can be made sufficiently flexible to accept data in many different layouts.

Forms for importing data must be capable of either screening data or trapping errors that occur when data rules are violated. Screening is the preferred approach because it affords an opportunity to provide better feedback to users. Screening means evaluating the data before an attempt is made to commit it to the database. If the data fails to meet one of the integrity conditions, the violation is conveyed to the user and no attempt is made to import the data. This, of course, mandates that the interface must include codes that perform the same validation as those in the database constraints. This seems redundant – and it is – but identifying the problem within the interface allows you to more easily identify the exact cause of the error and craft a more instructive message for the user. If you rely on an error handler, you may discover that the information returned by the DBMS does not adequately describe the cause.

The need to export data is somewhat less common but still valuable. This is especially true if you are required (or even just want) to share your data with another system. The external repository may use different identifiers for equivalent items, so the interface should automate the translations as much as possible. This can be accomplished through the use of additional columns or tables in your database. If there is only one external target, the most efficient approach is to include the name from the external system as an additional column. As an example, consider the case of exporting data to a system called the Water Quality Exchange (WQX). WQX recognizes parameters by very specific names which may differ from your preferred nomenclature. Adding a column called WQX_NAME to the parameters table and using that when exporting data to WQX works well. If you have multiple external targets, it may be more efficient to establish a separate table for documenting required naming conventions.

7.4.4   Data Review and Validation

Another common necessity for many environmental data management systems is a process for documenting quality assurance (QA) reviews of data. There are various ways to accomplish this. One obvious solution is to include this capability on the same form used to display the data for other purposes. In this scenario, the interface would, for instance, have a single form that shows all the metadata for all results associated with a sampling event. A good rule of thumb in user interface design, though, is to strive for simplification of forms as much as is practical. Creating a single form that serves all possible activities related to the displayed data may be more efficient from a development standpoint, but it introduces many opportunities for confusion and/ or unintentional mischief on the users' part. A better solution is to provide separate forms for distinctly different activities; QA review definitely meets that qualification. Furthermore, the forms should be similar but not identical. Similarity provides a sense of familiarity for users, but having multiple forms for different purposes that are visually too similar can lead to confusion.

Another aspect to consider is automation of some data validation checks. The types of checks we refer to here are not those that are part of the database schema constraints. This discussion instead refers to identifying and documenting characteristics of data that are noteworthy. The best example is related to value qualifiers. We've discussed this topic in previous chapters, but as a refresher: value qualifiers are markers that designate parameter results as having unexpected or unusual anomalies. Examples include qualifiers such as "detected in equipment blank" that are assigned by the lab and reported in the EDD. Managing data with a database affords an opportunity to detect a limited number of anomalous conditions and respond accordingly. For instance, your schema could include information that identifies, for a given parameter, the maximum time a sample can be held before analysis for that parameter is considered invalid. If the lab reports the date on which each analysis was performed, you can leverage this information to detect hold time exceedances. If the hold time is exceeded, you can either notify the user of this condition and reject the data or accept the data but mark it with the appropriate value qualifier. (You should first check if the lab already flagged this condition before marking it yourself.) Another common automatic validation check involves defining the range of expected values for parameters. If a value is entered that is not within the expected range, it can be rejected or flagged as "outside expected bounds."[4]

---

[4] This is often used for ensuring that temperature readings are entered in the appropriate units.

Note that some of these validation checks can be accomplished with stored procedures in the database. The more complicated a check becomes, however, the more likely it is to require processing that may be beyond the ability of the platform to evaluate it in a stored procedure. Also, troubleshooting and debugging complicated checks may be easier outside the confines of the database.

7.4.5 Querying and Reporting

The ability to retrieve data in a meaningful way is essential to the user interface and should not be confined to only the typical presentations (such as a table of all results for a given sample). We've continuously touted the importance of analyzing your business model, and that process should have revealed a number of queries and reports that are frequently generated. The interface should include as many of these as possible (see Section 7.6 for related comments). There may be a possibility of using a single form for generating more than one report, but more commonly you may need a separate form for each query or report.

One obvious question that is often asked is "what's the difference between a query and a report?" It's a good question but one that doesn't necessarily have a definitive answer. Some database professionals would argue that a query is used to retrieve the data and a report is the formatted presentation of the query results. This may be a case of a distinction without a difference. Realistically the two are hard to separate: you can't create a report without using a query, and you can't see the results of a query without generating a report.[5] Most users are more comfortable with the word "report" (perhaps because they associate "query" with the inner workings of the database) so that may be the preferred term of identification within the interface. Choose whichever you like – ultimately it doesn't really matter. What you are actually doing is retrieving data.

The process of retrieving data begins when the user is prompted to select or enter information that identifies the records they wish to retrieve. The specific entry requirements will vary depending on the purpose of the retrieval, but these should be known in advance for standard queries and reports. Strive to keep the number of entries to the minimum required to efficiently define the range of data. Avoid the use of coded selections – present choices using terms comprehensible to your users and organized in a manner to which they are accustomed. For many predefined reports, data can be identified with relatively few selections. Use previous selections to narrow subsequent choices when possible, but be prepared for users to select options in an unexpected order. As an illustration, suppose you have a standard format for reporting the results of a sampling event and that your data model associates each sampling event with a project. The required entries for identifying data for the report are the ones that identify a sampling event: the location, date, and time. The report form can therefore identify the data using only a series of dropdown list controls with the behaviors indicated in Table 7.1. The table describes the manner in which the contents

---

[5] True database geeks might argue that if you issue a query in a command window and don't rename columns or apply any additional manipulation, then you have not generated a report. I say this is a nit that's not worth picking.

TABLE 7.1

Controls Needed to Identify a Single Sample for Inclusion in a Report

The control receiving focus is the	If the status of other controls at the time is	then this control's list contains	Selecting an option in this control should
Project list.	location not selected, date not selected,	all projects.	populate the list of locations with those for which samples exist for the chosen project and populate the list of dates with the list of dates on which samples were collected for the chosen project.
	location selected, date not selected,	projects for which samples have been collected at the specified location.	populate the list of dates with those for which samples exist for the chosen project and the specified location.
	location not selected, date selected,	projects for which samples have been collected on the specified date.	populate the list of locations with those for which samples exist for the chosen project on the specified date.
	location selected, date selected,	projects for which samples have been collected at the specified location on the specified date.	perform no action.
Location list.	project not selected, date not selected,	all locations.	populate the list of projects with those for which samples exist for the chosen location and populate the list of dates with those for which samples exist for the chosen location.
	project selected, date not selected,	locations for which samples exist for the specified project.	populate the list of dates with those for which samples exist for the chosen location and specified project.
	project not selected, date selected,	locations for which samples exist for the specified date.	populate the list of projects with those for which samples exist for the chosen location on the specified date.
	project selected, date selected,	locations for which samples exist for the specified project on the specified date.	perform no action.

TABLE 7.1 Continued
Controls Needed to Identify a Single Sample for Inclusion in a Report

The control receiving focus is the	If the status of other controls at the time is	then this control's list contains	Selecting an option in this control should
Date list.	project not selected, location not selected,	all dates on which samples exist.	populate the list of projects with those for which samples exist for the chosen date and populate the list of locations with those for which samples exist for the chosen date.
	project selected, location not selected,	all dates on which samples exist for the specified project.	populate the list of locations with those for which samples exist for the chosen data and the specified project.
	project not selected, location selected,	all dates on which samples exist for the specified location.	populate the list of projects with those for which samples exist for the chosen date and the specified location.
	project selected, location selected,	all dates on which samples exist for the specified location and project.	perform no action.

of each list are determined when the list receives focus, which is based on information that is either present or missing from the other controls. The number of controls is limited, but their behaviors are connected in sometimes complex ways.

The list of behaviors reflects the universe of possible orders in which users might choose items and is an indication of the complexity of user interface design in a graphical user interface. Note that the project list becomes superfluous once a location is selected. Its purpose is simply to narrow the list of possible locations to a more manageable subset. If your description of sampling events includes depths, the form would also include a control for that attribute as well. Presence of a depth option adds extra levels of complexity to each of the behaviors described in the table. Additional controls could add more flexibility to the process. For example, the form could include boxes that define the beginning and ending dates that, if not blank, define a range that limits sampling events. While this example addresses all possible situations, it is not unreasonable to limit the selection pathways by forcing users to select items in a given order … within reason. For example, if the mindset of your organization is strongly project oriented, then users are likely always cognizant of the project for which samples were collected. In that case, you might opt to disable the other lists until the project is chosen. The overall approach described here is only one of several possible ways to choose a sampling event, all of which are equally viable and valid. The intention is to stimulate your creativity. Use your knowledge of the user community to craft a mechanism that is simple and understandable.

(You may be asking why we went through an elaborate breakdown of this relatively simple situation. We did it because this exercise is a good example of the type of procedural analysis required to create an effective GUI. You'll need to think in these terms a lot while creating the interface.)

No matter how many standard reports and queries you include in the interface, there will always be times when users will need something else. It's not practical to create an interface that addresses every data retrieval or formatting need of all users. For this reason, it's a good idea to include an *ad hoc* query option. The term *ad hoc* is Latin and translates as "for this." In database parlance, it refers to a query that is not preplanned but rather is constructed as needed to meet a specific goal. In practical terms it means giving the user the ability to select any number of columns from any set of tables and format the returned data in any manner. In reality this is only possible using raw SQL statements. Short of requiring users to learn SQL, how can you implement an *ad hoc* query capability? There are several strategies that can at least partially achieve this. One option is to provide selection lists and other controls that walk users through the process of constructing a standard SQL SELECT query. Figure 7.2 illustrates an example of how such a form might look.

Figure 7.2 shows the generator early in the process. The query text box is in its initial state, in which it contains only the word "SELECT." The user selects the query statement element from the list near the top of the form. The first step in defining the query is identifying the list of columns to be returned. When the user selects a table from the tables list, the list of columns is updated to show the columns in the selected table. The user adds the desired columns to the query by double clicking them one at a time. The next objective is to specify the WHERE clause. To accomplish this, the user selects the "match conditions" data element

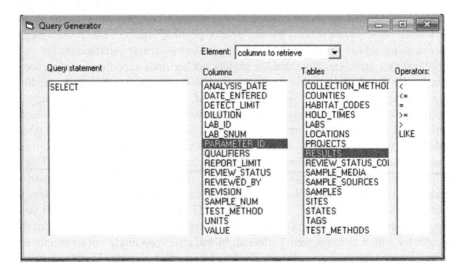

FIGURE 7.2   A conceptualization of an ad hoc SQL query generator.

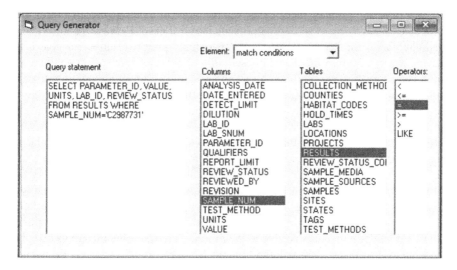

FIGURE 7.3 A complete, albeit simple, SQL statement has been created by the query generator.

option and selects the columns and operators as needed. Figure 7.3 shows the generator with the completed query.

There are several examples of this approach in various commercial products that interact with databases.[6] They occur mostly in products with limited scope and targeted objectives due to the many problems in both creating and using this method. First, the utility in SQL querying methods is that the complexity and richness of the language allows you to create elaborate views of the data. This complexity, however, makes it extremely difficult to construct a mechanism for guiding the uninitiated through the variations in the process. Thus, these tools are typically capable of producing only simple queries. Second, even providing the ability to construct simple *ad hoc* queries can require an inordinate amount of code. Finally, some allowance must be made for correcting mistakes in the generated query. This means either more controls for deleting portions of the statement or allowing direct editing of the query before execution. Creating a mechanism for managing the overall process becomes an intimidating task for anything beyond the simplest options.

Fortunately, when limiting our focus to environmental data, we can leverage the commonality of the schema. As a result, the most likely candidate components of an *ad hoc* query are limited and known (for instance, while a particular query may report test methods, it's unlikely that anyone will have the desire to make the test

---

[6] Many DBMS platforms include graphical interfaces for constructing complex queries. One issue with these tools is that they are available only within the confines of the DBMS management software. Another is that (in my opinion) they are just as difficult to learn and understand as using SQL statements, so it's often not worth the effort. At any rate, this chapter is focused on what you can develop within your own user interface, so we can ignore these examples.

methods table the primary focus of the query). We can therefore create a form that is capable of satisfying most impromptu data retrieval needs because the most likely candidate target for selection is the table that stores sample results. Our goal is to provide a way to return the desired descriptors of selected results by specifying as many characteristics as possible. This works because we know the query statement will begin with "SELECT (some fields) FROM (the results table)." Breaking down the structure of what might be needed to fill in the other parts of the query statement provides insight into how we can construct a query form that satisfies most needs.

First we need to identify the columns that will be returned. Controls similar to those shown in Figures 7.2 and 7.3 will suffice for this. Since we are confident that the main focus will be on records in the results table, we should begin by offering the columns in that table. Also, instead of listing all the tables in the schema as options for additional field selections, we can limit choices to only those tables that have schema-defined relationships with the results table. This will allow users to translate coded values in the results table to their more understandable meanings (e.g., by choosing the parameter name column from the parameters table instead of the parameter code from the results table). Tracking the list of tables referenced in the columns selected for the query will allow us to complete the FROM portion of the query by constructing appropriate JOINs. We have no incentive to complicate the situation by offering different types of JOINs because we're returning only information for records in the results table. All our JOINs are therefore INNER JOINs.

Now we get to the WHERE clause. This is a little more complicated but not overwhelming because once again the options for choosing records will all be based on columns in the results table. Obvious choices for selection basis are the spatial and temporal characteristics of the sampling event: location, date, and time. Controls described in Table 7.1 will work well for specifying these choices. Another obvious choice is parameter(s). For parameters and other translation tables that may have a large number of entries, a good strategy is to offer a list of all values and allow users to select one or more for inclusion. Just about every other column in the results table is a potential discriminator for selecting records. You can go so far as to allow users to select records based on options chosen for every column in the results table if you are so inclined. More likely, though, you will be able to narrow choices down to a limited subset. For each column used to select records, you also need a target value. There are nuances regarding how you solicit target values for columns; the nuances are based on the column's data type and usage. For columns that are coded values that refer to lookup tables, the preference is to offer all values in the lookup table. For numeric and date columns, you can solicit an explicit value or a range. For unconfined text columns (i.e., text columns on which there are no constraints on entries other than length), you can check for matches to an explicit string or use wild card characters in a LIKE clause. In the end, you will process the user's input into one long WHERE clause with multiple selection criteria joined by ANDs. Some of the individual components in the clause may also contain ORs.

The last segment of the query identifies the order in which records should be displayed. This is the ORDER BY clause, which is optional. Allowing users to specify the order is relatively easy because the choices are limited to the columns being retrieved. The clear solution for this is to show a list of the columns in the query and allow users to select the one(s) that establish the order. If you allow ordering by more than one column – and you definitely should – then you'll either have to keep track of the order in which columns were selected or show the chosen columns in a list that accommodates rearrangement.

7.4.6 DATABASE CLEANUP AND MAINTENANCE

The last category of functions we will discuss is reserved for administrators and involves database maintenance actions. Some common maintenance activities include:

- removal of records in tables that store data temporarily;
- identification of orphaned records; and
- resequencing of generated codes.

This list is not definitive, but it is representative.

Many databases include tables intended to store temporary data. A common practice is to queue data for important tables in temporary versions that have the same structure. For example, a system might upload incoming EDD data to a temporary table pending review for acceptance. If accepted, the data are moved to the results table; if rejected, the data are deleted. Another common practice is associated with particularly complex reports that require multiple processing steps before the final product. A system with this feature might use one or more temporary tables for the collection of interim data. In any event, communication failures or mistakes in the processes can result in records remaining in these temporary tables. Purging data from temporary tables should be done occasionally to free up storage space.

Orphaned records are child records for which the parent no longer exists. An example would be results that still exist for a sample that has been deleted. Theoretically this should never happen in a well-designed schema, and yet it does. One cause can be glitches in hardware or the DBMS software. These are rare but not impossible. Another cause can be database activity while a constraint is temporarily disabled. The most common cause, sadly, is human error such as failure to define a proper constraint during database creation. Regardless of the cause, orphaned records appear from time to time. Options for corrective actions are to either delete the orphans or recreate the parents. The appropriate action depends on the importance of the data.

If you have lookup tables in which the coded values are generated based on sequences of numbers or characters, there is a likelihood of developing gaps in the sequences. This occurs when older records are no longer needed and are deleted. This situation can be ignored in most cases but may become a problem depending on the size and type of the coded field. The risk lies in reaching the maximum planned value of the field. Addressing this is as simple as regenerating IDs so that the gaps are filled. (Note that this does not apply when you reach the maximum but there are no gaps – that's a different problem.)

Data maintenance functions can be performed as needed directly in the database, so why would you bother building them into the interface? Two situations suggest an answer. The first is that a particular issue may be difficult to identify – involving complex queries, for instance – or require review by others in order to resolve. The second occurs when you develop a database for someone else and won't be available to perform such activities. If either situation applies, consider including some maintenance functions as needed.

7.5   USER INTERFACE PLATFORMS AND COMPONENTS

The next step after the functional requirements have been identified is to select the specific operating system(s) for which the interface(s) will be created. Choices are driven primarily by factors associated with your analysis of user requirements (Section 7.2). You may discover that you have only a single option. If you have more than one choice, other considerations can include the availability and experience of computer programming staff, your own comfort level with software development, and budget.

Regardless of the platform(s), the generic description of typical user interaction remains the same and consists of a short set of components: a menu system or toolbar that enables navigation among the various options, data collection and presentation forms that are targeted to specific categories of data, and user feedback mechanisms such as message boxes and status indicators. Within these classifications, variations exist in the form of different discrete user interface items – components – that perform various functions. When choosing the specific components you will use, consider both their popularity and longevity. That flashy new grid control that is getting all the buzz right now might be tempting, but exercise caution before committing to it. Keep in mind that your interface may be in use for a long time. Maintaining software that includes components that are no longer supported or which never gain sufficient traction to attract a vibrant user base can be difficult.

If possible and appropriate, make your interface moderately adaptive – meaning that it can be customized to meet individual users' needs and preferences. This can be accomplished by allowing users to choose to which menu options and other interface components are available when they are logged in. Preferences may be applied to users or computers. Fully adaptive interfaces learn user preferences through tracking of actions and choices, but this capability is complicated to develop and probably beyond the reach of all but the largest environmental organizations.

The target platform(s) dictate the specifics of the types of controls and components the interface(s) will include, but also define expectations that users will apply when interacting with the software. The interface should adhere to appearance and procedural standards of the platform. Identifying these standards can be tricky depending on the operating system. For platforms with a long history, standards for user interaction are established and well documented. In Microsoft Windows, for instance, it is considered good practice to include (at minimum) three command buttons on all forms that interact with data – an Apply button that saves the data and keeps the form open, an OK button that saves the data and closes the form, and a Cancel button that closes the form without saving the data. Operating systems of more recent vintage (e.g., Android and others designed primarily for smart phones and tablets) are evolving very quickly, so the best source of intelligence about what works best may be a survey of popular applications for the platform (but stick to those with a business and/or professional focus).

As a final consideration, remember that there are limitations on some platforms that can affect overall capabilities. Web-based interfaces, for example, can be very tempting because they do not require installation. However, HTML places very strict rules on what a web page can and cannot do with respect to interacting with users' local data. This may prevent some desirable features from being obtainable through a web interface. Also, different browsers may interpret the same HTML commands differently. This may require that you limit users to a particular browser or else force you to include code that takes the browser into account when presenting data. And ultimately, controls that are part of standard HTML may not provide the desirable richness of the user experience. This can be overcome through the use of additional technologies (e.g., Flash, ActiveX, etc.), but these add an increased complexity to the development and support processes.

7.6   FINALIZING THE INTERFACE PLAN

The final step before initiating creation of the interface(s) is documentation of the interface plan. Throughout the planning process you will have gathered many pieces of information and made notes on ideas about how users interact with the data or how the database can best interact with users. Some of these ideas may be great, and some may be barely adequate. At this point they are probably not particularly well organized. It's time now to get the plan in writing (oh no, not another document!).

Generating a formal interface plan accomplishes several important objectives. First, it requires performance of the mental exercise of envisioning how the software will look and how it will interact with the database. A good interface plan will often include mockups (or hand drawings) of expectations regarding these aspects. This exercise forces you to think through each element in more detail. Fleshing out these activities that were previously only ideas will solidify your understanding of what is achievable and what may not be. You may also find that some elements that you previously considered discrete have enough overlap to be combined. Second, it affords an opportunity to weigh the costs and benefits of each element. Costs should include both the initial development and ongoing support. This can help in determining (with apologies to Bob Seger) what to leave in and what to leave out. Third, and perhaps most important, the interface plan serves as a communication tool between you and the software development team.[7] One situation that virtually guarantees problems with any software development project is the lack of communication. It leads to improper feature implementation and scope creep. Avoiding this pitfall is essential

---

[7] You should create the interface plan even if you are going to take the plunge and develop the interface(s) yourself. In this case it will serve as a guide to keep you focused on the entirety of the program. Experience demonstrates how easy it is to get so involved in one detail of the program that you completely forget to complete some other part.

for the successful creation of the interface(s). Putting the plan in writing and having it reviewed and approved by all concerned establishes clear expectations.

> **Best Practice #11**   Do not authorize anyone to start developing code related to the user interface(s) until the interface plan document has been approved by all parties. This should be denoted by signatures of the primary representatives of all affected participants – developers, management, and users. The interface plan constitutes the list of features and functions that has been agreed to by all participants.

7.7   TESTING

An integral – and essential – part of software development is testing. It is imperative that you include testing in your interface plan. There are numerous different philosophies and approaches to software testing. At one time the common software development paradigm separated coding and testing into distinct activities, with testing often being deferred until coding was completed. This approach has (thankfully) been replaced with a more integrated approach in which coding is done in incremental pieces and testing occurs throughout development. There are several development methodologies that adhere to this basic approach; one of the most popular methodologies at the time of this writing is called Agile Development. Agile Development breaks the software development project down into small milestones that can be reached in limited time spans. Agile Development also emphasizes demonstration of progress to users on a frequent basis and involves them in incremental testing and feedback. Following the Agile method – or one similar – is strongly recommended during creation of the typical environmental data management interface.

Even if you test frequently during development, an additional, more traditional testing approach may be beneficial. Comprehensive software testing involves creation of a thorough test plan. These plans describe every possible behavior of every form and control within the program and can run to hundreds of pages. Testers are given a step-by-step guide to follow. Each step identifies the expected outcome; testers record either success (achievement of the expected outcome) or failure (deviation from the expected outcome). When a failure occurs, testers identify the actual condition that resulted. [In an aside in Section 7.3.3 we discussed how creating a user interface has become more complicated with the advent of GUIs. The complexity of testing plans has increased exponentially because of GUIs.] This process is so burdensome that it deters many organizations from considering developing their own interface(s). In our opinion, this approach is overkill for most environmental data management systems unless the goal is to create a package that will be sold as commercial software. More commonly, the entire user community consists of in-house personnel. Thus, users form a more restricted group with established communications procedures and protocols. In such a situation, the penalty for post-deployment errors is less severe: the person responsible for the program gets a call or e-mail from Bob reporting the problem, the error gets corrected, and Bob gets notified. Work goes on.

Furthermore, if the error results in bad data in the database, appropriate resources are readily available to correct them. This doesn't mean, though, that you can skip testing entirely. If the software you put out is buggy, acceptance by the user community may be delayed or the package may be entirely rejected. It does mean, though, that you don't have to make testing an overwhelming endeavor. The incremental testing steps performed while following modern development methodologies (as described above) can be sufficient.

The important point to keep in mind during testing is that perfection is an unreasonable goal. You should strive to make the program as reliable as possible, but don't expect it to be flawless. A favorite quote from Douglas Adams is often cited by software developers when describing the creation of a user interface: "[a] common mistake that people make when trying to design something completely foolproof is to underestimate the ingenuity of complete fools."[8]

7.8   SUMMARY

We conclude this chapter with a best practice that summarizes the user interface development process.

> **Best Practice #12**   Development of the user interface should be treated like any other software development endeavor. Follow standards and best practices associated with that activity. If you aren't already knowledgeable in this area, read up on at least the basic principles. Stay in charge – work with the developer(s) to resolve questions or conflicting requirements, but don't allow anyone else to assume control of the entire process. Develop a plan and stick to it, but don't think of it as definitive at the outset – allow it to evolve. Structure the project in such a way that incremental development occurs and testing is done throughout the cycle. Engage representatives from all facets of the user community in testing.

---

[8] Mostly Harmless, Douglas Adams, Harmony Books, 1992.

8 Applying What We've Learned

8.1 PRELIMINARY COMMENTS

It has now come to the point where it's time to apply what you've learned. We'll do this by creating a custom application for managing environmental data. For brevity, we will limit the scope of the program, but we will attempt to be effusive regarding the capabilities that are present. Development and discussion of this application will demonstrate the concepts, principles, and practices you have learned throughout previous chapters and will (hopefully) stimulate ideas for how it can be expanded or adapted.

Be forewarned that some of the decision processes outlined in earlier chapters will not be included, but this is done because of a desire to avoid forced forays into distracting avenues. This will allow us to focus on the environmental aspects of the solution rather than wasting valuable pages on other topics. (Besides, since our application is for a situation that is complete fantasy, we would have ended up just concocting scenarios that guide us to the choices we knew we wanted.) One notable omission is that we will not attempt to survey existing commercial, off-the-shelf (COTS) software or other systems, and instead simply advance to the decision to create a custom database and user interface. We will trust that we have given you adequate instructions to prepare for a proper undertaking of these endeavors in your own real-world surroundings. In some cases, the choices for examples are driven by a desire to follow the path that best facilitates the sharing of information. For example, as much as possible, we wish to avoid forcing the user to acquire or download software from sources other those provided in this book. Resources related to the system created in this chapter are available online. The platforms and tools selected are the ones that are the least restrictive and therefore the most adaptable.

Accessing the Online Resources To download the files that support this chapter, point your browser to
www.routledge.com/Managing-Environmental-Data-Principles-Techniques-and-Best-Practices/Burnette/p/book/9780367654405.

DOI: 10.1201/9781003131953-9

Navigate to the section for Support Material. There you will find zip files that can be downloaded.

The specific choices for this development are as follows: first, the target operating system is Microsoft Windows. Second, Microsoft Jet (Access) is the chosen database platform. Within that framework, the database specifically uses the older .mdb format. Why Access? There are several factors that influenced this choice:

- It is the only platform that does not require installation of any additional software on our selected operating system. Since (at the time of this writing) Jet is still a standard component of Windows, you can be reasonably certain that the database platform is already installed. Use of any other DBMS would require readers to acquire and install additional software.
- The .mdb file format can be opened by numerous products. Thus, even if you don't have a license for Microsoft Access, you probably either have or can get another piece of software that allows you to at least open the database and examine its contents. Many of these software products also allow you to insert, edit, and delete data. In any case, the version of the interface posted on the web will allow you to interact with the database.
- The version of SQL in Jet does not support some standard features of ANSI SQL. You would think this would make it a poorer choice. However, despite all the things you can do with more robust implementations, it is likely that at some point you will encounter a need that exceeds your (or perhaps anyone's) database skills. You need to know how to work around these situations within the user interface. Choosing a version of SQL with some limitations guarantees us an opportunity to demonstrate techniques for alternative solutions without having to create unreasonable scenarios.

Finally, we will use Visual Basic for .NET (VB.NET) as our platform for creating the interface. It is commonly accepted that BASIC is the easiest programming language to read and comprehend without significant training. You should be able to understand the code even if you don't know VB or .NET functionality (especially with the helpful explanations provided). Furthermore, the .NET framework – like Jet – is a standard component of every current Windows installation. Thus, an application developed using VB.NET does not require an installation program that registers additional libraries and other files.[1] Note that despite the use of VB.NET, you will not be required to use Microsoft Visual Studio to view source code. The intention is not to teach you how to develop VB.NET programs that serve as database interfaces but rather to instruct you on the nuances required for creating a user interface that properly and effectively interacts with a database. Code will be presented in plain text,

---

[1] This is true even if you use additional custom controls in a .NET application. As long as the support files for the custom control are located in the same folder as the executable, the program will find them. No non-standard .NET controls will be used in this interface.

outside any specific development management system, and no attempt will be made to explain every last file required to create a .NET program. However, as various forms are discussed, it will be necessary to explain specific .NET components. As you read this information, keep in mind that the objects and methods used by other development platforms may be very similar in capabilities (and in many cases syntax).

8.2 THE BUSINESS MODEL AND THE DATA MODEL

In order to bookend Part 1, the original context from Chapter 3 will be revisited: an imaginary company called We Sample Stuff (WSS). As hinted in Section 8.1, an elaborate description of the WSS business model is not included. Instead, we will focus only on those aspects of the business model that most affect the data model. As it turns out, some things have changed at WSS while you've been learning about databases. You've therefore re-examined some of your original information through the lens of your newfound knowledge. The following discussion will begin by listing the original business model rules from Chapter 3, with updates noted as applicable. After the original list, notes will be included about some new concepts that must be addressed:

- Each sampling activity is associated with a specific project for a specific client. The company's accounting system tracks client information and contract details, and generates a list of projects. The data management system will need the list of project numbers and names, but otherwise will operate independently of the accounting system.
- UPDATE: You now have more details about the accounting system. Project numbers consist of four digits for the year, followed by a dash, followed by a five-character abbreviation that identifies the client, then another dash, and finally a four-digit sequence number for the combination of year, client, and project. An example would be 2021-BAUCM-0001 for the first project in 2021 for the client identified by BAUCM (Baucom Industries). The projects table will not require any data other than the name and standard ID for each project. Because project numbers are created in the accounting system, no validation of the project number structure is required in the database. An explicit clients table is therefore not needed.
- Each sampling location is associated with a site. When writing reports, project managers have varying requirements for grouping sampling events – individually, combined by site, and combined for the entire project.
- UPDATE: A sites table will be required. You've decided to use three-character abbreviations for sites. Since projects may involve multiple sites, a table will also be required that associates the two elements. A method is also needed to associate locations with sites. The obvious choice would be to include a site ID column in the locations table. However, this adds an extra column requirement to the primary keys for the locations, samples, and results tables (see the notes about these tables in Section 8.3 for more information). This is not a major issue, but an alternative idea emerged that accomplishes the goal without the need for an additional column – assign location identifiers that include the site ID as the first three characters.

- The locations sampled by WSS so far are all wells, but they have different purposes. Some are drinking water wells, some are used as industrial process water sources, and some are water quality monitoring wells.
- UPDATE: WSS has added capabilities for sampling of soils and surface water (both impounded and free flowing).
- For every sample, the date and time at which the sample was collected is noted on a field data sheet. Each sample is also assigned an identifier.
- UPDATE: You realized that the depth is also an important descriptor of each sample. Regarding sample IDs, consideration was given to the typical practice of just generating a sequential number for each sample. However, after contemplating the information in Chapter 4, the decision was made to create an identifier based on the combination of date, time, and depth. See the notes for the samples table in Section 8.3 for details.
- When performing sampling, the standard operating procedure (SOP) is to record a number of physical conditions at the site at the time the sample is collected. Examples include water temperature, well depth to water, and water pH. These are entered manually on a field data sheet.
- UPDATE: The format of the WSS field data sheet has evolved a bit based on the new sampling capabilities, but not that much. The company is looking into the use of tablets or smart phones for documenting field observations, but for now the goal is simply to try and mimic the format of the field data sheet within the interface. This should reduce the number of transcription errors from the paper form to the interface.
- The list of parameters for which analysis is performed varies with the purpose of the well. Analysis of wells with the same purpose may require analysis for different parameters based on client or project requirements.
- UPDATE: These same rules apply to the other sampling capabilities as well. The data model needs to include a mechanism for grouping parameters.
- WSS has existing contracts with two different analytical laboratories. These labs have the same capabilities and similar performance ratings. They charge nearly the same for corresponding analyses. The lab to which any given batch of samples is sent is therefore decided by each project manager based on factors related to how quickly results are needed and the current workload level at each lab. WSS also frequently evaluates other laboratories as potential partners, so more labs may be used in the future.
- UPDATE: No major changes to the concept, but more labs have already been added.
- WSS has SOPs that describe the actions required for collecting, preparing, and handling samples. Each SOP is specific to the type of equipment used to collect the sample. Another SOP describes the procedure for shipping samples to a laboratory. Clients are provided copies of these SOPs, and contracts state that WSS will reference the specific SOPs followed for each sampling event when reporting analysis results.
- UPDATE: No major changes in this idea either. The table that identifies these SOPs will be called "collection methods."

- WSS has a Quality Assurance (QA) officer whose responsibilities include validating all field and laboratory results.
- UPDATE: You've opted to not go crazy with this concept. You'll simply include column in the results table that indicates the review status of the record.
- Depending on the project, some sampling events include the collection of Quality Control (QC) samples. WSS offers a limited number of QC sample types: duplicate samples (collecting multiple samples from the same source), split samples (dividing a sample into multiple containers to be analyzed independently), blanks (reagent grade water), and spiked samples (reagent grade water spiked with a known quantity of a specific substance). The objective of collecting duplicate samples is to assess the performance of field personnel by helping determine if the samples are collected and processed correctly. Split samples, spiked samples, and blanks provide a basis on which to evaluate the lab's handling and analysis of the samples. WSS retains information about the relationships between QC samples and regular samples. This information is used for generating an analytical data QC report. Laboratories should have no way of recognizing that a sample is a QC sample.
- UPDATE: Your QA manager (Daryl) has been quite uncooperative regarding the database. Despite your most persuasive arguments, he insists that his QC analyses are too complicated for a database and he refuses to allow you to include them. For now you'll leave the QC samples out of the data model.
- NEW: By examining past field notes, comparing data in reports to field data sheets, and tracking down more information from project managers, you've learned that many sampling locations are known by multiple names. You will need some method for accommodating this practice.
- NEW: You've also realized that different labs use different names to refer to the same parameter. You have requested that labs use CAS numbers to identify parameters when possible, but some of the analyses include parameters that aren't chemicals and therefore don't have CAS numbers. The software will have to be able to recognize parameters by name when importing EDDs, and since parameters may have different names, some method for resolving these varying references to the appropriate analyte will be required.
- NEW: Another thing you've found is that occasionally EDDs indicate the use of test methods that are not appropriate for the reported parameters. These anomalies are attributed to lab recording errors rather than actual use of incorrect methods, but it would be beneficial to find some way to catch these during data import.
- NEW: It was noted in Chapter 3 that some clients provide results of prior sampling. You would like to import these into the database when available in order to provide background and parameter history for these locations. Some of the older data shows parameter results in inconsistent units or units different from what are normally used. Conversion of values based on different units will be required at some point in order to avoid the burden of checking and converting every file before importing the data.
- NEW: Management has identified two analyses that are requested often enough by clients that they should be included in the system immediately. One is a

comparison of sampling results with regulatory limits defined by various authorities. The regulatory limits of interest come in two varieties. First, there are simple limits based on the value of the regulated parameter (e.g., parameter A value > 0.5 mg/kg in soil). Second, there are combined limits defined by an exceedance value of the regulated parameter at the same time another parameter meets defined conditions (e.g., parameter A value > 5 µg/L when parameter B value < 100 mg/L in water). This requires the data model to include tables for recording these limits and that the interface provides a mechanism for evaluating and reporting exceedances. The second analysis used by WSS clients is a commonly applied tool for identifying trophic conditions in reservoirs: Carlson's Trophic State Index (TSI). The database and the user interface must support this evaluation.

- NEW: Attempts to convince Daryl that the database offered opportunities to automate certain QC checks failed. You had an idea for a simple check that might help convince him, and couldn't resist including it. You decided to include a table of hold times for parameters and compare the analysis date with the sample collection date in order to automatically flag results for which the hold time was exceeded.

These notes do not address every aspect of the business model and data model. Some of the very mundane aspects of the data model are omitted from the analysis. The elements that were skipped should be apparent from an examination of the completed database.

8.3 IMPLEMENTING THE DATA MODEL IN THE DATABASE

Let us now examine the completed database in some detail. In this section, we will describe key concepts and structures found in each table. Appendix A provides a complete data model for the database. This section is a more expository exploration of the tables. The tables are presented in alphabetical order. It may be beneficial to refer to the full data dictionary listing as you browse these comments. Note that in these explanations we will sometimes state that a particular constraint must be enforced through the interface. This is a true statement only because we are using Access. A more proper statement would be that a particular constraint could be enforced either through the interface or through a stored procedure. Recall from Chapter 7 that the equivalent of stored procedures in Access is accomplished using VBA. Since we are using VB.NET instead of VBA to create the interface, we will apply such constraints within that context.

ANALYTE_ALIASES

As with most environmental databases, we have a table of parameters (analytes); each record in the table specifies a parameter code and identifies the name we use for the parameter. The ANALYTE_ALIASES table is our acknowledgment that parameters may be known by other names. Because we will import results from a variety of labs, we may need flexibility in identifying parameters by name. The table contains only two columns. The PARAMETER_ID column is our internal coded identifier used throughout the database to denote specific analytes. The PARAM_ALIAS column is an alternative name by which the parameter is known. A parameter can have multiple aliases, but each alias must refer to only one parameter. The PARAM_ALIAS column must therefore be unique and is used as the primary key. The PARAMETER_ID is a foreign key into the ANALYTES table.

ANALYTE_GROUP_ELEMENTS

This table identifies all the parameters that constitute a selected parameter group. The GROUP_CODE column specifies the group and is a foreign key into ANALYTE_ GROUPS. The PARAMETER_ID column identifies one element within the group and is a foreign key into the ANALYTES table. The UNITS column is a foreign key into the UNITS table. The relationship constraint between UNITS and ANALYTE_ GROUP_ELEMENTS sets the child record UNITS column to the default value ("None") when the parent is deleted. A parameter can only be present once within a given group; the combination of GROUP_CODE and PARAMETER_ID is therefore the primary key.

ANALYTE_GROUPS

This table defines groups of parameters. GROUP_CODE is the coded identifier for the group and is the primary key. The GROUP_DESC column is free text used to describe the purpose of the group. The SHORT_NAME column is a free text short name for the group. This is used as the group name in the user interface. ANALYTE_ GROUPS is a parent table for ANALYTE_GROUP_ELEMENTS. The relationship constraint between these two tables cascades both updates and deletions.

ANALYTE_TEST_METHODS

The purpose of this table is to identify which test methods are acceptable for which parameters. Each combination of the two columns in this table must be unique, and hence the combination constitutes the primary key. PARAMETER_ID is a foreign key into ANALYTES and TEST_MTHD is a foreign key into TEST_METHODS. Both of these relationships cascade both updates and deletions, so deleting either the parameter or test method from the parent table deletes the record in this table.

ANALYTES

This table identifies all parameters known to the system. The parameter code is a five-digit number implemented as a text field to ensure five digits in every case. Rather than assign parameter codes sequentially, parameter codes are designated manually. This technique allows you to begin with an initial short list of analytes and then add related analytes in such a way that their ID numbers are near each other. For example, the original set of parameters included 5-day biological oxygen demand (BOD), but there are other variations such as 30-day BOD and ultimate BOD. The gap between the initial entry for 5-day BOD and whatever parameter is entered next enables the creation of the additional BOD parameter IDs with numbers close to the 5-day version. (The order of the parameter codes is obviously not that important.) The PARAMETER_

ID column is, of course, the primary key. Many other tables throughout the database refer to analytes and each of them has a relationship constraint with ANALYTES. The other columns are ANL_NAME, which is the full name by which we refer to the parameter, and ANL_SHORT which is a shorter version of the full name used for selection lists in the interface to conserve screen space.

COLLECTION_METHODS

This table identifies the equipment used to collect samples. The COLLECT_MTHD column is the internal ID used within the system for each collection method and is the primary key. In this case, a routine integer field is incremented for each new record. (This will be done via the interface due to the previously stated aversion to the use of autonumber fields and sequences.) The table is a parent in a relationship with SAMPLES, where collection methods are documented. The relationship does not cascade deletions. Instead, if the indicated collection method is deleted, the collection method is set to the default (0) in the SAMPLES table. The collection method record with an ID of 0 ("not on file") therefore serves an important role in the database and should be protected from deletion. The METH_NAME column serves the obvious role of providing a descriptive name for the method. The SOP_DOC column contains a path and file name that identifies the SOP that describes the specific actions performed when collecting a sample via this method. Cataloging the documents in this way provides an easy mechanism for identifying which SOPs are to be included when sampling results are reported to the client.

CONVERSION_FACTORS

This table serves the obvious purpose of providing factors to convert between different units. The conversion factor is determined by a unique combination of the units being converted, so the primary key is the combination of FROM_UNITS and TO_UNITS. To convert from the FROM_UNITS to the TO_UNITS, multiply by the FACTOR. To convert from TO_UNITS to FROM_UNITS, divide by the FACTOR. The foreign key situation provides an interesting conundrum. Both the FROM_UNITS and TO_UNITS must be present in the UNITS table, so two different constraints are needed. SQL does not allow you to create multiple constraints from the same column in one table to multiple columns in a second table. One constraint is therefore present in the database (FROM_UNITS must be present in UNITS). The second constraint must be enforced through the interface.

COUNTIES

It's desirable (but not required) to document the county in which each sampling location is located. Since the county is not a required entry in LOCATIONS, it would have been acceptable to simply created a free text field for the county name without any repercussions. Instead, a listing of all counties in all states was obtained from a government web site and incorporated for use as a lookup table. The advantage is that it allows users to select the county from a dropdown list instead of typing the county name, which both simplifies the user action and enforces referential integrity. (It also eliminates the need to create references to new counties when the first sampling occurs in them.) In the listing, the county codes are unique within each state but not unique throughout the data. The primary key is therefore the combination of POSTAL_STATE (which is the standard two-character state abbreviation) and CNTY_CODE. POSTAL_STATE is also a foreign key into the STATES table.

DATA_CONFIDENCE_FLAGS

This table contains coded values that represent the review status of individual results. There are only two fields, both of which are required. DCL_FLAG is the coded value (two characters) and DCL_DESC provides the interpretation of the code. DCL_FLAG is the primary key. DCL_FLAG is a required entry in the RESULTS table, so an entry in this table that designates "not reviewed" must be present and protected from deletion.

FIELD_FORM_PARAMETERS

An examination of the paper forms used by WSS to record field observations reveals an evolving process. The list of specific analytes recorded has changed over time, as has the order in which they appear on the form. Given this situation, it seems prudent to anticipate further evolution. This table introduces flexibility in the appearance of the form without forcing recoding of the interface to match each variation. The table specifies each parameter on the form (PARAMETER_ID), the UNITS in which it is to be recorded, and the SEQUENCE in which the parameters appear. Each analyte can occur only once on the form, so PARAMETER_ID is the primary key. It is also a foreign key into the ANALYTES table.

HOLD_TIMES

This table defines the maximum number of days a sample can be held prior to analysis before the analysis is considered invalid. PARAMETER_ID is the primary key and once again a foreign key into ANALYTES. MAX_DAYS is an integer. A value qualifier that signifies "hold time exceeded" should exist in the VALUE_QUALIFIERS table to enable automatic evaluation of this condition and flagging of results when the hold time is exceeded.

HUC_CODES

This is a lookup table for hydrologic unit codes (HUC). (Please overlook the redundancy in the table name.) The United States Geologic Survey created this hierarchical system for cataloging basins and watersheds in the United States. The system documents hydrologic units on six successively smaller scales from region to subwatershed. Each level is represented by two digits in the code. Codes can be any even number of digits up to 12; the total number of digits denotes the level for the code. For example, HUC 050102 is the second basin in subregion 1 of region 5. WSS management has decided not to delineate hydrologic units below the subbasin level, so eight digits will suffice for our purposes. Note that since leading zeroes are significant in the codes, this is a case that requires a text field for storing what appears to be numbers. HUC_CODE is the primary key.

LABS

A text column is used for the coded lab identifier in this case. This allows the use of codes that are potentially recognizable abbreviations for each lab. If all lab IDs are understandable without translation, the number of JOINs required to present retrieved data in a readable manner can be reduced. The LAB_ID column is the primary key. Other columns contain information regarding the address and point of contact for the lab, but all columns other than LAB_ID and LAB_NAME are optional. Because LAB_ID is a required entry in the RESULTS table, there must be a "not indicated" entry in this table to accommodate the import of older data in which the lab is not known. It is also useful to include a record to denote values that are observed in the field. This is designated with a LAB_ID of "FIELD" and a LAB_NAME of "Field Data."

LOCATION_ALIASES

For reasons explained in the notes for the LOCATIONS table (see below), the standard LOC_ID column entries may not be easily identifiable by field crews. This table translates the common names to their internal standard equivalents. Since sampling location designations tend to follow the same pattern at every site (e.g., monitoring wells are often designated as MW-1, MW-2, etc.), these common names will not be unique within the database. The combination of SITE_ID and LOC_ALIAS must be unique, however, so that is the primary key. The LOC_ID column then provides the database-standard designation as described below. A given location can have multiple aliases, so we designate one as the PRIMARY_ALIAS.

LOCATIONS

The database requires a unique designation for each sampling location, but the common names for locations tend to be the same for many sites (e.g., OUTFALL-1, Well-3, etc.). Furthermore, some mechanism is required for associating each location with the site at which it exists. A traditional approach to meeting these requirements would be to generate a sequential number as the location identifier, use the common designation as the location name, and create a foreign key into the table of site names. This is effective but will require multiple JOINs when retrieving data. We have created an alternative for this table that can help reduce the complexity of queries. The entries in the LOC_ID column are constructed in such a way that it can provide more context when viewed directly. The first three characters of each LOC_ID entry will be the SITE_ID of the site at which the location is found. The remaining characters can then be used for the common name. The LOC_ID field allows a total of only 12 characters, so some abbreviating of common names may be necessary in some cases. This approach comes at a cost within the user interface but is worth the effort. (See the notes in Section 8.4 that discuss user input of location information.) The LOC_ID is obviously the primary key, as well as a foreign key into other tables that link data to locations. It is desirable to view data from this schema in GIS, so entry of LATITUDE, LONGITUDE, and DATUM_REF are required to enable this capability. LATITUDE and LONGITUDE are numeric fields that contain their respective entries in decimal degrees. There aren't that many datum references, so these are identified strictly through the interface rather than creating a lookup table. These fields all have default values, which enables creating a location quickly and then providing coordinates later. There are numerous other descriptors for each location, some of which are required but most of which are optional. The coded descriptors have lookup tables, so these columns are foreign keys into their respective parents.

PHYSIOGRAPHIC_PROVINCES

This is a lookup table for information that classifies the overall geomorphology and other geophysical characteristics of regions. This information is useful in some analysis and modeling applications. This table has a fairly standard reference table configuration. The PHYSI_CODE column is the coded identifier and is the primary key. The PHYSI_NAME column is the textual description.

PREP_METHODS

Another standard lookup table, this one for the methods used to prepare samples for analysis. While not always reported in the EDD, the prep method can be a factor in determining a unique parameter result value (see notes regarding RESULTS below). PREP_MTHD is the primary key and coded identifier. Because PREP_MTHD is required in RESULTS but not always known, a "not on file" record should always be present in this table.

PROJECT_SITES

Most projects will be limited to a single site, but some may include multiple sites. This table relates the two entities. The combination of PROJECT_ID and SITE_ID is the primary key. Each column is also a foreign key into their respective parent. Because the PROJECTS table does not include a site reference, even projects that involve only one site must be present in this table.

PROJECTS

As noted in Section 8.2, there is no need in the schema for extensive information about each project. Columns are limited to the PROJECT_ID (primary key) and PROJECT_NAME.

REGULATORY_LIMITS

This table identifies values that define the regulatory limits for parameters. The REG_ID column is a sequentially assigned integer and primary key. Limits are defined by regulatory authorities (in the United States these are mostly states), so the POSTAL_STATE column is a foreign key into STATES. Similarly, PARAMETER_ID and UNITS are foreign keys into their respective parents. The RELATION column holds the standard math symbol (usually >) for the relationship to the numeric limit stored in the REG_VALUE column. The REG_NAME is a free text column used for selection and reporting of limits. An interesting situation arises when attempting to identify limits defined on the national level. There are at least three potential ways to address this situation. First, national standards could be assigned to the same code (*) used when the state is not indicated. Properly explaining this approach to users requires careful presentation within the interface. Second, the content of the STATES table could be expanded to include nation names. This, however, means that the table name is not representative of the actual contents of the STATES table (a bad idea). Third, a new table could be created for NATIONS and used as the authority reference in REGULATORY_LIMITS. This would also require the use of another field to indicate whether the regulatory authority is a state or a country. If we choose that option, it creates a conditional relationship in which the authority reference table varies. Creating such a conditional relationship is not permitted within SQL and would have to be managed within the interface. For now, we will use the first option for national standards.

REGULATORY_LIMITS_CONDITIONALS

This table identifies additional conditions that define a regulatory exceedance when the ADVANCED_FLAG for a regulatory limit is set to true. A given regulation can have multiple additional requirements, so the primary key is REG_ID and PARAMETER_ID. Each of these fields is also a foreign key into its parent, as is the UNITS column. As with the basic regulatory limit definition, the RELATION column entry is a mathematical symbol in most cases. However, some conditional checks specify a range of values, so the RELATION column may also contain the letter B to indicate "between." (This same paradigm could be implemented in the REGULATORY_LIMITS table if required, but we have not seen any primary limits defined as a range.) This possibility means we must provide an option for entering two discrete values, which we designate LOW_VALUE and HIGH_VALUE. If the limit is not a range, the LOW_VALUE column identifies the limit. It is therefore a required entry.

RESULTS

This is the main table for storing parameter values. Much consideration was given to what variations may be involved when labs analyze for a parameter, and those considerations resulted in the creation of a complex primary key to accommodate all the variations. The initial primary key fields are obvious because they associate the result with a specific sample: LOC_ID and SAMPLE_NUM. The PARAMETER_ID is another obvious choice. Beyond that, there may be results for different fractions (FRACTION) of the same parameter (total and dissolved), so that's another requirement for the primary key. It's not uncommon for one lab to send a sample to a second lab for a repeated analysis, so the LAB_ID should also be part of the primary key. The lab may choose to repeat an analysis using a different sample prep method (PREP_MTHD) or test method (TEST_MTHD), so these must taken into account as well. And finally, the lab may run an analysis multiple times using the same methods, so the internal ID assigned to each batch must be included as well (LAB_SNUM). If the lab does all these things, the database must be prepared to accommodate all variants. Our primary key is thus an aggregation of eight columns. All of these primary key columns except LAB_SNUM and FRACTION are also either complete or partial foreign keys into other tables. (The WSS database won't have access to the lab's internal sample numbers, so no reference table is possible for LAB_SNUM. The only options for FRACTION are T for total and D for dissolved, so we don't need a lookup table for that.) UNITS is a foreign key, as you would expect, as is DCL_FLAG. MDL and RL refer to the method detection limit and the reporting limit for the analysis. Note that there are two columns for storing the result: PARAM_VALUE and TEXT_VALUE. There is an interesting rationale behind this approach. At first glance, most people will choose to record parameter values in numeric fields. EDDs, however, often report non-detects as less than either the MDL or RL (e.g., <0.05), so if the value is a numeric field, the less than symbol must be stripped off and put in another field. Another EDD from another lab may report non-detects as "ND." In that case, the system must read the MDL or RL (and hope at least one of them is in the EDD) and generate the < symbol itself. That takes care of the non-detects, but there is yet another issue: computers store numbers in binary form, and binary numbers are sometimes inexact representations of the values they represent. When these values are retrieved, you can end up with numbers with obviously too many digits. This creates an issue with implied precision. Our solution to these problems is to store the entered (or imported) value in a text column (TEXT_VALUE). This offers wide latitude in capturing results exactly as they are reported. (Hey, we've even seen EDDs that say a parameter is "presumed present.") If the entry is actually a number, it is also saved in the PARAM_VALUE column. This improves the performance of analyses that process only numbers. When the data are presented back to users through the interface, the text version is used so there is no implied precision – what goes out is what came in. Our final note about this table regards the VAL_QUAL column. The codes for value qualifiers are single characters and this column is five characters. This enables storage of up to five qualifiers for any given result by concatenating all the qualifiers into a single string. This eliminates any option for validation of entries using standard SQL constructs, but it enables the ability to store more data.

SAMPLE_MEDIA

This standard lookup table identifies the various media from which samples are collected (water, soil, sediment, etc.). MEDIUM_CODE is the primary key. Because the medium is a required descriptor in the SAMPLES table, this is another case where the "not indicated" record must be protected.

SAMPLE_TYPE_CODES

Another standard lookup table. SAMPLE_TYPE IS the coded entry and primary key.

Sample Media, Types, and Sources

People who are less familiar with environmental sampling often confuse the meanings of sample media, sample types, and sample sources. These descriptors are linked in various ways but represent different aspects of the analysis.

- The sample medium refers to the physical "stuff" that was collected for analysis – soil, water, air, etc. There are a limited number of possible options for medium regardless of the situation and location.

- The sample source refers to the characteristics of where the sample was collected. The variations available for source are practically limitless and are frequently customized for the focus of a particular system. For instance, you can collect a water sample (medium) from a well, a reservoir, a stream, an industrial plant discharge, etc. A soil sample (medium) can be from a generic source such as "subsurface soil" or a very specific source such as "landfill with liner."
- The sample type refers to the type of analysis for which the sample was collected. (For this reason it is referred to as "analysis type" in some systems.) Here again the number of choices is limited and includes examples such as chemical, physical, radiological, biological survey, etc.

SAMPLES

This table stores all the characteristics for each sampling event. As with all tables, intelligent choice of a primary key is critical. Rather than relying on a sequential number by which to identify samples, the database uses a more meaningful identifier. The SAMPLE_NUM column consists of 17 characters that adhere to a pattern. The first eight characters are the date on which the sample was collected, using the format of year, month, day (e.g., 20210418 for April 18, 2021). The next four characters represent the time at which the sample was collected using a 24-hour clock reference with no colon (e.g., 1415 for 2:15 pm). The final five characters denote the depth at which the sample was collected, using three digits before and one digit after the decimal. The decimal is included. Thus, 010.0 indicates a depth of 10.0 units.[2] When collecting samples for which the depth is irrelevant, a depth of 000.0 is assigned. This sample number by itself contains all the information needed to place the sampling event spatially and temporally – except the location. The primary key for the table is therefore the combination of LOC_ID and SAMPLE_NUM. All the other columns in this table are foreign keys to various tables. A common practice for some categories of sampling activities is to collect samples at different depths and use them to report the vertical distribution of parameter values (reservoir sampling is an example). This is called a vertical profile, and in these cases it is desirable to consider the entire profile as a single event – at least as much as possible. To accommodate this, WSS assigns all the individual samples in the vertical profile to the time at which the profile was started. For instance, a vertical profile at a location called SNDHW1 that was conducted at 8:00 am on March 3, 2020 and included observations at the surface (identified as a depth of 0 by WSS), 2, 5, and 7 m would have SAMPLE_IDs of 202003030800000.0, 202003030800002.0, 202003030800005.0, and 202003030800007.0.

---

[2] Note that there is no specification of whether depths are measured in feet or meters. The assumption throughout the schema is that one or the other is used exclusively. If units are mixed, one or more tables will require modification so that the choice is specified at the appropriate level. For instance, if the choice varies by site, specify the units in the SITES table. If it varies by individual sampling location, specify the units in the LOCATIONS table. If it varies from sample to sample at the same location, then there are bigger issues than how to build a database.

SITES

As noted previously in this chapter, each sampling location is associated with a site. This table is a run-of-the-mill lookup table for site codes and names. The primary key is SITE_ID. The interface must enforce the use of the full three characters for each record since all locations associated with a given site have LOC_ID entries that begin with the site's ID.

SOURCE_CODES

Another lookup table. SOURCE_CODE is the coded value and the primary key.

STATES

This table contains a list of US states and their standard postal abbreviations. POSTAL_STATE is the primary key. Because there are required fields in some other tables that reference POSTAL_STATE, a "not specified" record is required and should be protected from deletion.

STREAM_CODES

For surface water sampling locations, identifying the stream or river on which they are located can be useful for context because a given stream may pass through multiple sites. Impounded areas are best identified by citing the original, unimpounded waterway, but a user may choose to define separate "stream" designations for them if desired. Combining information in STREAMS, LOCATIONS, and HUC_CODES can help identify even broader connectivity. STREAM_CODE is the primary key.

TEST_METHODS

As expected, this is a standard lookup table for the test methods used to evaluate parameter values in samples. TEST_MTHD is the primary key. It's worth noting that some methods may be known by more than one valid identifier. For instance, in the United States, the Environmental Protection Agency (EPA) maintains a publication called "Test Methods for Evaluating Solid Waste: Physical/Chemical Methods." This publication is also known as "SW-846." One example method in this publication is identified as 200.8, which is a method for determining trace elements in water and waste by inductively coupled plasma-mass spectrometry. Some labs will cite the method as "EPA200.8" while others will cite it as "SW846 200.8." If you place importance on this distinction – or simply want to limit what are essentially redundant entries in the test methods table – you could define a test methods alias table similar to the ones we've included for locations and parameters, or you could modify the interface to replace, say, "SW846" with "EPA" in test method citations during data entry and import. As with several other reference tables in the schema, there should be a "not on file" test method that should be protected from deletion. Another special test method that is noteworthy is used to indicate that the value of a parameter was calculated based on values from other known results. The code "CALC" is used as the test method code for this one.

TSI_PARAMETERS

This table is used for evaluation of Carlson's Trophic State Index (TSI) and is some-thing of an anomaly within the schema in that it has no relationships to any other table in the database. Carlson's method utilizes observations of Secchi depth, chlorophyll-a, and phosphorus. This table contains the PARAMETER_IDs for each of these constituents as indicated in the ANALYTES table. It always has exactly one record (and therefore no need of a primary key). There is one column for each constituent. The reason this table has no defined relationships is the same as we've seen in a couple of other cases: SQL will not allow you to define multiple relationships that associate a single column in one table with multiple columns in the same second table. The obvious question is "why bother with creating a table for this ... why not just code these parameter identifiers in the interface?" It's a choice. Doing it this way allows dynamic changes to the parameter numbers if necessary without having to recompile the interface.

TSI_RANGES

The purpose of Carlson's TSI is to assess the trophic state of a reservoir. The meth-odology returns a numeric score. This table translates ranges of TSI scores to more meaningful interpretations (e.g., 56 to 65 means eutrophic). The primary key is LOWER_VAL, which is the lower end of each range. It's up to the user interface to ensure that all possible values (0–100) are present in some range, that no ranges overlap, and that no ranges include values outside these limits. The necessity of this table lies in the literature: multiple studies have suggested that interpretation of the ranges should be tweaked based on characteristics of the region in which the reservoir is located.

TSI_SCORES

This table stores TSI scores after they have been calculated using the interface. TSI scores are typically calculated for conditions at one location on a specific date. It would therefore be reasonable to expect the primary key to be a combination of loca-tion identifier and sample number. However, reservoir sampling frequently involves collecting a vertical profile in which data and grab samples are collected at multiple depths. It may therefore be necessary to cite multiple samples in the profile in order to get valid values for chlorophyll and phosphorus. This means that a single sample ID cannot be cited as the source of data for the TSI score. The column for identifying samples used in calculation of the TSI is therefore SAMPLE_MASK and is only eight characters (the date and time for the profile). Using a different name for the column in this case helps distinguish that it is different from the standard SAMPLE_NUM. The primary key is, then, LOC_ID and SAMPLE_MASK. The other columns in this table contain the individual subscores for the three TSI components and the overall TSI score.

UNITS

This is a very simple table with only one column. UNITS (the column) is therefore the primary key. Its purpose is to provide a list of valid choices for recognized parameter value units. Numerous other tables include a UNITS column, most of which are foreign keys into this table.

VALUE_QUALIFIER_TRANSLATIONS

Our schema includes a table of standard value qualifiers. The labs used by WSS, though, have their own sets of qualifiers. Some qualifiers are the same in all cases by convention (for instance, U has come to designate "not detected"), while others differ between the various labs. For internal consistency, all qualifiers entering the WSS database must have the meanings found in the VALUE_QUALIFIERS lookup table, so this table translates qualifiers found in EDDs to their standard designations. The LAB_ENTRY column is the code indicated in the EDDs from the specified lab. The VAL_QUAL is the equivalent entry in our table. The primary key is the combination of LAB_ID and LAB_ENTRY.

VALUE_QUALIFIERS

This is the table of recognized standard value qualifiers. VAL_QUAL is the coded column and the primary key.

The Access version of this database is available for download from the website that contains supplemental materials. If you would like to create this schema on another platform, another file available for download includes the SQL commands for doing so. If the website is not available for some reason, Appendix B lists those same SQL commands. (The file downloaded from the web contains more INSERT commands and therefore creates more reference data in some of the lookup tables.)

8.4 THE USER INTERFACE

The user interface is a Microsoft Windows desktop program developed using Microsoft's Visual Basic language for .NET (VB.NET). The interface follows the standards for a multi-document interface application, which means there is a main window that serves as a container for other forms and dialogs that perform various functions. The main window has a menu system for selecting specific activities. Selecting a menu option launches the form or dialog that handles the action indicated by the chosen menu option. In most cases, multiple forms may be active at the same time.

The specific code used in the interface for a given purpose should not be considered the only correct way to do things, even when working with VB.NET. The .NET framework offers much flexibility and therefore alternative methods exist for some or all of the processes presented in the code. As noted in Section 8.1, the goal is to provide the reader with guidance regarding how to bridge the gap between users and data. The code is intended to illustrate techniques for data interaction, not to promote specific coding practices.

8.4.1 PRELIMINARY INFORMATION ABOUT WRITING A PROGRAM IN VB.NET

There are a small number of elements of which you need to be aware regarding the structure of a VB.NET program. Some are general .NET elements, while others are specific to accessing data. The following notes will help you grasp the meaning of some of the source code presented in this chapter:

- .NET adheres to the standards and practices of object-oriented programming. This means that a .NET program can create objects or use existing objects. In particular, the .NET framework includes a great many commonly used objects in its various libraries and components. Some of the statements in the interface source code create references to these libraries and components, thus providing the ability to use the objects in our program. In particular, the "Imports" statement at the beginning of a class definition enables use of the objects within the library noted in the statement.

- When connecting to a database platform, .NET programs use a variable called a connection string. The connection string has two parts. The first part identifies the specific DBMS to which connection is to be established – this is called the Provider. The second part identifies the specific instance of the DBMS for the connection – the database. Since we are using the Jet database engine, our database is the particular file to which we are connecting.

- There are two significant types of objects that make up a VB.NET program. The first type is the form object. Form objects are traditionally named as "frmXXX" where XXX is the name of the specific form (e.g., frmStreams). Forms are exactly what the name implies: presentations on the screen that serve as the primary method for connecting data and users. When designing a .NET program, you create forms using two activities. First, you define the appearance of the form. This is most often done through a visual designer of some sort where you draw the form and then add various controls to it by dragging, dropping, and (in some cases) sizing them according to your needs. Second, you create code (subroutines) that handles the various events generated by user interaction with the controls. There are many possible events, but you only have to write code for the ones that require actions related to your objectives. The second object type is called a module. Modules are traditionally named as "modXXX" where XXX signifies either the scope or purpose of the module (e.g., modChapter8). You can consider a module as a form with no visual representation – only code. Modules are used to create variables, functions, and procedures that are available throughout the program.

- The code in each form object consists of functions that handle events that occur for various user interactions with the controls. Because a single subroutine may be appropriate for handling events for more than one control, each event handler accepts two parameters. The first parameter identifies the specific control that generated the event (the class for this parameter is "Object" and the identity is passed as "sender"), and the second one identifies any arguments that are passed by the system that define conditions surrounding the event (the class is "EventArgs" and the name is "e"). The end of the subroutine declaration identifies the specific control and event that invokes the subroutine. This consists of the keyword "Handles" followed by the event(s). Events are specified by the control name, followed by an underscore character, followed by the action that initiates the event. An example is "Handles mnuFileExit_Click." If a procedure handles more than one event, the "Handles" keyword occurs only once and the specific events are separated by commas.

8.4.2 MODCHAPTER8

There is only one module for our interface, named "modChapter8." Its contents are shown in Figure 8.1.

Lines 2 through 5 define public variables that will be available to any process throughout the program. CurDataFile will hold the full path and name of the file that is currently in use. CurPath contains only the path portion of CurDataFile. ConnectionString is used throughout the program to connect the interface to the database. AccessType establishes the capabilities for the current user (see Sections 8.4.3 and 8.4.4 for more information).

Lines 7 through 24 define a subroutine that will be extremely valuable for the successful insertion and retrieval of data. Recall from Chapter 4 that quote characters are used in SQL statements to delineate strings, and as a result, strings that themselves include quote characters can cause problems. The solution is to add a second quote character following the first one. The SQL parser will interpret two consecutive quote characters as a single one that is part of the string itself rather than interpreting the first one as the end of the string. This subroutine accepts a string and then adds a second quote character everywhere a single one exists within the string. It is a good

```
1 Module modchapter8
2      Public CurDataFile As String
3      Public CurPath As String
4      Public Connectionstring As String
5      Public AccessType As String 'if FULL then full access, otherwise read-only
6      |
7      Public Sub InsertDblQuotes(ByRef Instring)
8          Dim EndPos As Integer
9
10         EndPos = Len(Instring)
11         For i = 1 To EndPos
12             If Mid$(Instring, i, 1) = "'" Then
13                 If Mid$(Instring, i + 1, 1) <> "'" Then
14                     Instring = Left(Instring, i) + "'" + Right(Instring, EndPos - i)
15                     EndPos = EndPos + 1
16                     i = i + 1
17                 End If
18             End If
19         Next i
20         If Right(Instring, 1) = "'" Then
21             Instring = Instring & "'"
22         End If
23
24     End Sub
25
26 End Module
```

FIGURE 8.1   modChapter8 is the only module in our program.

idea to call this subroutine any time you generate an SQL command that may include one of these characters.

8.4.3 The Login Process

In Chapters 4 and 6 we discussed different methods for managing user accounts through either a table of users or actual user objects in the database. In Chapter 7 we proposed a simpler alternative when the number of users and/or privilege categories is small. This interface follows the suggestion in Chapter 7, and in fact makes it even simpler. Only three possible privileges are available: system administrator, full access, or read only. Furthermore, the system administrator and full access passwords are coded into the interface as fixed strings. When a user selects "File" then "Open" from the main menu and selects the database, they are prompted to enter a password. If they enter the password that matches one of the strings embedded in the interface code, they are granted the appropriate access. This comparison is case-sensitive. If they enter anything else, they can still open the database but cannot enter new data, edit existing data, or delete data. Note that this allows us to give distinct read-only "passwords" to as many different users as needed.

The decision to differentiate between system administrator and full access privileges allows us to refine the level of control that can be exercised on some activities. In particular, in some cases we want to grant full access users the ability to enter and edit information, but not the ability to delete existing data.

8.4.4 Main Form and Menu Options

The main form (cleverly enough named "frmMain") contains only a single control – a menu strip. Its main purpose is to serve as a container for all the other forms and processes. The menu strip control appears and functions just like you would expect from any Windows program. It contains menu entries on three different levels. The menu structure is summarized in Table 8.1.

Most of the menu items are self-explanatory. One obvious difference from many Windows programs is the lack of "Save," "Save as," and "New" options on the file menu. These are inappropriate for the purpose of this interface. Also of note is that all the first level menu items other than "File" are originally disabled (this is done with a setting when the menu items are created). This avoids any attempts to perform database actions before the database is identified.

The code portion of frmMain is also relatively simple. The only events with which we need to concern ourselves are the click events that occur when the user selects each menu item. A portion of the code for frmMain is shown in Figure 8.2.

The first event handler addresses what happens when the user selects "File" then "Open" (lines 2 through 23). The purpose of this subroutine is to display the standard Windows File Open dialog box in order to solicit the user's choice of which file to open. Lines 3 through 5 set various aspects of the dialog and line 6 then displays the dialog. Lines 7 through 20 are executed only if the user selects a file. Lines 11 through 13 set the values for global variables defined in modChapter8. Lines 15 through 20 then enable the main menu items other than the File menu.

TABLE 8.1
The Menu Structure for Our Interface

Level 1 Items	Level 2 Items Available Under the Level 1 Item	Level 3 Items Available Under the Level 2 Item
File	Open	(None)
	Exit	(None)
Projects	Define Sites and Projects	(None)
Locations	Location Descriptions	(None)
	Location Aliases	(None)
Samples	Field Activities	(None)
	Sample Details	(None)
Results	Results for One Sample	(None)
	Results by Filter	(None)
	Import	(None)
Reports	Table of Results	(None)
	Trophic State Index	(None)
	Exceedances	(None)
Lookup Tables	related to Parameters	Names
		Groups
		Field Form Items
		Parameter Test Methods
		Regulatory Limits
	related to Locations	States and Counties
		Hydrologic Units
		Physiographic Provinces
		Streams
	related to Samples	Collection Methods
		Sample Media
		Sample Types
		Sample Sources
	related to Results	Labs
		Data Confidence Flags
		Prep Methods
		Test Methods
		Units
		Conversion Factors
		Value Qualifiers
Data Maintenance	Bulk Updates	(None)

The second event handler addresses selection of "File" then "Exit." This subroutine consists of a single command that terminates the program.

The remaining subroutines are event handlers for each of the other menu items (that do not themselves have submenus). The structure of each is the same. The first line creates an instance of the form that should be displayed when the menu item is selected. The second line specifies that the new form will be a child form of frmMain. The third line then displays the form.

```
 1 Public Class frmMain
 2     Private Sub mnuFileOpen_Click(sender As Object, e As EventArgs) Handles mnuFileOpen.Click
 3         OpenFileDialog1.CheckFileExists = True
 4         OpenFileDialog1.DefaultExt = "mdb"
 5         OpenFileDialog1.Filter = "WSS Analytical Data File (*.mdb)|*.mdb"
 6         If OpenFileDialog1.ShowDialog() = System.Windows.Forms.DialogResult.OK Then
 7             'get login info
 8             Dim LoginForm As New frmWSSLogin
 9             LoginForm.ShowDialog()
10             'set global variables
11             CurDataFile = OpenFileDialog1.FileName
12             CurPath = Strings.Left(CurDataFile, InStrRev(CurDataFile, "\") - 1)
13             ConnectionString = "Provider=Microsoft.Jet.OLEDB.4.0;Data Source=" & CurDataFile & ";"
14             'enable menu options
15             mnuLocs.Enabled = True
16             mnuProjects.Enabled = True
17             mnuSamples.Enabled = True
18             mnuResults.Enabled = True
19             mnuReports.Enabled = True
20             mnuLUTs.Enabled = True
21         End If
22
23     End Sub
24
25     Private Sub mnuFileExit_Click(sender As Object, e As EventArgs) Handles mnuFileExit.Click
26         End
27     End Sub
28
29     Private Sub mnuLUTResultUnits_Click(sender As Object, e As EventArgs) Handles mnuLUTResultUnits.Click
30         Dim UnitsForm As New frmUnits
31         UnitsForm.MdiParent = Me
32         UnitsForm.Show()
33     End Sub
34
35     *** (Additional code omitted from this Figure) ***
36
37 End Class
```

FIGURE 8.2   A partial code listing for frmMain.

8.4.5   LOOKUP TABLES

We now need to learn more details about how our interface manages data. Rather than jump in with a major activity such as documenting sampling events, we will ease into the process with the simpler forms – those that manage lookup table data. These forms provide a good introduction because they typically manage data for only one table, and the structure of those tables is usually simpler. Let us begin with the form for managing collection methods.

The form for managing sample collection methods is shown in Figure 8.3. The form contains a grid that lists all the records currently in the COLLECTION_METHODS table[3] as well as the standard Windows buttons labeled "Apply," "OK," and "Cancel." When the form opens, it should display the current list of collection methods in the grid. If the user has full access, they should be allowed to enter new methods and edit existing methods. (But we don't want to allow them to delete methods – that

---

[3] We are using the standard .NET DataGridView control. There are numerous other grid controls available for .NET in various third-party libraries, and many of them have features that most users consider superior to the DataGridView (e.g., options for sorting and data selection buttons in column headers). We opted to confine our development to only the standard .NET controls despite potential limitations on interface flexibility. This is consistent with our objective of conveying the concepts of managing data through the user interface rather than creating the most robust user experience.

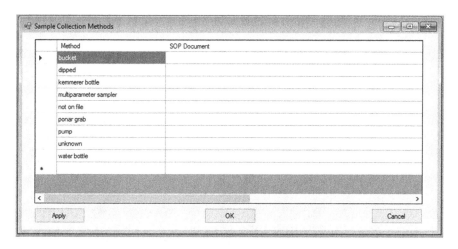

FIGURE 8.3   The form for managing sample collection methods.

capability is reserved for the system administrator privilege.) If the user is limited to read only privileges, we want to disable the "Apply" and "OK" buttons.

Figure 8.4 shows the portions of the code for the collection methods form that handles configuration of the form and one of the typical button click events. Lines 1 and 2 import the required standard .NET class libraries. Lines 5 through 10 define variables that should be accessible to all subroutines on the form. (Lines 6 and 7 in the figure are considered one line from a code standpoint. The underscore character at the end of line 6 signals to VB.NET that the next line is a continuation of the current line.) The form load event is defined in lines 12 through 36. Lines 19 through 25 define the layout of the grid, and lines 27 through 34 set the capabilities of the grid and availability of the buttons based on the current user's privileges. The other lines are related to data access and will be discussed shortly. Lines 38 through 41 define the subroutine that executes when the user clicks the Cancel button. Line 39 is the standard .NET command to close the form, and line 40 disposes of the instance of the form, thus freeing up memory.

Figure 8.5 shows the portions of the code for the form that handle some of the data management activities – the ones that are of most interest to us. The figure shows the code responsible for setting up the grid and displaying data within it. There are two key elements listed in this figure that are used to correlate the database records and the grid data. One is called a Data Adapter; it is associated with the data in the database. There are different classes of data adapters. The specific data adapter for a given situation depends entirely on the DBMS that is to be accessed. In our case, the adapter we need is the one for Jet; that object is called an OleDbDataAdapter. The OleDbDataAdapter is instantiated on lines 6 and 7 as an object named "DA." That line also defines the SELECT statement that returns the set of records loaded into the Data Adapter. The other element is called a Data Table and is not DBMS-specific. The Data Table is associated with the data in the grid. (Keeping these

```
 1 Imports System.IO
 2 Imports System.Data.OleDb
 3
 4 Public Class frmCollect
 5     Dim DBConn As OleDbConnection = New OleDbConnection(ConnectionString)
 6     Dim DA As New OleDbDataAdapter("SELECT collect_mthd, meth_name, sop_doc FROM _
 7     | [COLLECTION_METHODS] order by meth_name", DBConn)
 8     Dim DT As New DataTable
 9     Dim DataChanged As Boolean
10     Dim NextMethTempNum As Integer
11
12     Private Sub frmCollMeths_Load(sender As Object, e As EventArgs) Handles MyBase.Load
13         NextMethTempNum = 500
14
15         Call InitialiseDataAdapter()
16         Call GetData()
17         CollectGrid.DataSource = DT
18         CollectGrid.Refresh()
19         CollectGrid.Columns(0).Width = 25
20         CollectGrid.Columns(0).Visible = False
21         CollectGrid.Columns(1).Width = 200
22         CollectGrid.Columns(2).Width = 1000
23         CollectGrid.Columns(0).HeaderText = "ID"
24         CollectGrid.Columns(1).HeaderText = "Method"
25         CollectGrid.Columns(2).HeaderText = "SOP Document"
26
27         If AccessType = "READ" Then
28             ApplyButton.Enabled = False
29             OKButton.Enabled = False
30             CollectGrid.AllowUserToAddRows = False
31             CollectGrid.AllowUserToDeleteRows = False
32         ElseIf AccessType = "FULL" Then
33             CollectGrid.AllowUserToDeleteRows = False
34         End If
35
36     End Sub
37
38     Private Sub CancelButton_Click(sender As Object, e As EventArgs) Handles CancelButton.Click
39         Me.Close()
40         Me.Dispose()
41     End Sub
42
43 End Class
```

FIGURE 8.4   The non-data sections of the collection methods form code.

assignments in mind – Data Adapter links to the database, Data Table links to the grid – will help you understand the overall process.) The Data Table is created on line 8 as object DT. The GetData() subroutine uses the Data Adapter to fill the Data Table with records specified in the SELECT statement that is included in the Data Adapter definition.

The InitialiseDataAdapter() subroutine configures properties of the Data Adapter. In particular, we need to provide the Data Adapter with specific SQL commands to be executed when insert, update, and delete actions are required. These are defined as OleDbCommand objects on lines 11 through 15. Each command includes placeholders (denoted by question marks in the definition) that will vary for each affected record. The parameters for each command are defined on lines 17 through 24. One parameter must be defined for each question mark in the corresponding definition. The parameters must be defined in the order corresponding to their order in the command definition. For each parameter, a name must be created, the data type and size must be specified, and the source column in the object supplying the data

```
 1 Public Class frmCollect
 2
 3    *** (Much of the code in this Class definition are omitted from this Figure.) ***
 4
 5    Dim DBConn As OleDbConnection = New OleDbConnection(ConnectionString)
 6    Dim DA As New OleDbDataAdapter("SELECT collect_mthd, meth_name, sop_doc _
 7      FROM [COLLECTION_METHODS] order by meth_name", DBConn)
 8    Dim DT As New DataTable
 9
10    Private Sub InitialiseDataAdapter()
11        Dim delete As New OleDbCommand("DELETE FROM [COLLECTION_METHODS] WHERE collect_mthd=?", Me.DBConn)
12        Dim insert As New OleDbCommand("INSERT INTO [COLLECTION_METHODS] (collect_mthd, meth_name, sop_doc) _
13          SELECT MAX(collect_mthd)+1,?,? FROM [COLLECTION_METHODS]", Me.DBConn)
14        Dim update As New OleDbCommand("UPDATE [COLLECTION_METHODS] SET meth_name = ?, sop_doc=? _
15          WHERE collect_mthd = ?", Me.DBConn)
16
17        delete.Parameters.Add("p1", OleDbType.Integer, 4, "collect_mthd")
18
19        insert.Parameters.Add("p1", OleDbType.VarChar, 25, "meth_name")
20        insert.Parameters.Add("p2", OleDbType.VarChar, 255, "sop_doc")
21
22        update.Parameters.Add("p1", OleDbType.VarChar, 25, "meth_name")
23        update.Parameters.Add("p2", OleDbType.VarChar, 255, "sop_doc")
24        update.Parameters.Add("p3", OleDbType.Integer, 4, "collect_mthd")
25
26        Me.DA.DeleteCommand = delete
27        Me.DA.InsertCommand = insert
28        Me.DA.UpdateCommand = update
29
30        Me.DA.MissingSchemaAction = MissingSchemaAction.AddWithKey
31    End Sub
32
33    Private Sub GetData()
34        'Retrieve the data.
35        Me.DA.Fill(Me.DT)
36        DataChanged = False
37    End Sub
38
39 End Class
```

FIGURE 8.5   The sections of the collection methods form code that set up the grid.

must be identified. If the data types used in the parameter definitions don't match those of the columns with which they align in the database, an error will result that aborts the command.

It might clarify things to look at one of the examples in detail. Lines 14 and 15 create the update command for the Data Adapter. The SQL command is stated as

```
UPDATE [COLLECTION_METHODS] SET meth_name=?, sop_
doc=? WHERE collect_mthd=?
```

(The last part of the command definition identifies the data connection with which the Data Adapter is associated. "Me" refers to the current form and "DBConn" is the OleDbConnection object defined on line 5.) There are three question marks in the update command definition, so we need to define three parameters (lines 22 through 24). The first question mark occurs at the point where the UPDATE SQL command expects the value that will be inserted for the METH_NAME column, so the Parameters.Add statement includes these designations:

- name="p1" (The names here have no meaning outside the context of the definition of this specific parameter. For this reason, I typically just number them as shown.)
- data type="OleDbType.VarChar" (OleDbType is an enumeration in the .NET object model that identifies database column data types.)

- size=25 (Together with the data type, this means the parameter will be a VarChar of maximum length 25.)
- column="meth_name" (This refers to the column in the Data Table object.)[4]

The remaining Parameters.Add statements work the same way. The .NET command that updates the Data Adapter loops over the rows of the Data Table (see Figure 8.6), so let's see what happens when a row of the Data Adapter generates an insert action. Let's say the row contains the values 14, "Ponar Grab," and "Ponar.doc." The .NET command performs these actions:

- the first parameter for the UPDATE statement is determined from the "collect_ mthd" column of the Data Table;
- the second parameter for the UPDATE statement is determined from the "sop_ doc" column of the Data Table; and
- the third parameter for the UPDATE statement is determined from the "collect_ mthd" column of the Data Table.

The SQL UPDATE command that gets sent to the Data Adapter therefore becomes

```
UPDATE [COLLECTION_METHODS] SET meth_name='Ponar
Grab', sop_doc='Ponar.doc' WHERE collect_mthd=14
```

which is a valid statement and will execute successfully.[5]

The definition of the Data Adapter's insert command is more interesting. It has only two parameters – those corresponding to the method name and SOP document. To get the method code number, it uses the database's MAX() function to find the highest existing number and increments the value by 1. The INSERT command itself is adding a single record with values for all three columns, so the SELECT part of the command definition generates a set of values consisting of the next available method number, then the two values from the Data Table row – pretty clever. This means that the command ignores the value in the first column of the Data Table entirely. However, because the Data Table columns were created by filling the Data Table with data from the Data Adapter, the data types and other requirements are the same for the corresponding columns. We therefore must supply a value for each new row that gets added to the Data Table. This is accomplished with the NextMethTempNum variable and the GetNextMethNum subroutine, which is the DefaultValuesNeeded event handler for the grid (lines 37 through 41 in Figure 8.6).

---

[4] It can be confusing – especially at first – to assign the same names to the corresponding columns in associated objects. This example might be more clear, for instance, if we had called the columns in the Data Table by other names such as "column1" and so on. Once you understand the interactions between these entities, however, it is better when they have the same name (at least in my opinion). It makes it easier to keep the correspondence straight.

[5] Note that we don't include the terminating semicolon in any of the coded or generated SQL commands in this example. The reason we can omit them is because the .NET objects we have used thus far can only accept and execute a single SQL statement. The purpose of the semicolon in SQL is to designate the end of a statement. Since the statement in each case is known to be one statement in its entirety, no semicolon is necessary. (Also, remember that our DBMS is Jet, and semicolons are always optional in Jet.)

```
 1 Public Class frmCollect
 2
 3    *** (Much of the code in this Class definition are omitted from this Figure.) ***
 4
 5    Private Sub SaveButton_Click(sender As Object, e As EventArgs) Handles ApplyButton.Click
 6       Call SaveData()
 7    End Sub
 8
 9    Private Sub SaveData()
10       If Not DataChanged Then
11          Exit Sub
12       End If
13       'Save the changes
14       Me.DA.Update(Me.DT)
15       DataChanged = False
16    End Sub
17
18    Private Sub CollectGrid_CellContentClick(sender As Object, e As DataGridViewCellEventArgs) _
19       Handles CollectGrid.CellValueChanged
20       DataChanged = True
21    End Sub
22
23    Private Sub OKButton_Click(sender As Object, e As EventArgs) Handles OKButton.Click
24       Dim mAns As DialogResult
25       If DataChanged Then
26          mAns = MsgBox("Save changes before exiting?", MsgBoxStyle.YesNoCancel, "Save Data?")
27          If mAns = DialogResult.Cancel Then
28             Exit Sub
29          ElseIf mAns = DialogResult.Yes Then
30             Call SaveData()
31          End If
32       End If
33       Me.Close()
34       Me.Dispose()
35    End Sub
36    |
37    Private Sub GetNextMethNum(sender As Object, e As DataGridViewRowEventArgs) _
38       Handles CollectGrid.DefaultValuesNeeded
39       e.Row.Cells(0).Value = NextMethTempNum
40       NextMethTempNum = NextMethTempNum + 1
41    End Sub
42
43    Private Sub CollectGrid_ProtectDefault(sender As Object, e As DataGridViewRowCancelEventArgs) _
44       Handles CollectGrid.UserDeletingRow
45       If CollectGrid.SelectedRows(0).Cells(0).Value.ToString = "0" Then
46          e.Cancel = True
47       End If
48    End Sub
49 End Class
```

FIGURE 8.6 Additional code blocks in the collection methods form that perform data management.

The NextMethTempNum is a dummy variable that we initially set to a high value. The value must be sufficiently high to exceed any existing method number. We chose 500 because it is unlikely that WSS will have that many collection methods. The DefaultValuesNeeded event fires when the grid needs a value that is not provided by the user. Our collection method number column in the grid is not displayed because we want the methods sorted alphabetically. So when a new row is added, the required entry in the first column will not be present, hence a default value is needed. The GetNextMethNum subroutine inserts the NextMethTempNum value into the first column and increments the variable. This allows multiple rows to be added to the Data Table in the same session. The original value is meaningless because the Data Adapter actually determines the collection method number when it creates the INSERT statement. Thus, we can reset the GetNextMethNum back to 500 the next time the form is loaded.

The other important data-related subroutine in this class is called CollectGrid_ ProtectDefault (lines 43 through 48) and it handles the event that fires when a user attempts to delete a row. The SAMPLES table is a child of the COLLECTION_ METHODS table, and the collection method column in SAMPLES is required. The default value in the SAMPLES table is 0, which is the coded value for a record in COLLECTION_METHODS that translates to "not on file." We must therefore prevent users from deleting this particular collection method while on this form. (Even though only administrators are allowed to delete rows from this table, we must still prevent them from an unfortunate accident.) The CollectGrid_ProtectDefault subroutine does this, and fires in response to the grid event handler that responds to UserDeletingRow. This routine retrieves the value from the first column of the selected row and compares it to our protected code value. If the value is the important one (0), the delete event is cancelled.

There is one more item worth mentioning before we leave this form. While most of the other variables and subroutines are required, this one is not. It is, however, a good idea. The DataChanged variable can save some time during program execution. It is initialized to False when the form is first loaded. The CollectGrid_CellContentClick subroutine (lines 18 through 21) handles the event that occurs when a cell value in the grid is changed. It simply sets the value of DataChanged to True. The variable is used in the SaveData() subroutine to avoid having to save the data when no changes have occurred. You might be surprised at how much time these types of checks can save.

The same approach described here can be used for many of the other forms for handling lookup tables. Only minor changes are necessary in most cases. For example, the STREAM_CODES table is similar in structure to the COLLECTION_ METHODS table, except that the stream_code column is a text entry to ensure that it contains exactly four digits. As a result, we can apply all the same techniques in this form. The only changes are the syntax of the Data Adapter's insert command (we must format the stream code number) and the code that signifies "not on file."

The UNITS table form introduces an interesting twist. In this case, there is only one column (units) and it is itself the primary key. The challenge is how to properly craft an update command from the data in the grid. If you meant to enter units "mg/kg" but accidentally entered "mg/jg" and needed to subsequently change the entry, the syntax for doing so using an SQL command directly in the database is simple:

```
UPDATE UNITS SET units = 'mg/kg' WHERE units = 'mg/
jg';
```

Figure 8.7 shows the InitialiseDataAdapter subroutine for the units form. We know we need to define the syntax in a Data Adapter update command. We also know that we can use the question mark as a parameter for the command, and then get values from the grid to use as parameter values. In all our examples thus far we've simply retrieved a value from the grid. But in this case, we need the original value that was in the cell, not the current value. Fortunately, the grid control object remembers the original value in the row. All we have to do is to create a second parameter that references the same grid column and set the parameter definition to read the original value rather than the current one. This involves simply adding a second statement that sets the SourceVersion property of the parameter. The lesson here is that the controls

```
1    Private Sub InitialiseDataAdapter()
2        Dim delete As New OleDbCommand("DELETE FROM [UNITS] WHERE units=?", Me.DBConn)
3        Dim insert As New OleDbCommand("INSERT INTO [UNITS] (units) VALUES (?)", Me.DBConn)
4        Dim update As New OleDbCommand("UPDATE [UNITS] SET units = ? WHERE units = ?", Me.DBConn)
5
6        delete.Parameters.Add("p1", OleDbType.VarChar, 15, "units")
7
8        insert.Parameters.Add("p1", OleDbType.VarChar, 15, "units")
9
10       update.Parameters.Add("p1", OleDbType.VarChar, 15, "units")
11       update.Parameters.Add("p2", OleDbType.VarChar, 15, "units")
12       update.Parameters("p2").SourceVersion = DataRowVersion.Original
13
14       Me.DA.DeleteCommand = delete
15       Me.DA.InsertCommand = insert
16       Me.DA.UpdateCommand = update
17
18       Me.DA.MissingSchemaAction = MissingSchemaAction.AddWithKey
19   End Sub
```

FIGURE 8.7   The InitialiseDataAdapter subroutine for the units form.

you use in your interface need to be capable of managing typical data manipulation processes.

This technique of utilizing the original value in the Data Table can be applied to all our lookup tables that have non-sequential primary keys and for which a grid-based form is appropriate: test methods, states, hydrologic units, sample media, sample sources, sample types, data confidence flags, prep methods, and value qualifiers. We leave it as an exercise for the reader to create these forms in the Chapter 8 user interface (if so inclined).

Grid-based management of lookup tables is sufficient in many cases but not all. If a table has a large number of columns or is likely to include either a large number of rows, a tabular presentation can be overwhelming to users. An alternative method in these cases involves offering the user a list of items from which to choose. When a selection is made, data for the selected item is displayed in individual controls tailored to the entry or modification of each column. The interface program uses this approach for editing information about parameters. The form is shown in Figure 8.8.

The code behind this form utilizes the same Data Adapter object for saving data that we used in the grid-based forms, but instead of using a Table Adapter connected to a grid for interacting with the user, this approach uses more traditional text boxes. When a user selects an item from the list, the controls are updated using a new object called a DataReader. The overall result is that the code required to perform this interaction has more of the characteristics of traditional programming than our previous examples. Figure 8.9 shows the code that creates the dropdown list of parameter names.

The user chooses the parameter of interest from one of two dropdown lists at the top of the form. One list shows parameters sorted by number, and the other shows parameters sorted by name. The GetIDLists subroutine loads the contents of the selection lists. The primary key of the PARAMETERS table is the PARAMETER_ ID column, so we need an array that parallels the parameter name dropdown list and associates each parameter name item with its ID. In order to dimension that array, we need to know how many records are in the table. We accomplish this using a SELECT COUNT query. An OleDbConnection object is created on line 8 using the established

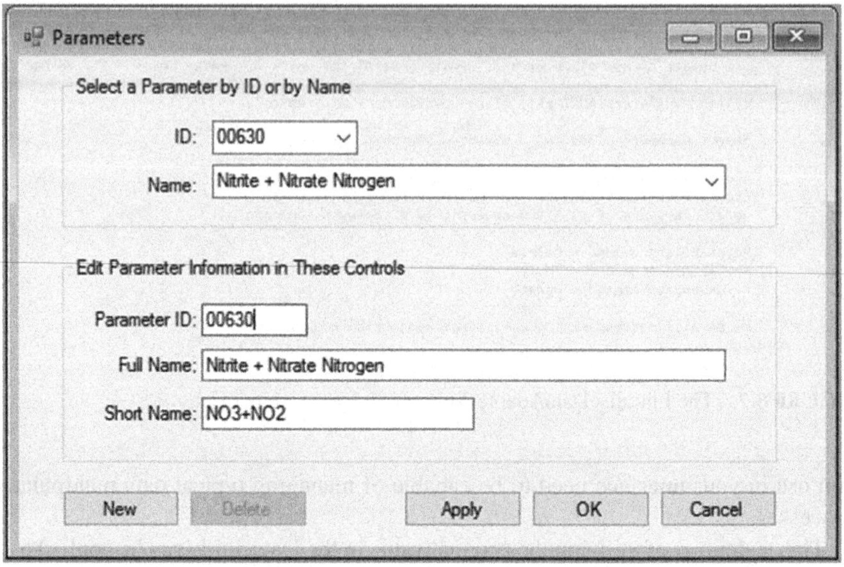

FIGURE 8.8   The form for managing information about parameters.

connection string. On line 9, an OleDbCommand object is created – the same object we previously used to create insert, update, and delete commands. Unlike before, we don't have to identify any query parameters because the command is simply a SELECT statement that retrieves all records. The new object – the DataReader – is created on line 11. That same line populates the Data Reader by executing the OleDbCommand's query. The Data Reader object is what is called a "forward only" data object, meaning that the data it retrieves can be accessed one record at a time, but only in the forward direction – you can't go back to records that have already been accessed. This type of object is common on other development platforms as well. They are used often and are popular due to their speed. We know from our experience with SQL that a query using SELECT COUNT will return only one record, so we obtain that record by issuing the Data Reader's Read method on line 12. We then use the results of the COUNT to dimension the parameter ID array. (It is dimensioned as one less than the number of records because the dropdown list element numbers start at 0.) The rest of the "Using" code block closes the various objects and disposes of them (lines 14 through 17). Next we repeat the process, this time retrieving all the parameter records in alphanumeric order. Our Data Reader object now has multiple records, so instead of requesting a single Read, we construct a loop (lines 28 through 32). Each parameter name is inserted into the dropdown list, and each parameter ID is inserted into the parallel ID array. The loop terminates automatically when the last record has been accessed. We then make a second pass through the PARAMETERS table, this time loading the parameter IDs into the ID list (not shown in the figure).

  We need the two selection lists to work in tandem – selecting an item from either list should automatically update the position of the other list to the corresponding

```
 1│   Private Sub GetIDLists()
 2        Dim QString As String
 3        Dim i As Integer
 4        Dim NumRecs As Integer
 5
 6        'get the number of existing parameter records
 7        QString = "SELECT COUNT(*) AS rc FROM [ANALYTES]"
 8        Using data1 As New OleDbConnection(ConnectionString)
 9            Dim d1cmd As New OleDbCommand(QString, data1)
10            data1.Open()
11            Dim DataReader As OleDbDataReader = d1cmd.ExecuteReader
12            DataReader.Read()
13            NumRecs = DataReader.GetValue(DataReader.GetOrdinal("rc"))
14            DataReader.Close()
15            DataReader.Dispose()
16            data1.Close()
17            data1.Dispose()
18            ReDim ParamNameIDs(NumRecs - 1)
19        End Using
20        'load the parameters into the list
21        i = 0
22        ParamNameList.Items.Clear()
23        QString = "SELECT * FROM [ANALYTES] ORDER BY anl_name"
24        Using data1 As New OleDbConnection(ConnectionString)
25            Dim d1cmd As New OleDbCommand(QString, data1)
26            data1.Open()
27            Dim DataReader As OleDbDataReader = d1cmd.ExecuteReader
28            Do While DataReader.Read()
29                ParamNameList.Items.Add(DataReader.GetValue(DataReader.GetOrdinal("anl_name")))
30                ParamNameIDs(i) = DataReader.GetValue(DataReader.GetOrdinal("parameter_id"))
31                i = i + 1
32            Loop
33            DataReader.Close()
34            DataReader.Dispose()
35            data1.Close()
36            data1.Dispose()
37        End Using
38        i = 0
39
40        *** (Code for loading the parameter number list is similar and is omitted here)
41
42    End Sub
```

FIGURE 8.9 The code that creates the parameter name dropdown list on the parameter data form.

item. Selection from either list should also retrieve the data for the parameter and display the information in the boxes. Once the lists are linked programmatically, we need only create code for record selection in the parameter ID list. Code that links the two lists and retrieves the data for display is shown in Figure 8.10. The ParamNumList_Selection subroutine repositions the parameter name list to the name corresponding to the selected parameter number (lines 9 through 17). Repositioning the parameter name list results in the execution of the ParamNameList_Selection subroutine. But selecting an element from the parameter name list repositions the parameter number list as well (lines 48 through 54). Without additional control, this would set up an endless loop where each procedure calls the other repeatedly. The ProcessClick Boolean variable prevents this from happening. The ParamNumList_ Selection routine updates controls on the form to display the contents of the selected record. This code uses another DataReader object, once again retrieving a single record. The ParamNameList_Selection subroutine simply forces selection of the corresponding parameter in the ID list, triggering the ParamNumList_Selection subroutine.

```
1   Private Sub ParamNumList_Selection(sender As Object, e As EventArgs) Handles ParamNumList.SelectedIndexChanged
2       Dim QString As String
3       Dim i As Integer
4
5       If ParamNumList.SelectedIndex = -1 Then
6           Exit Sub
7       End If
8
9       CurParamID = ParamNumList.Text
10      'update the name list item
11      ProcessClick = False
12      For i = 0 To UBound(ParamNameIDs)
13          If ParamNameIDs(i) = CurParamID Then
14              ParamNameList.SelectedIndex = i
15              Exit For
16          End If
17      Next
18      ProcessClick = True
19      'common form info
20      QString = "SELECT * FROM [ANALYTES] WHERE parameter_id='" & CurParamID & "'"
21      Using data1 As New OleDbConnection(ConnectionString)
22          Dim d1cmd As New OleDbCommand(QString, data1)
23          data1.Open()
24          Dim DataReader As OleDbDataReader = d1cmd.ExecuteReader
25          DataReader.Read()
26          ParamIDBox.Text = CurParamID
27          FullNameBox.Text = DataReader.GetValue(DataReader.GetOrdinal("anl_name"))
28          ShortNameBox.Text = DataReader.GetValue(DataReader.GetOrdinal("anl_short"))
29          DataReader.Close()
30          DataReader.Dispose()
31          data1.Close()
32          data1.Dispose()
33      End Using
34
35      RecMode = "EDIT"
36      DataChanged = False
37
38  End Sub
39
40  Private Sub ParamNameList_Selection(sender As Object, e As EventArgs) Handles ParamNameList.SelectedIndexChanged
41      Dim i As Integer
42
43      If Not ProcessClick Or ParamNameList.SelectedIndex = -1 Then
44          Exit Sub
45      End If
46
47      i = 0
48      For Each AItem In ParamNumList.Items
49          If AItem.ToString = ParamNameIDs(ParamNameList.SelectedIndex) Then
50              ParamNumList.SelectedIndex = i
51              Exit For
52          End If
53          i = i + 1
54      Next
55  End Sub
```

FIGURE 8.10   This code creates interaction between the two dropdown lists to select a record.

In addition to the standard Apply, OK, and Cancel buttons, these forms also require explicit buttons to initiate the processes of creating a new record and deleting an existing record. Figure 8.11 shows the code for handling the click events for three of the buttons. The OK and Cancel button handlers on this form are identical to the ones on the grid-based forms and so are omitted from the figure. The Apply button is similar to other iterations, except that it rereads the selection list and repositions it to the currently chosen item, if applicable (lines 12 through 20). The Delete button calls the SaveData procedure, which then deletes the current record. It then clears all the text boxes, reloads the parameter lists, and sets each list to reflect nothing is selected. The New button clears the text boxes for new input and places the cursor in the parameter ID box (line 43).

The SaveData subroutine (Figure 8.12) commits our changes to the database. It uses our now familiar Data Adapter, but in a different mode than what we've seen before. On our forms with grids, requesting that the Table Adapter's records be saved to the database triggers accessing the Data Adapter for each record. For

```
1      Private Sub ApplyButton_Click(sender As Object, e As EventArgs) Handles ApplyButton.Click
2          Dim CancelIt As Boolean
3          Dim i As Integer
4
5          CurParamID = ParamIDBox.Text
6          If DataChanged Then
7              Call SaveData(CancelIt)
8              If CancelIt Then
9                  Exit Sub
10             End If
11         End If
12         Call GetIDLists()
13         i = 0
14         For Each AItem In ParamNumList.Items
15             If AItem.ToString = CurParamID Then
16                 ParamNumList.SelectedIndex = i
17                 Exit For
18             End If
19             i = i + 1
20         Next
21     End Sub
22
23     Private Sub DeleteButton_Click(sender As Object, e As EventArgs) Handles DeleteButton.Click
24         Dim CancelIt As Boolean
25
26         RecMode = "DELETE"
27         Call SaveData(CancelIt)
28         'reset controls to empty
29         ParamIDBox.Text = ""
30         FullNameBox.Text = ""
31         ShortNameBox.Text = ""
32         RecMode = ""
33         Call GetIDLists()
34         ParamNameList.SelectedIndex = -1
35         ParamNumList.SelectedIndex = -1
36     End Sub
37
38     Private Sub NewButton_Click(sender As Object, e As EventArgs) Handles NewButton.Click
39         'reset controls to empty
40         ParamIDBox.Text = ""
41         FullNameBox.Text = ""
42         RecMode = "ADD"
43         ParamIDBox.Select()
44     End Sub
```

FIGURE 8.11   Subroutines for handling click events of buttons on the parameters form.

this reason, we had to create commands in the Data Adapter to handle INSERT, UPDATE, and DELETE events. On the parameter form we utilize the Data Adapter's ExecuteNonQuery method. This is appropriate for issuing specific SQL commands that do not return records (hence the "nonquery" portion of the name). In this case, we build a string that defines the SQL command to be executed based on how we got here (lines 16 through 30). We use a string variable called RecMode to identify whether our current activity should insert a new record, edit an existing record, or delete a record. The New and Delete buttons set the RecMode variable to "ADD" and "DELETE" respectively. Selecting a parameter from one of the selections list sets the mode to "EDIT."

We use the same method for lab information. Figure 8.13 shows portions of the code behind the form for managing lab data that contain noteworthy differences from the parameter information form. The lab data form uses only one selection list, which contains a list of lab names. As before, the LabList_Selection subroutine displays the data in the text boxes and other controls on the form. The assignment of the record values to the controls is similar to that on the parameters form, except for liberal use

```
1    Private Sub SaveData(ByRef bCancel As Boolean)
2        'update data based on control settings
3        Dim QString As String
4        Dim CT As OleDbConnection
5        Dim DA As OleDbDataAdapter = New OleDbDataAdapter()
6
7        If (RecMode = "ADD" Or RecMode = "EDIT") And (ParamIDBox.Text = "" Or FullNameBox.Text = "" _
8            Or ShortNameBox.Text = "") Then
9            MsgBox("Entries are required in all identification boxes.", MsgBoxStyle.OKOnly, "Cannot Save")
10           bCancel = True
11           Exit Sub
12       End If
13
14       bCancel = False
15
16       If RecMode = "EDIT" Then
17           'update existing data
18           QString = "UPDATE [ANALYTES] SET "
19           QString = QString & "parameter_id='" & ParamIDBox.Text & "', "
20           QString = QString & "anl_name='" & FullNameBox.Text & "', "
21           QString = QString & "anl_short='" & ShortNameBox.Text & "'"
22       ElseIf RecMode = "ADD" Then
23           'update existing data
24           QString = "INSERT INTO [ANALYTES] (parameter_id, anl_name, anl_short) VALUES ("
25           QString = QString & "'" & ParamIDBox.Text & "', "
26           QString = QString & "'" & FullNameBox.Text & "', "
27           QString = QString & "'" & ShortNameBox.Text & "')"
28       ElseIf RecMode = "DELETE" Then
29           QString = "DELETE FROM [ANALYTES] WHERE parameter_id='" & ParamIDBox.Text & "'"
30       End If
31       CT = New OleDbConnection(ConnectionString)
32       CT.Open()
33       DA.UpdateCommand = CT.CreateCommand
34       DA.UpdateCommand.CommandText = QString
35       DA.UpdateCommand.ExecuteNonQuery()
36       DA.Dispose() 'necessary because an open connection may inhibit availability of the latest data
37       CT.Dispose()
38       DataChanged = False
39       RecMode = ""
40   End Sub
```

FIGURE 8.12   The SaveData subroutine from the parameters form.

of the IsDBNull function. Recall from Chapter 4 that NULLs must be handled carefully in databases, and this is an example of why. For each non-required column in the table, we must anticipate that the column value will be NULL in order to avoid errors. A programming statement such as

```
If DataReader.GetValue(DataReader.
GetOrdinal("contact_name"))=""
```

would evaluate to FALSE in all cases because NULL is not the same as an empty string. The other noteworthy difference is in the SaveData subroutine. Here we must explicitly set columns to NULL if no value is present in the associated control when editing in order to ensure that existing data is purged. Standard practice is also to explicitly set columns to NULL if no value is provided during an INSERT operation.

It might seem logical to use this same approach for all of the remaining lookup table forms in the interface (i.e., all the ones we did not identify when discussing grid-based editing), and in fact this would be an acceptable approach. However, our preference would be to apply this method only to the parameters, labs, and conversion factors tables.

For the remaining lookup tables, we have an opportunity to introduce more complex forms that manage data in more meaningful ways. For instance, we can create forms that involve data from multiple tables. The form for defining and managing parameter groups is a good example. The form is shown in Figure 8.14.

```
 1   Private Sub LabList_Selection(sender As Object, e As EventArgs) Handles LabList.SelectedIndexChanged
 2
 3   *** (code removed here) ***
 4
 5           LabIDBox.Text = CurLabID
 6           LabNameBox.Text = DataReader.GetValue(DataReader.GetOrdinal("lab_name"))
 7           If Not IsDBNull(DataReader.GetValue(DataReader.GetOrdinal("contact_name"))) Then
 8               ContactNameBox.Text = DataReader.GetValue(DataReader.GetOrdinal("contact_name"))
 9           Else
10               ContactNameBox.Text = ""
11           End If
12
13   *** (code removed here) ***
14
15   End Sub
16
17   Private Sub SaveData(ByRef bCancel As Boolean)
18
19   *** (code removed here) ***
20
21       If RecMode = "EDIT" Then
22           'update existing data
23           QString = "UPDATE [LABS] SET "
24           QString = QString & "lab_id='" & LabIDBox.Text & "', "
25           QString = QString & "lab_name='" & LabNameBox.Text & "', "
26           If ContactNameBox.Text <> "" Then
27               QString = QString & "contact_name='" & ContactNameBox.Text & "', "
28           Else
29               QString = QString & "contact_name=NULL, "
30           End If
31
32   *** (code removed here) ***
33
34       ElseIf RecMode = "ADD" Then
35           'update existing data
36           QString = "INSERT INTO [LABS] (lab_id, lab_name, contact_name, address1, address2, city, _
37            state, zip, comments) VALUES ("
38           QString = QString & "'" & LabIDBox.Text & "', "
39           QString = QString & "'" & LabNameBox.Text & "', "
40           If ContactNameBox.Text <> "" Then
41               QString = QString & "'" & ContactNameBox.Text & "', "
42           Else
43               QString = QString & "NULL, "
44           End If
45
46   *** (code removed here) ***
47
48       ElseIf RecMode = "DELETE" Then
49           QString = "DELETE FROM [LABS] WHERE lab_id='" & LabIDBox.Text & "'"
50       End If
51
52   *** (code removed here) ***
53
54   End Sub
```

FIGURE 8.13   Snippets of code from the lab data form's selection list handler and SaveData routine.

The list of existing parameter groups is at the top of the form and is used to select a group for editing or deletion. When an existing group is chosen, the text boxes are updated to show the abbreviation, name, and short name of the group. All this information comes from the ANALYTE_GROUPS table. However, we also display the group's members (from the ANALYTE_GROUP_ELEMENTS table) as well. They are shown in a grid similar to the ones on some of the other lookup table forms. Another grid on the form contains the names of all the parameters present in the database. We code the form so that double-clicking a parameter in the "All Parameters" grid adds the selected parameter to the current group (after first confirming that it is not already a member of the group). Conversely, double-clicking a parameter in the "Parameters in this Group" grid removes it from the group. Each parameter within the group is also assigned specific units, so a dropdown list of all the units is available.

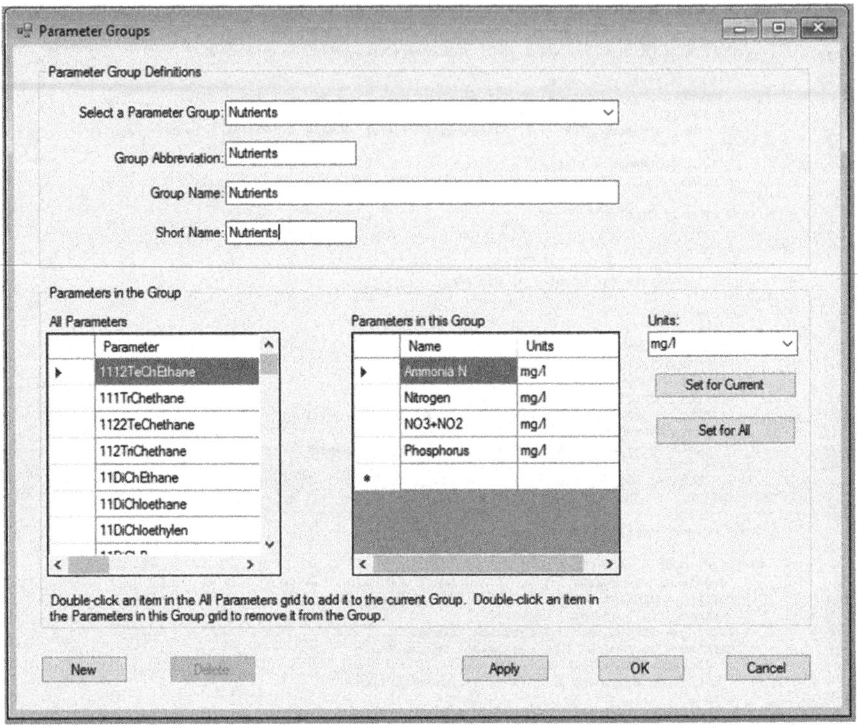

FIGURE 8.14 The form for managing groups of parameters.

Users select the desired units and click one button to establish the selection as the units for the parameter in the current row of the group parameters grid, or another button to assign the units to all parameters in the group. Thus, this form is used both to define the group and identify all its members.

Most of the code behind this form follows the same patterns we've seen on other forms. The most unique characteristic of the controls on this form is that the group parameters grid is not tied to a data set in either of the ways we've seen thus far. Grids operating in this mode are called unbound grids because they are not directly linked to either a Data Table object in the interface or a table in the database. Some of the code for managing this grid is shown in Figure 8.15.

The columns in the grid are established in the form's Load event handler (not shown in Figure 8.15) with a few simple lines of code. The first line establishes the number of columns in the grid (3). The next three lines provide names for each of the columns (ID, name, and units), and the last line hides the first column. That column contains the parameter code, which the user does not need to see. The contents of the name column will not be saved in the ANALYTE_GROUP_ELEMENTS table, but the column does serve the vital role of informing the user of the name of the parameter whose ID is in the first column. The GroupNameList_Selection subroutine updates the controls on the form when a group is chosen. The portions of that subroutine related to the group parameters grid are shown in lines 4 through 16 of Figure 8.15. Line 4 removes any existing data from the grid. Lines 5 through 7 define the query

```
1    Private Sub GroupNameList_Selection(sender As Object, e As EventArgs) Handles _
2        GroupNameList.SelectedIndexChanged
3        ......
4        GroupParamsGrid.Rows.Clear()
5        QString = "SELECT [ANALYTE_GROUP_ELEMENTS].parameter_id, anl_short, units _
6            FROM [ANALYTE_GROUP_ELEMENTS] INNER JOIN [ANALYTES] ON [ANALYTES].parameter_id= _
7            [ANALYTE_GROUP_ELEMENTS].parameter_id WHERE group_code='" & CurGroupID & "' ORDER BY anl_short"
8        Using data1 As New OleDbConnection(ConnectionString)
9            ......
10           Do While DataReader.Read
11               Dim rowId As Integer = GroupParamsGrid.Rows.Add()
12               Dim row As DataGridViewRow = GroupParamsGrid.Rows(rowId)
13               row.Cells(0).Value = DataReader.GetValue(DataReader.GetOrdinal("parameter_id"))
14               row.Cells(1).Value = DataReader.GetValue(DataReader.GetOrdinal("anl_short"))
15               row.Cells(2).Value = DataReader.GetValue(DataReader.GetOrdinal("units"))
16           Loop
17           ......
18    End Sub
19    Private Sub AllParamsGrid_CellMouseDoubleClick(sender As Object, e As DataGridViewCellMouseEventArgs) _
20        Handles AllParamsGrid.CellMouseDoubleClick
21        ......
22        If e.RowIndex > -1 AndAlso e.ColumnIndex > -1 Then
23            PNum = AllParamsGrid.Rows(e.RowIndex).Cells(0).Value.ToString
24            PName = AllParamsGrid.Rows(e.RowIndex).Cells(1).Value.ToString
25            For i = 0 To GroupParamsGrid.RowCount - 2
26                If GroupParamsGrid.Rows(i).Cells(0).Value = PNum Then
27                    MsgBox("That parameter is already in this group.", MsgBoxStyle.OkOnly, "Cannot Add")
28                    Exit Sub
29                End If
30            Next
31            Dim rowId As Integer = GroupParamsGrid.Rows.Add()
32            Dim row As DataGridViewRow = GroupParamsGrid.Rows(rowId)
33            row.Cells(0).Value = PNum
34            row.Cells(1).Value = PName
35            row.Cells(2).Value = ""
36        End If
37        ......
38    End Sub
39    Private Sub AddCurrentUnitsButton_Click(sender As Object, e As EventArgs) Handles AddCurrentUnitsButton.Click
40        ......
41        GroupParamsGrid.CurrentRow.Cells(2).Value = UnitsList.Text
42    End Sub
43    Private Sub AddAllButton_Click(sender As Object, e As EventArgs) Handles AddAllButton.Click
44        ......
45        For i = 0 To GroupParamsGrid.RowCount - 2
46            GroupParamsGrid.Rows(i).Cells(2).Value = UnitsList.Text
47        Next
48    End Sub
49    Private Sub GroupParamsGrid_CellMouseDoubleClick(sender As Object, e As DataGridViewCellMouseEventArgs) _
50        Handles GroupParamsGrid.CellMouseDoubleClick
51        If e.RowIndex > -1 AndAlso e.ColumnIndex > -1 Then
52            GroupParamsGrid.Rows.RemoveAt(GroupParamsGrid.CurrentRow.Index)
53        End If
54    End Sub
```

FIGURE 8.15　Code associated with the group parameters grid.

that will retrieve the data required to populate the grid. An OleDbDataReader object
is instantiated and initialized in code that is not shown. Lines 10 through 16 then loop
over the records returned by the Data Reader. Line 11 creates a new row in the grid.
This procedure returns an integer value that identifies the row number of the newly
added row. Line 12 creates a DataGridViewRow object that is tied to the newly added
row. Lines 13 through 15 then insert values from the DataReader into the cells in the
row. The GroupParamsGrid_CellMouseDoubleClick subroutine has the simple job
of removing the selected row from the group parameters grid, which is accomplished
on line 52. Double-clicking the All Parameters grid adds the selected parameter to the
group parameters grid, which is a little more complex (lines 19 through 38). First, the
values in the selected row are copied to variables (lines 23 and 24). Lines 25 through
30 examine the current rows of the group parameters grid and abort the procedure if
the selected parameter is already present. If not, lines 31 through 35 add the selected
parameter using the same process as that found in the GroupNameList_Selection subroutine. The buttons to update units in the group parameters grid set one or all values
in the third column, as shown on lines 46 and 52.

Saving the data in the group parameters grid can be a little tricky. We don't know specifically if new rows were added, existing rows were modified, or some rows were deleted. The very traditional approach to managing this situation requires two passes through the data. The first pass loops over the rows in the grid as it exists at the time data are saved. For each row, the parameter ID is obtained and the database table is queried to determine if a matching record exists. If so, the units are updated according to the grid value; if not, a new record is added to the database table using the values in the row. The second pass then retrieves all the database records and checks to see if each one is in the grid. If a database record is not present in the grid, it is deleted. There is no need to update units during this pass because those actions would have already been taken during the first pass. This is a thorough method but requires a bit of coding. Instead, our SaveData subroutine (not shown) takes an approach that is far less subtle but just as effective: all out, all in. By that we mean that we first delete all the existing records in the database table, then simply loop over the grid and add new records accordingly. It's a brute force approach, but it requires less code.

For what it's worth, the grid that contains the list of all parameters is loaded using a traditional DataSet object and the methods we've discussed on other forms.

Similar forms can be developed for the remaining lookup table menu items.

8.4.6 PROJECT AND SITE INFORMATION

The code examples in Section 8.4.5 illustrate the basic approaches to coding the processes of reading data from the database, presenting it to the user, and then saving back to the database. We've covered those abilities well enough that further presentation and dissection of code snippets should no longer be necessary. Instead, as we move beyond the basic lookup tables and into more complex aspects of the data model, we can now focus on describing the visual and operational aspects of interacting with the users. We begin with information about projects and sites.

This is a good choice for our first primary data form because of the relative simplicity of the tables. Given how these two tables interact, we can construct a form that bears some similarity with the parameter groups form both in appearance and function. The proposed form has two tabs, as shown in Figure 8.16. The first tab manages the project information. There are dropdown lists that allow a user to select a project either by name or by project number. The two lists should work in tandem just like the ones on the parameter information form. In that case, the user selected a parameter using one of

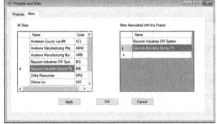

FIGURE 8.16   A potential form with two tabs for managing project and site information.

the lists and then edited the information in a series of list boxes. The projects table, however, contains only the two columns presented in the lists. The dropdown lists are actually combo boxes that allow editing directly in the list. Thus, the user can select an item from either list and edit all information about the selected project using just these two controls. The tab has its own set of standard buttons that behave as you would expect.

The second tab manages data for two different tables: SITES and PROJECT_SITES. Data for each table is presented in a grid. The grid on the left manages the SITES table. The two columns in this grid represent the entire SITES table. The grid on the right identifies the sites associated with the current project. These grids can be programmed to respond to the double-click events described for the parameter groups form. Because the user can intrinsically add and delete rows from each grid, no explicit New and Delete buttons are required on this tab. The form as described offers a very efficient method for users to enter a new project, define new sites as required, and assign the sites to the project all on the same form.

8.4.7 LOCATION INFORMATION

Next we move on to the forms for managing information about locations. First let us consider the primary form for records in the LOCATIONS table. This is another relatively simple form – the function is simply to provide a way to select a location and then offer controls to modify the descriptors as needed. Still, we have some ideas for improving the user experience, even on a form as straightforward as this. We propose a form with four tabbed sections, as shown in Figure 8.17.

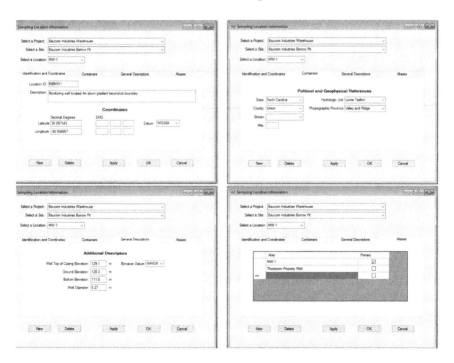

FIGURE 8.17   Our proposed form for managing location information has four tabs.

The process of selecting a location for editing follows the same logical data path that we would use in the real world: we need to know the site, and the site is associated with a project. We therefore require three steps to select the location. First, we choose a project from the top list. This loads all the sites associated with the project into the second list. Next, we choose the desired site, which in turn populates the list of sampling locations with all the ones from the selected site. This process offers our first opportunity for lightening the load the user must bear. If a project has only a single site, we can auto-select that site when the user selects the project. Likewise, if a site has only one sampling location, we can auto-select that as well.

All the controls within the tabbed areas of the form are updated when a location is chosen. The first tab displays the full ID for the location (this includes the first three characters, which identify the site), the location description (contents of the LOC_ DESC column), and the coordinate information. The code behind the location ID text box must prevent the user from modifying the first three characters, since this would signify assignment to a different site (which is not permitted). Regarding coordinates, recall that we store the latitude and longitude in decimal degrees in the database, as shown in Figure 8.17. Note, however, the set of boxes under the "DMS" heading. These allow users to enter the coordinates in degrees, minutes, and seconds (yes, there are still some techniques for determining coordinates in these terms). As entries are made in the DMS boxes, the decimal degree equivalents are calculated and used to update the boxes associated with the stored data.

The next tab displays political and geophysical boundaries that serve as containers for the sampling location. The state and county dropdown lists should be linked so that selecting a state populates the list of counties appropriately. The hydrologic unit and physiographic province (not required) dropdowns are self-explanatory. The stream references (water body name and river mile) are only appropriate for locations found in rivers, streams, lakes, and reservoirs.

The controls on the General Descriptors tab are mostly for locations that are wells of some sort, although the bottom elevation may also be appropriate for surface water sampling locations. The last tab shows all the common names (aliases) by which the location is known. One and only one alias may be designated as the primary alias. We have not defined a mechanism in the database to impose this restriction, so the code for the grid should enforce it. Other than that, the code behind this grid is relatively standard stuff. And finally, the buttons at the bottom of the form perform the usual functions and are coded much like previous examples already discussed.

The form and its controls interact with all the columns in both the LOCATIONS and LOCATION_ALIASES tables and do so in an obvious manner. The only consideration remaining is to ponder what other manipulations we can make in the code behind this form that will improve the user experience. Not a lot of options come immediately to mind, but there is one. We know that the presence of values in some of the descriptors columns is dictated by the type of location – in particular, wells and surface water locations. We opted not to define a column in the LOCATIONS table that specifies location type, but we could reconsider that now (which would require a new lookup table of location types). If we were to implement this change, the logical place to put the location type dropdown list would be immediately to the right of the location ID text box. Selection of certain location types might suggest manipulating some of the controls on the form to improve data entry. For example, if the location type is stream or reservoir, the controls on the Additional Descriptors tab that are not collected for this type of location (top of well casing, ground elevation, and well diameter) could be disabled or hidden. Similarly, if the location type is some form of well, the stream dropdown and river mile box are inappropriate.

The main menu of the interface offers one additional submenu choice related to locations: management of location aliases. This form is not absolutely necessary since management of aliases is performed on the main locations dialog. However, the use of the main form requires selection of each affected location in turn to enter or edit the aliases for each. The objective of the location aliases management form is to provide a single point of entry for multiple aliases related to all locations within a particular site. This is a courtesy to the user who may be tasked with defining multiple common names for many locations as quickly as possible (this is a common task during initial entry of data for a site). We leave it as an exercise for the reader to develop a form appropriate for accomplishing this task.

8.4.8 Sampling Events

Documentation of sampling events can occur during import of laboratory EDDs or other electronic files (see Section 8.4.9). However, in many cases, physical observations made during sample collection may be documented using more traditional methods such as field forms or log books. For this reason, a method for manually creating sampling events is essential. (Even if not explicitly required because of field observations, documenting sampling events prior to receipt of data from a lab can serve a valuable QA function.) A possible form for documenting sample collection activities is shown in Figure 8.18.

As you would expect, the dropdown lists beginning at the top of the form identify the location at which the sampling event occurred by drilling down through the project and site. As discussed in Section 8.4.7, we should apply the same automatic selections when only a single option exists for the next level items. Specification of the date and time at which the sample was collected could be done through simple text boxes. Using text boxes, however, imposes on the developer the necessity of writing validation code to ensure entries can be properly interpreted. Like many development frameworks, .NET offers controls specifically for selecting dates and times that eliminate the entry validation requirements. These both ease the burden on the developer and present the user with an easy alternative.

Recall that we generate our internal sample identifiers based on the date, time, and depth at which the sample was collected. A common practice when sampling reservoir or lake locations is to measure values at discrete depths from the surface to the bottom (a vertical profile). To facilitate assembly of the vertical data for analysis and presentation, best practice is to assign all samples in the profile to the same time. Each sample in the vertical profile then differs only in the depth portion of the sample ID. This explains why we have a grid instead of a single text box to capture depth information.

The collection method, source, and medium dropdown lists are constructed based on the values in their respective lookup tables. The operation of each of these lists is

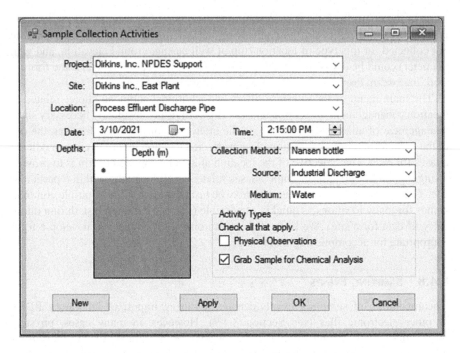

FIGURE 8.18   A simple form for capturing sample collection events.

independent and obvious. The Activity Types frame in the lower right portion of the form offers check boxes to specify the categories of activities that were performed for this event.

One difference between this form and the other forms we've presented thus far is that it does not retrieve any existing data – its function is solely to create new records in the SAMPLES table. That's why there is no Delete button on the form. This also simplifies the code that saves data, which would be invoked by the Apply and OK buttons.[6] The only unusual requirement when saving a sample is that a single sample may have multiple associated activities (e.g., both physical observations and a grab sample). The contents of the SAMPLE_TYPE column in the SAMPLES table makes this possible because it is a multi-character field and the individual sample

---

[6] It's possible – and perhaps even desirable – to modify this form so that it retrieves existing sampling events, thus offering an opportunity for editing details of samples. The most obvious change required is the replacement of the date and time selection tools with alternatives. Simple text boxes are still not a good solution. We need lists to select these elements, but they must function differently depending on the current mode of the form: are we choosing a sample for editing or are we defining a new form. If we're choosing a sample, the controls should be dropdown lists. Also, selection of the location should populate the date list, and selection of the date should populate the time list. On the other hand, if we're defining a new sample, then the controls should behave like text boxes and allow us to enter data as necessary. In our chosen development framework, the .NET control that serves as a dropdown list is called a Combo Box, and it has the ability to satisfy this operational need. Other platforms may or may not have an equivalent control.

type codes are single characters. Thus, the code that saves the sample record must generate the entry for the SAMPLE_TYPE by aggregating the coded values for the checked options.

Since the practice at WSS is to log physical conditions on a field data sheet, if the Physical Observations check box is checked on when the sample is saved, control should pass to another form for documenting the physical data when either the Apply or OK button is clicked. The intention is that the interface form for capturing field observations should mimic (as closely as possible) the paper form used by field crews. For this reason, the FIELD_FORM_PARAMETERS table includes a SEQUENCE field that is used to construct the interface's field observations form with parameters in the expected order. We leave it as an exercise for the reader to create both the form for defining the parameters and their sequence and the form for capturing the field data.

There are some potentially significant issues with the Sample Collection Activities form as proposed. From a design perspective, the Activity Type block must be expanded if we decide to offer additional categories of samples targeted at specialized analyses (e.g., radiological or biological). The form could remain statically defined (by simply adding check boxes for the new options), or it could be revised once in such a way that subsequent changes do not require modifications. To accomplish this, we could create a scrollable container into which the check boxes are inserted based on the contents of the SAMPLE_TYPE_CODES table. Another problem with this form occurs when the sample grid contains multiple depths and the Activity Types block has multiple boxes checked. In that case, we should clarify whether or not a grab sample was collected at every depth or only at some depths. This information is critical both to the documentation in the SAMPLES table and the ensuing display of the form for collecting field observations. There are multiple ways this could be addressed. One way would be to add another column to the depths grid – a check box to specify those depths at which a grab sample was collected. Another option would be to construct a secondary form that pops up prior to saving the data that requests clarification. Neither of these options is particularly appealing because they either complicate the depth grid unnecessarily or interrupt the flow of the interface. A better choice would be to modify the form such that it contains separate tabs for the physical observation documentation and the grab sample documentation.

Since this form only provides a mechanism for creating the sample records, we need a separate form for editing and deleting existing samples. The new form would be launched by selecting Samples and then Sample Details from the main menu. Because this form will access existing samples, we must provide a mechanism for selecting the sample to be retrieved. The sample collection activities form has lists for navigating through projects, sites, and locations, so if we then add new lists for date and time choices, we can build a form that provides the necessary functionality. Feel free to create such a form if you like, but we offer an alternative mechanism for sample selection. The alternative is shown in Figure 8.19.

The alternative accomplishes the same selection process except that instead of navigating through a series of dropdown lists, the user navigates the contents of a tree structure. The tree structure consists of a series of nodes at various levels. Nodes that

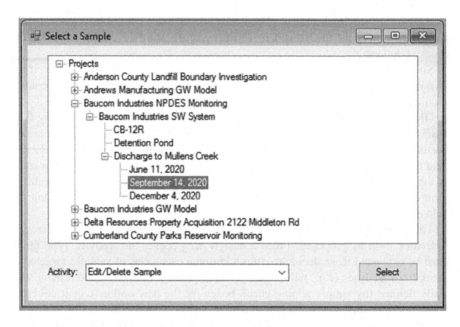

FIGURE 8.19   Selecting a sample for editing using a sample selection tree.

appear in the same branch are related and described as being parents or children of nodes immediately below them or above them in the structure. When the form first appears, it shows a root node that is labeled "Projects." Each node that has children displays a box that contains a + symbol. Clicking the box expands that node, showing its immediate children. If the children have their own children, each of them has a + box, and so on. When the + box for the Projects node is clicked, the tree displays a list of the projects in the database. The children of a project are the project sites, the children of the sites are sampling locations, and the children of the sampling locations are the samples collected at the location. The user navigates to the desired sample node and then clicks the Select button to display the details of the sampling event. From that form the event can be modified or deleted.

The advantage of this alternative is that this same form can be used for other selections with only minor modifications. Note the Activity list near the bottom left of the form. This list contains various other options that require selection of a sample (e.g., edit results). This form is loaded by choosing any one of several options from the main menu that require selecting a sample. The main menu option that is chosen determines the initial selection of the list, but the selection can be changed at any time to perform another activity. Selecting a sample and clicking the Select button displays the form appropriate for the currently specified activity. When the ensuing form is closed, control returns to the sample selection form. Thus, for instance, a user could select the main menu option for editing sample details, navigate to and select the desired sample, display the sample details form, edit details of the sample, return to the sample selection form, select the option to edit results, and then click Select again to display the form on which sampling results are displayed.[7] This type of multi-use form offers advantages to the developer (by reducing the number of forms required in the interface) and to the user (by providing a familiar method for performing different activities).

8.4.9 ENTERING AND IMPORTING RESULTS

There will always be a need for a form on which users can display results for a given sample. In this application, this form is launched by selecting Results and then Results for One Sample from the main menu. This form should enable all users to view the data, and users with appropriate privileges should be allowed to edit, insert, and delete results for the displayed sample. As with the sample details form discussed in Section 8.4.8, a form for this purpose may be displayed by the sample selection tree or it may itself contain sample selection controls.

For this form, the results are best presented in a grid with one row for each parameter and columns that correspond to the metadata columns in the RESULTS table. The form includes the usual Apply, OK, and Cancel buttons. New and Delete buttons are not needed since these functions are supported through normal grid interactions. Within this basic framework, there are opportunities to enhance the user experience. Since we have the ability to define parameter groups, one option would be to include a button that allows the user to select a group and add all the parameters in that group with one click. Another option involves the value qualifiers for results. Recall that the VAL_QUAL column in RESULTS is a multi-character field that allows documenting up to five separate qualifiers for any given result. When the user enters a cell in the column for managing value qualifiers, the interface could display a pop-up list of all value qualifiers in the lookup table, with those already applicable to the current record highlighted. The user could then modify the selections in the pop-up list as desired. When the user navigates to another cell, the pop-up list closes and the grid column is updated appropriately. These are some ideas for facilitating the optimal interaction between user and data; you can likely think of others as well.

In addition to a form that displays all results for a single sample, another view of the results is useful. In this view, results are retrieved not based on selection of a sample, but rather by selections from multiple filters. (For this reason, in our interface the form is found under Results and then Results by Filter on the main menu.) Likely candidates for the filters in our application include site, parameter, lab, test method, lab analysis date, value qualifiers, and the date on which the record was entered into the database. The filters are set using controls appropriate for the associated column: dropdown lists for columns with associated lookup tables (parameter, test

---

[7] When using the sample selection tree to identify samples, all forms displayed when the Select button is clicked should themselves display sufficient information to identify the sampling event. This information would be displayed already if the forms used the more traditional method of navigating through various dropdowns to specify the sample. Since selection of the sample has occurred in the tree, such controls would serve no purpose. Nonetheless, sample particulars – the project, site, location, date, and time at minimum – should still be shown on the form to eliminate the possibility of confusion.

method, etc.), lists of selectable items for the composite columns (value qualifiers), and text boxes for the untethered entries (dates). The form may be configured in such a way that the user sets the desired filters and then clicks a button to retrieve the data, or it may be configured so that each selection is applied and data are retrieved automatically upon completion of the selection. (This last option can produce slow response when the RESULTS table contains a large number of records.) Editing and deleting of data is allowed on this form, but addition of new records is not. For ultimate user control, a form such as this one should provide filters for every column in the RESULTS table. Moreover, the user should be able to determine which columns are shown in the grid and control the order in which the records are displayed.

The single sample results form can be used for manually entering all data associated with a given sample, but this can be a laborious and perhaps error-prone process. In reality, data in the RESULTS table should be imported instead of manually entered whenever possible. The issue with importing data is always format. If all analyses are performed by the same lab, you can easily craft a form that imports their EDDs (assuming they are consistent, of course). Like WSS, however, most organizations deal with EDDs from multiple sources. We could create separate forms for each lab, but that can be both a coding and tracking nightmare. A better solution is shown in Figures 8.20 through 8.22. The concept of this form is that it allows the user to load a file, describe the layout, and then import the data. Operations of the form are based on three steps, each on a successive tab.

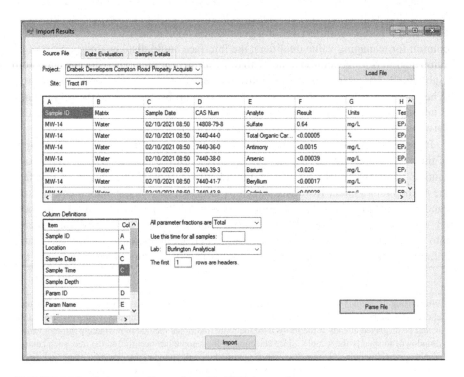

FIGURE 8.20   A dynamically configurable EDD import form.

Figure 8.20 shows the first tab (Source File). The purpose of the controls on this tab is to load the EDD data into a grid. When the form first loads, the upper grid is blank. The first column in the lower grid is populated (more on that will follow shortly). Few EDDs will include project and site information, so these must be selected from the typical dropdown lists at the top of the form. The user clicks the Load File button to start the import process. This launches the standard Windows File Open dialog in which the desired file is chosen. Each line in the file is then read and inserted into the grid. The exact process for reading the file varies with different source file formats. Most EDDs will be in one of three format variations: a comma-delimited American Standard Code for Information Interchange (ASCII) file (usually referred to as a comma-separated values file or CSV), a tab-delimited ASCII file, or a spreadsheet. The first two file types can be opened and read without any special requirements since all development languages are capable of reading simple text files. If the data are in a spreadsheet, an additional function library may be required in order to access the methods used for obtaining data from the file. (The .NET object library for Excel is an example; it gets installed automatically when Microsoft Excel is installed.) Regardless of the original format, we present the data in a grid that resembles a spreadsheet because most users are comfortable with this paradigm.

After the data are loaded into the grid, the objective is to describe the format of the data to the application. This is accomplished by defining mappings between columns in the upper grid and their meanings, which are shown in the lower grid. The rows in the lower grid are predefined and correspond to all the descriptive information that may be present in the EDD. This list should include all columns in the RESULTS table, but may include additional columns from other tables as needed. The user's goal is to enter into the lower grid the column identifiers from the upper grid that correspond to the data elements in the lower grid. If an element is not present in the file being imported, its column ID is left blank. Note that some data elements may either have the same identity or be combined into a single column. For example, in Figure 8.20, column A contains the sample ID as assigned by the field crew. The standard practice at WSS is to use the sampling location name as the sample ID in cases where samples are taken from only a single depth. Thus, column A is identified as containing both the sample ID and the location. If samples are collected from multiple depths, the sample ID consists of the location plus the depth(s) in parentheses (e.g., "SB-2 (2-4)" would indicate a sample collected from SB-2 with media from the range of depths from 2 to 4 units). If that were the case in the file shown, the sample ID, location, and sample depth columns would all be set to A. (This is a common practice among many organizations.) Similarly, in the example shown, column C contains both the date and time at which the sample was collected. Another noteworthy characteristic of the list of columns is that we include both the parameter ID and the parameter name. One or the other is essential, and both are useful. Some parameters may not have standard identifiers such as CAS numbers, so the import process should be capable of matching either element.

To the right of the lower grid are some additional controls that can be used to supplement the contents of the Column Definitions grid. This particular file does not contain a column that denotes the parameter fraction (total or dissolved). This designation is required in our data model, so we must assume that all results in this file are consistently one or the other. The dropdown list for fraction offers an alternative to reading the setting from the file. The time at which the sample was collected is also required by our data model, but the EDD may not include that information. A default time box is available to address those situations. The lab may or may not be identified in the EDD, so another dropdown list for is available for that selection as well. (If this option is selected, the assumption is that all data in this EDD is from the specified lab. If a single file contains data from multiple labs, then the lab must be included as a column in the file.) Finally, the user can identify how many rows at the top of the file contain headers. These will be skipped during import.

After the file structure is completely described, the user clicks the Parse File button. Parsing the file serves the critical function of evaluating all the entries to ensure that the data can be properly interpreted. The results of the evaluation are displayed in the grids on the Data Evaluation tab (Figure 8.21). The interface shows one grid for each data element that is checked. Each grid displays all the instances of the element associated with that grid that were found in the EDD but were not recognized in the database. For each unrecognized item, the grid identifies the first row in which the item appears. (Showing every row that has the same error is annoying to users.) In the case of unrecognized parameters, the row for each missing parameter includes both the parameter name and parameter ID. The elements in the other grids have only a single identifier. The objective on this tab is to use the information displayed to

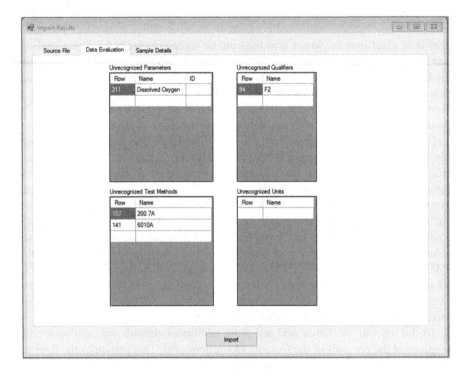

FIGURE 8.21   The import dialog's Data Evaluation tab.

correct any issues with the data before proceeding with the import. The resolution of each issue depends on the nature of the problem and varies by grid. For example, the only unrecognized parameter in our example has a name of "Dissolved Oxygen" and no ID. That means there was no entry in the parameter ID column of the EDD for this parameter, and so recognition could only be done on the name. In this case, we have a different name for the parameter in our ANAYTES table ("Oxygen, Dissolved"). The obvious solution in this instance is to create a new alias for the parameter that matches the text in the EDD.[8] There is one unrecognized value qualifier as well (F2). In order to address this, we must examine the EDD and/or other information provided by the lab to determine the meaning of F2 as a qualifier. If we find an existing quali- fier in our lookup table that has the same meaning, the corrective action is to modify the F2 entry in the EDD, changing it to our code for that qualifier. The two unrecog- nized test methods turn out to be variations on test methods already in the database. The A designation means a revised release of the method description. Based on this knowledge, a decision is required to determine if that level of distinction in the test methods table is desirable. If not, the EDD must be edited to remove the A at the end of these entries. If documentation of the variations is desired, the new variants must be entered as separate test methods. A third alternative would be to update the codes for the existing corresponding entries – change test method 6010 in the test methods table to 6010A – but that may be misleading moving forward because the database would cascade that change to existing records.

To verify that all the needed corrections have been made, the user returns to the first tab, reloads the file, and then clicks the Parse File button again. If all the issues have been addressed, all the grids on the Data Evaluation tab will be empty. Processing can then proceed to the final tab.

The interface has a form for documenting the sample collection activities (Section 8.4.8), but we must be prepared for situations in which the sampling event is not yet recorded in the database. The typical EDD does not include sufficient information to completely describe the sampling event itself, so a mechanism must be provided for entering this information when the EDD is processed. Figure 8.22 shows the Sample Details tab, which represents the final step before actually importing the data. The rows in this grid are created at the same time the EDD is parsed for errors. Each sample in the EDD is shown as one row in this grid. Some information about the sample can be gleaned from the EDD and added when the row for the sample is created. In the example, the sample ID, the location, the date, and the time are known. The code that parses the EDD also checks the SAMPLES table to see if samples in the file have already been recorded in the database. If a sample is already present, the row describing that sample can be completed entirely by reading the SAMPLES record. If the sample is not yet recorded, the user must complete as much of the grid

---

[8] Alternatively, since the data used during import is read from the grid and not the original file, we could allow users to edit entries directly in the grid. While simple, this solution is not effective. It requires users to find and correct additional erroneous entries (since we only show the first occurrence). Furthermore, subsequent EDDs from the same lab are likely to have the same errors, so the manual correction process must be performed over and over.

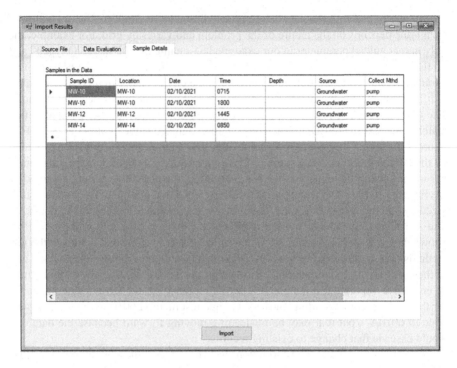

FIGURE 8.22 The final tab of the import form is used to describe the samples more completely.

as is applicable by entering any missing data. Some elements in this grid are optional and may remain blank if the appropriate values are unknown.

When data for all the samples is complete, the user clicks the Import button. As expected, this initiates the data import process. The data used during import is read from the grids on this form rather than the original file. This saves the time required to open and read the file a second time – not a large time saving for ASCII files, but some spreadsheet object libraries are notoriously laggard. The samples grid on tab three is processed first, creating all the samples present in the EDD (if not previously defined). The results grid on tab one is then imported, and all the data are captured.

The form as presented here is functional but offers many opportunities for improvement:

- It's very likely that many files from the same lab will be loaded, and those files will likely have the same format. The first tab could therefore include buttons that allow the user to save the contents of the column definitions grid. This information could be saved in a table in the database, or the settings could be recorded in a simple text file. We also then need a button to read this information from whatever storage approach is used. These options can significantly reduce the time needed to prepare a file for import.
- Times may appear in several different formats. When the source is an ASCII file, the code that reads the EDD can interpret different formats and take

appropriate action. Spreadsheets can pose a challenge. Data in a spreadsheet is often not what it appears to be due to formatting options that are applied when the data are viewed within the spreadsheet software. What appears to be a time (or a date/time) may be stored as text in the cell, or it may be stored as a decimal number (the date is the integer portion of the value, and the time is the decimal portion). The object library will usually return the raw value in the cell, so at the very least we need to account for the possibility that dates and times may have to be translated. A dropdown that identifies the format should be present that signifies if translation is necessary.

- As a courtesy to inexperienced users, it can be very helpful to include text that appears automatically as the column definition grid is traversed. The text can inform the user of additional nomenclature that may appear in an EDD column header that identifies an element. For instance, a standard name within the application might be "Detection Limit" but some EDDs might label the column as "MDL" or "Method Limit."

- It's also a best practice to notify users as early as possible if they have failed to provide a value for a required entry. The column definition grid should therefore be read before the user attempts to parse the EDD, and the user should be warned if any required entries are missing.

- The interface code can be written in such a way that it automatically modifies some of the entries that would otherwise show up as errors in the grids on the Data Evaluation tab. As previously discussed, some test methods are known by multiple identifiers: EPA 213.2 and SW846 213.2 are different designations for the same method. The interface can automatically check for and manipulate these designations, translating an entry for SW846 213.2 into EPA 213.2 if that is the preferred designation.

- Additional translation tables can be added to the database for some of the lookup tables (e.g., value qualifiers). In many cases, be cognizant of the need to make these translations lab-specific.

- There may be advantages to allowing users to ignore unrecognized entries. Suppose the lab includes in the EDD results for surrogate analyses that were performed based on decisions made by the lab instead of initiated by the client. This may introduce results for constituents that were used as surrogates, which may be undesirable. If these parameters are not in the parameters table, offering an option to ignore them can expedite import.

- If the EDD includes many samples, completing the samples grid can become monotonous. Adding mechanisms for populating multiple rows in a particular column while making only one selection would be popular. This could be done, for instance, by offering a dropdown list and a button for the sample medium because this descriptor is often the same for all the samples in an EDD. Selecting a medium and clicking the button to fill all the medium column in all rows is a good timesaver.

- Finally, the import process should generate a log file that records significant actions that occur during import. It should report, for instance, each new sample that gets created. If data are imported that replace existing values, this should also be noted.

The form as described is appropriate for EDDs because they almost always have one characteristic in common: each row is for a single parameter result and the columns contain various descriptors of that result. Other data formats may also benefit from similar import forms. One obvious other choice is often appropriate for observations recorded in the field using a multiparameter collector. Many units of these types are capable of exporting tabular data in which each row is a sampling event and the columns are for different parameters. A variation on the form above can be created relatively easily to import data in this format.

8.4.10 ANALYSES AND REPORTS

The analysis and reporting capabilities are limited for this first release of the WSS interface. There are three options available from the main form's Reports menu. In this section we examine each of these, one at a time.

The first choice is labeled "Table of Results." The goal of this report is to summarize results for a group of samples selected by the user. (The controls on this form and their respective operations are almost identical to controls and operations discussed for previous forms, so no image is included here. Use your imagination.) The user identifies the samples to be included in the report by making choices on a series of tabs. The tabs are named according to their associated data elements: locations, dates, depths, and parameters. Controls on the first tab (locations) specify the locations for which samples will be retrieved. A list on the right of the tab shows all the currently selected sampling locations. On the left are the typical controls required to select a location: first choose a project, then a site. When a site is chosen, the list of locations for that site is displayed in a grid. The user may select one or more locations from this grid. A button between the left side controls and the right side controls adds the highlighted location(s) to the grid of selected locations. A location can be removed from the selected list by double-clicking. Unlike other forms, this report can include results from any project or site. Selecting again starting with the project refreshes the controls on the left, allowing the ensuing locations to be added to the report in addition to others previously selected. As a shortcut, a button labeled "Select by Alternate Means" on the form launches another form that allows the user to populate the selected locations list using other criteria such as county, HUC, etc.

The controls on the second tab (dates) are used to choose the specific sampling events for each selected location that are to be included in the report. As with the locations tab, a list on the right displays the selected dates, and controls on the left are used to populate the list on the right. The controls do not distinguish sample dates for the locations on an individual basis, but rather as a whole. An illustration will clarify this. There are two date pickers on this tab which allow the user to specify the range of dates of interest. A button retrieves the samples collected between the two dates at any of the selected locations. A list on the left portion of the tab then displays the matching dates. The user then selects the specific dates of interest and adds them to the selected dates list by clicking a button. There are two additional controls on the left side of this tab that can affect choices. The first is a dropdown list of months. Selecting a month (in addition to the date range) before clicking the date retrieval button limits returned dates to only those in the selected month. This accomplishes a frequent goal of quickly being able to compare values at a location during the same period each year. The other control is an option that bypasses the selected dates list entirely and instructs the report to include all samples for the selected locations.

The third tab (depths) is useful when reporting soil boring or reservoir sampling results. It allows users to identify the depths for which results will be reported. Multiple options are available for specifying the depth(s) to be reported; the specific option is chosen by clicking a radio button. The default option is to include data for all depths. The second option allows the user to specify a depth range. As expected, this is accomplished by entering the beginning and ending depths that define the desired range. The third alternative allows users to select specific, discontinuous depths. If the user selects this option, the application does an initial retrieval of the sample identifiers for the previously chosen sampling events (locations and dates) and displays a grid that lists all the depths for those events. The user chooses the discrete target depths individually in this grid. (This grid serves as the "selected depths" list similar to the "selected locations" and "selected dates" lists on the first two tabs, except that this list is only a factor if this alternative is chosen.)

The fourth tab allows users to specify the parameters that will be included in the report and the units in which each will be shown. As with the other tabs, there is a grid on the right that displays the selected parameters and controls on the left for adding parameters to the selected list. Methods for choosing parameters include a list of all parameters and a list of parameter groups. If a group is chosen, all parameters in the group are added. A third method involves clicking a button that retrieves all the unique parameters found in the results for the sampling events that match the selection on the first three tabs. When a parameter is added to the list, the interface sets the units for it by retrieving results for the chosen samples. Additional controls on the right side of the form allow users to modify the reported units for any parameter. (These are similar to those on the form for defining parameter groups.) Because users like the option of defining a standard list of parameters, there is a button to save the currently selected parameter list and a button to retrieve a previously defined list.

Buttons are displayed across the bottom of the form below the tabbed area. Since this form has no ability to create, edit, or delete data, the standard Apply and OK buttons are missing. The function of the Cancel button is present, but the button itself is labeled "Exit this Form" for clarity. The button that generates the report is labeled "Tabular Report." Clicking it opens a pop-up form on which the user specifies the layout of the report. The content of the report is known at this point because of the sampling event and parameter specifications. Within this context, though, variations are possible regarding both the general layout and the order of the report rows. The controls on this pop-up form assign the four elements of the report data (locations, dates/times, depths, and parameters) to the four descriptors that define the report's appearance. The primary choice is which element will define the columns. The user may opt to assign any of the four elements to this role. The remaining three elements are then used to define the order of the rows. The top level of definition for the row order is the group. One of the remaining three elements is therefore chosen as the "group by" element. Breaks appear in the report after each group, and the user may choose an option to provide totals for each column on a new line below each group. That leaves the last two elements to determine the order of rows within each group.

After the user specifies their choices for the report format, the report appears in a new window. The new window contains a single large text box that displays the report data formatted as requested. It also contains a button to save a copy of the report. The report can be saved either as a fixed format text file, a CSV file, or a spreadsheet. If the report contains the correct data but the choices for formatting did not produce the required output, closing the form returns control to the main report form where a new button appears. It is labeled "Reformat." Clicking it retains all the previous data selections and redisplays the format pop-up, allowing the user to try again.

One more button is present on the form, labeled "Statistics Report." This generates a statistical summary of the data instead of a tabular report. This button retrieves the same data as the Tabular Report option and also displays a pop-up formatting dialog. When generating a statistical summary of the data, the format choices are more limited because data must be grouped by parameter. The options on this pop-up allow users to either lump all data for each parameter together, or to subgroup the data by location, date, or depth. Another option on the pop-up allows users to either include or exclude the raw data from the report. After the user chooses these options and closes this pop-up, one more pop-up appears. The new pop-up allows the user to control how to handle any non-detects that are encountered in the retrieved results. Options are the following:

- omit them from the analysis;
- substitute 0 for all non-detect values;
- substitute the MDL for all non-detect values (and omit results if no MDL is listed);
- substitute half of the MDL for all non-detects (and omit results if no MDL is listed); or
- substitute a random number between 0 and the MDL (or omit if no MDL is listed).

Based on the user's choices on the two pop-ups, the report appears in the same report window as that used for the Tabular Report. The analysis is limited to descriptive statistics: the number of values, minimum, maximum, mean, median, standard deviation, and standard error of the mean.

The versatility of the Table of Results report allows it to be used to generate a view of the data in just about any required format. The other two reports in the interface are more specialized. The second report option under the Reports menu generates an analysis based on Carlson's Trophic State Index (TSI).[9] The form that performs this analysis is shown in Figure 8.23.

The upper portion of the form is used to select samples to be analyzed. It behaves much like the sample selection form discussed in Section 8.4.8, except that when you get below the location level of the tree it only shows samples marked with the

---

[9] A Trophic State Index for Lakes, Robert E. Carlson, Limnology and Oceanography, Volume 22, Number 2, March 1977.

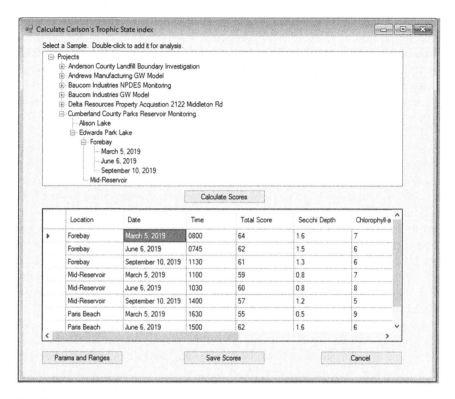

FIGURE 8.23 A form for calculating Carlson's Trophic State Index.

surface water source code. Users navigate to and double-click the desired sample to add it to the lower grid. When first added, the location, date, and time columns are the only ones populated. When all desired samples are in the lower grid, the user clicks the Calculate Scores button. The code behind this button steps through each row of the lower grid. The procedure retrieves the results for the three required parameters (Secchi depth, chlorophyll-a, and total phosphorus) for the sample and inserts them in the grid. Calculation of the TSI score for the sample then proceeds. Raw scores for each parameter are calculated and inserted into the grid (in columns not visible in the figure) and the final score is determined and displayed. After all rows are processed, data in the grid are available for copying and pasting into other formats such as client reports.

The Cancel button closes the form. The Save Scores button saves the contents of the grid in the TSI_SCORES table. The Params and Ranges button displays a secondary form that allows the user to determine actions taken when one or more of the parameters are missing for a given sample. The user may choose to insert a substitute value or opt to omit calculation of the subscore for that parameter. The user also chooses what to do if a subscore cannot be determined: calculate the score based on the remaining subscores, or abandon calculation of the TSI for that sample. If the user logs in with administrative privileges, this second form also provides the ability to modify the calculation by specifying the parameter to use for each requirement and define the textual interpretations for ranges of TSI scores.

The final choice under the Reports menu is a report of values that exceed regulatory limits. This report is accessed by selecting Reports and then Exceedances from the main menu. The form that generates this report has controls similar to those on the Table of Results report, except that the selection of samples is less complicated. As before, no image of this form is included here.

The form has three tabs. Samples are selected on the first tab. In this case, all samples to be included in the report must be from the same project and of the same medium. Furthermore, the assumption is that inclusion of all samples for all locations at the site within the specified date range is desired. The Samples tab therefore contains only the standard project and site dropdown lists to determine locations. The medium is chosen from another dropdown list. This is followed by two date controls used to define the date range of interest. When all the controls are populated, code in the form populates a grid that lists all dates within the specified range on which samples were collected for the site and medium indicated. Additional columns present the number of locations sampled on each date and the total number of samples collected on each date. (This is for informational purposes only.) Users may choose to delete dates from this grid if desired.

The second tab is used to select the regulatory standards against which the results will be compared. Regulations are established by various authorities (in the United States these are typically the individual states or the EPA), so the first choice on this tab is the selection of the authority from a dropdown list. Some authorities define different standards for different situations (e.g., residential or non-residential), so if these variations exist in the regulations from the selected authority and for the indicated medium, dropdown lists appear for selecting the options for this report. A button click retrieves the standards determined by these choices, which are added to a grid on the lower part of the tab. The report is limited to comparisons to no more than four standards, so processing may not continue to the next tab if more than four rows are present in the regulations grid. The user may remove a regulation from the report by selecting it in the grid and pressing the <Del> key on their keyboard.

At this point, all the information required to generate the report has been specified, but the form includes some options for formatting; these are available on the third tab. This report is hardwired to generate a spreadsheet file in order to provide more flexibility than would be available for a simple ASCII file. The formatting tab includes options that take advantage of these capabilities. Cells that contain values that exceed limits specified in the report can be color-coded to draw attention; controls on this tab allow the user to specify a desired highlight color for each standard. Another option allows users to de-emphasize cells in which the values are non-detects by displaying them in gray rather than black text. Users may also choose from several options that determine how non-detects are recorded. They may choose to include them as stored in the database, to show them as less than the MDL, or to show them as "ND."

A button near the bottom of the form generates the report. Because there are many steps required to retrieve data and format the output, a status box beside the Generate Report button is updated as processing proceeds The status box identifies the current operation (retrieving data, evaluating standards, formatting output, etc.). Providing

Constituent	Analytical Method	Units	Standards EPA MCL-based SSLs for Soil (Soil to GW)[1]	TPZ-10 02/10/2021 08:35 Depth: 15-16		TPZ-10 02/10/2021 09:11 Depth: 38-40		TPZ-11 02/10/2021 11:45 Depth: 13-14	
Inorganics and Metals									
Antimony	EPA6020	mg/kg	0.27	<	0.35	<	0.35	<	0.39
Arsenic	EPA6020	mg/kg	0.29		4.8		3.6		2.7
Barium	EPA6020	mg/kg	82		57		19		190
Beryllium	EPA6020	mg/kg	3.2	<	0.47		1.5		0.84
Cadmium	EPA6020	mg/kg	0.38	<	0.082	<	0.082		0.11 J
Chromium	EPA6020	mg/kg	180000		34		17		33
Cobalt	EPA6020	mg/Kg	--		3.8		26		8.9
Copper	EPA6020	mg/kg	46		6.9		3.8		5.9
Iron	EPA6020	mg/Kg	--		24000		5000		35000
Lead	EPA6020	mg/kg	14		9.2		6.3		14
Manganese	EPA6020	mg/Kg	--		97		29		15
Mercury	EPA7471	mg/kg	0.1		0.046		0.019	<	0.013
Nickel	EPA6020	mg/Kg	--		7.7		15		6.7
Selenium	EPA6020	mg/kg	0.26		0.63		0.42 J		0.67
Silver	EPA6020	mg/kg	--	<	0.035	<	0.035	<	0.039
Thallium	EPA6020	mg/kg	0.14		0.25		0.13		0.29
Vanadium	EPA6020	mg/Kg	--		42		20		33
Zinc	EPA6020	mg/Kg	--		26		92		21
Uncategorized Parameters									
Carbon, Organic	*	Percent	--		0.28		0.075 J		0.13
Percent Moisture	*	%	--		19		18.9		29.6
Solids, Sediment	*	%	--		81		81.1		70.4

Notes:
1. EPA Guidance (May 1, 2020) EPA MCL-based SSLs for Soil (Soil to GW) -- MCL-based SSLs, TR=1E-06, THQ=0.1
    ▓ Indicates an exceedance of MCL-based SSLs, TR=1E-06, THQ=0.1 criterion.
    -- Denotes that no standard is available.

FIGURE 8.24 The output of the regulatory exceedance report is a spreadsheet file.

this type of feedback during long operations such as this is helpful. This information not only assures the user that the program is doing something, it also helps them gauge how much time remains before the process completes.

An example of this report is shown in Figure 8.24, as it appears when loaded into the spreadsheet program.

8.4.11 DATA MAINTENANCE

The last item on the WSS application's main menu is for data maintenance. This menu option is only available when the user logs in as an administrator. There is only one submenu, labeled "Bulk Updates." When selected, this choice displays a form that allows an administrator to make changes to multiple records that can't be accomplished through relationships within the database. An example might be when, for instance, a lab notifies us that it reported the wrong MDL for results with a test method of EPA 200.7 that were analyzed between June 1 and June 10, 2019. The objective is to update all affected records without having to access them one by one.

The form contains controls that specify the table, column(s), and value(s) that identify the problematic condition, as well as the desired change(s) to be made. In our example, the administrator would define the date range, choose the lab, and select the test method as the identifying data, then specify the MDL column and new value as the modification to be completed. After setting all conditions, a button click performs the update action.

The obvious question is to ask why such a program is necessary. The answer lies in the incomplete implementation of SQL that is present in our chosen DBMS (Jet). In standard SQL, we could simply log into the database through the DBMS and issue a single update statement, to wit:

```
UPDATE RESULTS SET MDL=0.05 WHERE LAB_ID='TRS' AND
TEST_MTHD='EPA 200.7' AND LAB_ANLZ>=CDATE('06/01/
2019') AND LAB_ANLZ<=CDATE('06/10/2019');
```

Unfortunately, Jet does not support this type of statement. Specifically, Jet does not allow an UPDATE statement that includes a WHERE clause – hence the need for this process.

8.5   MOVING BEYOND THE BASICS

The interface as described above meets the basic needs of WSS and adheres to the company's business practices. In this final section, we examine potential modifications to the program driven by new corporate initiatives or changes in the user community.

For starters, let's consider some elements that are missing from the current iteration that become increasingly important as the number of users increases and their level of experience with the program increases. One obvious element that is missing from the existing code is extensive error trapping. Error traps are a vital part of any well-developed program, but in an attempt to get the database ready for use as quickly as possible, these features have thus far been omitted. The code included to this point performs the required functions correctly as long as events occur as anticipated. This is acceptable if the number of users is small and communication between administrators, developers, and users is frequent and effective. As more people start to use the database and interface, though, the likelihood of an unanticipated problem occurring increases. Without error trapping, any error will cause the interface to crash. This can lead to lost data, lost time, and annoyed users. It would therefore be a good idea to make a second pass through the entire program and implement graceful recovery capabilities when errors occur.

A second standard feature of most software that is missing from the interface directly affects the user experience. All the forms in the application are static – nothing changes on the forms when the user resizes a window. While not an absolute essential, tweaking the appearance of forms when they are resized increases the ability of the user to interact with the data efficiently. This is especially true with forms that contain grids that display many rows or columns. Effective form resizing involves as much art as science, but database applications with grid-based displays benefit greatly from the effort. At minimum, many of the forms in the interface should resize grids to take advantage of increased space when a form gets larger. Conversely, a minimum size should be established for each form in order to ensure that all controls on the form remain accessible.

A third element that is present in most desktop applications but missing in this program is context-sensitive help. While not absolutely necessary, creating a help file reduces the need for constant training and decreases the number of calls for assistance.

Another feature that is popular in Windows-based programs but missing from the application is a toolbar. Toolbars contain buttons with visual representations of activities that are performed when the user clicks the button. Toolbars typically contain shortcuts to frequently used functions. In this case, a toolbar was intentionally omitted from the initial release. The plan is to identify the most frequently accessed features from user feedback, and then create a toolbar for the interface based on that information.

Our database platform is Jet, which stores data in files that can be saved anywhere. The Jet database files also appear when viewing filenames in applications that browse the computer. Furthermore, Microsoft Access is installed on numerous WSS computers, so other Jet database files may exist on the network. For this reason, the interface should perform some form of validation when the user selects the database file to open. This code should check for the existence of one or more tables in the schema. If the tables are not present, the user has selected an invalid file and should be notified of this error. No other options in the interface should be enabled until the user selects an appropriate file.

Other enhancements to the application are necessary when additional data needs are identified. One obvious element not included in the initial version is related to chain of custody forms (COCs). The current scenario considers COCs only within their physical context: they are paper forms that are completed by field crews and packaged with the grab samples sent to the lab. However, COCs also contain information useful for our data management objectives. The specific bit of data to which we refer are the analysis requests. The COC provides instructions to the lab, which includes an indication of the requested analyses for each sample. If these requests are captured in the database, it makes it possible to subsequently compare EDDs with the analysis requests. This can identify any parameters for which analysis should have been performed but was not. Implementing this feature requires creation of a new table (a suggested name is ANALYSIS_REQUESTS), and creation of parameter groups that correspond to all the requests that can be documented on the COC. The field activity form is then modified to include the capture of all analysis requests noted for each grab sample. This information is then used in a new report (Sample Status) that compares the parameter analysis requests with the results table.

Breaking news ... Daryl (WSS's crusty QC manager) has finally decided to retire. Management has hired his replacement (Dan) to ensure a smooth transition. Dan is more tech-savvy than Daryl and is eager to include QC samples in the data model. There are several possible ways this can be implemented. One option would be to simply add a flag to the SAMPLES table to designate samples as QC. But since QC samples are collected for different purposes, we also need a way to identify each QC sample's type. Also, effective use of QC samples requires comparing results from QC samples to related regular samples. For these reasons, a better option is to create separate tables for QC samples and results. The structures of these tables will mostly mirror their regular sample and results counterparts, with some additions. An explicit QC flag column can be omitted from the QC_SAMPLES table (all the samples in this table are QC samples), but a QC_TYPE column will be necessary. A QC_SAMPLE_ TYPES lookup table will also be required in order to control QC type designations. An ASSOC_SAMPLE column will also be necessary in QC_SAMPLES; it will contain the sample number from the regular samples table for the sample to which this QC sample is associated (the assumption is that the QC sample is collected from the same location as the associated regular sample). The purpose of some QC samples is to ensure the quality of the lab's analyses (e.g., duplicates and spikes), so these QC samples should not be identified in such a way that the lab recognizes them as QC. This means that the results for them will likely be returned in the same EDD with regular samples. The EDD import form must therefore be modified to accommodate designating certain samples as QC so that the EDD data can be directed to the proper database tables.[10]

As described thus far, the QC tables work well for some QC types but not all. Specifically, there is a potential problem with QC samples such as blanks. The problem with blanks is that they should be associated with multiple samples – a trip blank, for instance, is associated with all samples collected during a particular trip into the field. To address this, the schema could be modified to include multiple ASSOC_SAMP columns to the QC_SAMPLES table (if you think this is a good idea, please reread Section 4.3.1). Note, though, that since the unique identifier for samples is the combination of LOC_ID and SAMPLE_NUM, this would require either also adding multiple ASSOC_LOC columns or creating a derived column that combines the two (which would also be a violation of normalization rules because the column would contain nonatomic elements). Alternatively, we could create a separate table that defines the association between regular and QC samples. This might actually require multiple tables (e.g., a TRIPS table), depending on how elaborate we wish to be. This general approach requires modifying multiple forms in the interface but turns out to be optimal for new data. It introduces a problem, though, if there is a desire to load data for QC samples collected previously. Capturing these QC samples involves poring over old log books and EDDs, and potentially migrating data from the existing SAMPLES and RESULTS tables to their QC counterparts.

---

[10] We also need some way of identifying them ourselves. A likely source of this information is the field log book, but if we rely on this source, the log book may not be available when we need to import data because the field crew is once again out collecting samples. One approach that doesn't rely on an additional data source involves tweaking the sample identification of the QC samples and modifying the EDD import code to recognize these alterations. For instance, we might log QC samples as being collected at a separate location (e.g., MW-12A instead of the actual MW-12). The EDD import form could be modified to recognize this as a flag and take appropriate action. This may be problematic, however, if we collect multiple QC samples associated with a single regular sample. A variation of this approach in which we alter the sample collection time might be better. Under this plan, we would issue a new SOP that states that all regular samples should now be designated as collected on the hour (e.g., 1400 instead of the actual 1405). The SOP then identifies minute portions of the time stamps corresponding to each of the QC types (e.g., a duplicate would be at 10 past the hour, a spike would be at 15 past the hour, etc.). This would allow the EDD import code to not only recognize these samples as QC, but also identify the specific QC type.

This is a tedious process, especially if the system has been in use for a long period of time. We therefore offer an alternative in this case that is not optimal but hopefully acceptable. The idea comes from the acknowledgment of how QC results are primarily used: in comparison to results from associated samples. Nothing in that statement requires the database to be responsible for making these associations. Instead, this association can be specified at the time of the comparison. Under this plan the original idea of having one ASSOC_SAMP column in the QC_SAMPLES table is retained (it is, after all, appropriate and adequate for many QC types). A QC Comparison Report form is then created (something that must be done anyway) on which the user is allowed to select QC samples and freely associate them with any regular sample(s). Some selections can be expedited and some restrictions may be placed on which regular samples can be chosen. One obvious option is to automatically select the one regular sample with which the QC sample is associated. Depending on how the field crews operate, we might want to consider limiting the regular samples to dates within a week of the date on the QC sample (but maybe not the project and/or site in case a trip involves visiting multiple sites for different projects). This approach can be effective, but note that it may still require some examination of existing data in order to move samples and results from the regular tables to the QC side.

More breaking news … WSS has a new project for a site that may have radioactive contamination. The question is: "can the existing schema handle these types of samples?" If the health safety aspects of this type of sampling can be ignored, the answer appears to be "yes." A new category of sample is required (in SAMPLE_TYPE_CODES) for radiological analysis, and some new parameters must be entered. But – unless the EDD includes some important metadata that was not anticipated – overall, the data model is capable of managing these data.

That may not be the case with the next blockbuster: WSS will expand its services to include biological monitoring. We know this will involve defining new collection methods, new sample types, and new test methods. Those are not problematic. What about what will actually be measured? Results for biological samples will not refer to anything in our existing ANALYTES table, but will instead refer to organisms. Can we just add organism names to the ANALYTES table? That turns out to be ineffective because biological results may return multiple measures for the same organism in the same sample (e.g., count, density, and biovolume may all be reported). The system must be prepared to capture each of these values if they are reported, and the RESULTS table is not structured to accommodate this. It appears, then, that new tables must be created to capture biological data. We will need:

- a separate table for biological samples (BIO_SAMPLES sounds like a good name) because the metadata associated with collection of these samples is significantly different (e.g., sampled area or volume is important);
- a separate table for biological results (BIO_RESULTS) because in addition to the issue about multiple values noted above, the metadata for biological results also includes some new concepts (e.g., life stage); and
- a separate table for the organisms themselves (TAXA).

The first two are relatively easy to construct by examining details of some example biological sampling events and the associated results. The last one requires more consideration. The first inclination might be to use an approach similar to the existing ANALYTES table: an identifying code number and a couple of names (in this case, instead of a long name and a short name we'll use a scientific name and a common name). More research into how biological monitoring is analyzed, however, reveals an important point: analysis of biological samples is often performed at a different taxonomic level than that at which results are reported. For instance, analysis of benthic macroinvertebrate samples may include documenting organisms at the genus or species level, but many of the standard analyses are conducted with results aggregated to the family level. Clearly some mechanism for defining the relationships between organisms will be required.

A first attempt at accomplishing this goal might involve a table that simply identifies parent–child relationships in the taxonomic breakdown, but the nature of these relationships should remind us of another structure implicit in our schema – projects, sites, locations, samples, and results. Recalling that relationship within the context of our form for selecting samples from a tree diagram provides the epiphany that taxa are organized in a tree structure as well. So instead of attempting to define relationships between organisms piecemeal, maybe we can construct a code that actually has some meaning. This turns out to be surprisingly easy. First, we decide how many taxonomic levels we want to include.[11] We'll call that number m. Next, we identify the order of magnitude of the maximum number of organisms at any given level we wish to accommodate for a single parent. To clarify with an example: assuming species is the direct child of genus in our taxonomy, how many organisms at the species level do we wish to allow for a given organism at the genus level? The choices for this answer are limited to the powers of 16: 16, 256, 4096, and so on. The important aspect of this answer is the power of 16 that identifies our choice. We'll call that number n. Then multiply the number of levels by the exponent. This product ($m \times n$) is the length of a text field that will accommodate your projected taxa needs (the actual maximum number is $m \times n - 1$). The individual taxa codes consist of m sets of n hexadecimal digits, each of which represents the organism's parent at the mth level. For analysis purposes, you may decide that some levels are required for each organism's hierarchy. Non-required entries that are missing are coded as all zeros.

An example might help illustrate how this works. Suppose that our taxa plan accommodates 14 levels (Kingdom, Phylum, Subphylum, Class, Subclass, Order, Suborder, Family, Subfamily, Tribe, Genus, Subgenus, Species, and Subspecies),

---

[11] This is not as trivial as it sounds. Many years ago we were taught the "basic" taxonomic levels of kingdom, phylum, class, order, family, genus, and species. As biological science has advanced, many additional levels have been added to this simple list. They have names that include designations such as "sub" (e.g., subphylum), "super" (superorder), and "infra" (infrafamily), and there are a lot of them. A good place to start when making this decision is to acquire example reports from the taxonomist(s) who will be performing the analyses. At minimum, you should include all levels found in the examples. In our experience, a good baseline includes these levels (in descending order): kingdom, subkingdom, phylum, subphylum, class, subclass, order, suborder, family, subfamily, tribe, genus, subgenus, species, and subspecies.

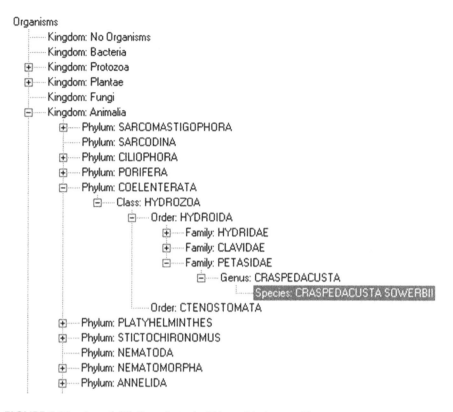

Organisms
- Kingdom: No Organisms
- Kingdom: Bacteria
- ⊞ Kingdom: Protozoa
- ⊞ Kingdom: Plantae
- Kingdom: Fungi
- ⊟ Kingdom: Animalia
  - ⊞ Phylum: SARCOMASTIGOPHORA
  - Phylum: SARCODINA
  - ⊞ Phylum: CILIOPHORA
  - ⊞ Phylum: PORIFERA
  - ⊟ Phylum: COELENTERATA
    - ⊟ Class: HYDROZOA
      - ⊟ Order: HYDROIDA
        - ⊞ Family: HYDRIDAE
        - ⊞ Family: CLAVIDAE
        - ⊟ Family: PETASIDAE
          - ⊟ Genus: CRASPEDACUSTA
            - Species: CRASPEDACUSTA SOWERBII
      - Order: CTENOSTOMATA
  - ⊞ Phylum: PLATYHELMINTHES
  - ⊞ Phylum: STICTOCHIRONOMUS
  - Phylum: NEMATODA
  - ⊞ Phylum: NEMATOMORPHA
  - ⊞ Phylum: ANNELIDA

FIGURE 8.25   A partial listing of a typical hierarchical taxa table.

that we anticipate no more than 255 children for any given organism, and that we require entries at the kingdom, phylum, class, order, family, genus, and species for all organisms. Figure 8.25 shows a hierarchical display of a portion of our taxa tree for kingdom Animalia. The tree lists organisms in taxa code order at each succeeding level. With this knowledge, we can determine from Figure 8.25 the specific 28-character taxa codes for each organism in the tree. Table 8.2 lists the codes for all organisms that are parents at some level for *Craspedacusta sowerbii*.

A few explanatory notes may be in order for both the figure and the table. The figure is from an actual system that stores biological sample results. You might notice the first Kingdom entry, which is labeled as "No Organisms." In this particular system, a special taxa code designation (all zeros) is used to indicate no organisms were found in the sample.[12] If you compare the entries in the table with the entries in the figure, you begin to better understand the construction of the taxa code. Each level in our taxonomic breakdown is represented by two characters in the code. Animalia is the

---

[12] Use of this code is reserved for targeted organism sampling as might be conducted for, for instance, harmful algal blooms. The proper interpretation of this code is not that there are no organisms in the sample but rather that no organisms from the target group were present in the sample.

TABLE 8.2

Taxa Codes for Organisms in Figure 8.25 That Define the Lineage for *Craspedacusta sowerbii*

Organism	Taxa Code
Animalia (Kingdom)	05000000000000000000000000000
Coelenterata (Phylum)	05050000000000000000000000000
Hydrozoa (Class)	05050001000000000000000000000
Hydroida (Order)	05050001000100000000000000000
Petasidae (Family)	05050001000100030000000000000
Craspedacusta (Genus)	05050001000100030000010000000
Craspedacusta sowerbii (Species)	05050001000100030000010000100

fifth kingdom in the figure (not counting the special code for No Organisms), so its code is 05 in the kingdom position and all the remaining digits are zero because they are not applicable to this entry. Now consider the code for Hydrozoa. Its kingdom is 05 (Animalia) and its phylum (Coelenterata) is the fifth phylum listed under Animalia; so its first four characters are 0505. There is no subphylum entry in this lineage, so the next two characters are 00. Hydrozoa is the first class under its phylum, so the code for Hydrozoa is 05050001 followed by 20 zeros.

Hopefully you now grasp how the coding works. Now consider the advantage of using this code for biological analysis. For any organism, you can determine its parent at any level by simply cutting off the taxa code for the organism after the number of characters required to define the desired level. Append zeros until you reach the total number of characters, and that is the taxa code of the parent at the target level. It also becomes very easy to aggregate results for children of any organism. If you need to know how many total organisms from family Hydridae were found in a sample, a single query can provide the answer:

```
SELECT SUM(ORG_COUNT) FROM BIO_RESULTS WHERE (…
identify sample particulars here…) AND TAXACODE LIKE
'0505000100001000l%';
```

Now back to other preparations for biological sampling. We mentioned above that new records in the COLLECTION_METHODS table must be added for methods associated with biological sampling. It turns out that there are a lot of interesting pieces of equipment for this purpose, and if we plan to use very many of them, our list of collection methods is about to get very long. This is not a problem in the database, but it might get annoying for users because now they have to wade through this lengthy list in order to select the appropriate one. We can do something to alleviate this issue, however. First, we need to define SAMPLE_TYPE_CODES for biological sampling at a level that indicates more than simply "biological." WSS plans to offer these services in three areas: phytoplankton analysis, zooplankton analysis, and benthic macroinvertebrate analysis. We therefore define codes for each of these types in SAMPLE_TYPE_CODES. Next, we add a column to the COLLECTION_

METHODS table that references the type(s) of samples for which this method is appropriate. We need to accommodate multiple entries because some methods are appropriate for more than one type. Theoretically, the column should be wide enough to denote every possible sample type, but more typically less than that will be sufficient. Next, we modify the interface form for documenting collection methods so that a series of check boxes are used to identify all the sample types for which the method is appropriate. Finally, we use this information on the form that documents field activities to limit the choices in the collection method list to only those marked as appropriate for the type of sample being documented. Users will appreciate the shorter list.

Our last bit of news is that WSS will begin purchasing and deploying continuous monitoring equipment for some projects. These are automated devices with probes that measure selected parameters on a regularly scheduled basis. How does this type of sampling fit into our schema? Frankly, it's a problem. You realize this when you acknowledge that our entire database structure is based on the collection of discrete samples. Consider how many columns there are in the tables required to capture data for a single parameter value. Now think about how many of those columns will be either blank or the same for all the results associated with continuously collected results. Finally, think about what our sample selection tree would look like if, for a particular location, there were samples listed every 15 minutes for 6 months. It becomes obvious that our current schema is not appropriate for these types of activities. We need a more efficient way to store and retrieve these results.

Fortunately, we have an answer for that situation as well. It involves treating the continuous collection as a single sampling event and creating a special table (or series of tables) that describes the particulars of the event. The description includes the depth(s) at which results are collected, the interval at which they are observed, and the parameters measured for each time step (including units). We also note the date and time of the first data collection for the event. To reduce size requirements further, the event description specifies the order in which the parameters will be reported by the equipment. The results table (a new one just for continuous results) then becomes very compact. It has columns for the event ID, the date/time stamp of observation, the parameter sequence number, and the value. That's it. An informative view of the results can be created using data from both the continuous sampling events table and the corresponding results table. This method will enable storage of what would otherwise be a massive amount of data (with a lot of blanks) in a much smaller footprint.

8.6   SUMMARY AND CONCLUSIONS FOR PART 1

This concludes our exploration of basic techniques and best practices for managing environmental data. From this portion of the book you have learned:

- why data management is important;
- why a database is the preferred method for managing environmental data;
- the basic concepts of how a database works;
- essential elements of SQL;

- how to analyze your specific data management needs;
- how to determine what type of solution is best for your situation;
- why every database needs a user interface;
- how to design a database that addresses your needs; and
- the basics of how to create an effective user interface for a custom database.

In Part 2 we will see how these concepts are applied in the real world.

Part 2

Environmental Data Management Realities

9 Prolog

9.1 PURPOSE

Part 1 included a lot of information about concepts, principles, and best practices related to managing environmental data, and concluded with a simple "real-life" example. Except that it wasn't – "real life" that is. The database and user interface described in Chapter 8 were created as a fantasy not actually tied to any physical person, place, organization, or endeavor. Like the rest of Part 1, it describes the optimal implementation of the data management paradigm. Unfortunately, nothing is ever quite that easy in actual "real life." The development of any data management system that will truly satisfy realistic requirements will be full of revisions, compromises, and changes in direction. The purpose of Part 2 is to give context to the ideas from Part 1 when those ideas meet with reality. Instead of attempting to generate a didactic list of specific implementation activities and the compromises they may entail, Part 2 will present examples from a single project – examining the history of the development of a truly (I mean it this time) "real-world" example.

A goal of this part is to provide the readers with food for thought. We will address issues related to both database design and user interface development. There will be some good things, some bad things, and perhaps even some ugly things. Regardless, the goal is to stimulate consideration of what it takes to accomplish a goal. The examples will (hopefully) prepare the reader for the types of challenges they will encounter as they manage environmental data, even though the specifics of their situation will vary.

Part 1 is written in the traditional style of a textbook or other reference work whose intention is to teach a subject. Part 2 takes a more personal approach and is presented in a more casual style. (I may even occasionally attempt to interject a little humor.) The voice is that of the author.

9.2 STRUCTURE

I have maintained a daily log of my work activities for many years. Early in my career I worked for small companies in which I – like just about every employee – had to wear multiple hats. In addition to writing code for various environmental modeling and other data-intensive pursuits, my responsibilities often included serving as the

DOI: 10.1201/9781003131953-11

Information Technology (IT) manager (and at times the sole occupant of the help desk). In that capacity, I found it helpful to jot down notes when I solved a particularly difficult hardware or software problem. Those sorts of things have a tendency to repeat themselves, and I found it saved time when I didn't have to recall the previous solution from memory. I began keeping the daily log as a way of retaining those notes. Over time, I began to document not only the IT-related items, but anything else on which I was working as well.

Because of this practice, the log contains a great many entries that illustrate the principles described in Part 1, the roadblocks posed to implementation, and how they were overcome (or subverted). The structure of Part 2 consists of a series of discussions based on this daily log, related in chronological order. Each segment will consist of one or more entries from the log that describe an activity or issue. This will be followed by commentary that may include more detail and a discussion of what is being described in the log. The intention is to show how each item relates to the principles from Part 1. Some items will include notes about lessons learned. Additional log entries and narrative passages may be included to provide context and continuity. I hope this approach makes the information both more engaging and more instructive.

The examples will be drawn from the development of the **D**ata management and **A**nalysis **S**ystem for **L**akes, **E**stuaries, and **R**ivers (DASLER). This is a comprehensive data management system for surface water quality data created for the United States Army Corps of Engineers. This system has a long history: development began in 1995 and has continued to the present. The history of DASLER includes examples of just about every principle discussed in Part 1. DASLER thus offers a comprehensive picture of the entire data management system development, deployment, and support processes.

10 Origins

10.1 CONTEXT

Not every database development project begins as such. In this case, the effort started much more simply.

In 1994, I was working for a small environmental consulting company in East Tennessee. The firm specialized in modeling – particularly groundwater modeling – but offered field services and other typical environmental support activities as well. Unlike large companies, small companies rarely draw a definitive boundary between responsibilities to clients (billable work) and responsibilities to the company itself (overhead activities). My role certainly bridged that gap: I was in charge of maintaining the company's IT resources as well as writing computer programs that supported a wide variety of projects. Much of my code was written in FORTRAN since that was the dominant language for models and other scientific programs. As our story begins, however, the company had migrated to an early version of Microsoft Windows as our primary desktop operating system, and I had begun branching out into other languages. In particular, the owner of the company was showing a lot of interest in Microsoft Visual Basic.

June 6, 1994

I discussed a job with my boss so he could put together an estimate for the Nashville District. They have two potential jobs for us, and there are Visual Basic tasks in each one of them. One involves modifying the existing W2 animation program slightly, and the other requires graphing some of their existing data.

This is the first entry in my log for what would become a major part of my career for many years. Such a simple beginning ….

May 30, 1995

I spent a fair amount of time today on the cost estimate for the programming portion of the project. I had to make several phone calls to get a handle on what is going on and find out more details regarding software, so it took me most of the day (off and on) to get this one done. I talked to the contracting office technical specialist in Nashville for a while about the project, where they are, and where they want to be. They are

DOI: 10.1201/9781003131953-12

using ArcView, which is a scaled down version of PC Arc/Info. It has a development language, called Avenue, for customizing the program and writing utilities. The client has the base maps and knows where to get the data sources, and they are just waiting on another contractor to deliver them a tool that will allow them to pick a sampling point and get some plots out. That contractor is using commercial software instead of developing something themselves, so they are taking the approach of working pretty much outside ArcView. Our part of the project will involve setting up ODBC [Open Database Connectivity] drivers for the client so they can access the Oracle database in Huntington, which holds their data.

Almost exactly a year later, things finally began to move, and I got more background about what was needed. In broad terms, our client (the Corps of Engineers) is responsible for managing water quality in a number of reservoirs. To meet that objective, some of the individual districts had requested that the Corps acquire or develop an appropriate data management system. The Corps had responded by licensing a commercial product. Our specific client (the Nashville District) was part of a regional test installation of that software. The commercial system consisted of an Oracle database and a user interface implemented as a terminal application.[1] At the time, only one of the districts (Huntington) had sufficient computing resources to host the system. The other districts participating in the evaluation had to connect remotely over telnet in order to manage their data.

The system had been in place long enough for each of the districts to have loaded a significant volume of data. Nashville now wanted to start generating some useful graphs of these data. The other contractor had been charged with creating a way for the client to generate four distinct graph types:

- a vertical profile x y graph of results for one or more parameters from a column of samples at one reservoir location, using elevation or depth as the y-axis and parameter value as the x-axis;
- an irregular time series x-y graph of results for one or more parameters for multiple samples at one location over time, with parameter value as the y-axis and date/time as the x-axis;
- a longitudinal contour of results for one parameter from samples for one reservoir collected during the same sampling trip, with parameter values contoured across a domain defined vertically by elevation and horizontally by river mile; and
- a time series contour of results for one parameter for samples from one location collected over time, with parameter values contoured across a domain defined vertically by elevation and horizontally by date/time.

---

[1] Few readers will be old enough to understand the phrase "terminal application." In the days before graphical user interfaces, much of the interaction with computers was accomplished through devices called terminals. Terminals had a keyboard and monochrome, text-only displays. They were connected to computers that might be miles away over dedicated lines. The user would type commands into the terminal (which were echoed to the screen), and the computer would respond accordingly. When personal computers began appearing in the workplace, one of the functions they offered was emulation of a terminal. When Microsoft Windows first appeared, continuation of the terminal emulator was practically essential. That was how our client communicated with their data.

The objective of the program from the other contractor was to identify data required for a plot, retrieve the data from the database and then generate the desired graph(s). My objective was simply to establish the connection from that program to the database. Around this same time, Geographic Information Systems (GIS) were becoming popular, and the Corps was eager to conduct their data retrieval within this framework.

June 9, 1995

I had more discussions with the other contractor today, and then more discussions with my boss later. Here's the bottom line on the situation: they are still about 2 months away from delivering the first version of their solution. When they do, it will work like this. They have a Visual Basic program that allows input of selections which define the search. The user enters the sampling point, constituent, etc., in response to dialog boxes. The Visual Basic program then builds an external file that defines the database query. The query must then be submitted to the remote database. When the query results are returned, the Visual Basic program takes over again and prepares the data for Excel and Surfer. Two of the plots are done by Excel, and the other two are done by Surfer. The statement of work that we are preparing addresses the next step in the process. There are two components here – installing and configuring the ODBC drivers to allow the other contractor's program to work with the remote database (Oracle) in Huntington and building an alternative map-based interface for defining the query. The other contractor is proposing that we will only do the ODBC installation and configuration, and they will do the map interface. Still, though, what they are proposing is to use ArcView to select only the sampling point. Specification of all other selections remains the same. This means that, at a minimum, getting the plots will require running ArcView, a Visual Basic program, Excel, and Surfer simultaneously.

A few days later, after much discussion with both the team in Nashville and the second contractor, I was able to get a more complete understanding of what was being created. I struggled to understand why the other contractor insisted on using GIS only for the selection of sampling location(s). I was convinced the Corps would much prefer an approach using only a single tool for selecting all data, but the other contractor was the lead on the project, so I deferred to their plan (for the time being).

June 14, 1995

I had a long talk with the contracting office technical representative this morning. I outlined my concerns about what the other contractor was proposing. She was very helpful, and also understanding. After talking to her, I have decided what I should do. I'm going to call the other contractor and suggest pursuing the Avenue path for further development. If they choose to participate, we'll set up things so that they develop the user interface part of the program and we handle the graphics. If they don't want to go along with that, we'll do it all ourselves.

It turned out that my concerns about the overall approach were shared by the District. There were two big concerns on their part. First, they really preferred to identify all the data required for a graph within a single interface – and wanted that interface to be GIS-based. Second, they were concerned about the ability of their computers to load all the elements needed in this endeavor simultaneously. My company had been experimenting with developing a graphics library based on Windows Application Programming Interface (API) calls. It was compact, it was fast, and we had been successful in using it for creating other plotting utilities. The Nashville team was already familiar with this approach from using our W2 animation program (referenced in the June 6, 1994 log entry above). In my discussions with them, they had asked about using this approach. We were therefore working on a backup plan in case the utility from the other contractor failed to perform.

September 20, 1995

Last week I spoke again with the contracting office technical representative in Nashville. She told me then that she was moving to a different group, and that she might not therefore have any further involvement in our GIS development efforts. She referred me instead to Bob Sneed (the head of the water management group) and suggested that I touch base with him this week. I called him this morning, and in our discussion he reminded me that this effort was his idea originally. So he was pretty well in touch with the process. He noted that they are still waiting on the other contractor to deliver the first iteration of their tool, and that we need to wait so we don't have to reinvent the wheel on this. He told me that they (the other contractor) expect to be another month to two months finishing up. So we're still in a holding pattern.

November 29, 1995

The boss and our reservoir modeling expert went to Nashville yesterday to meet with the Corps of Engineers about some modeling efforts and other tasks. To my surprise, they came back with the immediate word to proceed on the GIS development. We had a kick-off meeting this afternoon. I will be the technical lead, create the primary user interface, and provide the database connectivity. Our other developer will focus on the graphics library and creating the plots.

Finally, we got the authorization to proceed with the development. The other contractor had still not delivered their product at this time, but the District didn't want to wait any longer. I began to refer to this phase of development as "the GIS project" in my notes since I thought this would be the extent of the work.

November 30, 1995

Our team (one project manager and two developers) met for a while to discuss the GIS development project. I showed them copies of the plots (provided by Nashville) that would be required in the first iteration of the project and we discussed how to get to that point. We talked about the program flow. When the program is first opened, it will connect to the database immediately and obtain all the data it will initially need. These data will be used to build lists of parameters, sites, and dates. The program will maintain an internal "selection set" of each item type in memory. The last thing chosen will be the type of plot to be displayed. If too many items are selected for the indicated plot, the user will be notified and allowed to pare down the selection list dynamically. This gives us the flexibility to generate one graph, then immediately generate another one without forcing additional selections. I like the possibilities. The other big item of discussion was data access. We still have not been given access to the Oracle database in Huntington.

And with that, we were off and running. Over the next several months I gained a lot of experience coding in Avenue, which was the development language for ArcView at the time. Much of that experience proved painful because Avenue was a very new platform and was very buggy. Of course, I couldn't complain because our newly minted graphics library also had a lot of bugs. I also became well acquainted with Mark Campbell, who would be the primary user of the software and the technical lead on the project. He and I spoke often to ensure that our program would meet his expectations. Unfortunately, we were still having issues connecting to the Oracle database. Oh, and I also did not yet have the base maps for ArcView ....

February 1, 1996

I received some base map files from Mark today and I loaded them into ArcView. The files are for only one reservoir, but that should be enough for now. The next thing I need is some data to put behind the scenes so I can start testing the interface.

We eventually established connection to the Oracle database, only to learn of another potential stumbling block. Any layer in the ArcView map from which we wished to retrieve tabular data (i.e., sampling locations) had to be based on a shape file, and in this version of ArcView the only database format you could reference in a shape file was the .dbf format.[2] That meant an extra step would be required for our program: download the locations table from Oracle and insert the data into a .dbf file.

February 21, 1996

Bob Sneed wants to come here and meet with us to make sure we're all on the same page. We'll have a lot to talk about. So far, here's what it looks like we need in terms of software connections. ArcView will talk to an ODBC driver. But the ODBC driver still needs client rights with the Oracle database, so we need SQL*Net from Oracle. That will allow us client privileges, but it won't manage the ftp connection to the server. For that we need PC-NFS. Then, and apparently only then, can we query the database at will. Still, I think this is the solution we need to push for. If it will only work together ....

Looks like we've run into issues that were similar to what the other contractor was facing. Perhaps I was too harsh on them.

---

[2] The .dbf format was developed for dBase. This product was an early database for personal computers, and eventually dominated that market. Like Jet/Access, it stored data in individual files, but took an even more extreme approach: each table was in an individual file (.dbf) and indexes were also separate (.ndx). Obviously there was no effective way to establish relationship constraints in this scenario, so you couldn't really say dBase was a relational database. Still, it was powerful enough that a lot of desktop data management systems were created based on it. It had an interpreted language component, which meant that any interface or other program had to be run within the dBase program itself. Another vendor later created a compiler (called Clipper) for the dBase language, removing that limitation. I developed a lot of dBase and Clipper programs in my early career.

February 26, 1996

I spent the bulk of my day tinkering with data from the Oracle system in Huntington. I downloaded data from several of the tables, reformatted them and put them into dBase format. I had originally started downloading everything from the RESULTS table as well, but after about an hour I had 16M and it was still going. I stopped it at that point and decided I'd better limit my search. After spending all day getting the other data, I tried downloading for just one reservoir in the afternoon. That took almost 30 minutes, and I got 90,432 records. I think I might want to limit that further next time ....

This was an attempt to determine if we would be better off with an alternative solution that involved periodically downloading all the Oracle data and converting it to dBase format. This would eliminate some of the extraneous software pieces needed to make the system work, but would come at the expense of having to repeat the download and conversion activity over and over. This experiment was driven by competing software restrictions and ultimately the situation for the client: managing the data in one format but requiring use of the data by an analysis package that is not compatible with the original format. These types of competing interests are commonly the driving force behind compromises and work-arounds.

March 6, 1996

The group from the Corps (Bob, Mark, and their Unix system manager) arrived a little earlier than expected (about 10:30). We started by taking a look at the big picture on the project to make sure we were all thinking along the same route. We were. Then we got into a lot of discussion about specifics. They had some ideas that I had not thought about, and the reverse was true as well. Of particular interest were a couple of items. First, Mark thought we might be better off having multiple ArcView projects available: one for the overall river system, and others for the specific basins. That's because they are putting together more detailed maps of the specific basins, with more locations and more features. Second, Bob reminded us that we need to access data in other sources besides the Oracle database. They have HEC [Hydrologic Engineering Center]-format data (ASCII) for some stuff, and they also want to access recent data from DSS [Data Storage System, an HEC data management product]. This is the most troubling format, because it's not pure ASCII, and it's compressed. They have utilities for accessing these data, and our visitors claimed they could get us the source code for these utilities. We might then be able to incorporate some in-line code for accessing the information we need. That's not completely clear at this point. A new wrinkle in the program that I hadn't really anticipated was their desire to view their data in tabular format within the map as well. I think this should be fairly straightforward. Overall, it was a very productive meeting.

Meetings like this are absolutely essential when developing any sort of software. It's imperative to completely understand the client's needs and practices, and the best way to capture that information is through dialogue.

March 28, 1996

Bob Sneed called late in the day. He told me that the other contractor had finally delivered their version – and it wouldn't run on any computer in their office.

Looks like it's a good thing we had a backup plan.

April 12, 1996

I got some interesting responses from the mailing list this morning. First, someone pointed out that the on-line help has information that contradicts the printed documentation regarding how dates are handled. (To query, you have to use the Date. Make(datestring, formatstring) syntax.) So with that in mind, I went back to the Query Builder and looked again. I was able to select dates more successfully now, but there are still a few quirks. I could never select a date by requesting an exact match. I could, however, select an exact date by putting in two conditions: a >= condition and a <= condition using the same date. Apparently, the problem with querying date fields is well known and well documented .... Late in the day I showed the program to my boss for a reality check, and he had a couple of comments. First and foremost, he felt that there needed to be distinct tools for zooming and selecting. As I had things set up, there was one tool for selecting on the base map, and another for "select and zoom" to display the more detailed map. I trust him enough on this to follow his suggestion, so I did that.

As coding progressed, my log noted many issues encountered and overcome. Most don't offer any confirmation of the lessons from Part 1 or identify any compromises that had to be made. This one, however, is noteworthy because it refers to several topics from Part 1. First, note that I made use of resources beyond just the documentation and online help provided by the software vendor. (This was before everything was on the Internet, which explains the reference to "the mailing list." That's how information was frequently exchanged before the explosion of forums.[3]) Second, note that I was able to improve the interface by soliciting input from someone (my boss) with knowledge of the practices involved but no experience regarding this specific product. When you immerse yourself in development, it's easy to become locked in on a particular approach to a particular process. You can almost always get a better perspective by demonstrating things to someone less involved. And finally, this entry – coming on top of numerous omitted entries that discuss other problems encountered – summarizes nicely the danger of working with a very new development platform.

April 26, 1996

I spent all day in Nashville with two of our modelers. The idea of the trip was to discuss with the Corps any projects they want us to do in the closing year of this contract. The three of us met with Bob Sneed, Mark Campbell, and Richard Tippit. Richard is the biologist in their team. He was there for a reason. They want an expansion of the GIS programming that we're doing now, and Richard was there to provide details. They want to look at the option of linking their biological data to the GIS system as well. We talked in detail about how to go about that and what formats they have data in now. They also want to consider some enhancements to the basic product we're working on. After lunch, I gave a brief demonstration of where we are now on the interface. That went pretty well, even though we're still not done. I came away eager to get this thing completed so we can start the next phase.

---

[3] Don't give me any grief for not using "fora" as the plural of "forum."

This was the first real indication that the GIS interface would be only the tip of the iceberg.

10.2   SETBACK

May 14, 1996

Our PM called a meeting this morning to review the status of the GIS project. The status is: we are nearing completion, but it's going to be close on the budget. The other programmer is now to the point where she needs some of my live data to plot.

While I had been working on creating a user interface within ArcView, our other developer had been working with our graphics library to create the actual plots. So far she had been working with data she made up. As discussed in Part 1, this is not optimal, so now it was time to test her work with actual client data.

July 1, 1996

I spoke with Bob Sneed this morning. We talked at length about future directions for the GIS program; it was a very productive discussion. He continues to express interest in perhaps developing a complete interface to the database outside of the commercial product they are currently using. Also, the addition of a biological component could lead to more need for robust data entry elements, and these are definitely not going to be appropriate for ArcView. He also mentioned that they have now seen a demo of the Windows version of the commercial product, and it's still not exactly what they want. Bottom line: let's finish what we are presently working on, then see where things stand.

July 9, 1996

Bob Sneed informed me today that they now have a local copy of Oracle in Nashville, so they think they might be able to copy their data down to their office before we deliver this thing. That would certainly make things simpler.

September 13, 1996

Today I got the other programmer's code that she has done so far on the GIS program, so I could pick that up right away.

Our first major deviation from the plan. The other programmer asked to take an extended leave due to family matters. I now had to assume the additional responsibility of completing the portion of the program that generates the actual plots. This would almost certainly mean a delay in our final delivery. Fortunately, the Nashville folks were understanding about the situation and granted us an extension.

December 11–13, 1996

These were a frantic two days preparing for the delivery meeting in Nashville Friday, followed by a somewhat less frantic meeting itself. I discovered I needed to do another data filter to prevent problems I encountered with the longitudinal profiles – a column of data with a constant value. I filtered that out, and things got better. By 1:00 pm Thursday I had all the contouring working (to a point) and had the program compiled to work as a DDE [Dynamic Data Exchange] component. I then started testing the whole package together and ran into more problems. I found a couple of loose ends on the Avenue side that for some reason I had not completed. I quickly finished those, then tried running everything together. When I started picking information for plotting, though, I was reminded how dog-slow this process can be. I decided to switch all the selections over to the "non-daisy-chaining" type. So I coded right up to 2:30, ran a final, single test, then packaged everything up for the trip.

I expected the worst in Nashville because of the last minute changes, but it went surprisingly well. Bob was not all that happy with the graphics yet (they want smoothed contours, better labeling, more control, etc.), but they were pleased with the overall package. In response to some comments, I doctored some of the dialogs and forms while I was there. I also had to adjust some of the Avenue code to accommodate the fact that they were using the large fonts instead of the small ones I'm using. The only real problem I ran into was that I neglected to include the report files so we couldn't see or print the reports. Still, it went better than it could have.

I had thought I would try to persuade them to move this whole GIS thing to Visual Basic in the near future, but they had other ideas on priorities. We talked a while, and concluded that eventually it would be a good thing to do, but for now there are other things that are more urgent. The next phase of this project will be the database management system replacement for the existing commercial software. Their PM [Project Manager] wants the full-blown front end to the database so he and his people can do all the things the existing product does now, but with better performance. He wants me to write a scope of work right away for this effort so we can kick things off as soon as possible.

As final delivery meetings go, this one was not great, but it was good. We delivered the product the client wanted, although with much room for improvement. More importantly, it built on our relationship with the client and led them to immediately issue us more advanced work.

To summarize where we were at this point: we had a GIS interface that served as the single point of entry for generation of the plots, and that interface performed all the required data selections. The GIS interface then called a custom graphing application, which allowed users to further specify characteristics like the type of plot, assignment of colors to graphic elements, etc. In case you're interested, the four types of plots are shown in Figures 10.1 through 10.4. (I generated these images using the current version of the plotting utility, so these might be somewhat improved over the versions we could produce in 1996, but the overall effect is the same.)

10.3   MIDNIGHT

With the GIS interface to the existing database completed (at least a working first version), I now turned my attention to the more general database interface.

December 17, 1996

I wrote an outline for the new data management system this morning.

While waiting for the Corps to generate the scope of work for the database interface, I continued to refine the GIS interface/plotting program.

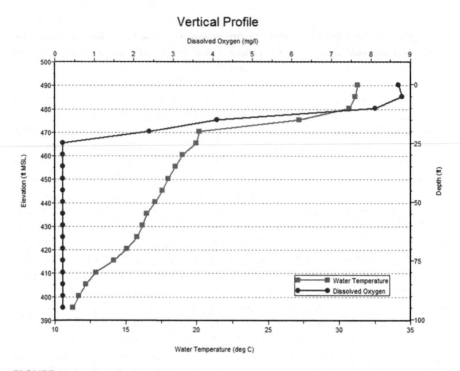

FIGURE 10.1   A vertical profile graph.

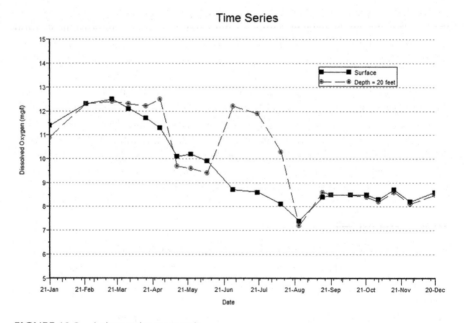

FIGURE 10.2   A time series x-y graph.

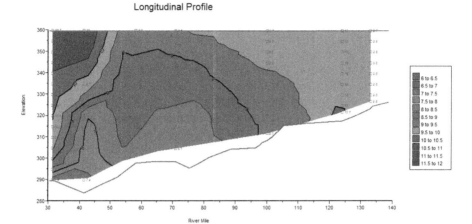

FIGURE 10.3   A longitudinal contour plot.

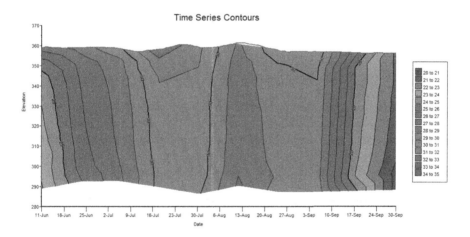

FIGURE 10.4   An irregular time series contour plot.

January 15, 1997
I talked to Bob today about delivering an update to the GIS interface. We agreed that sometime next week would be ideal.

January 27–28, 1997
Trip to Nashville these two days to deliver the updated GIS application. We failed in that effort while there because we were never able to connect Mark's computer to the Unix workstation. Their Unix admin was traveling to California on business, but we reached him near the end of the day Monday. He said he would connect remotely to the computer Tuesday morning and see if he could fix the problem.

Tuesday morning while we were waiting for him to work his magic on the connection, I met with Bob, Mark, and Richard to discuss future direction. We spent a lot of time on Richard's conceptual design and business requirements. We also discussed the biological sampling process in great detail. The Unix admin completed his work about 10:00 or so, and we were finally able to connect. But connecting was only the first issue, and we continued to have problems. It turned out that the Oracle TNS listener was not installed on the workstation. By this time the admin was not reachable, so we abandoned our efforts. I spent the last few hours in a detailed demonstration of the software on a laptop I had brought with me.

The existing Oracle database included all the tables and relationships associated with collection and analysis of physical observations and chemical grab samples, but nothing related to biological sampling. We all knew that additional tables would be required to support that, but we had not as yet identified details. From past experience, I had a pretty decent understanding of the physical and chemical samples, but I was not very knowledgeable about biological sampling. The discussions during the second day of this meeting were therefore absolutely essential in preparation for modifying the database. This was their opportunity to explain the biological portion of their business model, and my opportunity to begin translating it to a modified data model.

February 18, 1997

The trip to Nashville was long, but productive. There were three reasons for going, which I will outline below.

First: Some folks from the Pittsburgh District were coming to Nashville to see the program that we have developed. They were totally blown away by what we have done. They really, really want to get involved in furthering the development of this thing.

Second: I needed to meet with Richard to talk about philosophy on coding biological taxa. He had gathered some examples of coding schemes that various people use, and we reviewed them. One of the schemes had been used in Pittsburgh. That seemed to be the best approach, at least from a programming and data retrieval standpoint. We looked at the system Huntington uses, which would work but had some flaws from a programming standpoint. Richard also had some information on the coding used for STORET (EPA), but not a complete description of the system. What he described of that system seemed terribly cumbersome. We mutually agreed on some variation of Pittsburgh's system. They will send Nashville some files on disk, which we will use as a starting point for the development.

Third: I wanted to isolate the problem on Mark's connection to Oracle on the workstation, and I think I was successful. I installed SQL*Plus and discovered that I could connect there before the ODBC connection is made. That would seem to indicate that this is an SQL*Net problem, not an ODBC problem.

Oracle is a very powerful DBMS, but it demands a thorough knowledge of its many different parts. Many of these pieces have very specific roles because the database itself is platform-neutral. The continuing issues we had making what should have been a simple connection taught me a valuable lesson: the more robust the DBMS, the more challenging it may be to deploy. By the way, STORET stands for STOrage and RETrieval system.

February 27, 1997

I spent the bulk of the day today working on the preliminary definitions of the biological tables. I continued studying the Huntington information, as well as the sample report that Richard gave me. Eventually, I put together a written description of each of the tables in a document. I faxed this to the Nashville office, and about 3:00 in the afternoon Richard called me back. We spent over an hour discussing things. We added a few fields, and changed a few others. He wants to spend a couple of days looking this over and thinking about it. He should also receive the information from Pittsburgh in the next few days. Then he wants to come here about next Friday or so and hammer through this stuff to get a good, firm foundation.

March 7, 1997

*I spent most of the day today trying to figure out the meanings and usage of some of the tables in the existing Oracle database. I had tried several times to get information on all the tables by using "select * from tab" but could never get this to return any information (could this be a permissions issue?). Finally, I got an idea. I ran the export program on the entire database and chose not to export the data. When I looked at this file, it had exactly what I needed. It took a while to reformat this; but, now, I have a file that identifies all the fields in the entire structure and the indices as well. There are a number of tables that have no records in them, and there are still some whose purpose I cannot figure out, but this is an excellent start. Later in the day, I talked to some of the Nashville team about how they interact with the system, and that helped as well. I also downloaded (via export) some more of the data I need.*

March 10, 1997

I made a final review of the tables I have downloaded and/or drawn up from scratch and found a few holes. I filled those by going back to the Huntington system and getting the ones that were missing. Then I reviewed the structure of the menu system I had set up to make sure I had allowed for access to all the tables in the system. I found several more holes there, which I patched. These two processes took almost all day, but by the end of the day, I was fairly comfortable that I had the complete database and menu system set up.

It had become apparent that the new interface I was developing would be used for all the data – both the new biological information and the existing physical/chemical data. This made it imperative that I learn the structure of the existing schema in detail. The Nashville District had requested documentation on the database from the software vendor, but that request had so far not been granted. That left me in the unenviable position of having to work out the details of the existing schema purely by examining data and checking table structures. It was not an easy undertaking, but sometimes you're forced into taking the long route.

March 14, 1997

Mark Campbell called me this morning with some good news. They now have the SQL*Net connection working. They were able to use SQL*Plus to connect to the Oracle database on the workstation, but they still got an error when they tried to use

ODBC. We did a little checking over the phone for some files that we couldn't find. I was about to give up when I got an idea to go back to the basics. We went into the ODBC configuration and examined the connect string for the database. It was something like "t:###.###.###.###:WCDB" so I had them change it to simply "WCDB." Then, when we tried the ODBC test function, it worked!

The bad news is that it took us several months to connect the program to the live database. The good news is that efforts like this have been made much less intimidating in the last 20+ years. This is due to advances both on the software side (the software pieces that connect these components are a lot more mature and stable now) and on the information sharing side (the Internet makes it much easier to search for possible solutions).

April 4, 1997

I turned my attention back to the taxa code tables today. I had been working on the animal taxa codes, so that's where I went .... All the codes are now entered in the animal taxa table, and the programs are in place to do the same thing for the algae table.

This was the first major compromise I made in the design of the biological module. Richard Tippit was well known and had a reputation as an exceptionally talented analyst. I was impressed with his credentials and the knowledge he exhibited during our sessions designing the biology tables. One thing he consistently emphasized was that there were dramatic differences between the collection and analysis of phytoplankton samples and other types of biological samples (benthic macroinvertebrates and zooplankton). Based on his guidance and input, we had created different tables for these pursuits. We had separate taxa tables for kingdoms Plantae and Animalia, and we had two separate results tables – one for benthic macroinvertebrates and one for everything else. When I looked at what we had done, I knew intuitively that the differences were not significant enough from a data management perspective to justify the separation. The inherent problem this introduced in the database schema is that it prevented defining any direct relationship between the results and taxa tables for the non-benthic results table. This was because the taxa entries could refer to either one of the two taxa tables, depending on the sample type (phytoplankton sample = plant taxa table, zooplankton sample = animal taxa table). I can't fault Richard for this situation. His expertise was in the collection of samples and analysis of data, and he brought that knowledge into the database design discussion (as he should). I was confident that he knew things about the relationships between the data elements that I did not, and so I opted to go along and not worry so much about the implications in the database. I could code around it. It would be many years before we corrected this situation.

May 6, 1997

Today was the big meeting to view the software progress. Mark and Richard came in to see the stuff, and overall I think they were very impressed. We came up with a surprisingly short list of bugs and new ideas. They left with a good feeling, I think. The best comment I heard was from Mark. He said that when they first got into the other system, no one expected they would ever use it because it was just too daunting. He said he thought no one would be intimidated by this. He thought it was very friendly, even as it was becoming more robust.

This is the best compliment possible for someone who creates user interfaces. It means that I had been able to build a data model that adequately captured the complexities of their business model while still creating user interaction paradigms that were understandable and appropriate.

11 Birth

11.1 DAWN

Our existing contract with the Nashville District had expired, although we were still funded for a few tasks related to completing work that was awarded prior to the end of the contract period. We had already bid on a new support contract that would allow us to continue our development efforts with them and were still awaiting news of that outcome. Meanwhile, my boss had begun to explore whether we might be able to interest other clients in these types of endeavors.

August 4, 1997

My boss asked me today to spruce up my ArcView project files and make them look as good as possible. We now know that we won't be getting the new contract, but he still thinks we can market this product to other districts and possibly outside organizations. He wants to make a trip next week or so to some of the other districts, showing the product.

September 5, 1997

I got a call from Bob Sneed this afternoon. He wanted to discuss the plans for the AWRA paper, so we talked about that a little. We decided to have a poster session to go along with the talk.

Bob had asked me to collaborate with him on a joint presentation at a symposium hosted by the Tennessee Section of the American Water Resources Association (AWRA). He was eager to demonstrate the new GIS interface to a wider audience. I eagerly accepted the invitation, both to bolster our relationship with the Nashville District and to test the waters to see if any other organizations might be interested in a similar interface.

September 9, 1997

I spent a very long day today driving with one of our PMs to Louisville and back. We met with the PM and technical staff from the Louisville District to discuss our efforts in Nashville. I think the meeting went very well.

Word was spreading within the Corps about our work. There seemed to be some enthusiasm for the GIS interface among the districts that had been involved in testing the previous database. This increased our chances of being able to continue with the development after the end of our current work for Nashville.

September 24, 1997

I talked for a while today with the boss about the direction of our development efforts on the water quality database and plotting work I've been doing for the Nashville District. He wants to try and adapt that to commercial use, and he thinks he has a potential client interested. With that in mind, we discussed products, services, and names. I outlined my idea that there were really about three levels of things here. At the lowest level is the simple plotting package, which I have been calling the Hydrologic Information Plotting Program (HIPP). I told the boss that I thought this could be a stand-alone program that we sell fairly cheaply. The next step up from that is the full-blown data management system like the one I am in the process of developing. We talked about a name for that; his favorite was HIVAS – Hydrologic Information Visualization and Analysis System. I pointed out that there was more to the system than just hydrologic information – we also have water quality and biological components. He then asked me to figure out a name for the overall database product. I spent quite a bit of time on it, and the best I came up with was Data Management and Analysis System for Lakes, Estuaries, and Rivers – DASLER. (Some of the others I rejected were VADREL – Visualization, Analysis, and Data Management for Rivers, Estuaries, and Lakes, DARREL – Data Management, Analysis, and Reporting for Rivers, Estuaries, and Lake, and DAMFAS – Data Analysis and Management for Freshwater Aquatic Systems.) My boss didn't seem to be thrilled with the DASLER name, but he didn't object to it, either. As for the third level (the data management with GIS), it still seems to me that this will almost have to be a custom service rather than a product. We can demonstrate the capability of integrating our software (DASLER) with the GIS system, but it still seems like it will have to be a custom effort anytime we do it.

Any software developer will tell you that the most fun part of their job is trying to come up with a catchy name for their product.[1] I wasn't initially all that enthralled with the DASLER name (it's pronounced with a hard S ... like "dazzler"), but it grew on me pretty quickly. More importantly, Bob Sneed really liked it. More to the point regarding this log entry, we were still in the very early stages of the database interface. None of us knew at that point whether that part of the project would even be successful. I therefore tried to point out to my boss that we had two options currently in working order that we could try to promote. The worst possible outcome would have been for him to sell other clients on the idea of a complete data management

---

[1] Here is my all-time favorite name I ever came up with. I was developing software related to formerly used defense sites, which were abbreviated as FUDS. The particular application in this case was a database for cataloging documents that described the history of a particular site. These documents were used in determining who should be responsible for cleanup and restoration activities at the site. The name I came up with was the Electronic Library of Materials for Environmental Restoration at Formerly Used Defense Sites, or (wait for it) ELMER FUDS.

system for surface water quality data, only to have us fail in our attempt to properly create it.

11.2   MORNING

October 13–15, 1997

Road trip days. I came in to the office Monday morning and did a few last-minute updates to the program in preparation for taking it on the road to Huntington. I left with one of our PMs a little before 1:00. We arrived in Huntington around 7:00, checked in to a hotel, then went out for supper.

Our meeting Tuesday morning was at the lock and dam from which Huntington's water quality team operates. It took us about an hour to get there. The Huntington team's PM had called in sick for the day. Fortunately, his technical lead was in and available to spend a little time with us, so we proceeded. I showed him the plotting program and the database front-end. He was not interested in seeing the GIS component, so we skipped that. He had some interesting things to say, the most interesting of which was that the original commercial database interface was intended to be a temporary fix all along. Apparently, he has been waiting for something like this for quite a while. He really liked the plotting package, saying that he has to spend several hours preparing the plots that we can generate in minutes. All in all, he was very enthusiastic about the product.

All the districts that had been involved in testing the original commercial database – Nashville, Louisville, Huntington, and Pittsburgh – now seemed excited about our new design. Very encouraging. Meanwhile, I continued development of the primary database interface (DASLER) as described in numerous very boring log entries.

November 3, 1997

The person who will assume the technical lead for this effort in the Louisville office called this morning to set up the first meeting with me.

November 5, 1997

I talked to Bob Sneed today, and he kind of changed my thinking on a couple of issues. While we were talking, he said he would like for the system to go immediately from generating the sample numbers to entering the typical field data. After considering this, I decided they might rather have this whole field entry thing work a little differently. Instead of first identifying the locations and then generating the sample numbers and then entering the data, they might rather enter things one station at a time.

This note demonstrates the importance of a thorough understanding of all aspects of the business' practices before you start designing the interface. My thought process regarding the creation of sampling events and capture of field data was too database oriented: the process I originally created involved users first describing all the sampling events for a trip and then going back to enter the field observations for each one. I should have recognized before this point that the approach I had defined was not quite the same as the path taken by the field crews. Their mental picture compartmentalized all the actions taken at each location as a different event. It made sense, then, that they would think about entering the data that way. I had already designed forms and coded part of this process, but I had to abandon it in favor of what I learned during this conversation. The lesson in this (avoid imposing your own preconceptions) was one I try never to forget.

November 12, 1997

Today the boss and I traveled to the Nashville Corps offices to meet with both them and the Louisville group. The purpose of the meeting was to determine how to get Louisville up to speed and actively using the same capabilities that Nashville has and will have with the new database interface. The meeting went pretty well. We discussed the hardware requirements and the Unix system that Louisville is acquiring. We decided that Nashville's Unix administrator would provide the same setup and transition services to them that he provided to Nashville, and then we would take over and make similar changes to their data. By the end of the meeting, we had identified a ten-step process for this effort. Two of the steps were somewhat ill-defined: changing the database interface to incorporate differences in the way Louisville and Nashville operate, and changing the plotting program along the same lines. Key to the process will be getting a more complete definition of what is involved in those steps, which is part of another of the steps: visiting Louisville to determine how they operate differently from Nashville. I will travel to Louisville soon to do this analysis and return to write a comprehensive plan. Louisville will use the information I collect as they generate the scope of work and figure out how to fund the rest of the effort.

I would get to apply what I just learned almost immediately. I vowed to take steps to ensure that this would be a more comprehensive walk-through of the practices in Louisville than the one I had done with Nashville. (In fairness to me, I had gained more insight into the processes while creating the new database interface, so there was less information to take in with this second iteration.)

December 9, 1997

I had a very long, but productive, day. I flew to Louisville this morning. Louisville's technical lead picked me up at the airport. When we arrived at the office, we went to work immediately. We discussed in great detail the procedures they use, the nature of their data, etc. We spent all morning on the physical/chemical data and procedures. After lunch, we brought in their biologist for that part of the data. I think I got enough to write a fairly comprehensive scope of work.

Did I truly learn the lesson and actually get sufficient information to accurately and efficiently adapt our existing code to their needs, or would I run into additional differences as I progressed? I guess we'll see.

December 11, 1997

Mark and Richard were here today. We spent all day hashing out the data storage requirements for the biological tables. We discussed each item in detail, and in the end we came up with a few changes to the structures I had planned so far.

Up to this point I had been coding the portion of the interface that dealt with data previously managed by the original database (the physical and chemical data). Now we were starting to move into new territory. This would quickly determine whether or not I had properly modified the existing database schema.

December 16, 1997

Richard called me first thing this morning with questions about the document I sent that described the table structures. The biggest point of confusion was how to store the BIOSCORE records.

In Part 1 we mentioned several times that even very smart people can have trouble understanding how databases work. This was a classic example. Fortunately, Richard learned pretty quickly.

December 22, 1997

I spent all day working on the results dialog. Not much to report, as things are in a kind of routine mode now. I still have a few questions about the structure of the results table. There are several fields about which I know little or nothing. Nashville has no data in these fields, and I have no idea as to their purpose.

Oh, the joys of working with an existing schema for which no documentation has been provided. In retrospect, I should have realized that if the client was not using these columns – as evidenced by the lack of data – there would be no harm in ignoring them. That would not be the case if they were going to continue using the original interface, but since I was developing a new one, I needed assurance that removal of the columns would not result in any errors.

11.3 UPHEAVAL

February 2, 1998

I continue to struggle to find the answer to the Oracle performance question ….

February 3, 1998

*… [T]he gist of the conversation was that we had to upgrade the ODBC driver (no surprise there). The catch, however, was that the upgraded ODBC driver only works with a newer version of SQL*Net ….*

February 9, 1998

*… [W]ith the upgrade to NT 4.0, they have to upgrade the ODBC driver. But the new ODBC driver is not compatible with SQL*Net 2.2 ….*

This series of log entry excerpts describe an error that could have proven fatal to the entire process. More complete information about what was going on can be found in the discussion after the entries for March 10 and 11, 1998. (I was struggling to figure it out. I thought you might enjoy that same sense of confusion.)

February 13, 1998

Meanwhile, I spent much of the day working on the dialog that extracts data and prepares it for plotting. I made a couple of abortive attempts, then decided to go back and do it pretty much like the ArcView program does it. I printed off the

Avenue code to remind myself how that thing works, then started coding the VB program similarly.

This entry points to an interesting compromise that had we had to make. Nashville liked HIPP (the DASLER graphing utility that produces the four plots that started this whole project) and had decided they wanted to invoke it from either the GIS interface or the database interface. I developed it originally to work within the GIS, so it was programmed to get its data from .dbf files because that was the database format supported by ArcView shape files. The database interface, on the other hand, interacted with Oracle. We needed HIPP to communicate with both platforms. There seemed to be three options for how to meet this goal: (1) create a parallel version of HIPP that obtained its data from the database, (2) modify HIPP so that it was smart enough to get data from either source, or (3) make the database interface spit data out in .dbf format for HIPP's use. I opted for the third choice.

February 18, 1998

I spent all day on the rich text editor, and almost finished it in one day. It has limited capabilities – change fonts, cut, copy, paste, bold, underline, italic, and justification – but it works fine.

I knew from the outset that DASLER would include at least a handful of reports, and I was confident about how the Corps wanted to deal with them – bring them up in a report window, potentially manipulate the text a bit (e.g., adding bolding for emphasis), and then print them or save them from there. You would think that I could have found an existing control of some sort that provided all the necessary features. I tried several options early in the development process, but they all failed to meet one or more key requirements. I therefore did what you always have to do in that situation: I built a new one. This can be a challenge, but fortunately in this case the functional requirements were minimal (although very specialized in some respects). The report form I created during this period still serves as the primary report window in DASLER today.

March 10, 1998

I spent most of my time testing the Access vs. Oracle question ....

March 11, 1998

I spent the morning tinkering with the prospect of having ArcView get its data from Access ....

We hit a major glitch during this time frame, and it came from an unexpected source. When Nashville upgraded their computers from Windows NT 3.5 to Windows NT 4.0, their connection to the Oracle database suddenly got very, very slow – as in unusably slow. Beginning in mid-January, I had attempted with little success to reproduce the problem in my development environment (I did not yet have a copy of NT 4.0). In March I traveled to Nashville to troubleshoot the problem in person. Eventually we (Mark, the Unix admin, and I) traced the problem down to versions of software that were not compatible. This should have been resolvable with updates to one or more of the components, but after more than a month of downtime, no updates were on the horizon.[2] This sent our entire team scrambling for an alternative solution. Oddly enough, we did discover that the Jet database engine could somehow connect to Oracle using a different ODBC driver, so one proposal was to create a Jet/Access database that would act as a pass-through. I spent a lot of time testing the implications of this change. I knew it would have little effect on the database interface, but the big concern was whether or not we could make it work with ArcView. Ultimately the decision was made to proceed in that direction. We created two variations on this theme. Each district could opt to simply store their data in a native Jet file or have the Jet file act as a conduit to data stored in Oracle. This was originally intended to be a temporary solution.

March 31, 1998

One of the things I had suspected during this troubleshooting episode was index corruption. I went to Access, and there I discovered that none of the Oracle indices were converted.

Here's a handy tip: if you have to move data from one DBMS to another, NEVER trust a utility provided by either platform. I did, and assumptions I made about what it would and would not transfer were incorrect. The utility (I apparently did not document whether it was from Oracle or Microsoft) purported to replicate the complete data structure from Oracle in the Jet database and then move the data. It created the tables well enough, but it did not replicate any of the indices or constraints. I concluded that instead of using one of these tools, a better approach is to take the time to carefully create the schema in the new platform before moving the data.

April 28, 1998

After a long wait, we finally got a call from our contact at the power company today. He contacted us this morning, and we now have an appointment to show him the wonders of DASLER.

I had received a request from a major power company to provide more information on DASLER. They had heard about it during some of their work with the Corps. Bob had given them my contact information and tipped me off that they may be reaching out.

May 4, 1998

Richard called me back this morning and we talked about the missing biological data. He indicated that these taxa were kind of a mess and that there was no class or order assigned to these. After some discussion we decided to add the descriptions "class uncertain" and "order uncertain" in these cases.

---

[2] The specific elements that were out of sync were the ODBC driver, the version of SQL*Net, and the version of Oracle. Around this time Oracle had announced intentions to enter the desktop computing arena in a big way in an attempt to surpass Microsoft as the dominant vendor. This very public spat had each of them refusing to update their software to make it more compatible with products from the other. Ultimately it was the user community that paid the price.

Sometimes the migration to database-based information does not go smoothly. For our taxa tables, we had agreed that we would require entries for each taxon's hierarchy at the kingdom, phylum, class, order, and family levels. When we got into the process of loading the taxa information already in use, we discovered several issues. This was one of them: results recorded for organisms that were not identified to the level we expected. Our resolution was satisfactory from a database perspective, but unrealistic from a practical standpoint. Each taxon name had to be unique, so creating these entries required us to catalog a number of organisms in ways that were likely inaccurate. That is, we only had one "order uncertain" entry, so any results set that included that entry implicitly indicated the presence of some common organism. Fortunately, this was a stopgap measure. Subsequent research was required, but eventually we were able to properly identify the relationships for the organisms for which this information was missing. This was a compromise that allowed us to advance the process without having to pause while the issue was resolved.

May 5, 1998

I spent most of the day today on the biology data. I now have most of the work on the taxa tables done, but there is a slight hold up on the biotic indices table .... All the other biotic indices use numeric values, and that's what we have in the database. But the new list includes one index that uses letters. I tried to call Richard, but he is out today and tomorrow in the field. Hopefully he will get back to me soon so we can discuss this. The easiest fix will be to simply assign numeric values to these ratings.

The issue here is that the design of the biotic index scores table was done without examining a sufficient cross-section of the scores themselves. The initial examples that Richard found turned out to be limited in that they only included biotic indices whose scores were numeric. When the more complete set of data were provided for initial loading into the database, these indices would not import correctly. As errors go, this one was not terribly severe and was identified sufficiently early so that the impact on the project was minimal.

May 7, 1998

... I ended up writing a separate function for calculating the number of significant digits for an entry.

The schema in the existing database stored results in a numeric field. As a mathematician, that made sense to me. As I got further into the interface development, though, I began to realize the problems associated with this approach. (These are discussed briefly in Section 8.3, in the portion about the RESULTS table.) Recognition of the issue arose as I was developing some of the reports. Simply retrieving and presenting the values from the database tables resulted in the output including the number of digits inherent in the column's data type. Formatting was necessary, but the challenge was to determine how many of the digits were significant. This led to the creation of functions to determine the number of significant digits present when a value was first entered, inclusion of columns to store the number of digits, and functions to format the values accordingly at time of output. The functions had to be called in every instance where a value for a numeric field was entered or imported, and every instance where data were shown to the user. These restrictions produced a noticeable affect on overall performance. We ended up retaining these methods until Version 4.0.

May 14, 1998

The meeting with the power company went fairly well. We were supposed to meet from 8:00 to 10:00 and then leave, but when we got into it, they wanted to keep going. We ended up continuing through lunch and after, until 2:30. They were very impressed with the demo, and I think they want our help. Our next step is to put together an esti-mate for some first-round work to begin by the fall or so.

Expanding the clientele for which we perform data management services was cer-tainly the right choice from a business perspective. However, I did not completely anticipate how it would affect the software.

June 18, 1998

After talking with Louisville again about the particulars of some of the QC samples, we hit on a compromise. They were having trouble identifying the significance of some of the possible identified QC samples, so we decided to move all these question-able ones to a new table for dealing with later.

More misadventures related to migrating data. By now we had changed so many things from the original database that ours could correctly be called a new schema. Our schema differed even in some areas that had already existed in the original data-base. We now had two Corps Districts participating in the design, and we had all agreed on a minor change regarding how QC samples were identified. None of us recognized beforehand that this minor change could potentially affect records that had to be migrated from the previous database. In this case, everyone involved agreed to defer addressing this problem because there were more important issues that needed immediate attention. Sometimes you just have to set some of the data aside and deal with it later.

11.4   DELIVERY

June 30, 1998

I continued to plow through the users' guide today. I'm trying to keep this as short as possible, but it's hard. There's a lot that a user might need to know.

I was now getting close to delivering the initial version of the new database inter-face to Nashville. Because there would be multiple users both in Nashville and (hope-fully) in other districts, I felt that I should provide some reference material for them. The easiest option would be a users' guide. I was also looking into methods for cre-ating context-sensitive help files. I had a feeling that the alternative would involve me being on the phone constantly, explaining how things worked.

August 3, 1998

I talked to Mark for a while today. After some discussion, we decided that he should start the process of updating their database and getting things ready for full operation.

So far all the work done in the Nashville and Louisville districts with the new interface had been beta testing. We were now approaching the point where we could truly go live.

August 6, 1998

I talked to Bob at length today about our trip to DC next week.

The fact that there were now multiple districts that were pursuing using the revised database and our new interface had garnered the attention of the national water quality program manager. Bob had been asked to come to DC for a demonstration and bring me along.

August 12, 1998

It was a long day, but a worthwhile one. I arrived in DC about 9:30 and made my way to Corps headquarters .... I signed in and then headed up to a conference room to meet with the national water quality Program Manager, the Director of HEC, Bob, and several others .... They started the meeting by presenting a brief overview of their water control system development project, then we moved on to our water quality system. Overall they were fairly impressed, I think. They appear ready to sanction this thing nationally.

We appeared to be in a good position to support the water quality mission throughout the Corps. This would be a huge win, both for the Nashville District (for originating the development) and for my company (as the developer). But fate had other ideas.

August 13, 1998

I talked to the folks at STORET today. They are sending me a document which describes the export format I need to generate that enables STORET to read in the data.

There was one final piece of the puzzle that we had thus far ignored. As a federal agency, the Corps was obligated to share their water quality data with others. Nashville was, of course, aware of this obligation and had mentioned it during various discussions. As you might suspect, it became more important when we met in Washington. At this time, the best available mechanism for accomplishing that goal was EPA's STOrage and RETrieval system (STORET). STORET first appeared in the 1970s and was the first database EPA had created for managing water quality data on a national level. We needed DASLER to be able to send data to STORET; I just needed to get more information on the format. The format turned out to be relatively simple, so this feature was implemented quite quickly.

August 31, 1998

I got started on the field data collection planning module today. I reviewed the information from Louisville about how their process works, and spent a lot of time thinking about how to implement it in the database.

This was a late request from the Louisville office, and was one for which the database schema had not yet been prepared. All the districts that have water quality missions prepare a sampling plan at the beginning of each calendar year. They use this plan to track their progress toward completion of their water quality management goals throughout the year. Nashville had opted not to include this in the data model – focusing instead on the actual collection and analysis of data – but Louisville now wanted that process to be part of the database interface. I would have been justified in denying this request since it was not in the original scope. However, I determined that we had sufficient budget to at least attempt it, and under those circumstances I felt that pleasing the client was the wiser choice. I was able to capture the overall process, but I have to admit that the process I created was very unimaginative and quite kludgy.

The months between this post and the next one cited below were filled with stamping out bugs and tweaking the user interface to better adhere to the client's practices and procedures. I added some additional new features that were not part of the original plan. I also spent a good deal of time adapting the GIS interface to work with the Jet database rather than Oracle.

November 30–December 4, 1998

I spent the entire week in Louisville meeting the final delivery objectives for the DASLER project there …. Setting up the GIS interface for them got very interesting. They didn't have a base map layer established yet, and it took us some time to get an appropriate one created. I imported the sampling point theme and it appeared to be okay, but there did not appear to be as many locations as there should be. Upon closer inspection, I discovered that more than half their locations had coordinate entries in the database that were the same – the coordinates of the building where their office is located.

This presented a quandary: was there any way to control the latitude and longitude entries for the sampling locations? I briefly considered trying to make each location's coordinates be unique, but in the end that would not have solved the problem of entering values that did not actually correspond to the physical location. Ultimately I gave up on attempting to trap this in code and instead left it to the client to resolve this issue.

This was the final delivery of the product to Louisville. We now had two districts using the system for their actual data collection, management, analysis, and reporting. A minor celebration would not have been out of the question, but all of us recognized that this was truly just the beginning.

12 Growth

12.1 DIVERSIFICATION

December 7–9, 1998

Back from Louisville, I barely had time to catch my breath before heading out again. I was in the office until about 10:30 Monday morning. I filled out my expense report for the Louisville trip, and we had a staff meeting. I had little time for anything else, though, because I was getting things ready for the meeting with the power company. I printed five more copies of the DASLER manual, as well as multiple copies of the data dictionary. Then I hit the road.

The meetings went very well. The first major issue was a difference in how the power company identified sampling locations. It took most of the day Tuesday to work through the preliminaries and get a handle on how to designate them. We tossed out several options, and finally hit on one we thought would serve them well. Unfortunately, this method will require a fair amount of reprogramming of the interface, but I expected that.

The biggest change in DASLER is going to occur because of the tight integration they have within the organization. The lab is an integrated part of the operation, so there is a much higher degree of interaction. In fact, the lab generates numbers for the samples before they are even collected. The sampling plan is also a much bigger part of the picture here. I think I have a good understanding of the basic approach, but there might be some clarifications needed. I was also invited to go out sampling with them. I agreed to do this in January or February. That will help a lot in understanding the total picture.

There is a lot to digest here. I was beginning to realize that the ultimate question was whether our company was going to try to sell DASLER as software or as a service. If it was to be software, I had to find a way to build enough flexibility into certain parts of the code to accommodate varying practices. Selling it as a service would make the overall software coding easier, but the code itself would have to be adapted to each installation. Thus, the cost to clients would be higher. The last part of the last paragraph is very important. Observing a practice in the real world is frequently much more informative than just taking notes about it during a meeting.

DOI: 10.1201/9781003131953-14

December 14, 1998

I finished writing up the data dictionary for the power company's version this morning. Then I wrote another document which summarizes the differences in theirs and the other version. The two are intended to be read in tandem. I e-mailed the two documents to their technical lead, and he said they would probably get together tomorrow or Wednesday and respond by the end of this week. In the meantime, there are some things I can get started on already.

The boss had decided that we would pursue this work as a service, so I had to treat this iteration like a new endeavor. The two documents were important in effectively communicating our understanding of the requirements to the client. They formed the basis for our project plan.

December 16, 1998

I got a call from the technical lead at the power company. We discussed a couple of items, and then he approved the data dictionary as I had delivered it, with one exception. He still wants another day to allow others to comment on the project controls, which is the area we expanded the most. He expects to get back to me tomorrow with approval on that area.

I can't stress this enough: communication, communication, communication.

12.2   EXILE

January 7, 1999

I turned in my resignation today.

(Bet you didn't see that coming, did you?) Our company had been purchased by another one. The new owner imposed some very different policies, and I eventually determined I could not work under those conditions. (If this was the entertainment business, I guess you would say I left because of creative differences.) This was a difficult decision for me because of the relationships I had built with the DASLER user community. I also knew that what we had constructed to this point still needed a lot of enhancement and expansion, and I felt an obligation to see the development through. But in the end the working environment had become too toxic to stay. I had spent more than three years developing DASLER, and I admit to being emotionally invested in it. But sometimes you just have to let things go.

January 8, 1999

I kind of came to an impasse today on the power company's version of DASLER. The sticking point is their preference for determining the time of a sample from the automated collection equipment. This forces each depth to have a different time. I've gone back and forth on this issue several times over the past few days, and today I came down on the side of wanting them to change their ways. The problem is that all the code so far is set up to use a single time for an entire column of samples. That allows me to ask the user once for the date and time up front. Now, though, I'll have to make allowances for the time in every separate depth. I started tinkering with the field observations form today with this in mind, and it will get quite ugly.

In my resignation, I agreed to stay on for three weeks; therefore, I was still continuing my duties. This entry describes another situation of competing requirements. The client wanted to adhere to their existing policy of recording vertical profile data with different time stamps for each depth. Normally I would have agreed to accommodate their request, but in this case I had seen the effects this would have on the data model – and especially the interface – and I felt strongly that my way was better. They didn't see it before now because they had never been in a position of accessing all their data from a single point of entry. In the end they finally agreed to my approach. I think an important factor in that decision was when they realized that when they saved these vertical profile measurements in a spreadsheet, the name of the spreadsheet specified the date and time of the first observation in the profile – which is basically what I was proposing.

January 15, 1999

The boss told me today that he had hired the guy we interviewed on Monday. He will start a week from next Monday, which will be my last week. There will be a lot to cover that week.

If ever there was a need for a Vulcan mind meld in real life, this would be it.

January 28, 1999

The technical lead from the power company arrived early this morning, and we spent all day in our meeting. We went through the status of the data conversion efforts and the status of the code, then launched into his dealings with the program. It took most of the day, but we managed to get through the process in fairly good shape. I made about a page of notes on changes that need to occur, and we left it at that. I'll review this list with the new guy tomorrow.

My penultimate day at this company was spent with the client, documenting status and taking notes on what would need to change in their version. My objective was to get the new guy in the best position possible to be successful in completing the project to the client's satisfaction.

My new company was very similar to my old company in terms of capabilities and specialties. In fact, the two companies had worked together on the same project on at least one occasion in the past. The difference was that the new company was a little larger and still owned by its founder – someone whose expertise was moored firmly in the environmental field.

February 8–12, 1999

During the week I had several discussions about continuing work with the Louisville District.

My departure from the old company had created a difficult situation for the original DASLER clients. My old company was still under contract to deliver some updates to the Nashville District. Louisville still had a need for assistance with their data but had no current task orders with the old company; their preference was to engage my services through my new company. I was concerned that any changes I did for Louisville might involve changes to the code. Having two different contractors now potentially working on the product would make coordination more difficult. I cautiously agreed to assist Louisville with data, but tried to be careful about committing to making any changes to the code or data model.

February 24, 1999

I started work on the DASLER presentation materials this morning. There was also some discussion with my new boss about the need to rename DASLER.

My new company was interested in developing a variation of DASLER that could be sold as commercial off-the-shelf software (thus switching the business model from service to software) and was willing to invest their own research and development money in that effort. I was asked to prepare a presentation that would educate upper management about the current status of the system. We all also agreed that a new name for our product would be necessary to distinguish it from the previous version.

February 25, 1999

Last night I tossed around many possible acronyms for the new DASLER. My personal favorite was SPLASH (Software for Plotting, Linking, and Analyzing Surface Hydrology). Other possibilities included SWAMP (Surface Water Analysis and Management Program), HYDRA (Hydrologic Data management, Reporting, and Analysis), and TWINS (the Total Watershed INformation System). This morning I called my new boss with these suggestions. He had e-mailed me with his only suggestion: EDMAPS (Environmental Data Management And Plotting System). Anyway, at his suggestion I e-mailed some proposed names to the president of the company for his review and selection. To my surprise, he chose TWINS because he envisions eventually including groundwater and other types of data. So now I have a name, and just need to start working on the code.

I called Louisville today to let them know the new company had been successfully added to one of their existing contracts.

After some internal discussions, the new company decided that I should agree to Louisville's request for data support.

May 11, 1999

I found out today (from Mark) that Huntington has gone ahead with a task order to the old company for converting their data to DASLER. Meanwhile, the old company has delivered some code updates to Nashville, but there seem to be some problems with this iteration.

The first software update delivered by my replacement at the old company did not turn out well. Nashville was now very concerned about the future of DASLER if new arrangements were not made. Huntington apparently contracted with the old company to migrate their data before the code situation became apparent.

May 18, 1999

Today I visited the web site of a commercial software vendor who specializes in managing groundwater data. I met that company's owner/president at the New Jersey conference and, apparently after that, he contacted my new company's headquarters. He had some discussions with my new boss, and now is asking about teaming with us to get DASLER/TWINS rolled into their suite as a surface water product.

This seemed like an opportunity to jump start our push into the commercial software arena. Rather than having to create interest in an entirely new package, this would give us a chance to leverage the awareness of an existing system. The modified version of DASLER would become a part of a larger package of software for managing multiple types of environmental data. (Would it still be called TWINS? I really liked that name.)

May 20, 1999

I got a call from the Nashville Corps team today. They had just completed their conference call with the other districts within their Division and wanted to let me know what was discussed. They have all agreed to hold off any new development work until my former company's Huntington work is done. The deadline on that is August 1, and nothing else will happen until after that is done.

This conversation hinted at the possibility that future development of DASLER might land back on my desk.

July 1, 1999

I spoke today with Bob Sneed and he gave me the lowdown on the approach that is pending. There will be a conference call next week during which various scope items will be narrowed down. Then there will be a request for a quote from both companies.

The Corps had decided to contract the continued DASLER development to only one of the companies. This was the only logical approach, and the only one that had a chance of making DASLER successful. Each company would be asked to submit a proposal to address a specific list of requested changes. Since my former company had been modifying the code since my departure, the Corps provided me with a copy of the latest version so we could be responsive regarding the specific new requirements. I began the process of meticulously comparing my last version with the latest one.

July 2, 1999

I continued the comparison of the DASLER forms. Surprisingly, most of these have not changed significantly or at all.

July 8, 1999

I spent a couple of hours late in the day finishing up my analysis of the changes to DASLER. I now have a comprehensive list of the changes that were made since I left.

July 13, 1999

In my review of the changes in the DASLER code since I left the old company, I had made a note to myself to go back and check a few things in more detail because they looked interesting. I did one of those today. A new feature of the tabular report was a statistical option which returned statistics on the selected data. Good idea, but the implementation was not good. I got really worried when I saw some of the calculations. They were a mess (example: the code to calculate the median was exactly the same as the code for calculating the mean).

No wonder the client had been complaining about the revised interface. I began to grow confident that I would end up back on the project very soon.

July 20, 1999

I stumbled on to a fix for several of the problems that Louisville has encountered in recent weeks. I was talking to the technical lead there, and he was describing an error that occurred when he tried to import lab log files. The error was being caused by an index violation, but I couldn't find any code that would trigger this. Finally, he admitted that someone in their office had created some indices on their own in Access. I suggested he delete them. Later in the day I got a message from him saying that when he deleted his extra indices, the problem went away.

The problem with using a Jet database is that everyone thinks because they can open it in Access, they can make changes without repercussions. (Actually, this is a problem with any DBMS. With the right tools and passwords, any database can be opened and modified. It's just particularly easy with Jet.) Because this was actually the client's database – not mine – I was not comfortable putting controls in place to prevent them from opening the database any time they wanted. Perhaps that was a mistake.

12.3   REUNION

July 29, 1999

The contract person in our HQ called me to say we were awarded the next phase of the DASLER work and the task order had been received.

August 3, 1999

I heard back from the technical lead at the power company today. My old company has at last delivered a final version of their database and interface. They (the power company) can't go live yet, though, because my old company still wants the power company's technical lead to do more data manipulation.

While I didn't know the full details, I found it distressing in this case to "deliver" a database product that was unusable until further manipulation was performed by the client. Remember, the old company was selling DASLER as a service. Under those terms, I would have expected them to continue working with the client, providing guidance and assistance until the data were usable. This effort had begun before I left the previous company, and I knew the terms of the contract called for migration of existing data into the system.

August 6, 1999

More information today about the commercial software developer. The next meeting will take place in our HQ on the 23rd and 24th of August.

Meanwhile, my new company was moving forward with selling DASLER as software. I pondered what effect it would have to be simultaneously supporting one product peddled both ways.

August 10, 1999

I got a couple of e-mails from Huntington today. They are getting some pushback from my former company about the original data dictionary and wanted to know what my plans were on the new version.

This was my biggest concern given the current situation. My former company was still on the hook to complete work for the Huntington District while at the same time my new company was already under contract to remove many of the changes made after my departure and rebuild the system after first returning it to its state when I had left. Ideally the new development contract should not have been issued until all the work was completed by my former company. However, given that the Huntington work had already been authorized before the larger Corps team decided to abandon the efforts of the old company, I'm not sure there was a better solution available. The lesson here is that, when you are developing something for another party, you sometimes have to deal with situations that are beyond your control.

August 26, 1999

I called EPA today and ordered a copy of STORET. I want to test the import files that I'm generating with my code.

As noted previously, one of the features included in DASLER from the earliest version was the ability to export data that was then submitted to EPA's STORET system. Around 1999, EPA created a new version of STORET. I had not read that much about the new version, but I had made the assumption that the format for submitting files would not be significantly different. I was able to find a process for requesting a copy of the software, so I did that. The fact that you could get a "copy" of STORET should have been a clue that major changes had occurred, but I didn't make that connection at first. It turned out that this change was significant.

August 30, 1999

I got a phone call from the PM for the commercial software company this morning. He wanted to discuss the parameter numbering issue. We hashed out some of the ideas, but the ultimate decision will be theirs. They already have a CAS [Chemical Abstract Service] number for their parameters, but most physical observations don't have CAS numbers.

This was the first glitch in our work with the commercial software company. The issue was that the two systems used different numbering schemes for internal parameter identifiers. Theirs was based on CAS numbers, but ours was not because we managed so many parameters that were not part of the CAS registry. Not difficult to resolve, but something that had to be addressed. These types of issues are plentiful when you attempt to merge two systems.

September 9, 1999

Today I started taking a hard look at the new STORET situation, and things got ugly. After a couple of hours of digging through the documentation, I came to the realization that we simply can't interface with the new STORET with the way things are now.

STORET had undergone a major overhaul. The original database had been designed in the 1970s and was hosted on a mainframe. The data model was quite simple and included only three primary tables: locations, samples, and results. There were very few metadata columns in any of the tables. To submit data, you sent an ASCII file that contained data for one of these three tables. In the mid-1990s EPA decided (correctly) that there was insufficient information in the original STORET data model to support evaluating data quality, so they completely revised the database. The new database was much more comprehensive and (as a result) complex. This presented a major problem regarding allowing users to submit data. This is an easy problem to understand when you consider how many different tables are affected when you import data into any comprehensive database. EPA solved this situation in a very interesting way: they created a local version of STORET. When you received the STORET setup package, you ran an installation script that installed a copy of Personal Oracle, created a local copy of the STORET database, and installed their user interface. The process of getting data into the national STORET data warehouse now consisted of entering your data into the local STORET first, and then submitting the entire database (using the Oracle export function) each time you wanted to update the national database. When EPA received your file, they dumped all existing data for your organization and replaced it with what was in the latest file. That was no problem if you had no existing data management software and decided to use STORET as your data management system. But if you had something else you preferred (like DASLER), how were you supposed to get data into the local copy of STORET? I was stymied at that point.

September 14, 1999

The water quality manager from Division called me back today and we discussed the STORET situation. He had more of the background that I didn't know. Basically, this whole update situation was driven by the fact that the old STORET was not Y2K compliant. During the initial planning phase of the project to correct that, though, the government shutdown wreaked havoc and they got way behind. The current implementation is their shot at things, but it is being very, very poorly received, especially by the states. His advice was to basically wait it out. He expects that things will evolve through at least one more major iteration before long, so anything I was able to do now would just have to be redone in the future anyway.

Official sanction to ignore the problem. Good answer (for now).

September 20, 1999

My former boss called me this afternoon. He had sent a guy to Huntington last week to migrate their data, but the guy apparently went AWOL. He never showed up in Huntington and instead e-mailed the company to say that he was quitting. No notice, no nothing. My former boss told me that he was now the one who was going to Huntington to move their data.

My former boss was, from my experience, a good engineer and a very good environmental modeler, but he had little previous background working with databases. He ended up asking me later if I would go to Huntington with him to do the data migration. There were at least two reasons I had to decline his request. First, there was no contractual arrangement between the two companies and insufficient time available to establish one. Second, I was not comfortable installing data on the client's system when I had very little knowledge about the data. If I was part of the delivery team, I felt this implied that I had reviewed and approved the data. Since that was not the case, I was hesitant to participate.

By the end of September I had completed all the data migration work for Louisville. The next phase of development for the Corps was on hold until the situation between my former company and Huntington was resolved, so I had some time to focus on the version of DASLER that was to become part of the commercial software vendor's suite.

November 18, 1999

I got a quick reply from the software company about the controls I'm using. They requested that I get copies of a set of custom controls they like from a particular vendor.

This turned out to be a fortuitous suggestion. To this point I had been using all standard VB controls plus one additional item: a database-centric grid control. I thought the grid control I was using was pretty good, but our teaming partner was using one they thought was much better. This turned out to be excellent advice because the new one had numerous additional features that made coding easier and also made the user experience more enjoyable. (The comments in Section 7.5 about using custom controls still apply here. In this case, I was taking advice from someone with much experience with these controls.)

November 23, 1999

The big news today was that I started creating a utility similar to HIPP but for the biological graphs. I've decided to call it BOGG (Biological Observations Graphics Generator). I'm using some of the same dialogs from HIPP, but the main one is significantly different. There are a lot more options to set up front, so I have a tabbed dialog as the main one. I laid down the basic framework today and got started on some of the code.

The idea for a graphing utility for biological data arose as part of the commercial software version development, but it would be also find its way into the original version of DASLER.

December 7, 1999

I talked to the technical manager in Huntington today. He passed on some interesting news – they have officially notified my former company that they have until the end of this week to complete the work.

Almost three months after delivering the "final" product to Huntington, the District still did not have a working version. They had been very patient, but that patience was running out.

February 1, 2000

I traveled to Nashville today to meet with Mark and Bob at their water quality lab. There was also one person in attendance I had never met: their lab manager. I had some misunderstanding about the purpose of the trip. I thought the discussion was to revolve around a better connection between their existing lab system and DASLER, but it turned out to be much more than that. What they really want is a replacement for the current system, and part of that will be better connection to DASLER. The existing system is a cobbled-together set of dBase programs and other files that is staggering toward obsolescence. The lab manager took me through the whole process of what he does, and I think he was happy that I understood each step completely.

This was a new and unexpected wrinkle. The Nashville District had their own lab in which they did some of their analyses. They needed a new way to manage the analyses they performed in the lab, and what better way to expedite documenting of results than linking it directly to their DASLER database?

February 3, 2000

During the afternoon I got a call from Bob and Mark in Nashville. They are ready to proceed with the lab data system. It's kind of interesting the approach they have decided to take on getting this under contract. Like Louisville, Nashville has decided to request that another contractor add us to their contract.

This became a common paradigm over the years. The work I was doing on DASLER was never costly enough to justify the process of issuing a separate contract. Instead, my company would get tacked on as a subcontractor to a company that already had a contract.

February 8, 2000

I spent much of the day today hammering away at a Huntington problem. Requesting data for a particular report was returning nothing, even though the data were clearly present in the database. Huntington is using the Jet pass-through option, so at one point we opened that file in Access and tried doing some of these retrievals manually. They seemed to be working just fine. We finally noticed that there were extra spaces after the location ID that caused the query to not find a match.

This error was caused by differences in data types between Oracle and Jet. I had been working mostly with Nashville and Louisville, who had both migrated to pure Jet for their data storage. Huntington was still using the pass-through option, so their data were in Oracle. The column in question (LOC_ID) was defined in the LOCATIONS table as a CHAR(12) data type in Oracle (this column still retained its data type from the original database). Recall from Chapter 4 that this means a fixed length of 12 characters, even if some of the characters are blanks. Construction of our query involved allowing the user to select a location from a dropdown list, which was populated from the LOCATIONS table. Thus, all the entries in this list had trailing

spaces if the intended ID contained less than 12 characters. We had modified the
SAMPLES table (which was the target of the query), and in that modification had
switched the LOC_ID field to VARCHAR(12). So the query was trying to match
an entry that was 12 characters long with one that was shorter. The reason I had not
seen this before was because the columns in the two tables were the same type in
the stand-alone Jet version. This was a rookie level mistake about which I was very
embarrassed – I should have known better.

12.4   TRAVELS

February 23–24, 2000

*I spent these two days in Nashville at the Corps water quality workshop … The most
interesting thing that happened was an intense discussion about the proper way to
calculate the mean of a set of pH values.*

This discussion was about something that had not yet occurred to me. The
value of pH is determined by measuring the concentration of Hydrogen ions in
the sample; the pH value is the negative of the base 10 logarithm of this number.
The discussion – which at times was so heated that it could have been called an
argument – was how to calculate the mean pH from a set of pH values. One side
argued that the normal method of calculating a mean was appropriate. The other
side posited that, because this was an exponential relationship, the proper procedure
was to convert the pH values back to hydrogen ion concentration, calculate the
mean of those values, and then convert that back to a pH value. Eventually both
sides agreed that either could be appropriate, depending on the circumstances. If
you were calculating the statistics based on samples collected at different times
from the same location, the standard mean pH approach was more informative. If
you were combining results from samples from multiple locations and wanted an
overall picture of the total data set, the hydrogen concentration approach had some
value. In order to satisfy both concerns, I took the coward's way out: I modified
DASLER so that both values were reported. (In case you're interested, I ran some
tests. To no one's surprise, the two methods produce numbers that almost always
differ by about a factor of 10.)

March 16, 2000

*The technical lead from Huntington called about 9:00 and we talked for well over
an hour. This week he is attending a meeting of the Corps water quality guidance
committee. It's being held in Seattle. He clarified the reason for the meeting to me
first. Here was the situation that drove the meeting. A) The Corps is required to submit
their data to STORET. B) STORET is broken. C) What are they going to do about
this? The committee apparently thought that all the districts had been operating
in a vacuum and were pleasantly surprised to find that some of them were actually working together to address their collective needs. They liked what they saw in
the approach used in DASLER, and had received several good comments about the
product. They seem to be poised to make DASLER the default Corps water quality
data management software.*

This was exciting news. In a relatively short time (about five years) we had gone from creating a GIS utility for one district to potentially providing a new water quality data management system for the entire Corps. The committee had been made aware that other districts (beyond the original testers of the previous commercial software product) were starting to request installation and training for DASLER, so the official decision was to monitor how the next districts' migrations went before making a final decision.

April 13, 2000

Bob called about 11:00 to say he had been on a conference call this morning with the regular DASLER round table. Additions to the discussion this time around were people from Detroit and the head of water quality for the Corps (in DC). The most interesting portion of the discussion was the desire by HQ to have a meeting with representatives of EPA regarding making the connection between DASLER and STORET.

With the Corps moving to adopt DASLER nationwide, the need to make DASLER capable of sending data to the modernized STORET system suddenly became much more important.

April 17, 2000

The meeting with EPA is now all set for Thursday. I had hoped the meeting would take place soon, but I must admit I was a little surprised that it happened this quickly.

I talked with the big boss (owner and president of my company) today and he passed along info about a meeting with some folks who develop stuff for a particular brand of handheld computers. He wanted me to explore the possibility of making a program to run on their hardware that we could demo at trade shows to illustrate data collection and quick download to DASLER. This is certainly interesting and doable. However, after that discussion I talked at length to the Mark in Nashville and his counterpart in Huntington about this, and the response was less than positive. In fact, it was downright negative.

The handheld data collection option led to an interesting discussion. I believe the gist of the argument made by both technical guys was that almost all their data collection occurs from boats, and that they didn't trust the reliability of a handheld device in that environment (they were already using laptops in some cases, but these were hardened versions designed to protect against the elements). So while this was a tantalizing direction from a developer's perspective, there seemed little advantage in developing it if there was no interest from the known user community. Always listen to the users.

April 20, 2000

Trip to Washington to meet with the Corps water quality chief at HQ. I arrived at the office about 9:15, and by 9:30 everyone was there so we started the meeting. Attending were me, the HQ director, the technical lead from Huntington, and two guys from EPA – the top two people in the STORET program. The Corps HQ manager started with some background. He described the meeting in Seattle and touched on all the different approaches districts are using to manage their water quality data. He emphasized that a lot of this was driven by the fact that people can't make STORET work. Then he told them about DASLER and said that we were there to look each other over. I spent most of the next two hours showing them different pieces of the program. We stopped a lot to discuss various aspects of the program and the database. Overall, they were very impressed with what we had done, and they really liked the way some of the screens in DASLER worked. After I was through, they presented a lot of STORET in a similar vein. After looking at STORET, I see why they liked DASLER. The data models are very similar (except that DASLER's is more limited in scope). I also see why people don't like STORET. It has a very confusing interface. It harkens back to the old "one menu at a time, one page of data at a time" interface algorithm. The end result of the meeting was that we concluded it shouldn't be too difficult to make a connection from DASLER to STORET. The top STORET man acknowledged that a significant impediment would be me deciphering the STORET data model, but he offered to tutor me on that subject personally.

It was very exciting to garner this level of interest in our little program. If we could solve the STORET connection problem, we would be poised to take DASLER national. And that connection certainly seemed reasonable given the similarities between the DASLER and STORET data models. (Incidentally, I later learned the reason for the clunky interface for STORET. The original plan was for a more robust interface, probably somewhat like what we had in DASLER. The EPA team had just completed creating their database and were preparing to start designing the user interface when a bit of Congressional in-fighting resulted in a government shutdown. The STORET team ended up losing most of their programmers during that event, and when the government reopened, they were faced with a looming deadline. The interface they were using was created by a prototyping tool. The tool was designed to validate relationships in the database by automatically generating simple screens that displayed data for a single table. As a result, all their input forms were unimaginative – and worse, most of them looked almost identical. It was an unfortunate turn of events for them because they had an excellent data model but an almost incomprehensible interface.)

May 1–5, 2000

Trip to Baltimore for installation of DASLER.

This was the first installation at a Corps office that was not part of the original team that tested the commercial package. I spent the first day working with a very bright IT guy, creating the Oracle database and the Jet pass-through file (they opted for the same approach as Huntington). The rest of the week fell into a pattern of training sessions followed by data migration activities. I spent my nights tweaking the user interface code as needed to incorporate new information I gathered during the day. The most important consideration for these nightly coding sessions was to avoid modifying the program to address specific issues currently being encountered. I had to make sure that any changes I made did not affect the existing users or alter their normal practices. This is an easy trap into which many developers in this situation fall, and I was determined not to do so. Incidentally, this trip established the pattern that my future trips to other districts would follow.

June 7, 2000

Yesterday I drove to Virginia for a meeting today with some water quality folks from the North Atlantic Division. The HQ water quality chief was there for this meeting also. At the end of the meeting, he asked me if I was going to make the same presentation at their national water quality meeting in August.

DASLER was forcing me to become something of a road warrior.

June 8, 2000

I got started on the Nashville lab management system project today.

After many delays, I was finally starting to work on a new phase of the big picture: capturing data from Nashville's internal lab. I would end up creating a separate database for managing these data while in process. The interface for the lab system would include an option for uploading the data to the DASLER database.

June 20, 2000

The technical lead from the power company client called me just after lunch today, and it looks like they are ready to go another round. He said he has been testing the program over the past week or so, and it's in really bad shape. One thing he mentioned specifically was that it is possible to delete a reservoir ID even if there are results records on file for it. This makes him very nervous, so he wants me to give it the once over and fix the problems as best I can.

After a long hiatus, the power company had determined that their version of DASLER – which had finally been delivered by my former employer – was not going to work. This meant I might now be juggling three versions of the program.

July 6, 2000

It occurred to me today that Nashville's lab manager has a big problem at the moment, since he has no way of logging in the samples that are being collected. His old system hasn't worked since his hard drive crashed. So I talked to both him and Mark, and together we decided on a new course of action. I will try to get the first part of the program working as quickly as possible. That will give the lab manager something to use so he doesn't have such a backlog waiting when I complete the final version of the program. Also, it will give him time to work with the program and iron out any procedural preferences and/or bugs before the end of the project.

The reason Nashville had been interested in developing a new lab management system was that they could no longer get any support for the old one (based on dBase,) and they were struggling to keep it going. Originally, the lab manager had continued to use the old system while I worked on the new one. Then his hard drive crashed, and the old system became unusable. They needed something in a hurry, so we decided that I would give them what I had working so far. This was the best type of compromise – one that gets the client something they need and also serves a beta testing function. It felt good to help out, even though it wasn't in the original plan.

July 12, 2000

The power company technical lead was here today to take a look at the improvements I've made to the Corps version of DASLER and to discuss what we want to do with their version. I presented the summary of my findings in digging through their database and code in the context of showing him new features and telling him about the other differences. He seemed very impressed with what he saw, and we generally decided to make their version as much like the Corps product as possible, except with additional capabilities. I made a list of items to be accomplished, along with some other notes, while we were talking. One of the most exciting revisions is that I'm supposed to make their version read and write spreadsheet files directly, and I expect that feature to go over quite well with the Corps.

This discussion was noteworthy on two fronts. First, reducing the number of ways in which the power company's version would differ would make maintaining both versions simpler. Second, spreadsheet files were becoming the lingua franca of data exchange between labs and their clients. Prior to this point, all import and export operations in DASLER had been based on ASCII files. While effective, the approach required to manage import from text files was cumbersome. Our methodology forced careful examination of many rows in a given file in order to identify the positional boundaries for each data element (e.g., location is contained in columns 12–22 of the file). Spreadsheets offered a much more concise description (e.g., location is in spreadsheet column B). This also pointed out to me an unexpected advantage of working on the same program for different clients: the changes requested for one version would benefit users of the other version as well.

July 26, 2000

Today two guys came up from Chattanooga for a visit. They are from another consulting company that has a contract to provide support to the Mobile District. They were here to learn about DASLER, as they will be the ones actually using it. The specific application is for a reservoir in Georgia. This will be an interesting project because there won't be any new data collection activities involved – it's strictly a historic data activity. With that in mind, we covered the first parts of DASLER pretty quickly. I spent some time on the data dictionary, but then we just breezed over the processes that I normally spend a fair amount of time on – the data collection, tag number business, etc. Instead, we focused on the reporting and graphing capabilities. Both of them seemed very impressed with the possibilities here, and both laughed that they were currently spending many hours retrieving data from various sources when trying to answer a particular question that would now come quickly when they get their data into DASLER. We spent the last hour or so taking a look at some specific files they brought along. These are some of the files that they have gathered from other sources, and they are the ones that they want to import. We looked at a couple of examples and I gave them some notes about what they could expect and how to best import them. Overall I think it went very well.

I knew by this time that DASLER was starting to gain traction throughout the Corps. One thing I had not considered was that this would mean educating other contractors on how the program works. I was initially hesitant about this, primarily because I realized that it would almost always require a very compressed schedule.

I knew the time I would be allotted to bring them up to speed would be much more limited than what I typically allocated. Fortunately, I need not have been concerned about these particular people – they picked things up very quickly.

August 7–11, 2000

The trip to Omaha went pretty well .... Tuesday we started training. We spent all day in their conference room with my laptop hooked to a big screen monitor.

One thing that came up during the training seemed like a good idea, so I spent some time on it Tuesday night and had it implemented by Wednesday morning. You can now manually type "ND" as a valid value in either of the results dialogs. ND stands for "not detected," and one of the participants thinks this is a better approach than simply putting a less-than and indicating the detection limit. I think it's a judgment call, but it was easy enough to add that I decided to include it. It adds another option to the program. Since the value field is numeric, the program parses these entries and stores them as >999. Then, when data are loaded for viewing or reporting, the >999 is changed back to ND.

This trip generally followed the same pattern as the Baltimore installation trip (except that I had less time in the evenings to work on DASLER code because instead I was writing the users' guide for the Nashville lab system). The suggestion about using "ND" for a value foreshadowed other developments soon to follow, but since our results were still stored in numeric columns, you see how I created a workaround. There was also one other twist to this excursion. While I was there, a woman from the Northwest Division came down to check out DASLER as well. For the first time, I met someone who was not impressed by DASLER. Her major complaint was that it didn't store enough metadata – specifically all the details of the analyses performed in the lab. (We had hashed this out in the original design meetings with Nashville. The conclusion there – supported by all the other districts that had since started using DASLER – was that our system should be focused on accomplishing the districts' objectives rather than documenting every detail of the lab's actions. The metadata we had omitted from our data model was deemed not useful for the stated purposes.) Later I learned that she had been a lab analyst herself, which probably shaped her thinking. But the big lesson was not to get too much ego. No matter how good you think your system is, there will always be some who do not share your opinion.

August 14, 2000

I hit the road to Nashville early this morning.

This trip was to deliver and install the completed lab data management system. Except for some corrections and tweaks, I could now cross that item off my active list.

August 28–31, 2000

Trip to St. Paul for the Corps national water quality meeting. I was on the agenda in place of Mark because he had a scheduling conflict ... After my talk, people from three other districts came up to me and basically said "we're ready, where do we go to sign up?" The districts were New Orleans, Tulsa, and Philadelphia.

This made me hopeful that all this travel was beginning to pay some dividends.

September 7, 2000

I managed to find a way to implement the Shift-Click idea on the grids today, and it wasn't as hard as I had feared.

This was an idea I wanted to try in order to make life easier for the users. By this time, we had a bunch of these grids on all sorts of forms in DASLER. In some cases, some cells of the grid offered a dropdown list of options from which the user could select. Users would sometimes find themselves wanting to fill many (or all) the rows of the grid with the same value in a given column. This constant <select cell>, <dropdown list>, <click desired choice> was both time-consuming and annoying. I thought there should be a way to expedite this process, and I finally found it. I decided to code the grids so that if the user pressed the <Shift> key while clicking their selection, all blank cells in that column would get updated with the chosen value. This option proved very popular. The lesson here is to always be searching for ways to improve the user experience.

October 17–19, 2000

Trip to New Hampshire to plan the new ArcView interface.

The Corps' Cold Regions Research and Engineering Lab (CRREL) is in New Hampshire, and one of their specialties is developing GIS applications. With all the advances to the database interface in the last couple of years, I had been neglecting the part that started this whole thing – the GIS interface. My neglect was understandable because the GIS interface I had originally developed was always very district-specific, and it took a lot of time and effort to set it up for a new installation. Since my initial round of development, ArcView had migrated to a new programming platform. The folks at CRREL had more experience than I in creating GIS plug-ins and were eager to develop one that would serve as a generic GIS interface for DASLER. This would give all districts the option to use GIS without a lot of district-specific customization.

October 30, 2000

Today was a long day, but a productive one. I spent the day in DC, meeting with the Corps HQ director and the two EPA people we met with earlier. The purpose of the meeting was to discuss some of the details of what's missing in DASLER that STORET needs and to hash out an approach.

I had learned by now that STORET had quite a few more data elements than DASLER, but I did not yet know which ones would be required for import (many of STORET's data requirements were conditional based on the type and purpose of the sample being collected). The purpose of this meeting was to get a better handle on the situation. Both the Corps director and I took a cautious approach because we wanted to avoid imposing additional requirements on our users. That was the right thing to do, but I began to realize this could have the potential to set up another situation with competing requirements, since a primary goal of our current focus was to reinstate the ability to export to STORET.

November 13–17, 2000

Another week, another DASLER installation. In every other case there has been a special import filter to write, and in every other case it has been targeted at the current office only. Not so in this case. The only import filter I felt inclined to write here was one that has broad application. What I decided to do was to make a couple of generic imports, and I did the first one while on site. There will be one for data with analytes in rows and one for data with analytes in columns. I wrote the column one this week.

This installation was in Tulsa. The import filters referenced here were for data in spreadsheets, so I was actually getting a head start on the update that I started planning for the power company (that effort had been discussed in July but was still not under contract).

November 22, 2000

The most interesting stuff today was related to the commercial software vendor. They sent me a list of code changes they wanted, and they copied my boss. He is concerned that we have seen no revenue, and he is hesitant to authorize more work on my part until that situation changes. They offered to buy us out if we have no interest in continuing the relationship.

This was the beginning of the end of our relationship with that company. Over the past two years I had worked hard to integrate DASLER into their framework, but the integration never quite gelled. After all this work, we had only a very rough first version to show for the effort. I could see that the project was about to end unsuccessfully, but honestly I was not disappointed. I had spent the week before the Tulsa trip at a conference, manning a booth with them for the second year in a row. During that time, I had learned that they provided no information to their users regarding the structure of their database – it was essentially a closed book. Without these details, migrating data from their system to another would be extremely difficult. This was a fundamental departure from my philosophy, which has always been client-centric. I believe strongly that the data belongs to the client and that they should therefore have complete control over it. I was therefore relieved that we would not become partners with this company after all.

February 7–8, 2001

Both these days I made my way to downtown DC to meet with EPA. We spent all day Wednesday going through all sorts of details about the STORET database, concentrating on those issues directly related to surface water activities. A big aid to the process was a large printout of the ERD [Entity Relationship Diagram] they gave me of the STORET data model. I made copious notes on there as the day progressed. By the end of the first day we had gone over a lot of details, and I had taken a couple of pages of notes. The biggest decision in all this was that we would try to employ the SIM tool they are developing. It just makes sense, given the limited budget of the project, to not reinvent the wheel here. With that decision in mind, we set about identifying the missing pieces of the puzzle for DASLER and noting how to address each one.

The second day was less about STORET and more about DASLER. I spent most of the morning going over the latest incarnation of the product. The STORET Program Manager was especially keen on seeing the import function for multi-parameter samplers and the spreadsheet import function, so we spent some time there. The late part of the day was taken up with reviewing what we had covered, identifying tasks to be performed, and things like that. I updated my laptop with the latest version of the STORET database and code. Also, I recompiled the latest DASLER and left them a copy.

EPA was exceptionally helpful in explaining the data model for the modernized STORET during this meeting in DC. It would truly have been impossible to connect DASLER to STORET without their assistance. I was also happy to learn about their program called the STORET Import Module (SIM). This utility was a generic import program that would load data into the STORET database, so all I would have to do was create files that SIM could read. Given my new knowledge of the data requirements, this option suddenly made the effort far less intimidating. Lesson: if there is a reliable tool that will make your job easier, use it.

February 22–23, 2001

I met with a Corps group in Nashville to discuss the connection between DASLER and STORET. Attending the meeting were representatives from Nashville, Louisville, and Huntington. I kicked the meeting off by stating our purpose and then describing some of the details that STORET implements .... We spent quite a bit of time on Friday debating the merits of carrying along both text and numeric entries in the results table. In the end, we decided that advantages outweighed the disadvantages, so we're going with it.

One thing I had discovered while learning the STORET data model from EPA was that they had come up with a simple and elegant solution to a problem that had bedeviled me since the beginning of DASLER – the issue of implied precision and significant digits in numeric entries. I had always stored parameter results in numeric fields. There were a lot of problems with this approach, though. To capture an entry that was inexact (e.g., <0.05) you had to have a separate column for the < symbol. As noted elsewhere, there were additional issues with having to analyze entries and store the number of significant digits in order to overcome the problem caused by binary representations of real values. STORET's data model included both a text entry and a numeric version for parameter values. We decided to borrow this idea, and it allowed us to simplify both our data model and our interface. If an EDD indicated a value of <0.05, that's what went into the text version of the value column. It also gave us more flexibility for storing other non-detect designations (e.g., ND).

April 3, 2001

I spent much of the day today preparing to work on a generic version of DASLER for another consultant's clients. I copied the DASLER and HIPP source code into new directories and started making notes about what needs to be done.

Off and on for the past year I had been meeting with a guy I knew from my days working in Oak Ridge, Tennessee. He was now a partner in a firm whose primary owner was Native American. Their business catered to the environmental needs of other Native American organizations, and they had clients who needed help with environmental data management. After several months of kicking around ideas, he had hired me (through my employer) to create another custom version of DASLER.

So now I was about to start juggling a different third variation (the original commercial version having died by now).

April 18–19, 2001

I arrived in Louisville around 8:00, where I met a new database administrator. The PM and biologist from the Louisville District arrived around 10:30.

Another road trip, but this one had a distinctively different purpose. The Louisville District had decided that they no longer wanted to maintain their data in-house. Instead, they had contracted with another company to do it for them – one with which they had a long-standing relationship. The new company would perform all the data entry, and provide a copy of the database to the district on a regular basis. This would allow the district's personnel to focus on generating reports and performing analyses. I was there to get DASLER running on the new company's computers and do some training. This arrangement was something I had never considered, and I was skeptical at first. But they made it work, and continued that paradigm for several years.

May 23–24, 2001

I met with the power company all day on Wednesday. We started by trying to install DASLER on a laptop, but it didn't work. The installation seemed to go just fine, but when we ran it, the program reported an error and shut down. After a little investigating, I concluded that a likely suspect was the fact that Microsoft Office (and therefore Excel) was not installed on the laptop.

This was a trip to deliver the version of DASLER for the power company that would allow them to go live. The mistake I made was due to a faulty assumption: that Microsoft Office (of which Excel was a part) was installed on all their computers. It was easy to fix this problem – I just had to check to see if Excel was installed and if not, disable the program options that involved Excel – but it was an embarrassing omission on my part. Lesson: don't take anything for granted.

June 24–29, 2001

I made my way to Kansas City this afternoon.

This was an installation trip to get the Kansas City District started with DASLER. This was becoming old hat by this time.

August 15, 2001

I got started on the program that will do the database update for the Version 4 conversion today.

Among all the other activities going on over the past few months, I had also been working on the next release of the DASLER software. We now had a lot of different districts using the software, which had brought a rush of new ideas and perspectives. It also meant that – for the first time –I was going to be updating the databases of users I did not know as well. Adding to the pressure, this update was the first one that involved making nontrivial changes to the database structure. To facilitate the transition to Version 4, I decided to write a utility program that would perform the database updates. Previously, I had done this for each district individually by coaching each technical manager through the process. Even with the strong relationships I had with the original set of users, this process had at times been inefficient. I felt that having a program to perform the update was a better approach. It also occurred to me that I was being unfair to the technical team in the past, asking them to do something (albeit with my guidance) that made many of them uncomfortable. I used this approach for subsequent updates as well, and it proved very popular. My take on this was that I should not assume everyone is as comfortable tinkering with database structures as I.

September 27, 2001

I came to a hard realization today about the connection between STORET and DASLER. I was working through the code that exports the results (the last remaining export option to complete), and I hit a bit of a snag. Some of the results require clarification: you enter the name of the parameter, but you also need to specify the fraction, and for some the duration, etc. Now, I was aware of this from the beginning, but I had sort of thought I would be able to write code that extracts the pertinent parts and does all the work. After looking at the SIM example, and examining the Corps' revised analyte list, I began to have my doubts. It seemed like there were going to be an awful lot of item-specific code entries, which didn't seem like too good an idea. So after giving it some thought, I came to the conclusion that I should make one more fairly major change to the DASLER parameters table. I decided I would need to add fields for the proper STORET name, fraction, and possibly others.

Normally I would consider it unadvisable to modify the data dictionary for schema A just to meet some requirements in schema B, but in this case it was necessary in order to satisfy the requirement that we are able to export data to STORET. Realistically we had to do some modifications anyway because the SIM import process matched parameters by name only, and some of the names in STORET were different for the names we used for those same parameters. Rather than force our user community to use the names that were used in STORET, we had already decided to create a new column that listed the STORET name for each constituent. Chalk this up as a necessary concession.

October 25, 2001

The meeting with the second power company went well. We did a quick installation and even quicker tutorial.

The consultant referenced in the July 26, 2000 log entry was also working with a power company – a different one than the one that was already using DASLER. At the consultant's encouraging, the new power company had reached out to me to find out more. My experience working with our first power company client had made me aware that there were some minor variations in how they managed water quality data compared to the Corps, and those nuances were coded into the power company's version. I had gotten permission from our power company client to share their version of DASLER with new power company, so this was a very brief installation trip. The takeaway from this entry is subtle but important. In Part 1 we talked a lot about borrowing databases and applications from users with similar business operations and goals. This time I was on the other side of that: the one from which things would be borrowed. Lesson: sharing goes both ways.

November 13, 2001

The EPA PM called me back today with instructions on how to get around most of the problems I was having .... Apparently, SIM has a little problem that no one had thought of before now: the issue of duplicate parameters in different fractions (total, dissolved, etc.).

See, I told you this sharing thing goes both ways. I had been testing the connection of DASLER to STORET via SIM and had encountered a problem: if I had the same parameter in different fractions within an import file, SIM interpreted that as an error. So in a small way I felt like I helped EPA identify and fix a problem with their program.

December 28, 2001

This morning I sent out the notice that Version 4.0 was available. I got back two immediate responses from districts that claim to be ready now – Omaha and Huntington.

A major milestone achieved right at the end of the calendar year. This was the most significant and involved update so far. It reflected a big increase in capabilities, so I consider this to be when DASLER reached maturity.

13 Maturity

13.1 PLATEAU

January 9, 2002

The guy from the Native American company came over this morning about 9:00 and we discussed his situation until noon. We analyzed what had gone wrong with our initial attempts to get DASLER-X going for his clients. I decided that we tried too hard to modify the data model to fit the existing data.

My first attempt to create an independent version of DASLER for a broader audience (see the entry for April 3, 2001 in Chapter 12) had not gone well. That version was created as part of an arrangement with an old friend who was a partner in a company that catered to Native American clients. At his suggestion, we had dubbed it DASLER-X. As that code evolved, though, we had lost sight of the original objective (a version that was sufficiently adaptable to be used by practically anyone who collected surface water quality data) and instead focused too much on the specific data from his first known client. In essence, that effort had been executed much like the original development of DASLER when we considered it a service rather than a product. There was plenty of blame to go around for this outcome, but I shouldered a significant portion of it. The primary version of DASLER was very much still tailored to the Corps, and I was locked into thinking in that vein – make the program handle the data you see. Evidence from the DASLER-X sponsor had borne out this perception: the program seemed to work okay for the first client but faltered or outright failed when applied to others. In short, I didn't do enough homework. During this January meeting, we refocused our efforts for a second attempt.

March 18–20, 2002

I headed for Nashville around 7:00 am on Monday. The first session began at noon.

This was the first ever (sort of) DASLER users' meeting. The primary reason for this meeting was to disseminate information about the changes in Version 4. However, word had spread throughout the Corps, and we ended up with representatives from a number of districts that had not yet started using the database. It thus turned into a meeting that was partly new user training and partly old user updates regarding new procedures.

DOI: 10.1201/9781003131953-15

April 2, 2002

I decided to tweak DASLER a little bit this morning. During the training session in Nashville I realized I had omitted one of the things that we discussed way back when we were scouting out Version 4 – handling of non-detects during statistics processing. Louisville had some particularly pointed ideas about how to handle these, but I had forgotten about them while I was writing the original code. So today I went back and put in some options on what to do. There are now five possible choices. These only apply if the value is ND, Not Detected, or is a less-than value. The choices are: leave it out, insert zero instead, use the MDL (or other boundary value), use half the MDL or boundary value, or use a random number between zero and the MDL or boundary value. I coded that approach and tested it, and it all seems to be working just fine.

There is always disagreement when you start talking to a group of water quality professionals regarding how to perform statistical analysis on data when some of the values are inexact. The options I decided to include were the best ones our team could identify among the many options.

April 3–5, 2002

Days spent attending the AWRA symposium.... During one of the first breaks I was approached by a very tall gentleman who introduced himself and asked me if I was "the DASLER guy." He works for a federal agency and knows the two consultants who connected me up with the second power company. They had been talking up DASLER to him, and he was interested in finding out more. I gave him a quick overview and also noted that I had made previous attempts to interest his agency. We compared schedules and decided to sit down for a more detailed look on Thursday. When we did, we spent about an hour wandering through the program, hitting the high spots and discussing various issues. By the end he was convinced that this would be a very good tool for his use. When I returned for the banquet Thursday night, he had his boss cornered. He called me over and introduced me. She then informed me that they were ready to schedule a meeting and would be contacting me soon. Apparently, they're already convinced. Now all I have to do is sway the IM [Information Management] folks and we're off and running.

My initial hope was that their procedures would be similar enough to those of the Corps that they could use the existing version with no changes. I was already balancing things between three different versions: the original for the Corps, the one for the power company, and the generic one for the Native American company. I didn't relish the idea of adding a fourth version to the mix. Still, this was too good an opportunity to pass up.

May 29, 2002

I left around 11:45 and headed for a meeting with the federal agency. What I learned today was that the agency has a somewhat fractured water quality program, with different divisions collecting different data for different purposes. The project push now is an effort to gather much of the environmental data under one umbrella.... After that introduction, I jumped into DASLER. I started with a few slides from my AWRA slide show, just for background. After that I ran quickly through the ArcView interface before delving into some details about the DASLER program itself. I started with the data entry approach, but we didn't have much time to linger there because they were very interested in import routines. We hashed that awhile, then moved on to reports. After a break, we covered graphing, then biology, calculation of water quality indices, and finally STORET. Most attendees hung in there until the end, which was nearly 6:00. Near the end of the meeting we discussed services and rates and other things that you would not normally ask unless you were serious about doing business.

So the new agency was very interested, but there was still no indication as yet regarding whether I would be able to use any of the existing versions to meet their needs.

August 20–22, 2002

Trip to Montana for installation and training for DASLER-X. The first morning went pretty well, even though we ran over the allotted time in both sessions ....

This was a training session for the first organization to purchase our second attempt at a generic commercial version of DASLER. This second iteration had been done in cooperation with the same consultant who was involved in the first one. We were now delivering the product to a new client for this version, and the outcome might be the determining factor in whether or not our attempt to create this separate version would continue. The training went well and the client was favorably impressed. Now all we had to do was wait and see how things progressed after we departed.

September 3–5, 2002

I spent these three days in meetings with the federal agency to formally kick off their project.... The Program Manager started by describing the scope of work, and then we diverted to a discussion of the fish tissue database. That's an immediate need, so I thought we were about to decide to do it first as a side issue. But when we got into the meat of the discussion, most of the comments centered on best ways to integrate that data into the existing DASLER data structure.... At any rate, this all means a VERY customized product for them.

The first formal meetings of the project answered the question that had been on my mind since we first started talking: this would definitely be a separate version of DASLER. The deciding factor was the revelation that this organization did types of analyses that none of my other DASLER clients did. One example had come up right away: an extensive program that involved analyzing fish specimens for traces of chemical contaminants. Numerous other specialized activities were discussed during these meetings as well. That meant that I now had four distinct variants with which to deal.

November 5, 2002

This morning I spent a couple of hours doing a utility program for Huntington. It offers two passes through the database. The first compares the sample number depth to the sample depth in the field and reports errors. The second pass fixes the same.

This entry is an example of something that happened frequently throughout the early years of DASLER, and it illustrates a problem that occurs often when you create a new system that must capture past data in a variety of forms and formats. The issue here was that we had loaded a lot of historic Huntington records from old spreadsheets. The simplest path to loading the data was to use functions within the DBMS to directly insert data. The alternative would have been to write a custom import filter in the DASLER interface for each format, which would have given us more control over the process. It also would have busted the project budget, so the district had opted for direct insertion instead. Unfortunately, some of those source files did not conform to all the constraints we had established to ensure data quality. So once again we found ourselves with competing interests: data quality versus the need to capture all the historic data. The district made the call, and the call was to get the data in regardless of the consequences. As a result, we had disabled some of the constraints. This introduced a second problem, which was that the existence of these issues in the data prevented us from turning the constraints back on after the data were in. This utility was one of several I wrote over the years to try to correct issues that crept into the data in this way. The objective was to correct the errors so that we could reinforce our data rules in the database rather than the interface. Note that this introduced an additional problem in the interface as well: if there were records in the database that violated the standard business rules, I had to accommodate those variations in reports and analyses. The more glaring the violation, the greater the likelihood that it would create difficulties in other areas. Fortunately, most of our accessions to this demand were minor.

January 6, 2003

EPA's STORET Program Manager called today, and he enlightened me on something kind of important. Recall that I had trouble last week with the importing of a couple of parameters into STORET. Well, he offered some very good advice on that topic today. Since they are constantly tweaking their parameter names, if we try to keep our database in sync with theirs, we'll be forever issuing updates just to keep up. So instead of trying to stay ahead of the game that way, he suggested that we modify the way the import works by allowing for translations within SIM. It works this way. When a parameter name (or other lookup item, for that matter) gets rejected, SIM creates an entry for it in a lookup table. You can access these records from SIM and pick from a dropdown list of possible choices on how to translate them. That will be much easier to maintain than our internal lookup table.

This is an excellent idea, and one that I have implemented many times in DASLER and other programs over the years. I tend to call these "alias tables." For instance, I often create a parameter alias table that contains additional identifiers by which a given parameter is known. During data import operations, I check parameter entries against the name, any known identifying numbers (e.g., CAS numbers), and any aliases in this table. In a new system, it takes a while to populate this data source, but eventually the database "learns" to the point that you rarely have to add new aliases after a relatively short period.

February 13, 2003

I finished the bacteriological data form today.

This was for the version of DASLER for the second federal agency. It was a noteworthy effort because of a choice I made regarding how to code this form. The client's process for evaluating bacteriological samples involved the use of a specific brand of test trays. For analysis, you put fixed amounts of the sample media on these trays and after a specified amount of time you count the number of colonies that develop on two different areas of the tray. You then consult a reference list that translates the two values into an *E. coli* value for the sample. The reference list was very long and had tiny print. So instead of just providing a place to record the values, I took the time to convert the reference list to a lookup table and stored that in their database. This meant that instead of having to consult the reference list, they simply entered their raw numbers into the form and the program took care of the rest. It was a small thing, but one that made their work a little easier. That's the kind of thing that distinguishes an okay user interface from a great user interface.

March 24, 2003

I got some more good news today from the DC area: the Military Engineer is publishing our DASLER article next month. They needed a little more information, and I supplied it. I can't wait to see it in print.

Bob Sneed and I had talked many times about various ways we could spread the word to other Corps districts about DASLER. One option we pursued was writing an article for a publication of the Society of American Military Engineers – a bimonthly magazine called *The Military Engineer*. Each issue of the magazine has a focus, and our opportunity arose when an upcoming issue's focus was to be information management. We thought we were fortunate to get this article into the magazine, but to this day I have no idea if districts who later started using DASLER were influenced by it.

June 15–20, 2003

Trip to Portland to train Portland, Walla Walla, Seattle, and Sacramento Districts.

This was another milestone: training a large group of users from multiple districts at one time. Other than that, it simply marked a significant increase in the number of districts using the software.

13.2   STASIS

July 16, 2003

I made the trek today to sit in on a meeting of database junkies in the second federal client's office. After addressing some other, unrelated databases, we started talking about things they want to add to their version of DASLER: the benthic IBI [Index of Biotic Integrity], spring sport fisheries, sport fishing index, mosquito monitoring, and impingement and entrainment activities.

This version of DASLER was starting to veer off into some truly interesting new areas.

August 6, 2003

After that, I looked on my desk and saw a note I made to myself during the lull between phases 2 and 3 that commented on the fact that I didn't like the way the project results dialog was retrieving data. I had used the old traditional approach on that one – where I selected a project, then a location, etc. So I went back to that dialog today and introduced a more data-centric approach to retrieving. Now, you select a project at the top of the form. The code then looks for data types that are on file already for that project. (It ignores the project plan and goes straight to the samples.) Each data type that is found is then turned on. Each tab has its own location list, and some have date and time lists as well. Then the user can select the data type and narrow things down that way.

I'll start this commentary with the lesson from this post: always be looking for ways to improve the users' experience. Just because a process is working correctly doesn't mean that it can't be made better. In this case there had been no complaints about the way data were being retrieved for editing, but I had a gut feeling that there was room for improvement. This relatively minor tweak resulted in reducing the number of selections required to display data, and thus increased the efficiency of the process. This harkens back to what has been my philosophy ever since I started developing databases and user interfaces: my job is to make it easier for others to do their jobs.

November 4, 2003

Today was the day I went sampling with the Nashville crew.... I can't say that my impression of the process changed very much, because I had a pretty good idea of how things worked already. But it was definitely a worthwhile experience, and I was glad to have it. It helps me keep the process in mind as I develop the tools for managing the data.

There is nothing better for understanding the needs of users than working through some of their activities with them. If your job is to develop a data management system for some process, you really need a complete understanding of that process. And the best way to get that understanding is to actually do the work. I had been working with the Corps long enough that I had a pretty good idea about how they collected data, but going with them to perform sampling was still an excellent exercise. It's impossible to learn too much about an activity.

February 12, 2004

This morning I started thinking about the stand-alone fish data collection application. I created a new project and started tinkering with how I could present the captured data without any custom controls.

Another activity that the second federal agency performed that was unique among all the DASLER clients was fish population surveys. I had already completed the processes and forms inside DASLER itself to manage these data, but I had recently received another request. They wanted an application to use in the field to log results of their electrofishing surveys, and then have those results load into DASLER as simply as possible. The application would run on some new hardware they had just acquired. These were compact computers with minimal memory. They were hardened for protection during field conditions, and they ran a version of Windows called CE. This was much like standard Windows, except that there was no support for extra libraries and controls. The other consideration for this utility was that it had to be easy to use, and it had to be quick – cataloging the fish specimens collected during these sampling events was a fast and furious endeavor. I therefore had to come up with a good design that collected all the data without using anything beyond the simplest Windows controls (such as text boxes). There was not enough memory in these devices to support running any sort of database, so I had to be creative with how I saved the data. It was an interesting challenge, but I was able to rise to the occasion.

January 5, 2005

I took some time in the afternoon to check out the problem with the low DO [Dissolved Oxygen] calculation … there were two different parameters for water surface elevation. But then I also got another surprise when I discovered that the water surface elevations in the profiles were in meters and the geometry files had elevations in feet.

Sometimes the simplest things will catch you off guard. This was an interesting analysis that I had been trying to implement for several months (as time permitted) but just couldn't seem to get to work. The objective was to calculate the area and wetted perimeter of a reservoir cross-section that was exposed to low dissolved oxygen. The concept was pretty simple, combining data from a vertical profile sampling event and the geometry of the cross-section. I had gone over the math several times which gave me confidence in the validity of the code, but for some reason the process kept crashing. On this date I finally found the time to investigate things more completely and the solution (actually solutions … there were two problems) became apparent. I was a bit surprised to find that there were two parameters in the database for the same observation (water surface elevation), but I should not have been surprised given the number of different users involved over time and the number of parameters that were now in the lookup table. The issue of different units was more unexpected since all the data came from the same organization. Still, it was a relief to finally get this working. The takeaway, I guess, is don't assume anything.

October 18, 2005

I got up around 7:00 Tuesday morning and headed across the street to meet with the Omaha crew.… During the morning session I had mentioned the other versions of DASLER, and in particular DASLER-X. During lunch and then the afternoon session, we had a chance to discuss that version in more detail, and the new technical lead wanted to take a look at it. He was particularly interested in the continuous monitoring capabilities.

This was a sign of the maturity of DASLER, I suppose. I had been doing this long enough that there was now starting to be significant turnover in some of the districts. Some of these personnel changes resulted in lost institutional knowledge. The lead person in Kansas City had retired without any overlap with new personnel, so they were largely out of the DASLER business at this time. The new technical lead in Kansas City had reached out for more information, but to this point had not made any definitive plans. In Omaha, just about everyone who had been trained in the original session had moved on, then their replacements had also moved on. As a result, the DASLER user community in Omaha had turned over twice now. At least they were still operational and interested in remaining so. The purpose of this trip was to provide training for the folks who were now dealing with the software. As noted in the second part of this log entry, there turned out to be some interest in using DASLER-X instead of the Corps of Engineers' version. This was a twist I did not anticipate. My company was trying to sell the X version of the software (we had invested some internal R&D money in it), but much of the code base was derived from the original that the Omaha District had available to them for no charge. Because of the code overlap, I could not justify charging them for using it. In the end we reached a compromise that was suitable for everyone: Omaha agreed to pay a one-time licensing fee for DASLER-X and we did not charge them for the time I spent moving their data to the (slightly) different X schema.

November 4, 2005

I got a very interesting call just after lunch today. A guy I didn't know from the Corps called to ask me some questions about the software. The gist of the thing is that they need something to pour all the Hurricane Katrina data into, and so far nothing has been satisfactory. The data are coming from a variety of federal agencies. And the biggest issue is that the various users want to be able to just dump spreadsheet data into the system. This is a strength of DASLER, of course, so I think it will fit the bill nicely for them.

Not everything pans out the way you hope. By this time I was confident in DASLER's ability to capture data in just about any spreadsheet format, and I saw this as a golden opportunity to demonstrate the utility of DASLER in a prominent environment. Unfortunately, the Corps did not have the final say in this choice, and the opportunity never materialized.

November 7, 2005

I also spent some time on the phone with the second federal agency.... While we were talking, we did discover one thing that I overlooked. I had put in a dropdown for selection of the gear type, but they pointed out that this can change within a single series of drops. So I modified that approach and posted an update.

Here's a lesson for you: the processes for which you must craft a data model for environmental management are often quite complex. No matter how many times you go over procedures in great detail, there is always something you might miss. This particular feature was related to a special type of benthic sampling, and was something I had worked on for months. It was only after it had been used in the field that we (me and the technical team who had taught me about the process) realized we had not clearly identified one subtle nuance in the procedure. Fortunately it was an easy omission to address.

January 31, 2007

Huntington called me this afternoon and pointed out a flaw in DASLER. It's obscure, but important. We have never been reporting the depth units on the ad hoc report. This doesn't matter when all the units are consistent throughout the database, but they have some old data for some of their reservoirs where the depths are in feet, while the vast majority of their data has depths in meters. When you produce a report that includes both types of data the results are useless because the depth units are not identified.

Some lessons you have to learn more than once, I guess. The lesson here is to never, ever take anything for granted … no matter how sure you are of things. From the beginning, DASLER had included a setting that specified units for depth measurements. The assumption I made – which was reinforced by all the districts who were involved in the development – was that this would be consistent for all their data. That is, some districts measured depths in meters and others in feet, but whichever they used, that was what they always used. This turned out to be a mistaken assumption that was identified when Huntington imported some very old data. Fortunately, we at least had the foresight to explicitly record the depth units for each sampling event (not assuming it was the default in every case), so there was no issue with the actual recording of the data. The problem was in returning the data in a meaningful way. This encounter forced me to revisit all the reports that included depth and modify them so that the output was always shown using the office's default choice for depths.

13.3 EVOLUTION

If you've been paying attention to the dates of these log entries, you have probably noticed the time lag between the last two entries. DASLER had reached somewhat of a steady state. The districts that were using it were satisfied with the program, and no new districts were getting involved. I had gotten busy on some other projects for various clients, so the drop in DASLER activity had not really caught my attention. I still got occasional questions or just "remind me how to do this" phone calls, but otherwise there was very little communication with the Corps or any of the other organizations that were using DASLER (in any of its forms).

March 19, 2007

I spent the morning on follow-ups to e-mails that piled up last week. The most interesting issue to come up was related by a couple of messages from Portland and Omaha. Both were asking about the new Water Quality Exchange approach and how DASLER could be used to export data.

All that work sorting out how to export data to STORET was about to go out the window. EPA had moved away from using STORET for warehousing water quality data and had instead moved to a new paradigm: the Water Quality Exchange (WQX). This was actually just one part of a larger network (called the Exchange Network) that accommodated all sorts of environmental data. I was not thrilled that all our previous efforts were now useless, but I was intrigued to learn more about this new adventure. If you are fortunate enough to create a data management system that survives this long, you can expect to go through some major changes along the way.

August 15, 2008

My big effort for the day was more work on the DASLER update. I spent most of the day reviewing and reading about the new approach. Late in the afternoon came the

"Oh my" moment. It turns out that, according to all the information I have obtained thus far, it's not nearly as simple as I had planned. Nowhere in the instructions is there anything about submitting files directly to EPA. Instead, the described procedure for participation is considerably more involved. In order to get your data into the system now (at least as far as I can tell), you have to become a fully functioning node on the Exchange Network. If this does turn out to be the only path, then it makes my immediate task impossible. It will not be possible under those circumstances to simply write a modification for DASLER that meets the need. Instead, I would have to develop another application that reads the DASLER database and creates the XML [eXtensible Markup Language] file as a separate entity. Furthermore, this other application would have to be a web presence all the time, meaning a commitment of hardware and software that frankly I don't think any of the districts are going to be willing to make at this time.

After a long lull, a new DASLER effort had taken shape. EPA had officially dropped STORET, so the only mechanism now available for sharing water quality data was WQX. The districts in the Northwest Division pooled their resources and initiated an effort to create a mechanism for sending DASLER data to WQX instead of STORET. I was just getting started on this project when I discovered what looked like a major roadblock that could prevent this from ever being possible. I shouldn't have worried, though. EPA collects data from a lot of organizations that do not have either the financial resources or the technical capabilities to create a full-blown Exchange Network node. Instead, I should have recalled the STORET/SIM situation and realized that EPA already had a plan in place for such situations.

August 18, 2008

Crisis averted. I called a contact of mine in the EPA office in San Francisco this morning. I described the situation and asked him if there was a solution that did not involve a full-blown node deployment, and of course there was. He gave me a couple of names at EPA, and I was able to reach someone rather quickly. She was very helpful and gave me a full-blown demo of the solution. It's a piece of software called "Node Client Lite." It's a free download, and it apparently does exactly what is needed – it allows users to submit locally developed XML files directly to EPA for inclusion in WQX.

See, I told you. If you're looking for a lesson to learn from this situation, look no further than Douglas Adams: Don't Panic.

August 27, 2008

Today was the testing day for my first WQX export. The first couple of attempts failed because of schema validation errors. I had misplaced a couple of elements in the file – putting things in as sub-elements where they should not be, and vice versa – and so it took a couple of rounds to find and fix all of those. Once that was done, I had one last glitch, and it was something I had wondered about in the instructions. The times were listed as formatted like hh:nn:ss [where hh is the hour, nn is the minutes, and ss is the seconds], and the two example files followed this paradigm. I decided to push the envelope and see if it would accept simply hh:nn. It wouldn't, so that was one last fix. After that, my last submission came back as passing the validation. But there was also an e-mail saying the load had failed, and this confused me.

Files sent to STORET (or SIM) had been plain ASCII files, but WQX was more structured – the files were XML files. If you don't know, XML is a methodology for exchanging data that has some of the same characteristics as HyperText Markup Language (HTML) – the language that conveys and interprets data across the Internet. You can consider XML files to be a lot like database tables. An XML file has a schema comprised of major elements (essentially tables) and subsidiary sub-elements (essentially columns). These can go several levels deep – sub-elements can have their own set of sub-elements. Like a database schema, an XML schema defines relationships, so some sub-elements are universally or conditionally required. Also, valid entries for sub-elements might be determined by entries in another major element. A specific XML file is basically a snapshot of data from selected records in particular tables in the XML schema. I had a document that described the WQX schema, so generating the XML file was a pretty straightforward endeavor. I could submit the files using the Node Client Lite software, so I thought things were looking pretty good. My first submission confused me, though, because of something I didn't realize about the process. There were actually two levels involved in submitting a file. The first level was performed by the Exchange Network itself and simply validated the structure of the XML file. This would capture issues like a start tag for which the corresponding end tag was missing. If the file passed structural validation, the Exchange Network then passed the file to the target Exchange (WQX in our situation), where the file was then assessed for compliance with the schema. Clearly I still had much to learn about the WQX process.

September 2, 2008

I spent most of the day on the DASLER code, and was finally successful in getting the file to submit to completion. My contact at EPA sent me an e-mail late Friday saying that the first error was caused by having extra spaces in the activity type (I had used "Sample – Routine" when it should have been "Sample-Routine"). That appears to be what was causing the null function return, which was in turn causing the other non-parameter name-related problems. So I corrected that, and also fixed the parameter names that I had encountered that were wrong. Then I resubmitted, and it worked completely.

Okay, maybe not all that much to learn. Things came together very quickly, and I soon had a successful function that allowed users to select data in DASLER and generate a file to submit the data to WQX. Unfortunately, they still had to submit the data using the Node Client Lite application, but for now there was little I could do about that.

April 5, 2011

This morning I got an e-mail from a client in the DC metro area. He had gotten almost all of his lab data to load into DASLER. The exception was the QC data, and he wanted to know why it was being rejected. It took me a little while to figure it out, but I did it. The problem was with Excel. He had the associated samples entered properly, but they were entered as numbers. The display showed a proper sample number (including a digit after the decimal point), but Excel was storing this and serving it up like an integer. I converted the values to text by placing a single quote at the beginning. This had the effect of changing the display so the ".0" dropped off, so I had to add that back. I was then able to successfully import the data. I e-mailed some instructions.

I have a love/hate relationship with spreadsheet data. On the one hand, so much data is exchanged via spreadsheets these days that a developer can create one form with enough flexibility to load data that follows a general pattern but doesn't require columns in a specific order. On the other hand, if you look at the data in a file using the spreadsheet software itself, what you see may just be a big, fat lie. The formatting tools in spreadsheet software produce very misleading representations of numeric values. This specific case involved a private DASLER-X client who was befuddled because what he saw in the spreadsheet appeared to be correct when actually the underlying data was not correct. The import process reads the raw cell values, so it doesn't matter what the display shows – you're going to get the underlying value. The lesson I've learned over the years is to never trust what you see in a spreadsheet.

April 15, 2011

I fixed a DASLER bug that was reported by Baltimore District today. The report originally came last week, but I couldn't reproduce it. It turned out to be data-specific, which I suspected from the beginning. I had obtained their database, but still couldn't reproduce it since the cause turned out to be related to a specific sample. They had a life stage entry that was blank but no longer null. The query that looks for a match was looking for only null, so it never found it and then tried to add it again. That caused the error. It was an easy fix – I modified the query to look for null or empty string – but I would never have found it without detailed instructions that pointed out the offending sample.

The old "empty string is not the same as null" trap – it will eventually get you every time.

After the update that included exporting data for WQX, DASLER had once again lapsed into a sort of monotonous background during the last couple of years. There was still the occasional obscure bug that I would have to fix, but otherwise not much happened. The next flurry of activity occurred in late 2011 with a new assignment for more development work. There were two aspects of this effort. First, I would give DASLER the ability to export biological data to WQX. This would be our first foray into this area – the biological aspects of the modernized STORET system were only beginning to be viable when EPA shut that project down, so we had never made that connection in DASLER. WQX had now added some robust capabilities for accepting biological samples and results, so it was time to update our software. The second part of this new work involved creating a tool for the CE-QUAL-W2 model that used DASLER data for calibration. Both of these were new and exciting directions for the interface.

November 1, 2011

After some preliminary conversation, we started meeting around 9:00 or so. We began with the W2 discussion. A representative from the Corps' Engineer Research

and Development Center (ERDC) showed us some of the plots they currently generate during model calibration, and we talked about how they are using them. For a
long time it was just a general discussion about what sorts of things we wanted to do.
Eventually we determined the W2 files with which I would need to interact, so it was
a productive meeting.

When we got back to the office Mark showed the ERDC folks some plotting options
on his computer....

Then we went to a different conference room to discuss the WQX biological portion
of the project. Richard joined us during this part. This discussion was shorter, mostly
because everyone already knew what we needed to do. A lot of it involved briefing
Richard on how the procedure would work – or at least on the part we already knew.
I had suggested that we focus on the W2 part of the work first, but Mark suggested
that we do the opposite.

After the meeting broke up, Richard and I went with Mark back to his cubicle to
investigate some other aspects of this procedure.... Next we looked into downloading
some existing bio data. It took us a couple of tries to get some, but when we did
we discovered that all the existing records had species-level entries, but they also
included a field that contained a lookup reference on the ITIS web site. I'll need to
follow up that line of inquiry, but we think that might be the preferred method of identification. If so, we wanted to see if we could download the full ITIS list. We found it
in SQL Server format, so we should be able to get that.

The Integrated Taxonomic Information System (ITIS) is a US federally funded
repository of information about taxonomic identifiers and relationships. Some federal
agencies – including EPA – consider it the definitive reference for this sort of data.
I would have to get more familiar with ITIS in a hurry, and figure out some way to
reference it from within DASLER.

November 17, 2011

I called EPA and asked about how they update the ITIS taxa list. They do have a procedure. Users send them e-mails requesting that organisms be added and specify that
they are listed on ITIS or the Catalog of Life (Richard uses ITIS). EPA staff confirms
their status and updates the list. So that's one way that we can get things in that aren't
matched, and it will be appropriate for many of the unmatched entries.

Based on my evaluation today, I'm inclined to make only a single change to the
DASLER taxa tables – a flag to indicate that the taxon is present in EPA's list. I can
use the code I wrote today as part of the database update procedure and mark the
initial ones accordingly. But that means I'll also need to add a dialog in DASLER for
maintenance of that box. Or at least a report.

Comparison of the taxa cited in biological results in DASLER to the list of
organisms already in the WQX master list turned up a few hundred names that were
not found. Further investigation revealed that almost all of them were in ITIS, but not
WQX. Apparently the list of taxa in the WQX repository was not linked to ITIS, but
instead was just based on ITIS. This was troubling until I realized that there was not
much biological data in the WQX repository yet. And fortunately EPA had a procedure
for adding taxa pretty quickly. More interesting from a purely data perspective was that
we would now be modifying our schema for the first time in a couple of years.

November 28, 2011

Another thing I did today on the export dialog was to add a pre-export report function. This will tell the user which records won't be exported because the names have not been validated. That is, it will tell if there are any, since the data I've selected for testing apparently has none. It will be a good option, though.

I found another way to enhance the user experience. I had figured out by this time that, at least initially, our exports would fail frequently due to the inclusion of taxa that were in ITIS but not in WQX. When exporting physical/chemical data to WQX, our users would just generate the export file and submit it. Errors would only occur occasionally in that process. Because of the missing taxa, I knew files would get rejected a lot for the biological exports – at least for a while. By generating a pre-export report, I could warn them of these missing taxa beforehand and allow them to request updates to WQX before the files were actually submitted. It was an easy option to add that saved much frustration in the DASLER community.

January 5, 2012

Then I got the idea of allowing the user to designate the non-conforming names on the fly with each export. Richard and I discussed that, and we decided there should be about four options for dealing with these: export them as is anyway, do not export them, export using the "unidentified species identifier" tag, or map them to another taxon. Before I got into this very much, though, I had another thought that I considered to be even better. Instead of managing that stuff on the fly with each export, I should instead go further back and designate those settings in the taxa tables themselves. That meant some additional modifications to the DB structure (and another tweak to the DB conversion program), but I think it was the smart thing to do.

Once again, a chance to make life easier for the users. I'm big on taking advantage of all such opportunities.

February 8, 2012

I learned a valuable lesson today about re-using old forms in VB. I finished the coding of the year's biological data export dialog and started testing.... That's when I did a file compare on the entire contents of those two files, which revealed the problem: the physical/chemical exports are still using the WQX Version 1 schema, which doesn't include the biological activity description section. Ouch. Had I replaced the whole export operation code, I would not have run into this problem. Stupid mistake.

Ouch is right. Even an experienced programmer (like me, presumably) is capable of making rookie mistakes. In this case I was duplicating an export form for physical/chemical data that had been used successfully for so long that I was very confident that it worked. I had therefore just copied the existing code into the new form and tweaked the specifics to match the biological export requirements. The problem was that some of the more mundane sample description areas were now more complex for biological data. Lesson: don't take shortcuts unless you're prepared for them to fail.

March 8, 2012

Mid-afternoon I got a call from Richard Tippit saying he had a conference call with the Division water quality folks tomorrow and was wondering if there was anything to report. I decided it was time to poke the WQX team once again about the issue of exporting our non-count biological results. We identified three situations with which we needed to deal based on the data we most often have in our results: density and biovolume for phytoplankton, and density for zooplankton and benthics. We started with the benthics. Eventually we decided that our density numbers were just another way of reporting count because the units are #/m2. So we agreed that I would report the raw numbers and the density, both as characteristic count. Then we moved on to the phytoplankton. There again, density is really count, so that was addressed. But he couldn't answer the question about biovolume, so he got another guy on the phone. He couldn't answer it at first either, but he wanted time to think about it. Before I left for the day he had replied with an answer. The solution is to report the phytoplankton biovolume not as a bioresult but as a regular result. The characteristic is "phytoplankton biovolume" and the species name goes in the result comment field. I think I'm now ready to put this to bed.

One last roadblock came up before I could finalize the export of biological data to WQX. This was one issue I couldn't solve without input from the EPA team. The issue was that we collected multiple types of results for various kinds of biological samples: organism count, organism density, and organism biovolume. Unfortunately, WQX only accepted counts at this time. As noted above, they quickly realized that density was just another way to express count, so they tweaked their reference data a little bit to accept those units. The biovolume answer surprised me a bit, primarily because I would never have thought of it. It also meant, though, that I would have to create specific physical/chemical sampling events (that didn't actually exist in our data) in order to upload biovolume data. I complied and was now done with this part of the update. On to the W2 calibration tool!

14 Rejuvenation

14.1 CONNECTIONS

March 19, 2012

Then I spent the rest of the day on COW. This is getting interesting because it's kind of an open book for me. There are a lot of ways to accomplish the things I need to do, and unlike in many of these situations, I'm free to do things any way I want.

COW was the original name I had proposed for the W2 calibration tool. I apparently never recorded what that was supposed to abbreviate, but it was probably Calibration of W2 or some such. Thank goodness the team came up with a better name later. What was different about this tool when compared to all the other interface and utility programs I had developed for DASLER was that I was starting from a blank slate, at least with regard to the design. The objectives and procedures were defined by the overall purpose of the program – everyone involved understood the methods and practices associated with model calibration. But within that framework, I was unconstrained by preconceived notions about how to interact with the users. This would be a good test of my ability to do so efficiently and effectively.

April 2, 2012

We headed out to ERDC [Engineer Research and Development Center] a few minutes before 8:00. We met with three of the people who are most involved with the W2 model community in a conference room. I showed them what I had. It didn't seem like much as I was presenting it, but they all agreed that getting to that point was a lot of work. They provided some good feedback and suggestions.

I traveled with Mark Campbell and Nashville's lead W2 modeler to the ERDC lab in Vicksburg for a meeting with some of their top CE-QUAL-W2 folks. The objective was to demonstrate the progress we had made on the new calibration tool and get feedback to make sure we were moving in the right direction. In case you don't know much about model calibration, it works this way. After you set up your basic model, you run simulations that cover periods in the past for which you have observed data. You then compare the observed data with the model's predictions and refine the settings and configuration of the model. Repeat as necessary until the model is fine-tuned to minimize the difference between the model and observed data. It tends to

DOI: 10.1201/9781003131953-16

be a laborious and time-consuming endeavor. The objective of the program I was developing was to provide the comparisons between model output and observed data. The analysis of the program included both statistical and graphical comparisons. This was by no means the first W2 calibration tool, but because it was designed to interact with the DASLER database, it addressed one of the most time-intensive activities associated with calibration: obtaining and compiling the observed data. Other tools required the user to mine observed data from whatever resources are available and then format those data in whatever manner the tool expects. This program automated that step (at least partially – it did require the user to associate DASLER sampling locations with specific segments defined in the model). Another difference for our tool was that it worked with the "standard" W2 model. The most popular W2 calibration tool used a modified version of W2. The modified version was the standard model computationally but was altered to include some additional output files used by the calibration program. These were binary files, which made the analysis itself very fast. But it meant that there was a lapse in applicability each time a new iteration of the W2 model was released while the developer integrated the code that generated the files into the model and compiled the special version compatible with the tool. Furthermore, some users were uncomfortable that the files used in the comparison were binary, thus making it difficult to examine the values themselves. By contrast, our program used the standard ASCII files that were generated by the basic model itself. Performance suffered a bit, but we deemed the advantages worth the difference.[1] Development was not yet complete at the time this meeting occurred. The program was performing all the basic functions but was still pretty rough around the edges. Our main objective in showing it to the W2 experts was to confirm our approach and solicit suggestions for improvements.

April 4, 2012

*Apparently Bob Sneed doesn't like the designation of our program as "COW," which was discussed at length during the trip to Vicksburg. So today I suggested a few alternatives. His choice so far is **DASLER** **O**bservation and **C**alibration **T**ool using **O**utput of **R**aw **W**2 Files (DOCTOR-W2). Mark weighed in with **DASLER W2** **E**xtraction and **E**valuation for **B**ioengineers (DWEEB), but I think that was meant to be a joke. No definite decision yet.*

On the coding front, I modified the text-based reports to include all the statistical measures discussed in Vicksburg: mean error, absolute mean error, and Root Mean Square error. As I had hoped, that was relatively easy because of what I had already done. I then finished adding in the other forms for editing plot window objects. I tested all that and it seems to be working.

---

[1] The irony of this situation does not escape me. If you go back to the first log entry in Chapter 10, you'll recall that there were two tasks mentioned. In addition to the GIS task that would evolve into the creation of DASLER, there was a task that involved modifying a utility for the CE-QUAL-W2 model. My boss from way back then had created a utility to animate the output of the model, and he had used an early version of the graphics library we were developing. Now here I was, 18 years later, using that same library (albeit with many improvements and enhancements) to create graphics in a W2 calibration tool.

Thanks to Bob, we ended up with a much better program name (DOCTOR-W2). The meeting in Vicksburg also resulted in suggestions for slightly more advanced statistical comparisons, which proved easy to implement. In case you're interested, an example of one of the graphical comparison plots from DOCTOR-W2 is shown in Figure 14.1.

June 25, 2012

I worked on wrapping up the DASLER-X update. The big boss wants to change the name from DASLER-X to DASLER-PRO. It makes perfect sense, and I only wish I had suggested that from the beginning.

I was now working on releasing Version 6 of the generic version of DASLER, which would bring it up to the same version as the one for the Corps. The new name suggested by the president of my company was obviously a big improvement.

January 14–15, 2013

We met in a conference room and jumped into the training. I did all the preliminaries and was just starting to get into manual data entry when the representative from the other contractor arrived about 10:00.

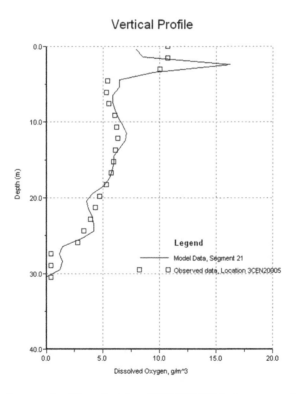

FIGURE 14.1   An example of the output from DOCTOR-W2 that compares observed vertical profile data with the output of the model.

I had long ago stopped hearing anything from the Louisville District regarding DASLER; I had learned over the last several months why this was the case. The original water quality crew there – the group that I had trained and then worked closely with for several years – had one by one retired, and eventually there was no one left who knew anything about DASLER. Unlike other districts (e.g., Omaha), they never asked for additional training, so I was not aware of the situation. At some point they had also stopped using the contractor that previously supported their data (see Chapter 12). So from a database perspective, things were a mess. Sometime in mid- to late-2012, word came down that they had a new water quality team leader and she was interested in resetting their data management efforts. Their plan was to accomplish this through another consulting company with which they already had a contract. The purpose of this session was to train both the new in-house team and the new contractor in the ways of DASLER. I assumed this meant a return to the previous paradigm.

July 18, 2013

I finished and tested the first continuous monitoring dialog today in DASLER (creating the event). Next up is importing the data, but I need some data to import.

In the first few months of 2013 Nashville had solicited input from the other districts that were using DASLER in preparation for a new work order for updating the software. Recall that Omaha was using DASLER-PRO instead of the standard Corps version. Apparently, they had shown some of the other districts some of that variation's unique features, which stimulated a lot of conversation. The end result was a decision to incorporate some of the features in PRO into the Corps version. This was actually a good deal for them: because these features were already vetted through use in PRO for many years, there was little cost involved because most of the code had already been written. The first activity in that effort was the addition of support for continuous monitoring data. Recycled code sometimes works just as well as fresh code.

July 22, 2013

I realized over the weekend that I needed one more table for the configuration info for the trophic state index calculation – to identify which parameter numbers should be used. I created that table and also wrote a dialog box to manage both that and the range definitions. Then I worked more on the dialog for doing the actual calculations. By the end of the day I had the calculations working, so all that's left now is to save them to the database and then generate a report format. I'm not planning on doing any graphics for that yet, but that might be coming later.

Another new feature that was included in this latest contract was a new analysis tool – calculation of Carlson's Trophic State Index (this should sound familiar from Chapter 8). Another exciting item in the new contract was a complete overhaul of the two main graphing programs (HIPP and BOGG). For the first time in years, I was once again expanding the capabilities of DASLER rather than just providing guidance and assistance related to data issues. It felt good.

September 24, 2013

At 10:00 I had a conference call with Louisville. I outlined the general approach that we have planned to take, and it was approved. We talked about how I can go about getting access to the database and other files, and we assigned some action items.

It turned out that the data situation in Louisville was more complex than I had thought. Apparently, no data at all had been loaded during the last few years of the former regime. As a result, the district had a massive backlog that needed to be incorporated if they were going to effectively use DASLER. Initially the new head of the water quality team in Louisville had followed the same approach as that used by the former team – engaging a contractor to handle all the data. Once the district got its full complement of water quality personnel, though, they realized their in-house team had the skills to perform these duties without involving the contractor. Still, the data backlog was intimidating. They hired my employer to help with this effort, and that work kicked off with this conference call. The data were in a myriad of formats, some of which were not compatible with any of the existing import procedures currently in the program. In addition to leading the project, my role would be to write custom programs to accommodate all the various formats. Meanwhile, I assembled a support team who would perform the actual data loading. For the first time I would now be essentially in charge of the full data cycle for a district. I was out of my comfort zone, but I was also the logical choice for the role. This would be the first of three contracts over the next few years that constituted a massive analysis and data correction effort. The sad part is that none of it would have been necessary if the original team had been more diligent regarding proper data management activities. (I have to say, though, that it's hard to fault someone in that situation. I learned early on that budgets sometimes impose restraints that force organizations to curtail all but the essential activities directly related to their mission.)

October 8, 2013

They have a whole set of samples and results for targeted sampling events – Harmful Algal Blooms or HABs. These analyses look for only organisms in the cyanophyta phylum (blue green algae), so the results list only those organisms. As a result, there are some events that report no organisms found. We have an entry in the taxa table for this, but so far it has implied that there are literally no organisms found. In this case, it means something different – no blue-green algae were found. I discussed this approach with Richard Tippit, and we agreed that the existing "no organisms" entry would be misleading given everything else being normal. So we have two choices. We can either create an entry in the taxa table under cyanophyta that says "no cyanophyta found" or we can create a new biological sample type. After some consideration I'm inclined to go with the latter.

Sorting through the Louisville data, I had discovered a type of biological sampling that (to my knowledge) no one in the Corps had yet been trying to record in DASLER. HABs were starting to happen more frequently and were becoming a very important concern for public health. Accommodating HAB sampling and analysis data resulted in the addition of many new capabilities in DASLER. Adding this support involved modifications to both the table structure and the interface.

January 30, 2014

The first session with Kansas City District was today.... We scheduled our next session for Monday at 2:00 pm.

Kansas City was another district where turnover had resulted in a lapse in continuity of DASLER usage. One thing that had not changed, though, was that it was still a one-person operation (for the time being). The latest occupant of that spot really wanted to get DASLER reinstated and working, and I was determined to make that happen if at all possible. However, due to budget constraints, there was no way to come up with the money for me to spend my traditional week on site. After many attempts to work out a way – any way – to get the training, we finally hit on a viable solution: I would conduct a series of two-hour webinar sessions that, over time, would cover everything I normally teach in the one-week class. I'm not a huge fan of remotely connected sessions – I feel that everyone gets better results with face-to-face training. However, I have to say that in this case it worked out better than what I anticipated. It might be because the guy was very sharp and picked up on things extremely quickly. Or it might have been because the lull between sessions gave him more time to explore the program in between, locking in the concepts and procedures presented in each meeting. For whatever reason, it truly worked well this time. I give credit to him for working so hard.

February 14, 2014

I fixed Nashville's database today. I started out by running several tests. Mark had sent me two copies of the database – one that demonstrated the problem, and an earlier backup that did not have the problem. However, if you ran a "compact and repair" operation on the good one, it became corrupted as well, showing the same symptoms. So I wrote a program that starts with a blank copy of the database and then copies all the records from one version to the new one. You have to do it in several passes due to data integrity constraints, but it eventually gets everything in there. I started with the good version, ran the program, then compacted it, and it then passed Mark's test. I then ran the program again on the one that was bad when I got it (because it had more data in it), and that one worked as well. I sent the updated database to Mark. His early tests seem to indicate that the problem is now fixed.

This was an interesting challenge. Mark Campbell had reported an odd situation. He sent me two copies of his database, one from late January and one from this week. The difference was that he had loaded some additional data and had also compacted the database. He described a complex data retrieval and report that worked on the original but not on the new one. Furthermore, when he compacted the one that worked, it also stopped working. After some tests, I became convinced that the problem was something structural in the database file itself. The best solution I could come up with was what is described here: start with a blank database and move data from each table from the old database to the new one. It worked. I don't know if this makes a case for or against a file-based database platform such as Jet. On the one hand, a more robust platform seems less likely to become corrupted. In all my years of doing this, I've never encountered a similar problem with Oracle or SQL Server. On the other hand, if such a problem were to occur on one of those platforms, the only opportunities for recovery would be a backup copy or possibly some data recovery tools provided by the vendor. I guess it's just food for thought.

November 5, 2014

I did more work on the TCImport program and completed the first batch of taxa updates on the live data. I'm happy now that this is a more robust solution.

This was an interesting solution to a mildly difficult situation related to the Louisville data project. The structure and schedule for this effort meant that our team included multiple individuals loading data simultaneously into a local copy of the database. I would periodically pull down Louisville's live database and update it by adding the latest batch of samples and results. The rub was that the data loading activities often required modifications to the taxa tables – entry of new organisms or corrections to existing ones. Since the district might also be modifying the taxa tables between updates, the challenge was to insert our changes without interfering with their changes. (I learned this lesson the hard way. Initially I thought I might get away with simply pushing our taxa table into the live database, but that corrupted the data the first time I did it. Next I tried doing a side-by-side comparison of the two tables and making our changes manually in the district's version. This was both time consuming and fraught with problems, the largest one being that it could result in incorrect taxa codes in the results data that would subsequently be uploaded.) The solution I came up with was to modify our custom off-line programs so that they logged each taxa table change in an external text file. I then wrote another program that parsed these files and made the corresponding changes to the live database at update time. The affected taxa codes in our copy of the data were noted, as well as the taxa codes in the live database for the corresponding organisms. These translations were applied to the results as they were loaded. It was a bit of a complicated process, but ultimately it saved a lot of time and greatly reduced the likelihood of introducing errors into the live database.

February 11, 2015

One of the things that distracted me today was a request from Omaha. The message described an interesting situation. They have some sampling locations in a marsh that is located in what is now a booming oil sand extraction zone. So they need to create a new watershed ID and move those locations to the new watershed. There are already samples and results on file. DASLER would allow them to change the location ID but not to one in another watershed. I offered to write them a quick utility with more flexibility. It took me less than an hour, including testing time. I was able to leverage the existing code for most of the work, so that was a definite time saver. I posted the utility and notified them.

If you're fortunate enough (as I have been) to maintain a particular system for a long time, eventually you'll see every possible oddity in the data. I thought I had already seen it all, then this came up. Location IDs in DASLER include the watershed/reservoir abbreviation as the first three characters (just like the example database in Chapter 8). Since the beginning we had allowed users to modify the location IDs, but as noted in this log entry, they couldn't move a location from one watershed/

reservoir to another. Until this message, I wouldn't have thought that would ever be needed. There was nothing the actual data model that prevented this – it was just a limitation of the user interface (and in my opinion, a wise one that could prevent mistakes). So now I truly could say I'd seen everything. I hoped.

November 4, 2015

And it was a very productive afternoon. I had identified three things we needed to cover: taxa table changes to make us more compatible with ITIS [Integrated Taxonomic Information System], review of the DASLER changes so far, and updates to the Louisville live data. We deemed the taxa table issue the most complex and therefore demanding of the most time, and so we jumped in there first. I started out by describing both our approach and the one in ITIS. I used the level information maps that I had generated, and they were helpful in developing the storyline. I passed them out one at a time, for good effect. I presented my case for sticking with our current paradigm – using "smart" codes for the taxa identifiers – but with potential changes. I think all were in agreement with that approach. We discussed what levels to add to our approach, and I think we were also all on the same page regarding omitting some of the more obscure levels in the ITIS version. We also fairly quickly came to the conclusion that we don't want to adopt the entire ITIS taxonomy with its 600k+ entries. The most lively and intriguing discussions centered on how we manage the update. I described some of the thoughts I had already had on the subject, but there were obvious issues with some of my ideas. Eventually we struck on what I think is a pretty good plan. I will convert the ITIS data to another database that the setup program (or maybe a separate utility) will access separately to manage the transition. (The concern is that the mapping transition might take some time and this will allow users to continue working in DASLER during the period. I ran an analysis to try and gauge how much trouble it might be to map things. I used Louisville's data. Of their 5,846 taxa, only 3,990 were exact matches to ITIS entries. That leaves 1,856 taxa that would require some manual interaction.) This external database will include a table that manages the new structural references, so when that is complete, the update to 7.0 can proceed. I think it will work, although it will take some clever doings on my part.

This is an unusually long entry (at least in the context of this book), but I left it intact because it contains a lot of important information related to having to manage information over which you have no control. The context here is that we were in the early stages of major revisions that would be part of DASLER Version 7.0. In this case, the objective was stated rather simply: the Corps wanted the DASLER taxa table to be more consistent with the ITIS taxa table, since ITIS was considered by EPA to be the definitive reference for taxonomic identification. I had spent some time over the last couple of weeks analyzing the ITIS database. That investigation turned up the information listed in the log. After much discussion during this three-day meeting, we had resolved most of the primary issues, but we also realized we were just starting to understand the implications. (At least there was one very positive side to this endeavor: we would finally – finally! – be consolidating all our organisms into a single taxa table.) By the end of this process, we had created links in the

DASLER interface to the ITIS database and had built a myriad of forms for tracking down organisms in ITIS in order to update DASLER names. It proved to be a good resource, but the sheer size of the ITIS repository had negative affects on the overall performance of DASLER whenever the two were linked.

February 8, 2016

Then I turned my attention to the WQX loading program.... By the end of the day I had the main form created (though not particularly working) and the first child form created – one for selecting a sampling event.

When EPA transitioned their water quality data repository from STORET to WQX, we had modified DASLER in such a way that it exported the XML files for WQX but relied on a utility from EPA (Node Client Lite) for the actual interaction with the Exchange Network. Part of the Version 7.0 overhaul was a task to eliminate the need for that extra piece. This was driven by the ever-tightening controls the Corps was enforcing on their computer resources (not that this was a bad thing). Because of these restrictions, it had become increasingly difficult to get permission to install Node Client Lite on Corps computers. It was time to remove that step. Fortunately, EPA provided a Dynamic Link Library (DLL) that included all the functions needed to interact with the Exchange Network. Unfortunately, there was little documentation included with the library. Nonetheless, this entry notes the beginning of an interesting period during which I created a custom application that linked directly to the DASLER database. With this program (which was a part of the DASLER suite and therefore on the Corps' approved software list), users could create the XML files, submit them, and then analyze the processing and loading reports all within one application. I even found a way to improve the user experience even more (if only slightly). I had always been annoyed that Node Client Lite stopped at the point at which the processing results were downloaded. The results were contained in an XML file, but this was presented just as raw text in Node Client Lite. It took a great deal of patience to dissect and read the report. Our DASLER utility (which we called the **W**QX **A**pplication for **L**oading **D**ASLER **O**bservations, or WALDO) actually parsed the report and summarized it, providing a much clearer picture of the outcome for the user. I've said it over and over, so you shouldn't be surprised that I'm saying it again: always look for ways to improve the user experience.

Another interesting aspect of the Version 7.0 project was that additional functions originally developed and implemented in DASLER-PRO were now to be incorporated into the standard Corps version. This raised my hopes that I would eventually only have to maintain a single version of the code.

May 25, 2016

The procedure I launched yesterday was still running this morning when I came in, and it was not even close to being done so it was time for a different approach.... The status column update went much more quickly after I created an index. Lesson learned: ALWAYS create an index.

This entry is more or less self-explanatory, but I'll provide a little context. I was working on capturing some data for one of the districts. This was continuous monitoring data, and there was a LOT of it. Still, I was expecting a relatively quick import – I had previously been clocking import of continuous data at a rate of about 500 rows per minute. However, in the new version of DASLER we had added support for multiple depths for continuous monitoring events. To clarify, our original data model for continuous data collection events specified a single depth because that was how the Corps was using the technology at the time. As probes and equipment became more cost-effective, they had begun collecting data at multiple depths for each event. So naturally we had modified the data model. This was the first big test of that revised model. The initial test results are obvious from the log entry, as are the solution and the lesson. The embarrassing part is that I failed to recognize the effect this relatively minor change – adding support for multiple depths – had on the speed with which records could be accessed. How careless was that?

14.2   ACME

May 31, 2017

First day at Civil and Environmental Consultants (CEC), and it was a long one.

I changed jobs again (after 18 years). This time my reasons for departure were less clear-cut but nonetheless valid. Let's just say that I had concluded my opportunities for interesting work at my previous employer appeared to be decreasing. Just as last time, the timing wasn't necessarily the greatest. Nashville was working on putting together a scope for another major DASLER update, and I had just started another round of updates for Louisville as we continued work on cleaning up their database. This was the biggest effort yet, and the contract was already in place. Fortunately, the company I just left was amenable to subcontracting the work to me at CEC, so there was no loss of momentum there. Unlike last time, this time the transition was quite smooth.

October 29, 2018

In the afternoon I was finally able to turn my attention to the work at hand and begin the merge process for CE and PRO.

The final merge of DASLER-PRO and the standard Corps version had finally kicked off. The week prior to this log entry had been spent in the Rock Island District. They were hosting a workshop of existing and prospective DASLER users within the Corps that was part of this new contract. The new contract – spearheaded by the Nashville, Louisville, and Omaha Districts – was funded through a cooperative effort involving many districts and was issued through the Engineer Research and Development Center (ERDC). The contract itself was thus an indicator of how DASLER had grown in importance to the Corps water quality community. There were three major activities required in the contract: the final merge of DASLER-PRO functionality into the main Corps version, a subsequent update that would add a list of new features to the program, and a workshop for all interested parties to present the capabilities that would ultimately exist at the end of the work. Because of timing, the workshop got scheduled first so as not to interfere with sampling activities. The workshop was attended by 17 people who represented seven districts and the analytical lab at ERDC. With the workshop now completed, I was ready to start down the path toward accomplishing something I had been hoping to do for a long time: reduce the number of supported versions of DASLER to one.[2] This would eliminate any opportunity to charge other organizations for use of the software because the only surviving version would be considered public domain. But the efforts to turn DASLER-PRO into a commercial product had never really gained traction anyway. By this time, I was only aware of one remaining non-government client who still used it. So the advantages definitely outweighed the disadvantages.

It did pose an interesting dilemma, however. Even though most Corp districts used the standard version, there were still those that preferred the PRO variant. The merger retained all but a very small handful of the features in PRO, but I didn't want to overwhelm users of the standard version with a lot of new menu options and dialog boxes. I finally settled on what I think was a good compromise. I created a table that managed system settings. Among the settings were flags for various components of DASLER. If a particular district opted to not avail themselves of a particular capability, they set that flag to off in the system settings table. All functionality related to components that were turned off disappeared from the menu system. If they opted to turn them back on later, they would reappear. This would allow existing users of either version to use the merged product without encountering the vertigo that sometimes happens when a familiar product suddenly has a new look. This is a simple idea, but one that made transitioning to the merged product much more palatable for everyone.

November 13, 2018

One form I removed today was the one for explicitly entering chlorophyll data. This has been around since the very earliest versions of DASLER, but I was pretty sure no one uses it anymore. I figured if anyone did, it would be Mark. So I e-mailed him to ask if he still used it. He does not, so there was no reason to retain it. It's gone.

Sometimes letting go of things is hard. Other times it's easy because you forget the thing was even there. That was the situation in this case. In the very early days of DASLER, we had put in a little feature that we all thought was pretty clever. Our original team had many discussions trying to resolve whether chlorophyll results belonged on the physical/chemical side or the biological side of the data model. In the end, we decided it should be in both, so we created an automatic process. It fired any time you manually entered data that included chlorophyll. If you were entering chlorophyll as part of the results for a physical/chemical sample, it created a phytoplankton sample with the same location, date, time, and depth characteristics. If you were documenting a biological sample, it would create a physical/chemical sample.

---

[2] I guess that's not absolutely accurate. It would actually be two because the other government agency was still using theirs. However, they had been limping along for years without any updates or ongoing support. They were still using Version 4.0, and this merged version would be 8.0. I had come to discount that version since they never asked for support. Also, the version for the power company had been relegated to the scrap heap. The company had reorganized at some point in the last several years, and during that reorganization their water quality mission became decentralized. The dispersal of the team that knew how to manage data to other assignments pretty much spelled an end to their use of DASLER.

The form identified in the log post popped up to notify you that this was happening (and give you a chance to cancel the second sample). We had eventually disabled it for most data activities (e.g., it no longer showed if the chlorophyll data were being imported), but it was still hanging around. I, like most DASLER users, had completely forgotten about it. I guess the lesson here is that a periodic review of the entire interface is a good idea. Or maybe that if you forgot something is there, you probably don't need it.

March 22, 2019

Back on the low DO [dissolved oxygen] process, I'm inching closer to a solution, but I'm still not quite there. I finally decided that the only way I was going to get all the issues worked out was to create some very simple examples and use those for testing. So I created three very simple examples. The first one is the simplest case – all decreasing elevations to the low point, then all increasing elevations to the far end … and with all elements covering only a single layer. The second example has some segments that cover two layers and also includes a single horizontal segment. The third one has a vertical jog in the middle, after the low point. I graphed each example and also calculated the perimeter and area values by hand. That way I have reference data with which to compare the program values. I got everything working on the first example before the end of the day.

Things can get pretty interesting when you start venturing off into more complex analyses. This was definitely happening to me here. Over the years I had programmed several different ways to identify low DO conditions. The simplest was just a report that looked for readings below a specified target value in the database, which was one of the first reports in the original version of DASLER. Another was a separate utility that analyzed vertical profiles and compared them with a lookup table of calculated reservoir capacity for various elevations. That one gave a rough estimate of the volume of water in the reservoir for which the DO was potentially below the target value. I had created that as a separate utility for one district several years back. When we were assembling the list of features to include in DASLER 8.1, I suggested that we combine those two items into a single category in the menu under "low DO values" and cite them as "points" and "volumes," respectively. Being a mathematician, my mind immediately noted that these were one-dimensional (1D) observations and three-dimensional (3D) calculations and I wondered if there was a two-dimensional (2D) version of this type of analysis also (and if so, was it appropriate for DASLER). Then I recalled that the version for the other federal agency included something that was probably the answer (see the log entry for January 5, 2005 in Chapter 13). That code also used a vertical profile but combined it with information about the cross-section geometry of the reservoir at or near the site where the profile was collected. The result was a calculation of the cross-sectional area and wetted perimeter that were exposed to the target low DO value. I offered to include that analysis in our suite, thus giving 1D, 2D, and 3D answers. After some discussion, this was approved based on the rationale that the perimeter calculation could be very important for biological analysis. My assumption was that I could more or less extract the code from the other version and drop it into the update – simple. It was only when

I went back and looked at the old code that I made an unexpected discovery. It turned out that in the original implementation I had been given an existing program and requested to just migrate the logic from it into their version of DASLER. I apparently never bothered to explore what was going on in detail. For the 8.1 update, I knew I would need to understand the code better, and that opened up a whole set of issues. There were several problems with the logic of the original, and ultimately I had to toss it all out and start from scratch. As I said, I'm a mathematician, but that doesn't mean I'm much of a geometer. This thing kicked my tail for what seemed like forever (but was actually only about a week) before I finally got something with which I was satisfied and confident in the results. I was proud of having accomplished it but still wasn't sure how popular it would be. Maybe the personal triumph was sufficient in this case.

August 9, 2019

This IBI [Index of Biotic Integrity] stuff is truly some of the most complicated (and therefore most interesting) stuff I've done in quite some time. It's interesting from at least two vantage points. First, the procedures for calculating the IBIs are themselves quite complex. Second, capturing all that in the simplest user interface possible is proving quite challenging. Today I made good progress on the interface up through the saving of the group elements. I did end up modifying things so that the data are saved each step of the way. That had some interesting challenges in and of itself, but I think I got them all worked out. I need to do more testing, but my initial attempts seem to be working. That got me all the way to the metrics themselves, but that's when I got a bit sidetracked. That process is one more step complicated than what I had originally determined. My original assessment was that each metric received a score in one of two ways: either by manipulating it with an equation, or by comparing its value to ranges and assigning a result. But a closer look at some of the examples shows that in some cases, both situations apply. That is, you apply a formula to the metric result and then compare that with the ranges (rather than just comparing the metric value). I think I have all the pieces defined, but I may not have them configured exactly correctly. Plus, I need to decode the Ohio information before I make a final decision.

If the 2D low DO calculation was a test of my geometric prowess, creating a system for defining and calculating an Index of Biotic Integrity (IBI) would be the ultimate test of my overall data management development skills – from both the database design and user interface creation points of view. I consider this to be the crowning achievement in the analytical capabilities within DASLER (at least so far), but understanding the magnitude of this achievement requires both background and explanation. IBIs started emerging toward the end of the 20th century as a way to use biological survey results to rate water quality. Our other federal agency actually created one of the first regionally accepted IBIs. It was based on benthic macroinvertebrate populations, so they called the Benthic IBI (BIBI). I had included calculation of the BIBI in their version of DASLER long ago. It found its way into DASLER-PRO, and was one of the items that was retained during the merge. But in the intervening years, the IBI process had really taken off, and now many states and other agencies were creating IBIs for application within their respective domains.

The feature list for Version 8.1 therefore included an item for managing additional IBI calculations.

On the surface this sounds relatively straightforward, but when you get into the details you discover that nothing could be further from the truth. The programming for the BIBI was hardcoded for a specific set of organisms and evaluations. Every other IBI was based on different organisms and calculations. More to the point, these things were proliferating almost daily. During the delivery meeting for Version 8.0, we had some lively discussions about the intimidating challenge ahead. We couldn't possibly hard code all those IBIs, and even if we could, maintenance would be a nightmare. I had a plan that I presented at that meeting, but at that point I wasn't sure if it was plausible.

To understand why, you need to know more about the IBI process. Here is a brief summary of how it works in general. The typical IBI score is determined by either adding or averaging scores from multiple individual component assessments (usually called metrics). Each metric is based on the characteristics of the results for the biological samples used to calculate the IBI score. Individual metrics are usually targeted at groups of organisms that share some common trait such as pollution tolerance. The organization that defines the IBI assigns values for these traits to individual organisms. Assignments may be made at any taxonomic level. Calculating the score for a particular metric typically requires identifying the specimens that apply to any groups defined in the metric out of all the organisms documented in the biological survey results, and then applying their respective trait scores. Additional mathematical manipulation is often also required. What you have at that point is the raw metric value. Combining the metrics may require some form of normalization, however, so in those cases the next step is to determine a score based on the metric's raw value. Scoring criteria are often defined in ranges (e.g., if the raw score is between 11 and 19, the score is 1 and so on), and many of the criteria have multiple ranges that are determined by additional factors (e.g., total drainage area contributing to the sampling location). Ultimately, all the metric scores are combined to produce the final IBI score, but then that score is also translated into a textual assessment based on ranges.

If it sounds complicated, it's because it is complicated. Maybe an example is in order. I'll describe an example based on fish population data. The IBI is composed of 25 metrics. The definitions of those metrics involve the enumeration of 17 different groupings of fish. Some groupings are based on taxonomy (e.g., Sunfish species), others are based on assigned characteristics (e.g., sensitive species), and still others are based on generic characteristics (e.g., omnivores). One of the metrics is described as "taxa richness of sucker species." Let's take a closer look at what it takes to calculate the score for that metric. First, we need the raw value. That's relatively easy. We start with an organism group (suckers). Members of that group are identified by the originating agency; in this case, it consists of all fish in the family Catostomidae. The raw value of the metric, then, is obtained by counting the total number of distinct taxa from the target group that were observed in the biosurvey results. Now we need to determine the metric score. In this particular IBI, each individual metric gets a score of either 1, 3, or 5. The instructions for calculating the taxa richness of sucker species includes six separate equations: two for each of the possible score values. The specific applicable equation is determined by the type of equipment used to conduct the survey. One set of equations is used when the survey was conducted using boat-mounted electrofishing equipment. The other set is used in all other cases. Let's say we used one of the non-boat-mounted methods. Then the IBI instructions state that the score for this metric is 1 when the raw value is less than a number derived from an equation involving some constants and the natural log of the contributing drainage area.

Based on this description, you should see that the level of complexity here is mostly in defining the IBI. Fortunately, I was able to meet the challenge. The database infrastructure was not terribly complicated, requiring the addition of only seven tables. Those changes were minimized because we already had tables capable of managing both the generic taxa characteristics such as mode of existence and feeding group (we called those characteristics "taxa descriptors") and the assigned ones such as pollution tolerance (we called those characteristics "biotic indices"). The seven additional tables managed the following data:

- general information about the IBI, including the organization that defined it, the type of biological samples involved, and so forth;
- identification of variables involved in the IBI, such as drainage area or equipment used;
- the definitions of organism groups found in the IBI;
- the membership of each group;[3]
- definitions of the individual metrics, including the equation(s) used to calculate the raw values;
- details of the scoring criteria for each metric; and
- the text interpretation of the overall IBI score.

The bigger challenge was the user interface. This was difficult for two reasons. First, as I trust you can tell from the discussion above, defining an IBI is just a complex process. Any activity this involved will be difficult for users to follow. The logical choice in this case was to use a tabbed dialog that works somewhat like a software wizard, guiding the user through each successively complicated part. I ended up with six tabs. The first tab captures the basic information. Variables are defined on the second tab, and organism groups are defined on the third tab. Metrics and the equations for calculating their raw values are defined on the fourth tab. Scoring criteria are defined on the fifth tab, and score interpretations are specified on the final tab.

Interestingly, once an IBI is defined, the calculation is comparatively simple, but this is only true because of some special processing code that also affects the definition process. The challenge arose when I started considering how to program the particulars of some of the metric equations – I needed a parser. Because many of the calculations involved assessing organism groups, the parser had to recognize several

---

[3] Identifying organisms that belong to any given group is not always trivial because the organizations that define IBIs often issue updates to their species characteristics lists. For that reason, I included the ability to dynamically determine group membership at calculation time for any groups based on assigned characteristics. I supplemented that with a form that accommodates the import of these updates rather than requiring manual corrections. This table therefore only captures membership in those groups that tend to remain stable, such as those based on taxonomic position.

new functions. The special functions I had to create had the following names and purposes:

- NUMTAXA(x) where x is either a specific group or the keyword "All" … this function counts the number of individual taxa in the specified group;
- MULTITAXA(x,y, …) which returns the total number of distinct taxa in the combination of the specified groups;
- NUMIND(x) which counts the number of individual specimens in the group;
- NUMIND(DOM) which returns the number of individuals in the dominant species for a sample;
- MULTIIND(x,y, …) which counts the number of individuals in the combination of multiple groups[4];
- EACHTAXONCT(x) which returns an array of individual taxa from the group and the number of individuals for each;
- TOTMASS(x) which returns the total mass of all specimens in the group;
- MULTIMASS(x,y, …) which finds the total mass of all individuals in the combination of the groups;
- EACHTAXONMASS(x) which returns an array of individual taxa from the group and the total mass of specimens for each;
- TRAITVALUE(x) where x is the name of a particular characteristic … this function returns the value of the specified characteristic for the taxon of interest (it's used exclusively within a loop over a series of taxa); and
- SUMOF(x) where x is an expression that returns a list of items.

These can be combined to produce most of the calculations that go into the determination of a given raw metric value. For instance, SUMOF(EACHTAXONCT(RG)* TRAITVALUE(TOL)) would identify all the taxa in the group RG, count how many individuals of each were found, then multiply each count by the value of the TOL index for the species, and return the sum of the total.

I have one more comment on this development process. In the heat of battle while trying to get all the IBI functionality working, I still managed to provide one more way to improve the data model and user experience. It was related to the fish survey data. The first implementation of support for fish survey data in the DASLER data model and interface was oriented toward collecting the raw data – recording the individual specimens observed during the survey. This worked great for organizations that did their own data collection, but it turned out that some of the Corps districts needed to calculate IBIs based on fish survey data from other sources. The problem was that these sources almost never provided the raw data. The only format available in many cases was what amounted to a summary report. Instead of listing every specimen, these reports listed only each species. For each, they included information such as the number of individuals, the length and mass of the largest specimen, the total mass of all the specimens, and so on. With this

---

[4] You can't just calculate the NUMIND of each group and add them up because group definitions may result in overlapping taxa.

in mind, I set up an alternative method for recording fish survey results data. Districts could record fish survey results in either the detailed or summary format. Ultimately, this allowed calculation of IBIs (and most, but not all of the other fish survey reports in DASLER) using either type of data. I had to force districts to choose one method for their database because of concerns about confusion over mixing both methods in the same system. But it accomplished the primary goal of enhancing the users' options and getting the job done.

It also turned out that the handling of the complex calculations for the IBIs was useful in addressing another item in the 8.1 update. The first approach to managing regulatory limits in DASLER consisted of very simple limits: an exceedance occurred if the value of parameter A was greater than X. Over the years, though, definitions of regulatory limits of physical and chemical constituents had become more complex. The first change we noticed was that some limits were now defined using a combination of values for multiple parameters (e.g., an exceedance for parameter A occurred if the value of parameter A was greater than X at the same time the value of parameter B was less than Y). We adapted DASLER to include this methodology beginning in (I think) version 7.0. More recently, some limits were now being defined with complex equations involving multiple parameters. The methodology developed for the IBI process allowed me to create a way for these new limit definitions to be entered and calculated.

March 10–12, 2020

The final delivery meeting for DASLER 8.1, at long last.

The focus of this meeting was delivery and acceptance testing of DASLER 8.1. At the time I'm writing this, 8.1 is the latest version, but likely not the final because a system like this is never truly finished. As evidence, note that I came away from this meeting with a list of 19 adjustments and tweaks based on the review conducted over these three days. All were minor, but you get the point. In the period after that meeting, I have continued to address minor adjustments to processes and provide additional guidance when necessary. The DASLER team continues to explore options for improving the functionality of the system. We haven't found any bugs lately, but we know they are there, just waiting for the inopportune time to present themselves.

14.3   REPRISE

March 4, 2021

We had an internal DASLER review today at 1:00 that lasted over 2 hours. The objective today was for me to walk through the process with folks from our Cincinnati office watching – I think to give them a better feel for how quickly things can come together. They sent me two files that were from a single project. It took quite some time to go through the first one, but that was because I was explaining everything as we went…. Near the end of the allocated time someone suggested that I go through the second file without comment and questions. We had 14 minutes left. This file was for the same site, but involved different sampling locations, so there was a bit of setup required before we processed the file. But that was a good demonstration because it's a more realistic scenario. The file contained both soil and groundwater samples. I was able to import the file and generate separate reports for each medium within the 14-minute window.

There is one more noteworthy development worth mentioning before concluding the story. Not long after delivering that most recent update of DASLER to the Corps of Engineers, I began the process of creating a new version for CEC's use. Now, you might infer from some of my statements in Part 2 that I would not enjoy going back to supporting multiple variations, but that turns out to not be the case. Instead I have become more exhilarated and excited about DASLER because of the interesting and challenging new directions the system has taken.

There are multiple areas where CEC's needs differ from the Corps. Some are associated with differences in mission and practices. Some relate to other factors.

First, CEC's activities include a more diverse range of environmental investigations than those performed by the teams in the Corps who use DASLER. To meet this need, I've modified the data model to better accommodate additional sample media, sample types, and analysis categories. Examples include soil chemistry, radiological analysis, and vapor intrusion monitoring. (Make no mistake: the Corps as an organization does many – maybe all – of these same categories of analyses, they just don't manage their data for these activities with DASLER.) In addition to database modifications, each new type of activity requires tweaks to the user interface as well: new forms, new reports, and new analyses. Some of these endeavors are in areas for which very specialized analytical software is available, so I've found myself working on new ways to export data. Another objective at CEC is streamlining of existing processes that already existed in DASLER. Thus, I've created new forms (e.g., wizards) that combine the functionality of existing forms, but tied everything together in one place so that users don't have to be as familiar with the overall interface to accomplish frequent goals. An example is a single form that allows users to create a new project, identify the project site, define sampling locations, import data, and generate a preliminary report of regulatory exceedances … all without having to click a menu option or open another dialog.

The second new thrust for DASLER is a focus on data collection using electronic devices. The capabilities of tablets and smart phones have increased exponentially in the past couple of years. Increasing cellular coverage areas have reduced the number and size of dead zones, providing field crews with greater opportunities to use these devices to collect data. Software vendors have introduced new and easier ways to create data entry applications that include options to upload data to web services that are now more widely accessible. All of these developments affect data acquisition strategies, and DASLER is adapting to use them.

Third, we are creating stronger integration with GIS. I love the fact that this is resulting in a sort of "circle of life" situation with DASLER. DASLER was born out of a GIS project, and now it's returning to that foundation.

Finally, with the CEC version, I am at last moving the primary DASLER interface to a newer programming language. Way back in 1995 when I started developing DASLER (see Chapter 10), Microsoft Visual Basic (VB) was a relatively new platform. It was based on the Component Object Model (COM), the most popular programming model for Windows applications at the time. VB continued to evolve and grow until around 2000; the last release was Version 6 (VB6). In the early 2000s, Microsoft introduced a new programming model (.NET) and a new version of VB (VB.NET), but the popularity of VB6 did not begin to wane until after 2010. Since you're now familiar with the history of DASLER, you understand that it grew from grass roots efforts within the Corps of Engineers. New features and capabilities were funded by individual districts as their needs arose and their budgets allowed. Throughout the history of the software, any money that was available for development was directed toward building on to the existing base. There was never an opportunity to update the foundation to newer technology.[5] The Corps of Engineers' version of DASLER is therefore still written in VB6 at this time.

Because the CEC version involves so many changes, I'm taking the opportunity to finally move the primary DASLER interface to VB.NET. (This is the logical choice rather than a completely different language due to the size and complexity of the code base.) The most exciting aspect of this transition is that it provides an opportunity to revisit code that is quite old. There are forms and functions in the VB6 version of DASLER that were written originally more than 20 years ago and have gone largely unchanged since their inception. (No need to tweak something that is working, right?) Rather than simply migrating all the existing processes to .NET, I'm taking the opportunity to re-evaluate them in an attempt to improve performance and/ or the user experience. (If you've been developing software for a long time, go back to something you did years ago. You'll probably find things that make you wonder why you ever did them that way.) This endeavor is at times challenging, but is always fun and interesting.

I am enjoying the challenges of adapting DASLER to these new practices and procedures. Creating new approaches stimulates the brain and revitalizes enthusiasm. I'm having a lot of fun with this new iteration.

My adventure continues. I wish you great success in yours, and hope that the instruction I've provided will contribute value to your pursuits. I also hope you learned something from reading about the development of DASLER. The most important point of Part 2 is that – like most endeavors related to science – developing, deploying, and supporting an environmental data management system rarely happens without some unexpected problems and diversions. The practices you learned in college – and in Part 1 of this book – are helpful guidelines, but they can never prepare you for the ultimate chaos that will greet you in real life. Rest easy in the knowledge that you can achieve many satisfying milestones along the journey.

---

[5] The only significant departure from this paradigm occurred when something entirely new was needed. WALDO – the utility that replaced Node Client Lite for exporting data from DASLER to WQX – was written in VB.NET.

Appendix A: Data Dictionary for the Database Developed in Chapter 8

This appendix contains a complete listing of the structure of all tables in the database created in Chapter 8. It also includes entity relationship diagrams that denote some of the important relationships between tables.

A.1 DATA DICTIONARY

Table A.1 lists each table in the data model. For each table, the columns are described and notes are given that provide further details. Because this database was created for the Jet database engine, the data types listed in this table are those referenced within that framework. Some Jet type names do not follow SQL standards. In particular, the TEXT(n) data type is equivalent to the more common VARCHAR(n) data type. You may also notice that some columns have a default value of "*." These are mostly foreign keys that cannot be NULL. In all cases, the * is the coded value for a related record that translates as "not on file" or "not indicated."

A.2 ENTITY RELATIONSHIP DIAGRAMS

Figures A.1 through A.4 are entity relationship diagrams for the example database. These diagrams indicate key relationships between some of the tables. The diagrams do not depict all relationships because not all tables are present in the diagrams. Each diagram shows the relationships between the tables that constitute a major concept within the database: parameters, locations, samples, and results.

TABLE A.1
The Example Database Data Dictionary

Table	Column	Data Type	Notes
ANALYTE_ALIASES	PARAMETER_ID	TEXT(5)	NOT NULL FK into ANALYTES
	PARAM_ALIAS	TEXT(50)	NOT NULL PRIMARY KEY
ANALYTE_GROUP_ ELEMENTS	GROUP_CODE	TEXT(12)	NOT NULL PRIMARY KEY FK into ANALYTE_ GROUPS
	PARAMETER_ID	TEXT(5)	NOT NULL PRIMARY KEY FK into ANALYTES
	UNITS	TEXT(15)	NOT NULL Default value: "None" FK into UNITS
ANALYTE_GROUPS	GROUP_CODE	TEXT(12)	NOT NULL PRIMARY KEY
	GROUP_DESC	TEXT(200)	NOT NULL
	SHORT_NAME	TEXT(10)	NOT NULL
ANALYTE_TEST_ METHODS	PARAMETER_ID	TEXT(5)	NOT NULL PRIMARY KEY FK into ANALYTES
	TEST_MTHD	TEXT(20)	NOT NULL PRIMARY KEY FK into TEST_METHODS
ANALYTES	PARAMETER_ID	TEXT(5)	NOT NULL PRIMARY KEY
	ANL_NAME	TEXT(70)	NOT NULL
	ANL_SHORT	TEXT(25)	NOT NULL
COLLECTION_ METHODS	COLLECT_ MTHD	INTEGER	NOT NULL PRIMARY KEY
	METH_NAME	TEXT(25)	NOT NULL
	SOP_DOC	TEXT(255)	A pointer to the file name of the SOP that defines how this method is used.
CONVERSION_ FACTORS	FROM_UNITS	TEXT(15)	NOT NULL PRIMARY KEY
	TO_UNITS	TEXT(15)	NOT NULL PRIMARY KEY
	FACTOR	SINGLE	NOT NULL Default value: 1
COUNTIES	POSTAL_STATE	TEXT(2)	NOT NULL PRIMARY KEY FK into STATES
	CNTY_CODE	TEXT(3)	NOT NULL PRIMARY KEY

TABLE A.1 Continued
The Example Database Data Dictionary

Table	Column	Data Type	Notes
	CNTY_NAME	TEXT(24)	NOT NULL
DATA_ CONFIDENCE_ FLAGS	DCL_FLAG	TEXT(2)	NOT NULL PRIMARY KEY
	DCL_DESC	TEXT(32)	NOT NULL
FIELD_FORM_ PARAMETERS	PARAMETER_ID	TEXT(5)	NOT NULL PRIMARY KEY FK into ANALYTES
	UNITS	TEXT(15)	NOT NULL FK into UNITS
	SEQUENCE	INTEGER	NOT NULL Default value: 0
HOLD_TIMES	PARAMETER_ID	TEXT(5)	NOT NULL PRIMARY KEY FK into ANALYTES
	MAX_DAYS	LONG INTEGER	NOT NULL
HUC_CODES	HUC_CODE	TEXT(8)	NOT NULL PRIMARY KEY
	HUC_NAME	TEXT(45)	NOT NULL
LABS	LAB_ID	TEXT(10)	NOT NULL PRIMARY KEY
	LAB_NAME	TEXT(25)	NOT NULL
	CONTACT_ NAME	TEXT(32)	
	ADDRESS1	TEXT(32)	
	ADDRESS2	TEXT(32)	
	CITY	TEXT(25)	
	STATE	TEXT(2)	
	ZIP	TEXT(10)	
	COMMENTS	TEXT(100)	
LOCATION_ ALIASES	LOC_ALIAS	TEXT(75)	NOT NULL PRIMARY KEY
	SITE_ID	TEXT(3)	NOT NULL PRIMARY KEY FK into SITES
	LOC_ID	TEXT(12)	NOT NULL FK into LOCATIONS
	PRIMARY_ ALIAS	TEXT(1)	
LOCATIONS	LOC_ID	TEXT(12)	NOT NULL PRIMARY KEY
	LATITUDE	SINGLE	NOT NULL Default value: -99

(continued)

TABLE A.1 Continued
The Example Database Data Dictionary

Table	Column	Data Type	Notes
	LONGITUDE	SINGLE	NOT NULL Default value: -99
	DATUM_REF	TEXT(8)	NOT NULL Default value: "*"
	POSTAL_STATE	TEXT(2)	NOT NULL Default value: "*" FK (with CNTY_CODE) into COUNTIES
	CNTY_CODE	TEXT(3)	FK (with POSTAL_ STATE) into COUNTIES
	HUC_CODE	TEXT(8)	FK into HUC_CODES
	STREAM_CODE	TEXT(4)	FK into STREAM_CODES
	STREAM_MILE	SINGLE	
	PHYSI_CODE	TEXT(2)	FK into PHYSIOGRAPHIC_ PROVINCES
	BOTTOM_ELEV	SINGLE	
	GROUND_ELEV	SINGLE	
	TOP_OF_ CASING	SINGLE	
	WELL_ DIAMETER	SINGLE	
	LOC_DESC	TEXT(200)	
PHYSIOGRAPHIC_ PROVINCES	PHYSI_CODE	TEXT(2)	NOT NULL PRIMARY KEY
	PHYSI_NAME	TEXT(50)	NOT NULL
PREP_METHODS	PREP_MTHD	TEXT(20)	NOT NULL PRIMARY KEY
	PREP_DESC	TEXT(200)	NOT NULL
PROJECT_SITES	PROJECT_ID	TEXT(15)	NOT NULL PRIMARY KEY FK into PROJECTS
	SITE_ID	TEXT(3)	NOT NULL PRIMARY KEY FK into SITES
PROJECTS	PROJECT_ID	TEXT(15)	NOT NULL PRIMARY KEY
	PROJECT_ NAME	TEXT(100)	NOT NULL
REGULATORY_ LIMITS	REG_ID	INTEGER	NOT NULL PRIMARY KEY
	REG_NAME	TEXT(75)	NOT NULL

TABLE A.1 Continued
The Example Database Data Dictionary

Table	Column	Data Type	Notes
	POSTAL_STATE	TEXT(2)	NOT NULL FK into STATES
	PARAMETER_ID	TEXT(5)	NOT NULL FK into ANALYTES
	UNITS	TEXT(15)	NOT NULL FK into UNITS
	RELATION	TEXT(2)	NOT NULL
	REG_VALUE	SINGLE	NOT NULL
REGULATORY_ LIMITS_ CONDITIONALS	REG_ID	INTEGER	NOT NULL PRIMARY KEY FK into REGULATORY LIMITS
	PARAMETER_ID	TEXT(5)	NOT NULL PRIMARY KEY
	UNITS	TEXT(15)	NOT NULL FK into UNITS
	RELATION	TEXT(2)	NOT NULL
	LOW_VALUE	SINGLE	NOT NULL
	HIGH_VALUE	SINGLE	
RESULTS	LOC_ID	TEXT(12)	NOT NULL PRIMARY KEY FK (with SAMPLE_NUM) into SAMPLES
	SAMPLE_NUM	TEXT(17)	NOT NULL PRIMARY KEY FK (with LOC_ID) into SAMPLES
	LAB_ID	TEXT(10)	NOT NULL PRIMARY KEY Default value: "*"
	LAB_SNUM	TEXT(17)	NOT NULL PRIMARY KEY
	PARAMETER_ID	TEXT(5)	NOT NULL PRIMARY KEY FK into ANALYTES
	PARAM_ FRACTION	TEXT(1)	NOT NULL PRIMARY KEY
	PREP_MTHD	TEXT(15)	NOT NULL PRIMARY KEY FK into PREP_METHODS Default value: "*"
	TEST_MTHD	TEXT(15)	NOT NULL PRIMARY KEY FK into TEST_METHODS Default value: "*"

(continued)

TABLE A.1 Continued
The Example Database Data Dictionary

Table	Column	Data Type	Notes
	UNITS	TEXT(15)	NOT NULL FK into UNITS
	PARAM_VALUE	DOUBLE	
	TEXT_VALUE	TEXT(15)	NOT NULL
	MDL	SINGLE	
	RL	SINGLE	
	DILUTION	SINGLE	
	LAB_ANLZ	DATE	
	DCL_FLAG	TEXT(2)	NOT NULL Default value: "*"
	DATE_ ENTERED	DATE	NOT NULL
	VAL_QUAL	TEXT(5)	
SAMPLE_MEDIA	MEDIUM_CODE	TEXT(2)	NOT NULL PRIMARY KEY
	MEDIUM_ NAME	TEXT(15)	NOT NULL
SAMPLE_TYPE_ CODES	SAMPLE_TYPE	TEXT(3)	NOT NULL
	TYPE_NAME	TEXT(30)	NOT NULL
SAMPLES	LOC_ID	TEXT(12)	NOT NULL PRIMARY KEY FK into LOCATIONS
	SAMPLE_NUM	TEXT(17)	NOT NULL PRIMARY KEY
	SAMPLE_ DEPTH	SINGLE	NOT NULL
	SAMPLE_TIME	DATE	NOT NULL
	COLLECT_ MTHD	INTEGER	NOT NULL FK into COLLECTION_ METHODS Default value: 0
	SOURCE_CODE	TEXT(2)	NOT NULL FK into SOURCE_CODES
	MEDIUM_CODE	TEXT(2)	NOT NULL FK into SAMPLE_MEDIA Default value: "*"
	PROJECT_ID	TEXT(15)	NOT NULL FK into PROJECTS
	SAMPLE_TYPE	TEXT(3)	NOT NULL FK into SAMPLE_TYPE_ CODES
SITES	SITE_ID	TEXT(3)	NOT NULL PRIMARY KEY

TABLE A.1 Continued
The Example Database Data Dictionary

Table	Column	Data Type	Notes
	SITE_NAME	TEXT(120)	NOT NULL
SOURCE_CODES	SOURCE_CODE	TEXT(1)	NOT NULL
			PRIMARY KEY
	SOURCE_NAME	TEXT(30)	NOT NULL
STATES	POSTAL_STATE	TEXT(2)	NOT NULL
			PRIMARY KEY
	STATE_NAME	TEXT(24)	NOT NULL
STREAM_CODES	STREAM_CODE	TEXT(4)	NOT NULL
			PRIMARY KEY
	STREAM_NAME	TEXT(100)	NOT NULL
TEST_METHODS	TEST_MTHD	TEXT(20)	NOT NULL
			PRIMARY KEY
	TEST_DESC	TEXT(200)	NOT NULL
TSI_PARAMETERS	SECCHI_PARAM	TEXT(5)	
	CHLOR_PARAM	TEXT(5)	
	PHOS_PARAM	TEXT(5)	
TSI_RANGES	LOWER_VAL	INTEGER	NOT NULL
	UPPER_VAL	INTEGER	NOT NULL
	RANGE_LABEL	TEXT(50)	NOT NULL
TSI_SCORES	LOC_ID	TEXT(12)	NOT NULL
			PRIMARY KEY
			FK into LOCATIONS
	SAMPLE_MASK	TEXT(12)	NOT NULL
			PRIMARY KEY
	TSI_SCORE	SINGLE	NOT NULL
	SECCHI_SCORE	TEXT(5)	
	CHLOR_SCORE	TEXT(5)	
	PHOS_SCORE	TEXT(5)	
UNITS	UNITS	TEXT(15)	NOT NULL
			PRIMARY KEY
VALUE_QUALIFIER_ TRANSLATIONS	LAB_ID	TEXT(10)	NOT NULL
			PRIMARY KEY
			FK into LABS
	LAB_ENTRY	TEXT(3)	NOT NULL
			PRIMARY KEY
	VAL_QUAL	TEXT(1)	NOT NULL
VALUE QUALIFIERS	VAL_QUAL	TEXT(1)	NOT NULL
	VAL_MEANING	TEXT(100)	NOT NULL

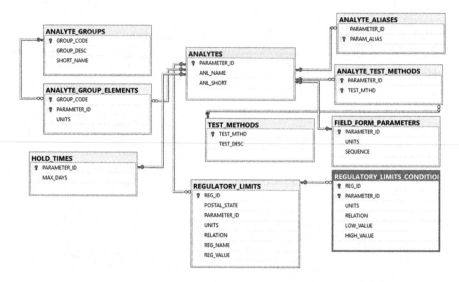

FIGURE A.1   Entity relationship diagram for tables associated with parameters.

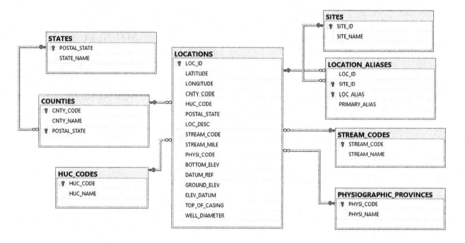

FIGURE A.2   Entity relationship diagram for tables associated with sampling locations.

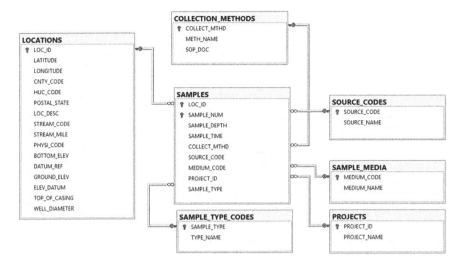

FIGURE A.3 Entity relationship diagram for tables associated with sampling events.

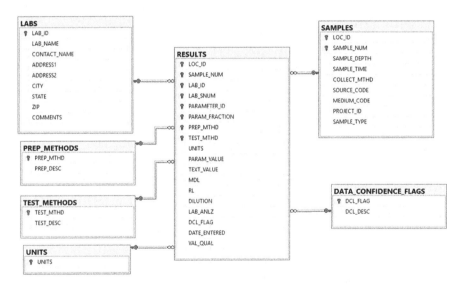

FIGURE A.4 Entity relationship diagram for tables associated with sampling results.

Appendix B: SQL Commands for Creating the Database and Inserting Data

This appendix contains SQL commands that can be used to create the example database described in Chapter 8 and insert data into some of the tables. The Access version of the database is available for download from the web (see the boxed text in Chapter 8 for details), as are the contents of this appendix. Given that, why would the reader be interested in these commands, and why would we reproduce them here? The primary reason is to provide more definitive examples of some of the categories of SQL statements we discussed in Chapter 4. In the interest of brevity, we did not offer very many actual examples at that point. We presented generic forms and a few hypothetical versions. By the end of Chapter 8, the reader has experienced a more realistic scenario first hand. It is therefore our hope that reviewing the commands in this appendix with the deeper understanding of purpose gained in working with the example database will solidify the concepts and lead to a greater grasp of the material.

B.1 COMMANDS FOR CREATING THE TABLES

The following commands create the tables in the example database discussed in Chapter 8. These commands create the basic tables, set default values, and define primary keys.

```
CREATE TABLE ANALYTE_ALIASES (
      PARAMETER_ID varchar(5) NOT NULL PRIMARY KEY,
      PARAM_ALIAS varchar(50) NOT NULL
);

CREATE TABLE ANALYTE_GROUP_ELEMENTS (
      GROUP_CODE varchar(12) NOT NULL,
      PARAMETER_ID varchar(5) NOT NULL,
      UNITS varchar(15) NOT NULL DEFAULT 'None',
CONSTRAINT PK_ANALYTE_GROUP_ELEMENTS PRIMARY KEY
(GROUP_CODE, PARAMETER_ID)
);
```

```
CREATE TABLE ANALYTE_GROUPS (
     GROUP_CODE varchar(12) NOT NULL PRIMARY KEY,
     GROUP_DESC varchar(200) NOT NULL,
     SHORT_NAME varchar(10) NOT NULL
);

CREATE TABLE ANALYTE_TEST_METHODS (
     PARAMETER_ID varchar(5) NOT NULL,
     TEST_MTHD varchar(20) NOT NULL,
CONSTRAINT PK_ANALYTE_TEST_METHODS PRIMARY KEY
(PARAMETER_ID, TEST_MTHD)
);

CREATE TABLE ANALYTES (
     PARAMETER_ID varchar(5) NOT NULL PRIMARY KEY,
     ANL_NAME varchar(70) NOT NULL,
     ANL_SHORT varchar(25) NOT NULL
);

CREATE TABLE COLLECTION_METHODS (
     COLLECT_MTHD smallint NOT NULL PRIMARY KEY,
     METH_NAME varchar(25) NOT NULL,
     SOP_DOC varchar(255) NOT NULL
);

CREATE TABLE CONVERSION_FACTORS (
     FROM_UNITS varchar(15) NOT NULL,
     TO_UNITS varchar(15) NOT NULL,
     FACTOR real NOT NULL DEFAULT 1,
CONSTRAINT PK_CONVERSION_FACTORS PRIMARY KEY (FROM_
UNITS, TO_UNITS)
);

CREATE TABLE COUNTIES (
     CNTY_CODE varchar(3) NOT NULL,
     CNTY_NAME varchar(24) NOT NULL,
     POSTAL_STATE varchar(2) NOT NULL,
CONSTRAINT PK_COUNTIES PRIMARY KEY (CNTY_CODE,
POSTAL_STATE)

);
CREATE TABLE DATA_CONFIDENCE_FLAGS (
     DCL_FLAG varchar(2) NOT NULL PRIMARY KEY,
     DCL_DESC varchar(32) NOT NULL
);
```

```
CREATE TABLE FIELD_FORM_PARAMETERS (
     PARAMETER_ID varchar(5) NOT NULL PRIMARY KEY,
     UNITS varchar(15) NOT NULL,
     SEQUENCE smallint NOT NULL DEFAULT 0
);

CREATE TABLE HOLD_TIMES (
     PARAMETER_ID varchar(5) NOT NULL PRIMARY KEY,
     MAX_DAYS smallint NOT NULL
);

CREATE TABLE HUC_CODES (
     HUC_CODE varchar(8) NOT NULL PRIMARY KEY,
     HUC_NAME varchar(45) NOT NULL
);

CREATE TABLE LABS (
     LAB_ID varchar(10) NOT NULL PRIMARY KEY,
     LAB_NAME varchar(25) NOT NULL,
     CONTACT_NAME varchar(32),
     ADDRESS1 varchar(32),
     ADDRESS2 varchar(32),
     CITY varchar(25),
     STATE varchar(2),
     ZIP varchar(10),
     COMMENTS varchar(100)
);

CREATE TABLE LOCATION_ALIASES (
     LOC_ID varchar(12) NOT NULL,
     SITE_ID varchar(3) NOT NULL,
     LOC_ALIAS varchar(75) NOT NULL,
     PRIMARY_ALIAS char(1),
CONSTRAINT PK_LOCATION_ALIASES PRIMARY KEY (SITE_ID,
LOC_ALIAS)
);

CREATE TABLE LOCATIONS (
     LOC_ID varchar(12) NOT NULL PRIMARY KEY,
     LATITUDE real NOT NULL DEFAULT -99,
     LONGITUDE real NOT NULL DEFAULT -99,
     CNTY_CODE varchar(3),
     HUC_CODE varchar(8),
     POSTAL_STATE varchar(2) NOT NULL DEFAULT '*',
     LOC_DESC varchar(200),
     STREAM_CODE varchar(4),
```

```
        STREAM_MILE real,
        PHYSI_CODE varchar(2),
        BOTTOM_ELEV real,
        DATUM_REF varchar(8) NOT NULL DEFAULT '*',
        GROUND_ELEV real,
        ELEV_DATUM varchar(5),
        TOP_OF_CASING real,
        WELL_DIAMETER real
);

CREATE TABLE PHYSIOGRAPHIC_PROVINCES (
        PHYSI_CODE varchar(2) NOT NULL PRIMARY KEY,
        PHYSI_NAME varchar(50) NOT NULL
);

CREATE TABLE PREP_METHODS (
        PREP_MTHD varchar(20) NOT NULL PRIMARY KEY,
        PREP_DESC varchar(200) NOT NULL
);
CREATE TABLE PROJECT_SITES (
        PROJECT_ID varchar(15) NOT NULL,
        SITE_ID varchar(3) NOT NULL,
CONSTRAINT PK_PROJECT_SITES PRIMARY KEY (PROJECT_ID,
SITE_ID)
);

CREATE TABLE PROJECTS (
        PROJECT_ID varchar(15) NOT NULL PRIMARY KEY,
        PROJECT_NAME varchar(100) NOT NULL
);

CREATE TABLE REGULATORY_LIMITS (
        REG_ID smallint NOT NULL PRIMARY KEY,
        POSTAL_STATE varchar(2) NOT NULL,
        PARAMETER_ID varchar(5) NOT NULL,
        UNITS varchar(10) NOT NULL,
        RELATION varchar(2) NOT NULL,
        REG_NAME varchar(75) NOT NULL,
        REG_VALUE real NOT NULL
);

CREATE TABLE REGULATORY_LIMITS_CONDITIONALS (
        REG_ID smallint NOT NULL,
        PARAMETER_ID varchar(5) NOT NULL,
        UNITS varchar(10) NOT NULL,
        RELATION varchar(2) NOT NULL,
```

```
     LOW_VALUE real NOT NULL,
     HIGH_VALUE real,
CONSTRAINT PK_REGULATORY_LIMITS_CONDITIONALS PRIMARY
KEY (REG_ID, PARAMETER_ID)
);

CREATE TABLE RESULTS (
     LOC_ID varchar(12) NOT NULL,
     SAMPLE_NUM varchar(17) NOT NULL,
     LAB_ID varchar(10) NOT NULL '*',
     LAB_SNUM varchar(17) NOT NULL,
     PARAMETER_ID varchar(5) NOT NULL,
     PARAM_FRACTION varchar(1) NOT NULL,
     PREP_MTHD varchar(20) NOT NULL DEFAULT '*',
     TEST_MTHD varchar(20) NOT NULL DEFAULT '*',
     UNITS varchar(15) NOT NULL DEFAULT 'None',
     PARAM_VALUE float,
     TEXT_VALUE varchar(15) NOT NULL,
     MDL real,
     RL real,
     DILUTION real,
     LAB_ANLZ datetime,
     DCL_FLAG varchar(2) NOT NULL DEFAULT '*',
     DATE_ENTERED datetime NOT NULL,
     VAL_QUAL varchar(5) NULL,
CONSTRAINT PK_RESULTS PRIMARY KEY (LOC_ID, SAMPLE_
NUM, LAB_ID, LAB_SNUM, PARAMETER_ID, PARAM_FRACTION,
PREP_MTHD, TEST_MTHD)
);

CREATE TABLE SAMPLE_MEDIA (
     MEDIUM_CODE varchar(2) NOT NULL PRIMARY KEY,
     MEDIUM_NAME varchar(15) NOT NULL,
CONSTRAINT [PK_SAMPLE_MEDIA] PRIMARY KEY
);

CREATE TABLE SAMPLE_TYPE_CODES (
     SAMPLE_TYPE varchar(3) NOT NULL PRIMARY KEY,
     TYPE_NAME varchar(30) NOT NULL
);

CREATE TABLE SAMPLES (
     LOC_ID varchar(12) NOT NULL,
     SAMPLE_NUM varchar(17) NOT NULL,
     SAMPLE_DEPTH real NOT NULL,
     SAMPLE_TIME datetime NOT NULL,
```

```
        COLLECT_MTHD smallint NOT NULL DEFAULT 0,
        SOURCE_CODE varchar(1) NOT NULL DEFAULT `*',
        MEDIUM_CODE varchar(2) NOT NULL DEFAULT `*',
        PROJECT_ID varchar(15) NOT NULL,
        SAMPLE_TYPE varchar(3) NOT NULL,
CONSTRAINT PK_SAMPLES PRIMARY KEY (LOC_ID, SAMPLE_
NUM)
);

CREATE TABLE SITES (
        SITE_ID varchar(3) NOT NULL PRIMARY KEY,
        SITE_NAME varchar(120) NOT NULL
);

CREATE TABLE SOURCE_CODES (
        SOURCE_CODE varchar(1) NOT NULL PRIMARY KEY,
        SOURCE_NAME varchar(30) NOT NULL
);

CREATE TABLE STATES (
        POSTAL_STATE varchar(2) NOT NULL PRIMARY KEY,
        STATE_NAME varchar(24) NOT NULL
);

CREATE TABLE STREAM_CODES (
        STREAM_CODE varchar(4) NOT NULL PRIMARY KEY,
        STREAM_NAME varchar(100) NOT NULL
);

CREATE TABLE TEST_METHODS (
        TEST_MTHD varchar(20) NOT NULL PRIMARY KEY,
        TEST_DESC varchar(200) NOT NULL
);

CREATE TABLE TSI_PARAMETERS (
        SECCHI_PARAM varchar(5),
        CHLOR_PARAM varchar(5),
        PHOS_PARAM varchar(5)
);

CREATE TABLE TSI_RANGES (
        LOWER_VAL smallint NOT NULL PRIMARY KEY,
        UPPER_VAL smallint NOT NULL,
        RANGE_LABEL varchar(50) NOT NULL
);
```

```
CREATE TABLE TSI_SCORES (
     LOC_ID varchar(12) NOT NULL,
     SAMPLE_MASK varchar(12) NOT NULL,
     TSI_SCORE real NOT NULL,
     SECCHI_SCORE varchar(5),
     CHLOR_SCORE varchar(5),
     PHOS_SCORE varchar(5),
CONSTRAINT [PK_TSI_SCORES] PRIMARY KEY (LOC_ID,
SAMPLE_MASK)
);

CREATE TABLE UNITS (
     UNITS varchar(15) NOT NULL PRIMARY KEY
);

CREATE TABLE VALUE_QUALIFIER_TRANSLATIONS (
     LAB_ID varchar(10) NOT NULL,
     LAB_ENTRY varchar(3) NOT NULL,
     VAL_QUAL varchar(1) NOT NULL,
CONSTRAINT PK_VALUE_QUALIFIER_TRANSLATIONS PRIMARY
KEY (LAB_ID, LAB_ENTRY)
);

CREATE TABLE VALUE_QUALIFIERS (
     VAL_QUAL char(1) NOT NULL PRIMARY KEY,
     VAL_MEANING varchar(100) NOT NULL
);
```

B.2 COMMANDS FOR CREATING RELATIONSHIPS

As noted in the main text, attempting to create constraints within the statements that create the tables can be difficult because the order of creation becomes important. We prefer therefore to create the relationship constraints after all the tables have been established. The following statements generate the relationships needed to construct the database.

```
ALTER TABLE ANALYTE_ALIASES ADD CONSTRAINT FK_
ANALYTE_ALIASES_ANALYTES FOREIGN KEY
  (PARAMETER_ID)
  REFERENCES ANALYTES(PARAMETER_ID)
  ON UPDATE CASCADE
  ON DELETE CASCADE
;
```

```
ALTER TABLE ANALYTE_GROUP_ELEMENTS ADD CONSTRAINT
FK_ANALYTE_GROUP_ELEMENTS_ANALYTE_GROUPS FOREIGN KEY
  (GROUP_CODE)
  REFERENCES ANALYTE_GROUPS(GROUP_CODE)
  ON UPDATE CASCADE
  ON DELETE CASCADE
;

ALTER TABLE ANALYTE_GROUP_ELEMENTS ADD CONSTRAINT
FK_ANALYTE_GROUP_ELEMENTS_ANALYTES FOREIGN KEY
  (PARAMETER_ID)
  REFERENCES ANALYTES(PARAMETER_ID)
  ON UPDATE CASCADE
  ON DELETE CASCADE
;

ALTER TABLE ANALYTE_TEST_METHODS ADD CONSTRAINT FK_
ANALYTE_TEST_METHODS_ANALYTES FOREIGN KEY
  (PARAMETER_ID)
  REFERENCES ANALYTES(PARAMETER_ID)
  ON UPDATE CASCADE
  ON DELETE CASCADE
;

ALTER TABLE ANALYTE_TEST_METHODS ADD CONSTRAINT FK_
ANALYTE_TEST_METHODS_TEST_METHODS FOREIGN KEY
  (TEST_MTHD)
  REFERENCES TEST_METHODS(TEST_MTHD)
  ON UPDATE CASCADE
  ON DELETE CASCADE
;

ALTER TABLE COUNTIES ADD CONSTRAINT [FK_COUNTIES_
STATES] FOREIGN KEY
  (POSTAL_STATE)
  REFERENCES STATES(POSTAL_STATE)
  ON UPDATE CASCADE
  ON DELETE CASCADE
;

ALTER TABLE FIELD_FORM_PARAMETERS ADD CONSTRAINT FK_
FIELD_FORM_PARAMETERS_ANALYTES FOREIGN KEY
  (PARAMETER_ID)
  REFERENCES ANALYTES (PARAMETER_ID)
  ON UPDATE CASCADE
  ON DELETE CASCADE
;
```

```
ALTER TABLE [HOLD_TIMES] ADD CONSTRAINT FK_HOLD_
TIMES_ANALYTES FOREIGN KEY
  (PARAMETER_ID)
  REFERENCES ANALYTES(PARAMETER_ID)
  ON UPDATE CASCADE
  ON DELETE CASCADE
;

ALTER TABLE LOCATION_ALIASES ADD CONSTRAINT FK_
LOCATION_ALIASES_LOCATIONS FOREIGN KEY
  (LOC_ID)
  REFERENCES LOCATIONS(LOC_ID)
  ON UPDATE CASCADE
  ON DELETE CASCADE
;

ALTER TABLE LOCATION_ALIASES ADD CONSTRAINT FK_
LOCATION_ALIASES_SITES FOREIGN KEY
  (SITE_ID)
  REFERENCES SITES(SITE_ID)
  ON UPDATE CASCADE
  ON DELETE CASCADE
;

ALTER TABLE LOCATIONS CONSTRAINT FK_LOCATIONS_
COUNTIES FOREIGN KEY
  (CNTY_CODE, POSTAL_STATE)
  REFERENCES COUNTIES ([NTY_CODE, POSTAL_STATE)
  ON UPDATE CASCADE
  ON DELETE SET DEFAULT
;

ALTER TABLE LOCATIONS ADD CONSTRAINT FK_LOCATIONS_
PHYSIOGRAPHIC_PROVINCES FOREIGN KEY
  (PHYSI_CODE)
  REFERENCES PHYSIOGRAPHIC_PROVINCES(PHYSI_CODE)
  ON UPDATE CASCADE
  ON DELETE SET NULL
;

ALTER TABLE LOCATIONS ADD CONSTRAINT FK_LOCATIONS_
STREAM_CODES FOREIGN KEY
  (STREAM_CODE)
  REFERENCES STREAM_CODES(STREAM_CODE)
  ON UPDATE CASCADE
  ON DELETE SET NULL
;
```

```
ALTER TABLE REGULATORY_LIMITS ADD CONSTRAINT FK_
REGULATORY_LIMITS_ANALYTES FOREIGN KEY
  (PARAMETER_ID)
  REFERENCES ANALYTES(PARAMETER_ID)
  ON UPDATE CASCADE
  ON DELETE CASCADE
;

ALTER TABLE REGULATORY_LIMITS_CONDITIONALS ADD
CONSTRAINT FK_REGULATORY_LIMITS_CONDITIONALS_
REGULATORY_LIMITS FOREIGN KEY
  (REG_ID)
  REFERENCES REGULATORY_LIMITS(REG_ID)
  ON UPDATE CASCADE
  ON DELETE CASCADE
;

ALTER TABLE RESULTS ADD CONSTRAINT FK_RESULTS_DATA_
CONFIDENCE_FLAGS FOREIGN KEY
  (DCL_FLAG)
  REFERENCES DATA_CONFIDENCE_FLAGS(DCL_FLAG)
  ON UPDATE CASCADE
  ON DELETE SET DEFAULT
;

ALTER TABLE RESULTS ADD CONSTRAINT FK_RESULTS_LABS
FOREIGN KEY
  (LAB_ID)
  REFERENCES LABS(LAB_ID)
  ON UPDATE CASCADE
  ON DELETE SET DEFAULT
  ;

ALTER TABLE RESULTS ADD CONSTRAINT FK_RESULTS_PREP_
METHODS FOREIGN KEY
  (PREP_MTHD)
  REFERENCES PREP_METHODS(PREP_MTHD)
  ON UPDATE CASCADE
  ON DELETE SET DEFAULT
;

ALTER TABLE RESULTS ADD CONSTRAINT FK_RESULTS_
SAMPLES FOREIGN KEY
  (LOC_ID, SAMPLE_NUM)
  REFERENCES SAMPLES (LOC_ID, SAMPLE_NUM)
  ON UPDATE CASCADE
  ON DELETE CASCADE
;
```

```
ALTER TABLE [RESULTS] ADD CONSTRAINT FK_RESULTS_
TEST_METHODS FOREIGN KEY
  (TEST_MTHD)
  REFERENCES TEST_METHODS(TEST_MTHD)
  ON UPDATE CASCADE
  ON DELETE SET DEFAULT
;

ALTER TABLE RESULTS ADD CONSTRAINT FK_RESULTS_UNITS
FOREIGN KEY
  (UNITS)
  REFERENCES UNITS(UNITS)
  ON UPDATE CASCADE
  ON DELETE SET DEFAULT
;

ALTER TABLE SAMPLES ADD CONSTRAINT FK_SAMPLES_
COLLECTION_METHODS FOREIGN KEY
  (COLLECT_MTHD)
  REFERENCES COLLECTION_METHODS(COLLECT_MTHD)
  ON UPDATE CASCADE
  ON DELETE SET DEFAULT
;

ALTER TABLE SAMPLES ADD CONSTRAINT FK_SAMPLES_
LOCATIONS FOREIGN KEY
  (LOC_ID)
  REFERENCES LOCATIONS(LOC_ID)
  ON UPDATE CASCADE
  ON DELETE CASCADE
;

ALTER TABLE SAMPLES ADD CONSTRAINT FK_SAMPLES_
PROJECTS FOREIGN KEY
  (PROJECT_ID)
  REFERENCES PROJECTS(PROJECT_ID)
  ON UPDATE CASCADE
  ON DELETE CASCADE
;

ALTER TABLE SAMPLES ADD CONSTRAINT FK_SAMPLES_
SAMPLE_MEDIA FOREIGN KEY
  (MEDIUM_CODE)
  REFERENCES SAMPLE_MEDIA(MEDIUM_CODE)
  ON UPDATE CASCADE
  ON DELETE SET DEFAULT
;
```

```
ALTER TABLE SAMPLES ADD CONSTRAINT FK_SAMPLES_
SAMPLE_TYPE_CODES FOREIGN KEY
  (SAMPLE_TYPE)
  REFERENCES SAMPLE_TYPE_CODES(SAMPLE_TYPE)
  ON UPDATE CASCADE
  ON DELETE CASCADE
;

ALTER TABLE SAMPLES ADD CONSTRAINT FK_SAMPLES_
SOURCE_CODES FOREIGN KEY
  (SOURCE_CODE)
  REFERENCES SOURCE_CODES(SOURCE_CODE)
  ON UPDATE CASCADE
  ON DELETE SET DEFAULT
;
```

B.3 COMMANDS FOR INSERTING DATA

After the tables and relationships are in place, data can be inserted. The following commands insert data from the example database. We do not include every record found in the online version of the example database, but we do include all the records in reference tables that have a special purpose (mostly the "not on file" and "not indicated" placeholders). We also choose to limit data in some of the tables with many records (e.g., states and counties). The downloadable version of these statements includes the complete data from the example database.

```
INSERT INTO ANALYTES(PARAMETER_ID,ANL_NAME,ANL_
SHORT) VALUES ('00000','Lake Depth','Lake Depth');
INSERT INTO ANALYTES(PARAMETER_ID,ANL_NAME,ANL_
SHORT) VALUES ('00004','Stream Width','Stream
Width');
INSERT INTO ANALYTES(PARAMETER_ID,ANL_NAME,ANL_
SHORT) VALUES ('00009','Distance from left
bank','Sample Location');
INSERT INTO ANALYTES(PARAMETER_ID,ANL_NAME,ANL_
SHORT) VALUES ('00010','Temperature','Temperature');
INSERT INTO ANALYTES(PARAMETER_ID,ANL_NAME,ANL_
SHORT) VALUES ('00060','Stream Flow, Mean
Daily','Stream Flow, Mean');
INSERT INTO ANALYTES(PARAMETER_ID,ANL_
NAME,ANL_SHORT) VALUES ('00061','Stream Flow,
Instantaneous','Stream Flow, Inst');
INSERT INTO ANALYTES(PARAMETER_ID,ANL_NAME,ANL_
SHORT) VALUES ('00076','Turbidity','Turbidity');
INSERT INTO ANALYTES(PARAMETER_ID,ANL_
NAME,ANL_SHORT) VALUES ('00077','Secchi Disk
Depth','Secchi');
```

```
INSERT INTO ANALYTES(PARAMETER_ID,ANL_NAME,ANL_
SHORT) VALUES ('00299','Oxygen, Dissolved','Dis
Oxygen');
INSERT INTO ANALYTES(PARAMETER_ID,ANL_NAME,ANL_
SHORT) VALUES ('00301','Oxygen Saturation,
Dissolved','Dis Oxygen Sat');
INSERT INTO ANALYTES(PARAMETER_ID,ANL_NAME,ANL_
SHORT) VALUES ('00400','pH','pH');
INSERT INTO ANALYTES(PARAMETER_ID,ANL_NAME,ANL_
SHORT) VALUES ('00410','Alkalinity','Alkalinity');
INSERT INTO ANALYTES(PARAMETER_ID,ANL_
NAME,ANL_SHORT) VALUES ('00500','Residue,
Total','Solids, Tot');
INSERT INTO ANALYTES(PARAMETER_ID,ANL_NAME,ANL_
SHORT) VALUES ('00505','Residue, Volatile','Solids,
Volatile');
INSERT INTO ANALYTES(PARAMETER_ID,ANL_NAME,ANL_
SHORT) VALUES ('00515','Residue, Dissolved','Solids,
Dissolved');
INSERT INTO ANALYTES(PARAMETER_ID,ANL_NAME,ANL_
SHORT) VALUES ('00520','Residue, Volatile,
Dissolved','Solids, Vol Diss');
INSERT INTO ANALYTES(PARAMETER_ID,ANL_NAME,ANL_
SHORT) VALUES ('00530','Residue, Suspended','Solids,
Suspended');
INSERT INTO ANALYTES(PARAMETER_ID,ANL_NAME,ANL_
SHORT) VALUES ('00535','Residue, Volatile
Suspended','Solids, Vol Susp');
INSERT INTO ANALYTES(PARAMETER_ID,ANL_NAME,ANL_
SHORT) VALUES ('00546','Residue, Settleable','Solids
Settleable');
INSERT INTO ANALYTES(PARAMETER_ID,ANL_NAME,ANL_
SHORT) VALUES ('00600','Nitrogen','Nitrogen');
INSERT INTO ANALYTES(PARAMETER_ID,ANL_NAME,ANL_
SHORT) VALUES ('00605','Nitrogen, Organic,
Total','Nitrogen, Organic');
INSERT INTO ANALYTES(PARAMETER_ID,ANL_NAME,ANL_
SHORT) VALUES ('00610','Ammonia, Nitrogen (as
N)','Ammonia N');
INSERT INTO ANALYTES(PARAMETER_ID,ANL_NAME,ANL_
SHORT) VALUES ('00615','Nitrogen, Nitrite (as
N)','Nitrite');
INSERT INTO ANALYTES(PARAMETER_ID,ANL_NAME,ANL_
SHORT) VALUES ('00619','Ammonia, Nitrogen,
Unionized','Ammonia, unionized');
```

```
INSERT INTO ANALYTES(PARAMETER_ID,ANL_NAME,ANL_
SHORT) VALUES ('00620','Nitrogen, Nitrate (as
N)','Nitrate');
INSERT INTO ANALYTES(PARAMETER_ID,ANL_NAME,ANL_
SHORT) VALUES ('00625','Kjeldahl Nitrogen (as
N)','Kjeldahl N');
INSERT INTO ANALYTES(PARAMETER_ID,ANL_NAME,ANL_
SHORT) VALUES ('00630','Nitrite + Nitrate
Nitrogen','NO3+NO2');
INSERT INTO COLLECTION_METHODS(COLLECT_MTHD,METH_
NAME,METH_TYPE) VALUES (0,'not on file',NULL);
INSERT INTO COLLECTION_METHODS(COLLECT_MTHD,METH_
NAME,METH_TYPE) VALUES (1,'unknown',NULL);
INSERT INTO COLLECTION_METHODS(COLLECT_MTHD,METH_
NAME,METH_TYPE) VALUES (2,'pump',NULL);
INSERT INTO COLLECTION_METHODS(COLLECT_MTHD,METH_
NAME,METH_TYPE) VALUES (3,'multiparameter
sampler',NULL);
INSERT INTO COLLECTION_METHODS(COLLECT_MTHD,METH_
NAME,METH_TYPE) VALUES (4,'dipped',NULL);
INSERT INTO COLLECTION_METHODS(COLLECT_MTHD,METH_
NAME,METH_TYPE) VALUES (5,'kemmerer bottle',NULL);
INSERT INTO COLLECTION_METHODS(COLLECT_MTHD,METH_
NAME,METH_TYPE) VALUES (6,'bucket',NULL);
INSERT INTO COLLECTION_METHODS(COLLECT_MTHD,METH_
NAME,METH_TYPE) VALUES (7,'water bottle',NULL);
INSERT INTO CONVERSION_FACTORS(FROM_UNITS,TO_
UNITS,FACTOR) VALUES ('cm','m',0.01);
INSERT INTO CONVERSION_FACTORS(FROM_UNITS,TO_
UNITS,FACTOR) VALUES ('cm3','liter',0.001);
INSERT INTO CONVERSION_FACTORS(FROM_UNITS,TO_
UNITS,FACTOR) VALUES ('cm3','m3',0.000001);
INSERT INTO CONVERSION_FACTORS(FROM_UNITS,TO_
UNITS,FACTOR) VALUES ('JTU','NTU',1);
INSERT INTO CONVERSION_FACTORS(FROM_UNITS,TO_
UNITS,FACTOR) VALUES ('liter','cm3',1000);
INSERT INTO CONVERSION_FACTORS(FROM_UNITS,TO_
UNITS,FACTOR) VALUES ('liter','m3',0.001);
INSERT INTO CONVERSION_FACTORS(FROM_UNITS,TO_
UNITS,FACTOR) VALUES ('m','cm',100);
INSERT INTO CONVERSION_FACTORS(FROM_UNITS,TO_
UNITS,FACTOR) VALUES ('m','mm',1000);
INSERT INTO CONVERSION_FACTORS(FROM_UNITS,TO_
UNITS,FACTOR) VALUES ('m3','cm3',1000000);
INSERT INTO CONVERSION_FACTORS(FROM_UNITS,TO_
UNITS,FACTOR) VALUES ('m3','liter',1000);
```

```
INSERT INTO CONVERSION_FACTORS(FROM_
UNITS,TO_UNITS,FACTOR) VALUES ('m3/day','m3/
hr',4.166667E-02);
INSERT INTO CONVERSION_FACTORS(FROM_
UNITS,TO_UNITS,FACTOR) VALUES ('m3/day','m3/
min',6.94444E-04);
INSERT INTO CONVERSION_FACTORS(FROM_UNITS,TO_
UNITS,FACTOR) VALUES ('m3/day','m3/sec',0.0000116);
INSERT INTO CONVERSION_FACTORS(FROM_UNITS,TO_
UNITS,FACTOR) VALUES ('m3/day','mgd',2.64E-07);
INSERT INTO CONVERSION_FACTORS(FROM_UNITS,TO_
UNITS,FACTOR) VALUES ('m3/hr','cfm',0.5885778);
INSERT INTO CONVERSION_FACTORS(FROM_UNITS,TO_
UNITS,FACTOR) VALUES ('m3/hr','cfs',9.80963E-03);
INSERT INTO CONVERSION_FACTORS(FROM_UNITS,TO_
UNITS,FACTOR) VALUES ('m3/hr','mgd',0.0063393);
INSERT INTO CONVERSION_FACTORS(FROM_UNITS,TO_
UNITS,FACTOR) VALUES ('m3/min','cfm',35.31467);
INSERT INTO CONVERSION_FACTORS(FROM_UNITS,TO_
UNITS,FACTOR) VALUES ('m3/min','cfs',0.5885778);
INSERT INTO CONVERSION_FACTORS(FROM_UNITS,TO_
UNITS,FACTOR) VALUES ('m3/min','m3/day',1440);
INSERT INTO CONVERSION_FACTORS(FROM_UNITS,TO_
UNITS,FACTOR) VALUES ('m3/min','m3/hr',60);
INSERT INTO CONVERSION_FACTORS(FROM_
UNITS,TO_UNITS,FACTOR) VALUES ('m3/min','m3/
sec',1.666667E-02);
INSERT INTO CONVERSION_FACTORS(FROM_UNITS,TO_
UNITS,FACTOR) VALUES ('m3/min','mgd',0.38036);
INSERT INTO CONVERSION_FACTORS(FROM_UNITS,TO_
UNITS,FACTOR) VALUES ('m3/sec','m3/day',86400);
INSERT INTO CONVERSION_FACTORS(FROM_UNITS,TO_
UNITS,FACTOR) VALUES ('m3/sec','m3/hr',3600);
INSERT INTO CONVERSION_FACTORS(FROM_UNITS,TO_
UNITS,FACTOR) VALUES ('m3/sec','m3/min',60);
INSERT INTO CONVERSION_FACTORS(FROM_UNITS,TO_
UNITS,FACTOR) VALUES ('m3/sec','mgd',22.821);
INSERT INTO CONVERSION_FACTORS(FROM_UNITS,TO_
UNITS,FACTOR) VALUES ('mg/kg','mg/l',1);
INSERT INTO CONVERSION_FACTORS(FROM_UNITS,TO_
UNITS,FACTOR) VALUES ('mg/kg','ug/kg',1000);
INSERT INTO CONVERSION_FACTORS(FROM_UNITS,TO_
UNITS,FACTOR) VALUES ('mg/kg','ug/l',1);
INSERT INTO CONVERSION_FACTORS(FROM_UNITS,TO_
UNITS,FACTOR) VALUES ('mg/l','g/cm3',1);
```

```
INSERT INTO CONVERSION_FACTORS(FROM_UNITS,TO_
UNITS,FACTOR) VALUES ('mg/l','g/l',0.001);
INSERT INTO CONVERSION_FACTORS(FROM_UNITS,TO_
UNITS,FACTOR) VALUES ('mg/l','g/m3',1);
INSERT INTO CONVERSION_FACTORS(FROM_UNITS,TO_
UNITS,FACTOR) VALUES ('mg/l','mg/kg',1);
INSERT INTO CONVERSION_FACTORS(FROM_UNITS,TO_
UNITS,FACTOR) VALUES ('mg/L','mg/l',1);
INSERT INTO CONVERSION_FACTORS(FROM_UNITS,TO_
UNITS,FACTOR) VALUES ('mg/l','ppb',1000);
INSERT INTO CONVERSION_FACTORS(FROM_UNITS,TO_
UNITS,FACTOR) VALUES ('mg/l','ppm',1);
INSERT INTO CONVERSION_FACTORS(FROM_UNITS,TO_
UNITS,FACTOR) VALUES ('mg/l','ug/l',1000);
INSERT INTO CONVERSION_FACTORS(FROM_UNITS,TO_
UNITS,FACTOR) VALUES ('mgd','m3/hr',157.75);
INSERT INTO CONVERSION_FACTORS(FROM_UNITS,TO_
UNITS,FACTOR) VALUES ('mgd','m3/min',2.6291);
INSERT INTO CONVERSION_FACTORS(FROM_UNITS,TO_
UNITS,FACTOR) VALUES ('mgd','m3/sec',0.043819);
INSERT INTO CONVERSION_FACTORS(FROM_UNITS,TO_
UNITS,FACTOR) VALUES ('mm','m',0.001);
INSERT INTO CONVERSION_FACTORS(FROM_UNITS,TO_
UNITS,FACTOR) VALUES ('NTU','FTU',1);
INSERT INTO CONVERSION_FACTORS(FROM_UNITS,TO_
UNITS,FACTOR) VALUES ('NTU','JTU',1);
INSERT INTO CONVERSION_FACTORS(FROM_UNITS,TO_
UNITS,FACTOR) VALUES ('ppb','g/cm3',0.001);
INSERT INTO CONVERSION_FACTORS(FROM_UNITS,TO_
UNITS,FACTOR) VALUES ('ppb','g/l',0.000001);
INSERT INTO CONVERSION_FACTORS(FROM_UNITS,TO_
UNITS,FACTOR) VALUES ('ppb','mg/l',0.001);
INSERT INTO CONVERSION_FACTORS(FROM_UNITS,TO_
UNITS,FACTOR) VALUES ('ppb','ppm',0.001);
INSERT INTO CONVERSION_FACTORS(FROM_UNITS,TO_
UNITS,FACTOR) VALUES ('ppb','ug/l',1);
INSERT INTO CONVERSION_FACTORS(FROM_UNITS,TO_
UNITS,FACTOR) VALUES ('ppm','g/cm3',1);
INSERT INTO CONVERSION_FACTORS(FROM_UNITS,TO_
UNITS,FACTOR) VALUES ('ppm','g/l',0.001);
INSERT INTO CONVERSION_FACTORS(FROM_UNITS,TO_
UNITS,FACTOR) VALUES ('ppm','mg/l',1);
INSERT INTO CONVERSION_FACTORS(FROM_UNITS,TO_
UNITS,FACTOR) VALUES ('ppm','ppb',1000);
INSERT INTO CONVERSION_FACTORS(FROM_UNITS,TO_
UNITS,FACTOR) VALUES ('ppm','ug/l',1000);
```

```
INSERT INTO CONVERSION_FACTORS(FROM_UNITS,TO_
UNITS,FACTOR) VALUES ('ug/Kg','mg/kg',1000);
INSERT INTO CONVERSION_FACTORS(FROM_UNITS,TO_
UNITS,FACTOR) VALUES ('ug/Kg','ug/kg',1);
INSERT INTO CONVERSION_FACTORS(FROM_UNITS,TO_
UNITS,FACTOR) VALUES ('ug/l','g/cm3',0.001);
INSERT INTO CONVERSION_FACTORS(FROM_UNITS,TO_
UNITS,FACTOR) VALUES ('ug/l','g/l',0.000001);
INSERT INTO CONVERSION_FACTORS(FROM_UNITS,TO_
UNITS,FACTOR) VALUES ('ug/l','mg/l',0.001);
INSERT INTO CONVERSION_FACTORS(FROM_UNITS,TO_
UNITS,FACTOR) VALUES ('ug/L','None',1);
INSERT INTO CONVERSION_FACTORS(FROM_UNITS,TO_
UNITS,FACTOR) VALUES ('ug/l','ppb',1);
INSERT INTO CONVERSION_FACTORS(FROM_UNITS,TO_
UNITS,FACTOR) VALUES ('ug/l','ppm',0.001);
INSERT INTO CONVERSION_FACTORS(FROM_UNITS,TO_
UNITS,FACTOR) VALUES ('ug/L','ug/l',1);
INSERT INTO CONVERSION_FACTORS(FROM_UNITS,TO_
UNITS,FACTOR) VALUES ('um3/ml','#/ml',1);
INSERT INTO CONVERSION_FACTORS(FROM_UNITS,TO_
UNITS,FACTOR) VALUES ('um3/ml','mg/l',1);
INSERT INTO CONVERSION_FACTORS(FROM_UNITS,TO_
UNITS,FACTOR) VALUES ('um3/ml','umho/cm',1);
INSERT INTO CONVERSION_FACTORS(FROM_UNITS,TO_
UNITS,FACTOR) VALUES ('umho/cm','mho/cm',1);
INSERT INTO CONVERSION_FACTORS(FROM_UNITS,TO_
UNITS,FACTOR) VALUES ('umho/cm','UM/CM',1);
INSERT INTO CONVERSION_FACTORS(FROM_UNITS,TO_
UNITS,FACTOR) VALUES ('umho/cm','um3/ml',1);
INSERT INTO CONVERSION_FACTORS(FROM_UNITS,TO_
UNITS,FACTOR) VALUES ('umho/cm','uS/cm',1);
INSERT INTO COUNTIES(CNTY_CODE,CNTY_NAME,POSTAL_
STATE) VALUES ('001','Anderson','TN');
INSERT INTO COUNTIES(CNTY_CODE,CNTY_NAME,POSTAL_
STATE) VALUES ('003','Bedford','TN');
INSERT INTO COUNTIES(CNTY_CODE,CNTY_NAME,POSTAL_
STATE) VALUES ('005','Benton','TN');
INSERT INTO COUNTIES(CNTY_CODE,CNTY_NAME,POSTAL_
STATE) VALUES ('007','Bledsoe','TN');
INSERT INTO COUNTIES(CNTY_CODE,CNTY_NAME,POSTAL_
STATE) VALUES ('009','Blount','TN');
INSERT INTO COUNTIES(CNTY_CODE,CNTY_NAME,POSTAL_
STATE) VALUES ('011','Bradley','TN');
INSERT INTO COUNTIES(CNTY_CODE,CNTY_NAME,POSTAL_
STATE) VALUES ('013','Campbell','TN');
```

```
INSERT INTO COUNTIES(CNTY_CODE,CNTY_NAME,POSTAL_
STATE) VALUES ('015','Cannon','TN');
INSERT INTO COUNTIES(CNTY_CODE,CNTY_NAME,POSTAL_
STATE) VALUES ('019','Carter','TN');
INSERT INTO DATA_CONFIDENCE_FLAGS(DCL_FLAG,DCL_DESC)
VALUES ('*','result has not been rated');
INSERT INTO DATA_CONFIDENCE_FLAGS(DCL_FLAG,DCL_DESC)
VALUES ('1','Not Rated');
INSERT INTO DATA_CONFIDENCE_FLAGS(DCL_FLAG,DCL_DESC)
VALUES ('3','Probable');
INSERT INTO DATA_CONFIDENCE_FLAGS(DCL_FLAG,DCL_DESC)
VALUES ('5','Acceptable');
INSERT INTO DATA_CONFIDENCE_FLAGS(DCL_FLAG,DCL_DESC)
VALUES ('9','Validated');
INSERT INTO HOLD_TIMES(PARAMETER_ID,MAX_DAYS) VALUES
('00076',2);
INSERT INTO HOLD_TIMES(PARAMETER_ID,MAX_DAYS) VALUES
('00410',14);
INSERT INTO HOLD_TIMES(PARAMETER_ID,MAX_DAYS) VALUES
('00500',14);
INSERT INTO HOLD_TIMES(PARAMETER_ID,MAX_DAYS) VALUES
('00515',14);
INSERT INTO HOLD_TIMES(PARAMETER_ID,MAX_DAYS) VALUES
('00530',14);
INSERT INTO HOLD_TIMES(PARAMETER_ID,MAX_DAYS) VALUES
('00610',28);
INSERT INTO HOLD_TIMES(PARAMETER_ID,MAX_DAYS) VALUES
('00625',28);
INSERT INTO HOLD_TIMES(PARAMETER_ID,MAX_DAYS) VALUES
('00630',28);
INSERT INTO HUC_CODES(HUC_CODE,HUC_NAME) VALUES
('*','not specified');
INSERT INTO LABS(LAB_ID,LAB_NAME) VALUES ('*','not
indicated');
INSERT INTO LABS(LAB_ID,LAB_NAME) VALUES
('FIELD','Field Data');
INSERT INTO PREP_METHODS(PREP_MTHD,PREP_DESC) VALUES
('*','not on file');
INSERT INTO PREP_METHODS(PREP_MTHD,PREP_DESC) VALUES
('EPA130.1','Hardness');
INSERT INTO PREP_METHODS(PREP_MTHD,PREP_DESC) VALUES
('EPA160.1','Solids, Dissolved');
INSERT INTO PREP_METHODS(PREP_MTHD,PREP_DESC) VALUES
('EPA160.2','Solids, Suspended');
INSERT INTO PREP_METHODS(PREP_MTHD,PREP_DESC) VALUES
('EPA160.3','Solids, Total');
```

```
INSERT INTO PREP_METHODS(PREP_MTHD,PREP_DESC) VALUES
('EPA160.4','Solids, Volatile');
INSERT INTO PREP_METHODS(PREP_MTHD,PREP_DESC) VALUES
('EPA200.7','Metals in Water by ICP-AES');
INSERT INTO PREP_METHODS(PREP_MTHD,PREP_DESC) VALUES
('EPA2540E','Volatile Solids');
INSERT INTO PREP_METHODS(PREP_MTHD,PREP_DESC)
VALUES ('EPA300.0','Nitrogen, Nitrate + Nitrite /
Sulfate');
INSERT INTO PREP_METHODS(PREP_MTHD,PREP_DESC) VALUES
('EPA350.1','Nitrogen, Ammonia');
INSERT INTO PREP_METHODS(PREP_MTHD,PREP_DESC) VALUES
('EPA350.2','Ammonia Nitrogen');
INSERT INTO PREP_METHODS(PREP_MTHD,PREP_DESC) VALUES
('EPA351.2','Total Kjeldahl Nitrogen');
INSERT INTO PREP_METHODS(PREP_MTHD,PREP_DESC) VALUES
('EPA351.4','Total Kjeldahl Nitrogen');
INSERT INTO PREP_METHODS(PREP_MTHD,PREP_DESC) VALUES
('EPA353.2','Nitrogen, Nitrate+Nitrite');
INSERT INTO PREP_METHODS(PREP_MTHD,PREP_DESC) VALUES
('EPA3545','Organochlorine Pesticides in Sediment');
INSERT INTO PREP_METHODS(PREP_MTHD,PREP_DESC) VALUES
('EPA365.1','Phosphorus');
INSERT INTO PREP_METHODS(PREP_MTHD,PREP_DESC) VALUES
('EPA6010B','ICP Metals');
INSERT INTO PREP_METHODS(PREP_MTHD,PREP_DESC) VALUES
('EPA6020','Phosphorus');
INSERT INTO PREP_METHODS(PREP_MTHD,PREP_DESC) VALUES
('EPA7471A','Total Mercury in Water');
INSERT INTO PREP_METHODS(PREP_MTHD,PREP_DESC) VALUES
('EPA8270C','Semi-Volatile Organics in Sediment');
INSERT INTO PREP_METHODS(PREP_MTHD,PREP_DESC) VALUES
('EPA9.2','Dissolved Metals');
INSERT INTO PREP_METHODS(PREP_MTHD,PREP_DESC) VALUES
('EPA9.3','Total Metals');
INSERT INTO PREP_METHODS(PREP_MTHD,PREP_DESC) VALUES
('EPA9056','Sulfate');
INSERT INTO PREP_METHODS(PREP_MTHD,PREP_DESC) VALUES
('EPA9060','Total Organic Carbon');
INSERT INTO PREP_METHODS(PREP_MTHD,PREP_DESC) VALUES
('EPA9060A','Total Organic Carbon');
INSERT INTO PREP_METHODS(PREP_MTHD,PREP_DESC) VALUES
('SM2340B','Hardness, Total as CaCO3');
INSERT INTO PREP_METHODS(PREP_MTHD,PREP_DESC) VALUES
('SM2340C','Hardness, Total as CaCO3');
```

```
INSERT INTO PREP_METHODS(PREP_MTHD,PREP_DESC) VALUES
('SM2540B','Solids, Total');
INSERT INTO PREP_METHODS(PREP_MTHD,PREP_DESC) VALUES
('SM2540C','Solids, Dissolved');
INSERT INTO PREP_METHODS(PREP_MTHD,PREP_DESC) VALUES
('SM2540D','Solids, Suspended');
INSERT INTO PREP_METHODS(PREP_MTHD,PREP_DESC) VALUES
('SM2540E','Solids, Volatile');
INSERT INTO PREP_METHODS(PREP_MTHD,PREP_DESC) VALUES
('SM4500NH3B','Nitrogen, Ammonia');
INSERT INTO PREP_METHODS(PREP_MTHD,PREP_DESC) VALUES
('SM4500NH3G','Nitrogen, Ammonia');
INSERT INTO PREP_METHODS(PREP_MTHD,PREP_DESC) VALUES
('SM4500NO3F','Nitrogen, Nitrate+Nitrite');
INSERT INTO PREP_METHODS(PREP_MTHD,PREP_DESC) VALUES
('SM4500Norg','Nitrogen, Total Kjeldahl');
INSERT INTO PREP_METHODS(PREP_MTHD,PREP_DESC) VALUES
('SM5310C','Total Organic Carbon');
INSERT INTO SAMPLE_MEDIA(MEDIUM_CODE,MEDIUM_NAME)
VALUES ('*','Non-specific');
INSERT INTO SAMPLE_MEDIA(MEDIUM_CODE,MEDIUM_NAME)
VALUES ('EL','Elutriate');
INSERT INTO SAMPLE_MEDIA(MEDIUM_CODE,MEDIUM_NAME)
VALUES ('SE','Sediment');
INSERT INTO SAMPLE_MEDIA(MEDIUM_CODE,MEDIUM_NAME)
VALUES ('SL','Soil');
INSERT INTO SAMPLE_MEDIA(MEDIUM_CODE,MEDIUM_NAME)
VALUES ('WA','Water');
INSERT INTO SAMPLE_TYPE_CODES(SAMPLE_TYPE,TYPE_NAME)
VALUES ('*','(Not indicated)');
INSERT INTO SAMPLE_TYPE_CODES(SAMPLE_TYPE,TYPE_NAME)
VALUES ('C','Chemical');
INSERT INTO SAMPLE_TYPE_CODES(SAMPLE_TYPE,TYPE_NAME)
VALUES ('Y','Physical');
INSERT INTO SOURCE_CODES(SOURCE_CODE,SOURCE_NAME)
VALUES ('*','(Not indicated)');
INSERT INTO SOURCE_CODES(SOURCE_CODE,SOURCE_NAME)
VALUES ('1','Stream');
INSERT INTO SOURCE_CODES(SOURCE_CODE,SOURCE_NAME)
VALUES ('2','Lake');
INSERT INTO SOURCE_CODES(SOURCE_CODE,SOURCE_NAME)
VALUES ('3','Monitoring Well');
INSERT INTO SOURCE_CODES(SOURCE_CODE,SOURCE_NAME)
VALUES ('4','Wastewater Plant Discharge');
INSERT INTO SOURCE_CODES(SOURCE_CODE,SOURCE_NAME)
VALUES ('5','Industrial Discharge');
```

```
INSERT INTO SOURCE_CODES(SOURCE_CODE,SOURCE_NAME)
VALUES ('6','Potable Water System');
INSERT INTO SOURCE_CODES(SOURCE_CODE,SOURCE_NAME)
VALUES ('7','Groundwater');
INSERT INTO SOURCE_CODES(SOURCE_CODE,SOURCE_NAME)
VALUES ('8','Surface Soil');
INSERT INTO SOURCE_CODES(SOURCE_CODE,SOURCE_NAME)
VALUES ('9','Subsurface Soil');
INSERT INTO SOURCE_CODES(SOURCE_CODE,SOURCE_NAME)
VALUES ('A','Other Source');
INSERT INTO STATES(POSTAL_STATE,STATE_NAME) VALUES
('*','not specified');
INSERT INTO STATES(POSTAL_STATE,STATE_NAME) VALUES
('TN','Tennessee');
INSERT INTO STREAM_CODES(STREAM_CODE,STREAM_NAME)
VALUES ('*','Not on file');
INSERT INTO TEST_METHODS(TEST_MTHD,TEST_DESC) VALUES
('*','not on file');
INSERT INTO TEST_METHODS(TEST_MTHD,TEST_DESC)
VALUES ('CALC','Calculated Value from other known
results');
INSERT INTO TSI_PARAMETERS(SECCHI_PARAM,CHLOR_
PARAM,PHOS_PARAM) VALUES ('00077','32210','00665');
INSERT INTO TSI_RANGES(LOWER_VAL,UPPER_VAL,RANGE_
LABEL) VALUES (0,35,'Oligotrophic');
INSERT INTO TSI_RANGES(LOWER_VAL,UPPER_VAL,RANGE_
LABEL) VALUES (36,50,'Mesotrophic');
INSERT INTO TSI_RANGES(LOWER_VAL,UPPER_VAL,RANGE_
LABEL) VALUES (51,55,'Moderately Eutrophic');
INSERT INTO TSI_RANGES(LOWER_VAL,UPPER_VAL,RANGE_
LABEL) VALUES (56,65,'Eutrophic');
INSERT INTO TSI_RANGES(LOWER_VAL,UPPER_VAL,RANGE_
LABEL) VALUES (66,100,'Hypereutrophic');
INSERT INTO UNITS(UNITS) VALUES ('%');
INSERT INTO UNITS(UNITS) VALUES ('% as C');
INSERT INTO UNITS(UNITS) VALUES ('% as N');
INSERT INTO UNITS(UNITS) VALUES ('% as P');
INSERT INTO UNITS(UNITS) VALUES ('cm');
INSERT INTO UNITS(UNITS) VALUES ('cm3');
INSERT INTO UNITS(UNITS) VALUES ('deg C');
INSERT INTO UNITS(UNITS) VALUES ('deg K');
INSERT INTO UNITS(UNITS) VALUES ('FTU');
INSERT INTO UNITS(UNITS) VALUES ('g');
INSERT INTO UNITS(UNITS) VALUES ('g/cm3');
INSERT INTO UNITS(UNITS) VALUES ('g/g');
INSERT INTO UNITS(UNITS) VALUES ('g/kg');
```

```
INSERT INTO UNITS(UNITS) VALUES ('g/l');
INSERT INTO UNITS(UNITS) VALUES ('g/m2');
INSERT INTO UNITS(UNITS) VALUES ('g/m3');
INSERT INTO UNITS(UNITS) VALUES ('JTU');
INSERT INTO UNITS(UNITS) VALUES ('l/min');
INSERT INTO UNITS(UNITS) VALUES ('liter');
INSERT INTO UNITS(UNITS) VALUES ('m');
INSERT INTO UNITS(UNITS) VALUES ('m/sec');
INSERT INTO UNITS(UNITS) VALUES ('m2');
INSERT INTO UNITS(UNITS) VALUES ('m3');
INSERT INTO UNITS(UNITS) VALUES ('m3/day');
INSERT INTO UNITS(UNITS) VALUES ('m3/hr');
INSERT INTO UNITS(UNITS) VALUES ('m3/min');
INSERT INTO UNITS(UNITS) VALUES ('m3/sec');
INSERT INTO UNITS(UNITS) VALUES ('meq/L');
INSERT INTO UNITS(UNITS) VALUES ('mg');
INSERT INTO UNITS(UNITS) VALUES ('mg/cm3');
INSERT INTO UNITS(UNITS) VALUES ('mg/g');
INSERT INTO UNITS(UNITS) VALUES ('mg/kg');
INSERT INTO UNITS(UNITS) VALUES ('mg/l');
INSERT INTO UNITS(UNITS) VALUES ('mg/m2');
INSERT INTO UNITS(UNITS) VALUES ('mg/m3');
INSERT INTO UNITS(UNITS) VALUES ('mgd');
INSERT INTO UNITS(UNITS) VALUES ('mho/cm');
INSERT INTO UNITS(UNITS) VALUES ('ml');
INSERT INTO UNITS(UNITS) VALUES ('ml/l');
INSERT INTO UNITS(UNITS) VALUES ('mm');
INSERT INTO UNITS(UNITS) VALUES ('mm H2O');
INSERT INTO UNITS(UNITS) VALUES ('mm Hg');
INSERT INTO UNITS(UNITS) VALUES ('mm2');
INSERT INTO UNITS(UNITS) VALUES ('mm3');
INSERT INTO UNITS(UNITS) VALUES ('ms');
INSERT INTO UNITS(UNITS) VALUES ('mS/cm');
INSERT INTO UNITS(UNITS) VALUES ('mV');
INSERT INTO UNITS(UNITS) VALUES ('None');
INSERT INTO UNITS(UNITS) VALUES ('NTU');
INSERT INTO UNITS(UNITS) VALUES ('PCU');
INSERT INTO UNITS(UNITS) VALUES ('pg/g');
INSERT INTO UNITS(UNITS) VALUES ('pg/l');
INSERT INTO UNITS(UNITS) VALUES ('ppb');
INSERT INTO UNITS(UNITS) VALUES ('ppm');
INSERT INTO UNITS(UNITS) VALUES ('SU');
INSERT INTO UNITS(UNITS) VALUES ('ug');
INSERT INTO UNITS(UNITS) VALUES ('ug/cm3');
INSERT INTO UNITS(UNITS) VALUES ('ug/g');
INSERT INTO UNITS(UNITS) VALUES ('ug/kg');
```

```
INSERT INTO UNITS(UNITS) VALUES ('ug/l');
INSERT INTO UNITS(UNITS) VALUES ('ug/m2');
INSERT INTO UNITS(UNITS) VALUES ('ug/m3');
INSERT INTO UNITS(UNITS) VALUES ('UM/CM');
INSERT INTO UNITS(UNITS) VALUES ('UM/ML');
INSERT INTO UNITS(UNITS) VALUES ('um3/ml');
INSERT INTO UNITS(UNITS) VALUES ('umho/cm');
INSERT INTO UNITS(UNITS) VALUES ('uS/cm');
INSERT INTO VALUE_QUALIFIERS(VAL_QUAL,VAL_MEANING)
VALUES ('B','analyte detected in associated blank');
INSERT INTO VALUE_QUALIFIERS(VAL_QUAL,VAL_MEANING)
VALUES ('E','concentration exceeds the calibration
range of the instrument');
INSERT INTO VALUE_QUALIFIERS(VAL_QUAL,VAL_MEANING)
VALUES ('I','matrix interference');
INSERT INTO VALUE_QUALIFIERS(VAL_QUAL,VAL_MEANING)
VALUES ('J','estimated value');
INSERT INTO VALUE_QUALIFIERS(VAL_QUAL,VAL_MEANING)
VALUES ('U','not detected');
INSERT INTO VALUE_QUALIFIERS(VAL_QUAL,VAL_MEANING)
VALUES ('X','hold time exceeded');
```

Appendix C: Bibliography
References and Recommended Reading

Webster's New Universal Unabridged Dictionary, Jean L. McKechnie, ed., Dorset and Baber, 1983.

The Associated Press Stylebook and Libel Manual, Christopher W. French, Eileen Alt Powell, Howard Angione, eds., The Associated Press, 1984.

Applied Mathematics for Database Professionals, Lex de Haan and Toon Koppelaars, Apress, 2007.

An Introduction to Database Systems, Bipin C. Desai, West Publishing Company, 1990.

Designing Data-Intensive Applications, Martin Kleppmann, O'Reilly Media, Inc., 2017.

www.iso.org/standard/63555, "ISO/IEC 9075-1:2016 Information Technology – Database Languages – SQL – Part 1: Framework (SQL/Framework)," accessed October 12, 2020.

https://standards.globalspec.com/std/6769/ANSI X3.135, "Information Technology – Database Languages – SQL," accessed October 12, 2020.

CodeNotes for Oracle 9i, Gregory Brill, ed., Random House Trade Paperbacks, 2002.

Fundamentals of Data Normalization, Alan F. Dutka and Howard H. Hanson, Addison-Wesley Publishing Company, 1989.

"A Simple Guide to Five Normal Forms in Relational Database Theory", Communications of the ACM 26(2), Feb. 1983, 120–125.

Developer to Designer: GUI Design for the Busy Developer, Mike Gunderloy, Sybex, Inc., 2005.

Microsoft Jet Database Engineer Programmer's Guide, Second Edition, Dan Haught and Jim Ferguson, Microsoft Press, 1997.

Applied Discrete Structures for Computer Science, 2nd Edition, Alan Doerr and Kenneth Lavasseur, Macmillan Publishing Company, 1989.

Oracle Essentials: Oracle Database 10g, 3rd Edition, Rick Greenwald, Robert Stackowiak, and Jonathan Stern, O'Reilly Media, Inc., 2004.

Standard Methods for the Examination of Water and Wastewater, 19th Edition, Mary
   Ann H. Franson, Managing Editor, American Public Health Association, American
   Water Works Association, and Water Environment Federation, 1995.
Mostly Harmless, Douglas Adams, Harmony Books, 1992.
A Trophic State Index for Lakes, Robert E. Carlson, Limnology and Oceanography,
   Volume 22, Number 2, March 1977.

Index

Printed in the United States
by Baker & Taylor Publisher Services